Interrogating Boundaries of the Nonhuman

ECOCRITICAL THEORY AND PRACTICE

Series Editor: Douglas A. Vakoch, METI

Advisory Board

Sinan Akilli, Cappadocia University, Turkey; Bruce Allen, Seisen University, Japan; Zélia Bora, Federal University of Paraíba, Brazil; Izabel Brandão, Federal University of Alagoas, Brazil; Byron Caminero-Santangelo, University of Kansas, USA; Chia-ju Chang, Brooklyn College, The City College of New York, USA; H. Louise Davis, Miami University, USA; Simão Farias Almeida, Federal University of Roraima, Brazil; George Handley, Brigham Young University, USA; Steven Hartman, Mälardalen University, Sweden; Isabel Hoving, Leiden University, The Netherlands; Idom Thomas Inyabri, University of Calabar, Nigeria; Serenella Iovino, University of Turin, Italy; Daniela Kato, Kyoto Institute of Technology, Japan; Petr Kopecký, University of Ostrava, Czech Republic; Julia Kuznetski, Tallinn University, Estonia; Bei Liu, Shandong Normal University, People's Republic of China; Serpil Oppermann, Cappadocia University, Turkey; John Ryan, University of New England, Australia; Christian Schmitt-Kilb, University of Rostock, Germany; Joshua Schuster, Western University, Canada; Heike Schwarz, University of Augsburg, Germany; Murali Sivaramakrishnan, Pondicherry University, India; Scott Slovic, University of Idaho, USA; Heather Sullivan, Trinity University, USA; David Taylor, Stony Brook University, USA; J. Etienne Terblanche, North-West University, South Africa; Cheng Xiangzhan, Shandong University, China; Hubert Zapf, University of Augsburg, Germany

Ecocritical Theory and Practice highlights innovative scholarship at the interface of literary/cultural studies and the environment, seeking to foster an ongoing dialogue between academics and environmental activists.

Recent Titles

Interrogating Boundaries of the Nonhuman: Literature, Climate Change, and Environmental Crises, edited by Sune Borkfelt and Matthias Stephan
Avian Aesthetics in Literature and Culture: Birds and Humans in the Popular Imagination, edited by Danette DiMarco and Timothy Ruppert
Shamanism in the Contemporary Novel, by Özlem Öğüt Yazıcıoğlu
Modernism and the Anthropocene, edited by Jon Hegglund and John McIntyre

The End of the Anthropocene: Ecocriticism, the Universal Ecosystem, and the Astropocene by Michael Gormley

Trees in Literatures and the Arts: Humanarboreal Perspectives in the Anthropocene edited by Carmelina Concilio and Daniela Fargione

Lupenga Mphande: Eco-critical Poet and Political Activist by Dike Okoro

Environmental Postcolonialism: A Literary Response edited by Shubhanku Kochar and M. Anjum Khan

Reading Aridity in Western American Literature edited by Jada Ach and Gary Reger

Reading Cats and Dogs: Companion Animals in World Literature edited by Françoise Besson, Zelia M. Bora, Marianne Marroum, and Scott Slovic

Turkish Ecocriticism: From Neolithic to Contemporary Timescapes edited by Sinan Akilli and Serpil Oppermann

Interrogating Boundaries of the Nonhuman

Literature, Climate Change, and Environmental Crises

Edited by Matthias Stephan
and Sune Borkfelt

LEXINGTON BOOKS
Lanham • Boulder • New York • London

Published by Lexington Books
An imprint of The Rowman & Littlefield Publishing Group, Inc.

4501 Forbes Boulevard, Suite 200, Lanham, Maryland 20706
www.rowman.com

86-90 Paul Street, London EC2A 4NE

Copyright © 2022 by The Rowman & Littlefield Publishing Group, Inc.

All rights reserved. No part of this book may be reproduced in any form or by any electronic or mechanical means, including information storage and retrieval systems, without written permission from the publisher, except by a reviewer who may quote passages in a review.

British Library Cataloguing in Publication Information Available

Library of Congress Cataloging-in-Publication Data Available

978-1-6669-0378-2 (paperback)

Acknowledgements

The editors would first like to thank all the contributors for their enthusiasm, hard work, and patience at various stages of this project. It has been inspiring to work with you all.

We would also like to thank many colleagues at the Department of English at Aarhus University for continuing encouragement and interesting conversations.

In addition, we would like to acknowledge the editorial and production team at Lexington Books for their assistance with the project.

Matthias Stephan would like to thank Sune Borkfelt for his commitment to his scholarship and depth of knowledge in the field of critical animal studies, without which this project would be the poorer. His effort, attention to detail, and friendship has made editing this collection enlightening and rewarding. I could not operate without the love and support of my lovely wife, Maria, and my inquisitive children, Philippa and Tristan, who constantly interrogate me and those around us with questions as to why we do things the way we do, and provoke me to do so as well. I would also draw attention to the many inspiring writers, scholars, activists and leaders who, for generations if not lifetimes, have challenged limits and deconstructed boundaries to allow us to consider a better future, despite the enormous environmental challenges we face together, and hope this small contribution makes some small impact on that effort.

Sune Borkfelt would like to thank Matthias Stephan for his hard work and dedication in relation to this volume, and for pleasant co-work on this and other projects. Exploring, questioning, and interrogating the boundaries and binaries through which we often view the world is a continuing project for me in seeking to understand others and enhance my ethics. In this, I draw inspiration from many of the human and nonhuman animals I have been fortunate to encounter and share the planet with. I dedicate this work also to my favourite human animals, Deva and Dicte, and to those who continue to work for a future with fewer arbitrary boundaries and greater harmony.

Chapter 8 was written while the author was a fellow at the Internationale Jugendbibliothek in München.

Contents

Acknowledgements   vii

Introduction: Writing the Nonhuman amidst Environmental Crises   1
    Matthias Stephan and Sune Borkfelt

PART I: PAST NARRATIVES OF ENVIRONMENTAL CRISIS   31

Chapter 1: The Peculiar Associations of Melville's "Encantadas": Nature and National Allegory   33
    Kristen R. Egan

Chapter 2: Making a Difference? Richard Jefferies's *After London*, E. M. Forster's "The Machine Stops," and Climate Change Fiction   53
    Adrian Tait

Chapter 3: Stories of "Being-with" Other Animals: A Case of Humans and Horses   69
    Mary Trachsel

PART II: WITNESSING   89

Chapter 4: Animal Texts: How *Coyote America* and *American Wolf* Embody the Literary Animal through a Cross-Disciplinary Approach   91
    Lauren E. Perry

Chapter 5: Beautiful and Sublime: Embracing Otherness in Mary Oliver's Ecopoetry   109
    Anastasia Cardone

Chapter 6: The Sea's Witness: Narration, Texturisation, and Reader
   Responsibility in Rachel Carson's Oceanalia   129
   Lauren O'Mahony

**PART III: NONHUMAN AGENCY/REPRESENTATION OF
THE NONHUMAN**   145

Chapter 7: The Posthuman Return: Transformation through
   Stillness in Richard Powers's *The Overstory*   147
   Owen Harry

Chapter 8: Classifying Monsters   165
   Vera Veldhuizen

Chapter 9: "'There Isn't Anything That Isn't Political.' It's an
   Expression That Sounds Human, but Everything in Her Voice
   Indicates That She Is Not": The Nonhuman in Ellen Van
   Neerven's 'Water'   183
   Clare Archer-Lean

PART IV: MUTATION AND POST-APOCALYPSE   203

Chapter 10: "We've Made Meat for Everyone!": The Ideology of
   Distinction and Becoming Flesh in Cormac McCarthy's *The
   Road* and Joseph D'Lacey's *Meat*   205
   Samantha Hind

Chapter 11: "There Would Be Monsters, Some Hopeful": Viral
   Agencies and Mutational Posthuman Politics in Post-Millennial
   Science Fiction   221
   Clare Wall

Chapter 12: "A Reign of Community and Harmony": Envisioning a
   Multispecies Society in a Post-Nuclear World   239
   Elizabeth Tavella

Index   257

About the Editors   269

About the Contributors   271

Introduction

Writing the Nonhuman amidst Environmental Crises

Matthias Stephan and Sune Borkfelt

The world is in crisis: socially, politically, environmentally. While climate change and other environmental crises are often framed as human concerns, or as nature's retaliation for human over-use and abuse of its resources, the growing environmental crisis implicates the fates of nonhuman animals too, raising questions of how current environmental crises may stem from our historical disregard for the interests and capacities of other species. As a whole, this collection asks whether literary works that interrogate and alter the terms of human-nonhuman relations can point to new, more sustainable ways forward.

Boundaries and categorizations are under pressure. In recent years, theorists across fields and disciplines—from posthumanist scholars and new materialists to scholars drawing on Deleuzian ideas of indiscernibility or on Anat Pick's notion of '"creaturely poetics"—have increasingly questioned or challenged boundaries between subjects and objects, between humans and nonhumans, between the real and the artificial, between nature and culture. Concurrently, environmental crises are also challenging perceived boundaries; indeed, if grand scale environmental collapse, extinction crises, and climate change teach us anything, it is arguably both the interconnectedness of all life on the planet and the fact that there is no nature out there distinct from or unaffected by human culture.

In this introduction to *Interrogating the Boundaries of the Nonhuman*, we explore the possibilities of connecting the ongoing interrogation of boundaries with environmental crises in literature—past, present, future—while introducing and connecting the collection's chapters through the ways in which they all work within this frame of the blurred, renegotiated, and interrogated boundaries affected by the challenges currently facing the world.

Drawing on some of the theoretical approaches mentioned above, we argue that the interrogation of boundaries and dichotomies, traditionally sanctioned through anthropocentric modes of thought, is both inevitable and crucial to truly address the various environmental and biodiversity crises currently facing the world. The selection of chapters that follow are organized in a loosely historical direction, moving from consideration of climate change and the human/nonhuman boundary as allegory in the works of Melville through considerations of postapocalyptic futures in speculative and science fiction. They also represent a diversity of variants of Anglophone scholarship, maintaining the spelling and grammatical styles of scholars from the US, UK, Canada, Australia, and Europe.

INTERROGATING THE ANTHROPOCENE

> I along with others think the Anthropocene is more a boundary event than an epoch. (Haraway 2015, 160)

In 2000, in a discussion in the Global Change Newsletter, two scientists proposed a new geological era, based on the many changes since the then current era, Holocene ('Recent Whole' as they note). In their respective fields—Paul J. Crutzen a scholar in the Atmospheric Chemistry division of the Max-Planck-Instutite in Mainz, Germany, and Eugene R. Stoermer at the Center for Great Lakes and Aquatic Sciences at the University of Michigan—the importance of the impacts of man on the growing environmental changes needed to be forefronted. They write, "[c]onsidering these and many other major and still growing impacts of human activities on earth and atmosphere, and at all, including global, scales, it seems to us more than appropriate to emphasize the central role of mankind in geology and ecology by proposing to use the term 'anthropocene' for the current geological epoch." They go on to stipulate that they do not see these effects diminishing, but rather suggest "[t]he impacts of current human activities will continue over long periods" (Crutzen and Stoermer 2000, 17).

Elizabeth DeLoughrey, in 2019, also notes the severity of the crisis, emphasizing "[t]he rapid increase in atmospheric carbon; extreme weather events such as drought, flooding, fire, and hurricanes; cataclysmic species extinctions; sea-level rise; ocean acidification; and a warming planet all testify to a crisis of global climate change" (2). She, however, rightly notes that the primary use of the term is as it is seen through the hard sciences, and not as presented in cultural spheres and drawing on scholarship in the arts and humanities. She also notes its geographical focus centered on the global north. She argues that "[t]he lack of engagement with postcolonial and Indigenous perspectives has shaped Anthropocene discourse to claim the *novelty* of crisis rather than being attentive to the historical *continuity* of dispossession and disaster caused by empire" (2). In this way, DeLoughrey is interrogating the geographical boundary of this discourse, wanting to decenter the debate (and its response) from the global north, or more accurately, following (as she notes) Chakrabarty in provincializing Europe. In this she is, again rightly, cautious in worrying that "much Anthropocene scholarship" resurrects the notion "of the 'Age of Man,' . . . a figure who reigns as a singular (masculine) 'species'" (3).

Yet, just as she argues that the term Anthropocene dismisses the concerns of vast parts of the globe (and a majority of the world's human population), we further want to interrogate this concept—as focusing primarily on the *Anthropos*, or 'man' in both terminology and effect. Not only does this challenge need to be placed in terms of who is represented in the discourse among humans, but provide further recognition that the effects brought on by the actions of men (even if primarily in the global north, or primarily through imperialism and colonialism) have an effect broader than 'man' but across the human-nonhuman binary.

The term *Anthropocene* has been interrogated in a variety of ways. Andreas Malm and Alf Hornborg, in considering the global climate crisis, also interrogated the specific origins of the crisis and its universal framing of 'human activities' and any potential implication that this was not driven by choice:

> Realising that climate change is 'anthropogenic' is really to appreciate that it is *sociogenic*. It has arisen as a result of temporally fluid social relations as they materialise through the rest of nature, and once this ontological insight—implicit in the science of climate change—is truly taken onboard, one can no longer treat humankind as merely a species-being determined by its biological evolution. (2014, 66)

In a footnote, they also suggest the Capitalocene as an alternative to *sociogenic*, which further focuses the era on human activities, but presents a deliberate framing on particular socioeconomic activities which function disproportionately across the globe, and in between both men and nonhuman species alike. Jason Moore, picking up on this term, asks: "Are we really living in the Anthropocene—the 'age of man'—with its Eurocentric and techno-determinist vistas? Or are we living in the Capitalocene—the 'age of capital'—the historical era shaped by the endless accumulation of capital?" (2017, 596). In making the distinction, Moore is picking up on a number of factors. The Anthropocene itself represents an interesting liminal category, as it presents two different aspects of the crisis simultaneously, "recognizing humans as part of nature whilst separating Humanity from Nature," a dichotomy that "troubles Anthropocene thinking at every turn" (597). This gets to the heart of the man/nature divide, as the term itself absorbs into a geological category, historically fashioned as larger in scale than humans' development as a species, the very assemblages by which humans operate. Essentially we have written 'nature' into our own conception of time and space. At the same time, it presents a techno-optimist frame, as much of the discourse, especially from the hard sciences, is about human intervention to 'solve' the environmental crises we face. Moore argues that the focus on capital is useful in specifically challenging this unwarranted position:

> Capitalocene names capitalism as a system of power, profit, and re/production in the web of life. It thinks capitalism as if human relations form through the geographies of life. Far from refusing the problem of political economy, however, it highlights capitalism as a history in which islands of commodity production and exchange operate within oceans of Cheap—or potentially Cheap—Natures. Vigorous accumulation depends on the existence—and the active production—of human and extra-human natures whose costs of reproduction are kept 'off the books'. (2017, 606)

Moore's framing argues for an important focus on the consequences not only for human but 'extra-human natures' which we agree are often kept 'off the books,' not only in economic terms. There are few economic or social consequences for contributing to the climate and environmental crises we face, and even those known consequences disproportionately fall on those least able to meaningfully mitigate them. His notion of 'cheap nature' encapsulates an unfortunate attitude towards ecosystems and their assemblages both historically and today, as many of the chapters of this collection discuss.

Donna Haraway argues that "[t]he boundary that is the Anthropocene/Capitalocene means many things, including that immense irreversible destruction is really in train, not only for the 11 billion or so people who will be on earth near the end of the twenty-first century, but for myriads of other critters too" (Haraway 2015, 161), placing an important focus on the nonhuman animals that she refers to as 'critters.' In a larger discussion Haraway also presents the idea that the Capitalocene has more explanatory power than the Anthropocene:

> What I think the term Capitalocene does that the term Anthropocene does not do, and cannot do, is to insist that it is an historically situated complex of metabolisms and assemblages. The people that I know who use Anthropocene tend to emphasize the history from the mid-eighteenth century forward, and tend to take the use of fossil fuel as the key historical moment. The Capitalocene suggests a longer history. I think we are looking at slave agriculture, not coal, frankly, as a key transition. (Haraway et al. 2015, 21)

The question becomes not whether there are environmental crises, but how they have come about—especially with a focus on social and cultural practices which have, in many ways, contributed to this development. This is an important challenge to the hard science approach to the Anthropocene. Crutzen and Stoermer importantly highlight the continuing impact of man-made activities, but the intervention of the Capitalocene forefronts the mechanisms of discourse, and the blindspots entailed therein.

Part of the discussion, as the quote from Haraway et al. suggests, is the timeline in which one considers the Anthropocene—whether this begins in the Industrial Age (her reference to coal), the Neolithic Age (the beginning of farming and repurposing of land for anthropocentric purposes) or the global era represented by the slave trade, in which populations of both human and nonhuman animals have been transplanted across the seas, at great cost (in many senses) to contribute to capitalist enterprise. The term *Plantationocene* was coined in this conversation: "In a recorded conversation for *Ethnos* at the University of Aarhus in October, 2014, the participants collectively generated the name Plantationocene for the devastating transformation of diverse kinds of human-tended farms, pastures, and forests into extractive and enclosed plantations, relying on slave labor and other forms of exploited, alienated, and usually spatially transported labor" (Haraway 2015, 162, footnote 5). Interestingly, the conversation did not limit the discussion to the concept of plantations, with its combination of exploited human and nonhuman animal labor, but also to considerations beyond the nonhuman animal. For example, Norburu Ishikawa suggests that "plantations are just the slavery of plants" and Donna Haraway chimes in to say "and microbes" (Haraway et al. 2015, 22, 23). Essentially, this term seems to crystallize the exploitive nature of the current relationship to the environment, conceived as a resource for anthropocentric endeavours, with little value placed on the consequences of this framing—in terms of the human (people) or the nonhuman, here conceived as animals, plants and microbes alike: "The Plantationocene makes one pay attention to the historical relocations of the substances of living and dying around the Earth as a necessary prerequisite to their extraction . . . The plantation system depends on the relocation of the generative units: plants, animals, microbes, people" (23). In coining the term *Plantationocene*, Anna Tsing, Donna Haraway, and others have opened up a discourse about not just a universal man's involvement in the global crises we face today, but of how and in what ways this process has come to play out, and what are the consequences for human and nonhuman alike.

Yet, this term, like *Anthropocene* and *Capitalocene*, still forefronts human endeavors and human frames. Despite a resignation to the use of Anthropocene as the most likely candidate for a term moving forward (one palatable to the hard sciences in ways in which these 'cultural' concerns seem not to be), Haraway further suggests other terms that put the concept more in touch with the nonhuman:

> I am calling all this the Chthulucene—past, present, and to come. . . . 'My' Chthulucene, even burdened with its problematic Greek-ish tendrils, entangles myriad temporalities and spatialities and myriad intra-active entities-inassemblages—including the more-than-human, other-than-human, inhuman, and human-as-humus. . . . namely, the webs of speculative fabulation, speculative feminism, science fiction, and scientific fact. It matters which stories tell stories, which concepts think concepts. (Haraway 2015, 160)

In this Haraway pushes for a term that decenters man, and reads crises through our various entanglements. While we agree that the term Anthropocene seems a *fait accompli*, the interrogation of the term as a boundary is important. So too is reading the Anthropocene on both of its faces, focusing on man-made crises while also criticizing any limitation on which entities—humans, animals, plants, viruses, the nonhuman—need to be considered in looking 'beyond' such crises, to a reconstituted and reconstructed future.

It is in the context of ideas such as these that one must consider the word "nonhuman" in the title of this book. "The nonhuman," as we use it here, should not be understood as a monolith, nor should it be understood as merely encompassing the multiplicity of nonhuman animals, nor should it be read as enforcing a strict boundary between ourselves as human and everything else. Rather, it is perhaps closer to what Jacques Derrida calls "a heterogeneous multiplicity of the living, or more precisely (since to say 'the living' is already to say too much or not enough), a multiplicity of organizations of relations between living and dead, relations of organization or lack of organization among realms that are more and more difficult to dissociate by means of the figures of the organic and the inorganic, of life and/or death" (2008, 31). Derrida positions this "[b]eyond the edge of the *so-called* human, beyond it but by no means on a single opposing side" and famously objects to the monolithic idea of "the animal," emphasizing instead plurality and multiplicity (31). Despite its grammatically singular form, we mean for "the nonhuman" here to do similarly encompassing work, to emphasize heterogeneity. But since we are simultaneously "interrogating boundaries" it is important to also note the fluidity of the term, how the "human," so to speak, flows into the "non" or remains part of the "non*human*." The term *nonhuman*, for us, is in this way also a term in which "species meet," just as the human body is deeply entangled with and reliant upon other species and entities (Haraway 2008, 3–4). In other words, the term "nonhuman"—and particularly in our title's combination with "interrogating boundaries"—is meant to also invoke the recognition of interrelations that some theorists have called posthumanist (e.g., Wolfe 2010; Nayar 2014). As one such scholar phrases it, the human is seen as "co-evolving, sharing ecosystems, life processes, genetic material, with animals and other life forms" in ways that lead to an interrogation and questioning of the "[n]ormative subjectivity, which defined and categorized life forms into 'animal,' 'plant' and 'human'" (Nayar 2014, 8–9).

Thus, while much of what one can read in this volume concerns nonhuman animals and human relations with these in light of environmental crises, it also reaches beyond this and touches upon the nonhuman in this broader sense. Chapters in this volume consider, for example, literary relations to viruses, to plants, to hybrid species that break down traditional boundaries between human, animal and plant, between natural and artificial, as well as considering environments more broadly. It is part of the overall idea of this book to explore why and how texts deal with such a variety of nonhuman entities, to challenge such categories, and to engage the entanglements that they imply. This, we contend, offers us new insights that are useful in relation to the crises we all—human or not—face as well as relations between humans and nonhuman animals, humans and our environments, humans and all with which we are entangled.

Bringing insights from the field of literary animal studies to bear upon urgent issues of climate change and environmental degradation, individual chapters by a diverse and international group of junior and senior scholars examine literary contributions to the ecological framing of human-nonhuman relationships. Collectively, the chapters contemplate the role of literature and other arts in the setting of environmental agendas and in determining humanity's path forward in the company of nonhuman others.

These twelve chapters all focus on looming environmental crises and examine how nonhuman entities figure in literary responses to the challenges they pose. The authors use a diverse set of methodologies, with each chapter presenting cases that spotlight various aspects of human-nonhuman relations. The collection is divided into four parts, each highlighting a different conversational focus within the discussion: narrating past environmental crises; witnessing environmental events and states of being; recognizing and representing nonhuman agency; and mutating and adapting to a postapocalyptic environment. These parts are ordered loosely on a trajectory from past to future, demonstrating that the setting of human-nonhuman relationships is not a new topic of discussion and illustrating the long sweep of interventions that are possible. Each part is intended to prompt further discussion of literature's role in formulating human responses to more-than-human environmental problems.

PAST NARRATIVES OF ENVIRONMENTAL CRISIS

The chapters in the first part, *Past Narratives of Environmental Crisis*, take their starting points in the nineteenth and early twentieth centuries. They draw on those primary sources to speak to contemporary issues, from a nationalist assumption of land boundaries, to the use of technology to mitigate environmental crises, to the relationship between human and nonhuman animals developed in literature over time. Mary Trachsel's consideration of human-horse relations, with a focus on symbiosis, moves towards the focus of the following part, Witnessing.

Each of these chapters considers texts that predate the contemporary, and predate the debate around anthropogenic climate change. Yet, as each of the chapters suggest, they speak to the current moment meaningfully, and due to their distance, provide specific insight into the situation and how we can read our current era as part of an ongoing tradition of our relationship to each other—human and nonhuman alike. They do this while also drawing on the debates of the era of each author they consider, and their relationships to land, nature (human and nonhuman) and each other. In so doing, they expand on the notion of which texts, and which eras, can be seen to provide insight into our current crises. As with the discussion of the Anthropocene in the preceding part, one can see that legacies of historical decisions, assumptions, and values have long-reaching effects not only on our current challenges, but on their framing and potential solutions. The notion of the Plantationocene specifically interrogates the legacy of slavery and colonialism, which is present in Kristen R. Egan's consideration of Melville's "The Encantadas" . The Capitalocene is infinitely entangled with notions of progress and technology, which Adrian Tait interrogates in his consideration of two texts from the Victorian era—itself a champion of not only progress but its spread globally. Mary Trachsel, however, draws on E. O. Wilson's concept of the Eremocene (2016) in considering the connection between human and horse, and their increasingly entangled conception as traced historically, from a framing of human dominance to a co-created relationship that requires a reconsideration of the status of both parties, and potentially destabilizes the anthropocentric assumptions entailed within.

The collection starts off with Kristen R. Egan's consideration of Herman Melville's "The Encantadas", set in a series of South American islands, and framing it in terms of nation building as well as environment. As she states, "Melville describes an island environment that does not resemble a pure Edenic landscape containing the perfect raw and metaphorical material to build a nation; instead, he creates a dystopia that represents the unstable and contested battleground between environment and empire." She also notes that, historically, critics also disagree as to the intention and interpretation of Melville's tale, read as a travelogue and a series of fictional sketches, as well as both an exploration of Melville's psyche and a consideration of the collection of islands often designated the Galapagos, contributing to its liminal nature.

Through close reading and analysis of Melville's text, Egan interrogates the very categories by which we tend to understand physical location—as a product of a national or regional space, as tied to a grounded, fixed entity, and as a stable marker. She states, "[p]lace naming, mapping, generating a national allegory, and employing hierarchies of 'civilization' are all necessary to nation formation, but this text disrupts these processes, subverting national production and revealing the 'peculiar associations' between nationalism and environment, associations that are forced rather than natural." This notion of nation formation is also parallel to our idea of natural spaces—which are constructed 'as' nature and then designated for use or protection. Arguably, one should consider the ecosystem as existing in tandem with humanity, and as such designating separate spaces to nature and 'man' falls into the trap of anthropocentrism.

In Egan's reading, Melville's text can be seen as a foreshadowing of the conservation movement in the US (and elsewhere) which set aside land for 'nature reserves' only if they had been left untouched by humans. She argues that, "[p]lace naming is one of the preliminary steps to configuring the borders of the nation and controlling nature, and Melville subverts this act." In this, she suggests that Melville's text itself interrogates the ways in which man, especially in the colonial and imperial tradition, labels and then lays claim to the land. His text suggests that the land itself resists such classification, and draws attention to the relative nature of any such logic—contingent on perspective, national tradition, and historical context. Through this reading, Egan's chapter presents Melville's text as also foreshadowing our shifting relationship to nature, and the need for a reconsideration not only of the designation of a particular island group, but for our relationship with nation, land, and environment—and the notion that even our current relationships are a historic legacy which needs to continually be interrogated as we face ever-growing environmental crises.

Adrian Tait looks at past 'future histories,' stories from the early twentieth century that posited future scenarios of environmental crisis and our interrelations with humans and nonhumans. As he states, "even before environmental impacts such as enhanced global warming were identified and understood, and long before the term 'cli-fi' was coined to describe the kind of fiction that engages directly with climate crisis (Johns-Putra 2016, 266), writers were speculating about the potential outcome of a modernizing process that was generating unexpected and often unseen risks." How we once considered the future, as Egan's chapter also attests, affects our future readings of the current situation, as it exposes and allows us to interrogate those previous frameworks and envisionings, specifically in how we interact with the nonhuman. For example, in his reading of E. M. Forster's "The Machine Stops," Tait notes, "what is at fault is humanism itself: through its fantasy of exceptionalism—of humans as somehow independent of an embodied existence—humanism has proven to be humanity's undoing." His readings of both Forster and Richard Jefferies's *After London* interrogate the technopositive framework of the Victorians, which was picked up and championed in the modernist era by Futurism and associated movements across the arts. The readings question not only the underlying logic of this positivist frame, but also its lack of consideration of the nonhuman, "and the unintended consequences that are its side-effect, the nonhuman, agential reality [. . .], ready to resume its own self-willed trajectory."

Yet, interestingly, Tait also draws on research into empirical ecocriticism, by Schneider-Mayerson and his colleagues, in looking for more empirical ways to evaluate the impact of such past 'future narratives.' Tait's use of reception studies is potentially a model for such analysis—which paired with his discourse and textual analysis of the stories by Jefferies and Forster, adds much to the conversation about the nonhuman and its relationship to environmental crises. He shows how we conceived of the future, how we have learned from that speculation, and what we can now see as the consequences of this literary output. Furthermore, he considers how descriptions of the past allow us to interrogate those assumptions we carry forth from the modernist era—and how those have consequently shaped our response to contemporary crises. So, while his chapter "assumes, imaginative fiction is an innately innovative and flexible medium, perfectly capable of escaping what Clark has described as the 'anthropocentric delusion' (2015, 191), or the 'potentially destructive projections of the personal scale' (192)," he also interrogates those claims and suggests that more empirical data, and more innovative methods, could help shed light on the efficacy of such literary narratives—and especially, given the growing threat of environmental crises, the ability for them to intervene in time.

Mary Trachsel, in the final chapter of this part, situates a historical overview of human-animal entanglement in a consideration of the nonhuman and its agency, specifically focusing on human-horse narratives over time. As she writes: "A historical survey of these books and the interspecies relationships they depict reveals the development over time of an increasingly biocentric representation of humans as relational beings embedded in webs of life that reach beyond humanity, reconceptualizing the state of human being as human being-with more-than-human others." In the presentation, Trachsel invokes cultural critic and feminist scholar Joanna Zylinska, and her notion of the counter-apocalypse, tracing the typical responses to anthropogenic environmental change and the usual suspects of how one can avoid it—escape to a new planet, the type of technopositivism Tait discusses, and geo-engineering. Yet, as Trachsel notes, "[a]ll three of these popular problem-solution narratives of the Anthropocene distinguish human subjects as doers from the rest of nature, which is done unto; all presume human exceptionalism as justification for human dominion and control."

Rather, Trachsel recounts a story of a co-evolution of human and nonhuman, and through a tracing of the human-horse literary narrative, demonstrates an evolving relationship towards a co-creating, mutually beneficial framework. The evolution of this corresponds, as Trachsel attests, to a period of redefinition of the role of nonhuman animals in our society—the once ubiquitous feature of land and countryside—as modernity has slowly excluded all but the most domesticated of animals from acceptable parts of social life. Trachsel's chapter explores the shifting nature of the horse narrative, one of continued entanglement, and one which has survived the shift from the horse as creature of burden—supportive of the rural economy—to a part of both leisure and *bildung* for certain classes. She cites Birke stating, "[b]y replacing human dominance and aggression with attitudes of respect and cooperation, [Birke] explains, natural horsemanship transforms human culture one human being at a time, not simply by teaching 'a different way of being-with horses,' but more fundamentally by teaching 'a different way of being' (Birke 2007, 227)." Trachsel focuses on being-with and becoming to explore the boundary between horse and rider—the potential for this to be a symbiotic relationship, and one in which the human is not presented as clearly the dominant force. Louise Boscacci champions Bracha Ettinger's notion of "wit(h)nessing" "as a waymaker that enriches and extends the work of witnessing by embracing the teachings of *affect* and *more-than-visual sensing* and mattering in our humanimal encounters" (2018, 343). This parallels Trachsel's call for a more relational approach to the nonhuman-human encounter, which suggests that "Smiley's Oak Valley series encourages young readers to renounce human exceptionalism in order to practice new ways of human being-with nonhuman others." In her tracing of history, we see the growing entanglement and affect between horse and human. As Boscacci claims, "when we wit(h)ness, we *risk* being affected—a-bodily moved, grown more capacious or stilled and undone" (2018, 346). Each of the chapters in this part gives us reason to pause, expand our sensibilities, and make us more attuned to the entanglements and interrogations of boundaries we are witness to.

WITNESSING

Paying attention to others is to witness their existence, and nonhuman others are not exceptions from this. Yet there tend to be different degrees of attention and care put into our witnessing of the details of others' lives, and nonhumans often get the shorter end of the stick as the complexities of their lives are ignored or overruled by anthropocentric interests. This is perhaps also the reason attention given to witnessing in animal studies is often in relation to the violence other animals are subjected to at the hands of humans, just as much work on witnessing in general focuses on atrocities (e.g., Gillespie 2016; Hatley 2000).

Taking her starting point in ideas of witnessing in relation to past violence, Deborah Bird Rose leans on the scholarship of James Hatley, who argues that to "witness is . . . a mode of responding to the other's plight that exceeds an epistemological determination and becomes an ethical involvement. One must not only utter a truth *about* the victim but also remain true *to* her or him" (Hatley 2000, 3). By witnessing, one is thus "summoned to attentiveness, which is to say, to a heartfelt concern for and acknowledgment of the gravity of the violence toward particular others" (3). Rose sees in this a sort of moral command, in which "[m]oral claims are thrust upon one, and then a response is due," which means there is "dialogical potential at work" in the process of witnessing (2004, 30–31). Or, as she neatly summarizes the process and its call to the witness: "the moral claim, the response, the recognition of connection, the commitment" (31). In Rose's decolonial thinking, she ties such witnessing to loss of place, arguing that witnesses to such loss "take up a moral burden" and that this

> burden of witnessing to ecological loss brings Nature into the moral community, implicitly asserting in the context of place the injunction described by Hatley . . . : not only to speak truthfully, but to remain true *to* the place. In remaining true to place, one remains (or seeks to remain) true to non-human living things, ecosystems, and processes of resilience. (51)

Melville's "The Encantadas", considered by Kristen R. Egan in the first part of this book, could perhaps be read as an attempt to balance such an effort to be true to place with the demands on the writer and the colonial politics of his time. Rose's articulation of witnessing in relation to place also opens the door to considering witnessing as *not solely* about suffering, but of bearing witness to lives as they are. To be *true* to the individuals whose lives (and deaths) one witnesses is also to bear witness to their actual lives, as important irrespective of the amount of concrete suffering they include. This is witnessing as acknowledgment of presence, and can be a powerful tool in resisting the marginalization of others. As Rose points out, "[t]he terms 'non-human living things,' 'ecosystems,' and 'processes of resilience' are abstract; we encounter their reality in the world, in place" (51). This reality may include more or less suffering, but always includes the vulnerability of the living to suffering; witnessing life is thus always to be attentive to the vulnerability of others, even if removed from suffering in the present moment.

In this sense, witnessing the lived lives of other animals and beings in their environments, as they are, also works to decenter the human. Paying close attention to another's life can be a way of acknowledging their place in the world, not in relation to oneself, but in and of itself. In the first chapter of the *Witnessing* part, Lauren Perry considers works on wolves and coyotes that further give voice to these animals, while the focus also moves from fictional representation to considerations of other genres, here the non-fictional, documentary style focus of what she names 'Animal Texts.' These texts, she argues, "successfully bridge chasms between disciplines" by bringing humans' fascination with other animals to the forefront. Pointing to precursors such as Aldo Leopold and Rachel Carson, Perry points out that "[e]nvironmental writing has chronicled animals for decades, but we sometimes miss what is right in front of us on the page in our myopic literary analysis." As Perry argues, Animal Texts by Dan Flores and Nate Blakeslee "use literary tropes to give narrative agency to wildlife" and as such the "the narratives no longer present [the animals] as symptoms or victims of human action but as agents of their own future. Animals infiltrate the text through layered representations." There is, in other words, a serious attention to bringing the lived lives of specific wolves and coyotes home to the reader in such texts, to let their agency affect the writing, and thus to bear witness to their existence through a genre of texts designed to do just that.

Theorists draw attention to the double meaning of witnessing as both "a sensory experience—the witnessing of an experience with one's own eyes and ears" and "the discursive act of stating one's experience for the benefit of an audience" (Peters 2001, 709), while philosopher Kelly Oliver argues that, in addition to "the juridical connotations of seeing with one's own eyes," witnessing also has "the religious connotations of testifying to that which cannot be seen" (2015, 483). Indeed, for Oliver, the tension between what is seen by the witness and *bearing witness* to something beyond recognition . . . is the heart of subjectivity" (483). In other words, witnessing is not—or not solely—about documenting the lives of others; it is also about the way the witness is attentive and able to acknowledge those lives; as such, the moral claim invoked by Hatley and Rose comes into being also in relation to the subjective experience and openness to the subjectivity of others' experience. In Perry's chapter, part of this openness consists in a rewriting of "outdated and absurd regional boundaries [which] should be viewed for what they are: meaningless to all wildlife other than humans." This seems especially poignant to recognize in a time of environmental crisis, which is presently converging with the "critical moment in our world where the questions of nonhuman intelligence, environmental literature, and wildlife have reached a pinnacle." Animal Texts, as Perry defines the genre, rise to meet that challenge.

Subjectivity is equally important to the ecopoetry of Mary Oliver, which is the subject of the subsequent chapter in the part, written by Anastasia Cardone. Oliver's poetic response to human-nature entanglements draws, in Cardone's analysis, on kinds of closeness and attentiveness akin to those described as part of witnessing above. John Shoptaw has argued that ecopoetry needs to live up to two distinct criteria: it "needs to be environmental and it needs to be environmentalist" (2016, 395). The first criterion, which Shoptaw describes as needing "to be about the nonhuman natural world . . . really and not just figuratively" (395) is easily and obviously fulfilled by Oliver's poetry, yet for the criterion of being environmentalist to be fulfilled, Shoptaw argues, "the environment" of a poem in question must be "implicitly or explicitly, impacted by humans" (400).

One might here glimpse in Shoptaw's definition the possibility of an objection to some of Oliver's poems being described as ecopoetry, not just because the human is not always (even if often) impacting what is described, but also since the impact is often not perceived as negative when it *is* there. What Cardone shows, however, is how Oliver "recovers an organic language by rooting poetry in the earth, while including her readers to trigger a change in human perspective." In doing this, Oliver's poems depict "wholesome inclusion in nature through the physical and sensual contact with the other," Cardone argues. These are, arguably, methods of witnessing. Oliver is at once expressing a respect for the separateness of the other, with whatever positive and negative sides there may be to nature, and seeking to come closer in harmonious ways, to recognize and to commit. It is in this willingness to come closer that there is, in Cardone's words, a "fostering" of "aesthetic and ethical experiences" that allows for the subject to "feel an intrinsic part of nature, so that . . . the more the subject takes a step outside of their self, the more nature draws nearer, in a mutual and cordial embrace." The arguably environmentalist move in Oliver's poems, then, is less a matter of critiquing human impacts, and more a matter of imagining and forming other, more genuinely ethical and attentive, relations.

Like the 'Animal Texts' in Perry's chapter, Rachel Carson's three books about the ocean move beyond abstractions to be witness to lives lived in particular environments and the circumstances of those lives. It is these books—Carson's 'oceanalia'—that are the focus of Lauren O'Mahony's chapter, which concludes this volume's second part. As O'Mahony demonstrates,

"Carson illustrates witnessing in action" in her works about the sea. However, Carson employs a wealth of different narrative strategies and perspectives in her works, allowing for different methods of witnessing and recognizing the ocean's living beings. As O'Mahony writes, the shifting perspectives "modulate the distances between reader and text, in some cases making readers feel as if they are experiencing the sea through the narrator's eyes, dipped below its surface with its creatures or travelling through time observing its history." Indeed, Carson inventively employs anthropomorphism and nonhuman characters in her non-fictional works, occasionally depicting the dangers to creatures posed by human activity. This arguably prefigures the later influential work of cognitive ethologists such as Marc Bekoff, who argue for the use of anthropomorphism in science (e.g., 2013), and also arguably clashes with more conservative notions of witnessing. Yet it also speaks to Hatley's notion that in the attentiveness found in witnessing "the wounding of the other is registered in the first place not as an objective fact but as a subjective blow" (2000, 3).

Taken together, O'Mahony argues, Carson's sea narratives "challenge the perceived boundaries between reader, text(s) and world to offer a three-dimensional texture of the ocean that seeks reader engagement and ideally, future action," thus acting from the moral claim's call to response of which both Hatley and Rose write. In addition, as Marnie O'Sullivan has suggested elsewhere, Carson's works also challenge boundaries in other ways, for instance because "the edge of the sea is an elusive and indefinable boundary" in her representation (2012, 78). Indeed, O'Sullivan has argued, "Carson's persistent preoccupation with marginal landscapes and their inhabitants model patterns of engagement with the 'other' that fosters an ethic of care that avoids domination or exploitation," thus mirroring the ethical dimension of the attentiveness found in witnessing (78). Arguably, this is what we see when Carson, in O'Mahony's words, "makes the strange and unfamiliar less so while conjuring a substantive representation that shifts 'the ocean' from object to subject."

"Centering the animal as a subject of witnessing allows us to see with particular clarity the importance of witnessing and the role of emotion in witnessing," Kathryn Gillespie has argued (2016, 574). In their respective chapters, Perry, Cardone, and O'Mahony give very different, yet all inspiring, examples of textual attempts to produce such clarity and emotion.

NONHUMAN AGENCY

Nonhuman agency has always been part of human epistemologies—from spiritual ideas about the agency of God, angels, or other ephemeral beings, to the Cartesian emphasis on reason as uniquely human, which effectively distinguished human agency as inherently different from any nonhuman animal agency, by claiming the latter arose solely from "passions" (Descartes 2007, 60). Yet the line between human and nonhuman agency has also continually been blurred throughout history. When the Scottish Romantic Age reformer John Oswald pleaded animals' cause in his *The Cry of Nature* (1791), for instance, he declared, "O that [man] would listen to the voice of nature! For powerfully she stirs within us; and, from the very bottom of the human heart, with moving voice she pleads," thus rhetorically blending the cries of nonhumans outside humans with the metaphorical call of conscience within (2000, 28). Others have heard in concrete animal voices the agency of expression and have reacted affectively, even while limiting the exercise of animals' agency in other ways (e.g., Borkfelt 2019, 229–232). Still others have chronicled and contemplated the actions of animals, and some have chosen to punish animals for exercising agency even as prevailing philosophies dismissed such agency as purely instinctive (Girgen 2003; McFarland 2018).

In the last couple of decades, however, the debate seems to have shifted significantly: Karen Barad "calling into question the presumed alignment of agency and subjectivity" (2007, 217) and arguing for an "agential realism" (393); Jane Bennett's notion of "vibrant matter" and declaration that "encounters with lively matter can chasten my fantasies of human mastery, highlight the common materiality of all there is, expose a wider distribution of agency" (2010, 122); the arguments of numerous posthumanist scholars which unseat the traditional human subject (e.g., Nayar 2014; Wolfe 2010); animal studies scholars across disciplines paying close attention to nonhuman animals' agency (e.g., Bekoff and Pierce 2009; Carter and Charles 2011; McHugh 2009, 2010; Roscher 2019; Colling 2021). Through all these diverse strands of thinking, the general notion of the human as the only true agent—whether in philosophical, biological, or moral terms—has been thoroughly critiqued, questioned, and undermined.

It makes sense, at this point, to view agency as relational rather than bound to the subject (whether that subject is human or not). As others have argued, doing so frees the concept from ties to particular kinds of subjectivity or capacities, while at the same time resisting the idea that anything that has an effect has agency (Carter and Charles 2011, 9–14; Roscher 2019, 150–152). If agency is plural, and agents are thus collectivities, in this sense, then exploring agency almost by definition becomes about interrogating the boundaries between those entities found in the relations in/from which agency arises. While it is clear that nonhumans are agents in this conceptualization of agency, it also, for instance, means that nonhuman agency is not solely nonhuman when it happens in relation to humans, making for a complex notion of agency that immediately questions boundaries in human-nonhuman relations of any kind. Such a position can also be combined relatively seamlessly with various posthuman(ist) and other non-essentialist ontologies in which the human is always-already embedded, entangled, part of assemblages, and was indeed never 'just' human to begin with, given our very embodiment's reliance on other organisms (e.g., Haraway 2008, 3–4; Wolfe 2010, xv-xiv). Or, as anthropologists Alan Smart and Josephine Smart have put it, "[w]ithout non-humans, there would have been no humans, because our nature is tied up with them as far back as we can trace humans" (2017, 2).

Agency, then, is contingent on others and becomes relevant only in relation, and for humans in the relations with the creatures that live with us, on us, and in us. Yet, as Carter and Charles point out, it also arises from (and is restricted by) the wider contexts and hierarchies in which we are all enveloped. In human societies, this includes the distribution of resources, and since "we are born into a certain place at a certain moment" and the "distributions predate our arrival, they do not require our consent or complicity," various advantages or disadvantages follow from this (2011, 10–11). For nonhuman animals, this distribution tends to be highly disadvantageous, as they

> are profoundly affected by their locations within a distribution of resources that is deeply anthropocentric, where their habitats and ecologies are subject to human interests and depredation, where their lives are subordinated to the carnivorous needs and desires of humans and where the material and ecological conditions for their survival are frequently disregarded by the pursuit of human commercial advantage. (Carter and Charles 2011, 11)

The three chapters in this volume's part on *Nonhuman Agency* speak in different ways to these considerations as well as to the identification and transgression of boundaries.

Owen Harry's consideration of Richard Powers's *The Overstory* presents a story of receptivity to the agency of trees, a form of being-with and witnessing, while also considering the nature of communication between nonhuman entities (Powers's communicative trees) and where the line is drawn. Yet, being vulnerable to cutting and commercial use by humans, the trees in the novel are clearly also enveloped in the power structures and hierarchies which humans have established. Harry views the novel through the posthumanist work of Rosi Braidotti which, as he states, "views humanism's erasure of agency from the nonhuman world as contributing directly to global environmental degradation." Reading it through such a posthumanist lens, Harry argues that Powers's novel "demonstrates the potentially generative role of literature in affirming nonhuman agency, suggesting also the kinds of posthuman subjectivities required to escape the inherently teleological and exploitative narratives of humanism." As a way of broadening our attention to nonhuman agency, Harry's analysis suggests an attentiveness to kinds of agency perhaps not immediately recognizable to humans, and focuses specifically on the role of stillness in *The Overstory*.

As Harry argues, given the traditional association of agency with expression, voice, and indeed language, Powers's use of stillness offers an in some ways radical departure from anthropocentric notions of agency in that it "subverts associations of agency with activity," "encourages receptivity to slower timescales," and "allows for a non-teleological recognition of connections between humans and nonhumans." Through his innovative analysis, Harry thus suggests an expansion of current frameworks for considering nonhuman agency, by pushing beyond animals and highlighting Powers's "radical move which encourages us to take plant life seriously but also has clear consequences for animal agency."

Vera Veldhuizen's presentation of Orson Scott Card's novels also presents ethical boundaries between creatures not normally considered animal, providing an interrogation of alien encounters, and of the liminal nature of AIs and viruses, and the ethics of policing these lines. As Veldhuizen states, "aliens discovered and described in science fiction go beyond nonhuman animals; they are truly Other, both far removed from our reality and monstrously, uncannily close to our Earthly cohabitants." In Card's novels, such alien beings are classed according to a protocol known as the "Hierarchy of Exclusion" to ensure moral treatment of the species encountered, yet as Veldhuizen argues "a protocol which is based entirely on Othering (and thus potentially limiting empathy) forces the Other to be morally colonised, and to classify themselves in a system which considers humanity as the peak of existence." Carter and Charles have argued that a key difference between human and nonhuman animal agency is that the former is politicized within human social life because "who gets what, when and how requires the manipulation and mobilization of symbolic resources and representations" (2011, 13). As Veldhuizen shows, the nonhumans in Card's novels are precisely politicized in this way, as they are co-opted into a hierarchy that is exactly such a representation.

Notably, Veldhuizen explores how the humans in the novel respond to a virus that is part of a planet's ecosystem and forms "[p]erhaps the most explicit and complex challenge to anthroponormativity regarding the Hierarchy of Exclusion." In Veldhuizen's words, this virus, called "the descolada," "destroys the DNA of anything it comes into contact with," yet there is speculation that it may be both conscious and intelligent, and attempts to communicate with it are made. Hence, as Veldhuizen notes, the virus forms a very special challenge for the protocol of behavior to encountered species, and the legitimacy of such anthroponormative categorizations, which reflects ways in which perceived dangers to human safety often overrule morality.

As Sarah McFarland has noted, "oftentimes the human response to predatory animal agency is to impose human moral values upon the nonhuman, reinforcing the human supremacist illusion upon both worlds rather than recognizing . . . mutuality" (2018, 95).

Where Veldhuizen focuses on works that depict extra-terrestrial colonization, Clare Archer-Lean's chapter engages more earthly colonial issues in her consideration of Australian Aboriginal and their interactions with creatures who again challenge nominal lines between plant and animal, and provide representation to nonhuman agencies. As Archer-Lean states, the works she considers "share [a] revoking of the epistemological dominance of realism and a conjuring of the nonhuman entity to develop agential representation." The chapter's primary focus is on Ellen van Neerven's short story "Water," which Archer-Lean argues "dissolves anthropocentric and imperial oppositions and hierarchies, centralising Indigenous world views to cast new knowledge on the crises of the Anthropocene through representation of nonhuman/human relationships as increasingly sensual and mutable." This is done not least through the story's "plant people," who as the name implies suggest other ontologies than those based in Eurocentric, colonialist taxonomies and categorizations, thus also blurring the lines of who are considered agential. In Archer-Lean's words, van Neerven's narrative "mobilises tropes of armed resistance, speculative futures, and the hybrid nonhuman entity to queer and destabilise colonial authority and speciesism."

As Archer-Lean notes, "the agential force of the nonhuman," which appears in van Neerven's story (and in the TV series *Cleverman* also briefly considered) "is derived from rich and continuing Indigenous cultural traditions." Here, the nonhuman as a person is real, not symbolic, and hence the story is able to mobilize "the nonhuman entity in service of an ethos of respectful engagement and interagency across species lines," thus also emphasizing the relational aspects of agency for those willing to see them.

In the end, discussions on nonhuman agency often come down to what we as humans are willing or able to notice—and are willing to imagine as agential beyond the human, not just symbolically but in reality. In his seminal essay "Why Look at Animals?" John Berger famously complained that "[t]he fact that [animals] can observe us has lost all significance" (2009, 27). Humans may look at animals through various cultural lenses, not recognizing the animals (or other nonhuman beings) looking back or otherwise reacting to our presence, which would otherwise reveal their role in the agential relation. In the various narratives analyzed by Harry, Veldhuizen, and Archer-Lean the nonhumans look back—they react and interact—and thus affirm their (role in) agency.

MUTATION AND POST-APOCALYPSE

The final part, *Mutation and Post-Apocalypse*, considers texts set in various iterations of the future, in landscapes ravaged by cataclysms both known and unknown, but which upend social structures and landscapes and depict a world in which life has changed dramatically—human and nonhuman alike. The texts considered by each of the contributors have been variously classified as science fiction, dystopian, speculative fiction, and post-apocalyptic, each of which has its own generic history, tropes and definitions. Yet, what the chapters share is an interrogation of the norms within these frames, not only causing us to reconsider the pessimism associated with the apocalypse and its aftermath, or the inevitability of reified patriarchal norms in a dystopian future, but also positioning these narratives as opportunities to reconsider, and reformulate, our society in the wake of these catastrophic changes, to provide a better future for those that remain.

In looking at these global changes, such as the climate crisis, artistic expression turns towards narratives in genres like science fiction because of their ability to show its scope. In an interview in Screen Daily, Bong Joon Ho, director of *Snowpiercer*, explains his choice of science fiction to depict the climate crisis, stating that "[s]cience fiction is a genre where you can express the human condition and systems in which we live much more directly and symbolically" (Noh 2013), which Shelley Streeby notes "helped him explore questions about climate change and global class inequalities and stage them for a global audience" (Streeby 2018, 4). This collection is particularly interested in this entanglement of the climate and inequality, and how literary scholars are able to highlight the potential in these narratives to not only depict the disastrous, but use that framing to model change for the future, not for humanity in particular (in an anthropocentric mode), but in creative constellations that destabilize and interrogate. Teresa De Lauretis has called this capacity of "potentially creative of new forms of social imagination, creative in the sense of mapping out areas where cultural change could take place, of envisioning a different order of relationships between people and between people and things, a different conceptualization of social existence, inclusive of physical and material existence" (De Lauretis 1980, 161).

Science fiction, in particular, has long been given the place in the cultural imaginary where one can explore questions of otherness. The very premise of Darko Suvin's definition of the genre hinges on the idea of 'cognitive estrangement' in which the world is altered from a verisimilar representation of our own world through implementation of a 'novum,' a plausible technological difference. Sherryl Vint credits that grounded nature with the relevance of the genre to these concerns: "In addition to this specific concern with science, sf's long history of exploring questions of alterity and particularly the boundary between human and other sentient beings—frequently explored through robot or other AI characters—further positions it as uniquely suited to interrogating the human-animal boundary" (Vint 2010, 6). However, she champions the idea with a note of caution—that we must not lose sight of the alterity of the Other in presenting a futuristic or scientific tale which only serves to enlighten us about ourselves: "If our readings of such texts forget or minimize their animal being—transforming them into analogues of robots or images of technoscience or 'just' aliens who might share some features with animals—then we foreclose the texts' radically other utopian impulses" (Vint 2010, 16). In the chapters in this collection, all natures of nonhuman entities are depicted and interrogated, and even viral and hybrid beings are shown in their radical alterity, from the 'plant people' and gene-changing virus presented in the previous parts by Clare Archer-Lean and Vera Veldhuizen respectively, to the hybrid entities, gene mutations, multispecies communities, and even indistinction of the nonhuman/human presented in this final part.

Amitav Ghosh, in *The Great Derangement*, however, challenges the efficacy of science fictional tales to add to our understanding of global climate change. While he agrees fervently that "the climate crisis is also a crisis of culture, and thus of the imagination" (Ghosh 2016, 9; see also Clark 2015, 73; Nixon 2013, 3; Heise 2008, 208; Kainulainen 2013, 111), he also argues that literary representations have failed to deliver along these lines. His argument aligns certain narratives to their origins at the beginning of the nineteenth century, along with the rise of the novel, following Ian Watt and others—which also corresponds to at least some definitions of the Anthropocene. The novel and industrialization have similar cultural antecedents, and thus, following Ghosh's reasoning, the novel may not be the best suited medium with which to address this particular cataclysm. Yet, even when acknowledging the growing genre of climate fiction, he claims that it is "made up mostly of disaster stories set in the future" and that, for him, "the future is but one aspect of the Anthropocene: this era also includes the recent past, and, most significantly, the present" (Ghosh 2016, 72). We, however, argue that this may misrepresent the genre. Samuel Delany reminds us that "[s]cience fiction is not about the future; it uses the future as a narrative convention to present significant distortions of the present" (Delany 2012, 26).

Moreover, it is precisely as an expression of the present crisis that there is such a proliferation of cli-fi stories. Jonathan Elmore argues that "[o]ne way to understand the explosive proliferation of cli-fi is as a sociocultural response *en masse* to climate change" (2021, 2) and not only that it is a response to the present, but that it may contribute meaningfully to the future: "We must deliberately and with rapidity learn to tell this story, our geostory, well and widely. In fact, many thinkers have argued that cli-fi (stories of, and about, climate change) may be the most important tool available for understanding and surviving the Anthropocene" (3). Despite the urgency, we also need to pause and take stock of which tales we choose to tell, and whose stories are privileged and presented. Ursula K. Heise argues so, even in considering the value of nonhuman entities, and

> however much individual environmentalists may be motivated by a selfless devotion to the well-being of nonhuman species, however much individual conservation scientists may be driven by an eagerness to expand our knowledge and understanding of the species with whom we co-inhabit the planet, their engagements with these species gain sociocultural traction to the extent that they become part of the stories that human communities tell about themselves: stories about their origins, their development, their identity, and their future horizons. (2016, 5)

The chapters in this collection, and this part in particular, highlight responses to the anthropocentric notion that Heise cautions us about. Our world is entangled; as the global climate and environmental crises increasingly demonstrate, our ecosystems cannot be separated into a 'good' for humanity and consequences for others. Our stories, from the Galapagos to distant planets, need to reflect this entanglement. Shelley Streeby, drawing on Indigenous logic and culture, argues that "people of color and Indigenous people use science fiction and other speculative genres to remember the past and imagine futures that help us think critically about the present and connect climate change to social movements" (Streeby 2018, 5). While Streeby is focused on connecting Indigenous and people of color to sf and speculative stories as a matter of praxis and exploring alternative worldings, this is true both outside the United States (see Nnedi Okorafor, or Ellen Van Neerven as referred to in this collection) but also true of speculative fiction in general. Vint argues that "speculative fiction operates at a different ontological level, positing a new world with its own taken-for-granted truisms. Speculative texts invite us to inhabit such worlds, to share their 'estranged' assumptions, and perhaps to recognize through this that the material, given world is also not as fixed as we might once have believed" (Vint 2021, 501), which one can read in each of the chapters in this part, by Samantha Hind, Clare Wall, and Elizabeth Tavella.

In addition to being read as speculative fiction, each of the texts also interrogate the notion of the post-apocalyptic, asking how we can envision futures that help us stage a post-apocalyptic life. These final chapters interrogate that possibility, showing that considerations after the 'end times' envisioned in apocalyptic thinking need not be a reversion to the base or worst traits of humanity, but rather can open up the possibility of a rethinking of our relationships with each other—human and nonhuman alike—and a recognition of our shared participation in an ecosystem and society moving forwards. Stephen Joyce argues that "[t]he word 'apocalypse' does not refer to the end of time but to the revelation that comes once history has ceased and assumed its final shape" (Joyce 2018, 48). In this, the apocalypse is staged as the end of times. Sarah Dillon, however, suggests that this frame has also been about the dawn of a new era: "it may seem strange to suggest that apocalyptic narratives are a strategy for confronting and deferring the threat of remainderless destruction. But it does not seem so strange if one recalls that in the biblical tradition, apocalyptic narratives predict both the end of the world and the coming of a new age" (Dillon 2007, 376). Each of the three chapters in this part focus on life after this end—and imagine, in various iterations, this new age. Hind's presentation of *The Road* follows what Joyce presents as typical of the post-apocalyptic, namely, takes that are "often morally ambiguous, dystopian, and told in formats that favour infinitely suspended narratives" (Joyce 2018, 51). Yet, each of the other chapters present a future in which there is potential for optimism, an ability to carve out a utopian space in the dystopian aftertimes—akin to the critical dystopia suggested by Moylan and Baccolini (2003).

Those chapters interrogate our notions of the pessimism often presented in the post-apocalyptic—with assumptions that humanity will break down, and we will be 'reduced' to a series of baser instincts. However, there are other options found in this reduction of our contemporary way of life. When the Australian philosopher and ecofeminist, Val Plumwood, was famously attacked by a crocodile, she was confronted with a revelation, that she—by virtue of her humanity—is not outside of the discourse of consumption. As she recalls, "[i]t was a shocking reduction, from a complex human being to a mere piece of meat" (2002); an experience that in Matthew Calarco's words carried out a shift "from her privileged subject position to a shared zone of coexistence with other edible beings" (2015, 60). That reduction is informative, as it helps to destabilize the privilege of the anthropocentric position. It is a moment of revelation that we are all connected, and that there are consequences for our (in)action(s). Since we are all in this equally, the privileging of any species should be interrogated and that perhaps, the only way 'forward,' as suggested in several of the chapters, is a path that we don't all share for the benefit of those who remain. Amitav Ghosh argues that "[t]he knowledge that results from recognition, then, is not of the same kind as the discovery of something new: it arises rather from a renewed reckoning with a potentiality that lies within oneself" (Ghosh 2016, 5). We are aware of our connectedness, but as these chapters point out—we need that moment of realization, a reminder that the nonhuman world is a part of the human world, and that our future speculations can reflect on that and propose new ways forward, a new future for us all.

This starts with Samantha Hind's postapocalyptic interrogation of the concept of flesh, exemplified by considering consumption and representation of meat in speculative fictional texts by Cormac McCarthy and Joseph D'Lacey. It is not clearly presented, in either of the novels, that the conditions are a result of the global climate crisis—however, each of the speculative futures presents a landscape eerily denuded of nonhuman life, invoking the imaginary that in a destabilized ecosystem somehow only human animals have the capacity to survive—though often thought with consequences for our ethical consideration of what it is to be human. Hind argues that, like Margaret Atwood's theoretical line of speculative fiction, this presented future scenario is more realistic than we would like to consider: "Such speculative fiction worlds, where whole cities have crumbled and starvation looms like an unwanted omen, are, at least for their creators, not such an inconceivable possibility, since the climate crisis puts the future of every species on Earth in danger." However, rather than focusing on the ethical implications, Hind's analysis focuses on the unstable ontological categories between the human and the nonhuman, with their concomitant assumptions behind edibility and the inconsumable. In drawing this boundary to interrogate, she uses McCarthy not only to challenge the line between, but the status supposedly belonging to each side, deconstructing the assumptions behind being human and the 'ideology of distinction' that maintains this unwarranted assumption.

In contrast to McCarthy's novel, Hind also draws on the community of D'Lacey's *Meat*, in which the boundaries between the human and the nonhuman are entangled with the consumption of flesh and the designation of individuals on either side of the line. She considers how the text produces the 'Chosen,' those individuals who must undergo transformative surgery "in order to *become* edible flesh," and further notes that "[d]espite the obvious human species identity of the Chosen, then, *Meat* acts as an ideological allegory, placing mutilated humans in the conditions and positions typically reserved for farmed nonhuman animals." The novel, however, is not a simple portrayal of this post-apocalyptic community, but suggests the cracks in its own logic. The idea of un-becoming demonstrates the arbitrariness of the categories, making the distinction even more 'ideological': "Such an un-becoming shows the instability of the ideology of distinction and directly challenges it—despite taking many years to fully manifest." This, more than anything, seems to underscore the critique implicit in Hind's argument, as she draws connections between the two novels she analyses, as well as between the frames of the post-apocalyptic and the critical dystopia frames it interrogates.

Clare Wall's chapter continues the theme of destabilizing an anthropocentric frame, focusing on future 'plague' narratives—examining three authors who present scenarios of post-apocaptic life and using new materialist and posthuman lenses to interrogate the relative positioning of human and nonhuman actors within the narratives: "Examining Watts's, Bacigalupi's, and Atwood's post-millennial plague narratives through a posthumanist lens, it becomes clear how their nuanced accounts of interspecies partnerships, nonhuman entanglements, and transformative 'mutational politics' decenter the human subject and position the human as part of an environmentally situated assemblage." Wall considers these texts through a broad lens, looking across multiple volumes in considering the ways in which human and nonhuman actors (AI, viruses) need to work together, as well as emphasizing the instability of these categories in the first place. As considered in previous chapters, any intervention into an ecosystem has consequences, some foreseeable and many not—and what is foreseeable is dependent only on the perspectives and biases inherent in that perspective, that bodily experience, and embodied frame. Wall's presentation draws on numerous posthumanist thinkers, arguing for a process of becoming—one which is embedded in a 'zone of coexistence' to use Calarco's terms (2015), or a product of 'making kin' to use Haraway's term (2015).

Importantly, Wall's chapter presents the notion of considering both the global climate crisis and, increasingly, environmental crises, as notions of concern not for the present circumstances, but for an ethical reading of the future in which we consider the good of all, not just the good of the few—the human population. By using these future apocalypses, the extrapolation of potential scenarios—not even as distant as Atwood assumes science fiction implies, but potential based on our own technology and society—Wall presents narratives that treat the human and nonhuman as equal in deserving ethical consideration, as entangled in the same ecosystem and with each an equal claim to survival. She argues that, "[i]n this sense, both Watts's and Atwood's narratives resist anthropocentric apocalypticism by recognizing that what survives may not be human beings—at least not as we know them—and that a restoration of biodiversity, even if it is radically different than it was before, is still worth celebrating." This need not necessarily be read as pessimistic, even from an anthropocentric position, but as an opportunity to reconsider our thinking, our entanglements, and as a suggestion that the future, perhaps, still remains open to optimism: "By challenging anthropocentric biases in their narratives, Watts, Atwood, and Bacigalupi underscore the importance of imagining potential new symbiotic partnerships and hybrid ecologies that negotiate environmental effects under climate change with attention to our entanglements with nonhuman agencies."

Finally, Elizabeth Tavella looks at Paolo Volponi's projected post-apocalyptic scenario on a devastated planet, with a consideration of escaped circus animals—providing a focus on non-anthropocentric society in a future world "destroyed by atomic devastations and climatic mutations." His 1978 Italian novel, *Il Pianeta Irritabile*, is analyzed in this chapter through the intersecting lens of "critical animal studies, disability studies, and ecocriticism." The aim is to demonstrate how the novel exposes the inherent limits of the nature/culture dichotomy as well as the urgent need to build a society based on new ethical foundations." With a series of characters that already interrogate notions of verisimilitude, an elephant that can recite Dante and a goose that can perform calculus, Volponi's novel is often taken as falling into the trap highlighted by Heise, of presenting the nonhuman actors as a metaphorical extension of humanity—and yet, as Tavella rightly notes, the novel does not fall into this trap. Rather, what is highlighted is "the author's ability to explore the real nature and place in the world of nonhuman animals, who should not be understood, within this theoretical framework, as mere projections of the renewal of 'humans.'"

The novel itself is also set in a post-apocalyptic scenario, reflecting not only McCarthy's *The Road*, as discussed earlier, but also Rachel Carson's *Silent Spring* in its speculative fiction 'A Fable for Tomorrow,' through its absence of bird song. Volponi uses this to disorient the reader, following a nuclear catastrophe, but it is also eerily relevant in our pandemic filled present, in which we are simultaneously engaged with rethinking our world in order to deal with anthropocentric climate change. Tavella harkens back to ecofeminist discourse, in which nature is meant to cover up for the atrocities of man, but rather than laying blame, looks towards a new, positively framed future. Tavella argues that "[w]ith *Il Pianeta Irritabile*, Volponi manages to disrupt the conventional binaries of nature/culture and human/animal, particularly through linguistic experimentation and metamorphic processes extending to the corporeal dimension and the natural environment, which leads to the obsolescence of hierarchies and the establishment of a new social and ecological order."

In conclusion, the series of chapters in this final part see the power of speculative fiction to not only reflect, but to change our common outlook for the future. The results of our actions, in the post-industrial Anthropocene, or the post-modern Capitalocene, have led directly to our current predicament. Yet, in addressing both climate and its concurrent environmental crises, these chapters argue fervently that we need to rethink not only our relationship to 'nature' but to each other—across the human-nonhuman binary, and consider the entangled nature of all things. Shelley Streeby argues that "[o]ur answers about the future of climate change must not come solely from the sphere of science and technology, or they will be too narrow, not capacious enough.

The work of imagination is critical and culture is a crucial contributor to that conversation" (Streeby 2018, 30). It is the work of the imagination, presenting the possibilities of the future, that will help us to challenge the assumed frames and make our future more conducive to life, in all its forms.

REFERENCES

Barad, Karen. 2007. *Meeting the Universe Halfway: Quantum Physics and the Entanglement of Matter and Meaning.* Durham, NC: Duke University Press.
Bekoff, Marc. 2013. "Animal Consciousness and Science Matter: Anthropomorphism Is Not Anti-Science." *Relations* 1 (1): 61–68. doi: 10.7358/rela-2013-001-beko.
Bekoff, Marc, and Jessica Pierce. 2009. *Wild Justice: The Moral Lives of Animals.* Chicago: University of Chicago Press.
Bennett, Jane. 2010. *Vibrant Matter: A Political Ecology of Things.* Durham, NC: Duke University Press.
Berger, John. 2009 [1977]. "Why Look at Animals?" In John Berger, *Why Look at Animals*, 12–37. London: Penguin.
Birke, Linda. 2007. "'Learning to Speak Horse': The Culture of 'Natural Horsemanship.'" *Society and Animals* 15 (3): 217–39.
Borkfelt, Sune. 2019. "Sensing Slaughter: Exploring the Sounds and Smells of Nonhuman Literary Encounters." In *Animal Encounters: Kontakt, Interaktion und Relationalität*, ed. Alexandra Böhm and Jessica Ullrich, 225–40. Berlin: J. B. Metzler.
Boscacci, Louise. 2018. "Wit(h)nessing." *Environmental Humanities* 10 (1): 343–47.
Calarco, Matthew. 2015. *Thinking Through Animals: Identity, Difference, Indistinction.* Stanford: Stanford Briefs (Stanford University Press).
Carter, Bob, and Nickie Charles. 2011. "Human-Animal Connections: An Introduction." In *Human and Other Animals*, ed. Bob Carter and Nickie Charles, 1–27. Houndmills: Palgrave Macmillan.
Clark, Timothy. 2015. *Ecocriticism on the Edge: The Anthropocene as a Threshold Concept.* London: Bloomsbury.
Crutzen, Paul J., and Eugene F. Stoermer. 2000. "The 'Anthropocene.'" *Global Change Newsletter* 41: 17–18.
Davis, Janae, Alex A. Moulton, Levi Van Sant, and Brian Williams. "Anthropocene, Capitalocene, . . . Plantationocene?: A Manifesto for Ecological Justice in an Age of Global Crises." *Geography Compass* 13(5): e12438.
De Lauretis, Teresa. 1980. "Signs of W[a/o]nder." *The Technological Imagination: Theories and Fictions,* ed. Teresa De Lauretis, Andreas Huyssen, and Kathleen Woodward, 159–174. Madison, WI: Coda Press.
Delany, Samuel. 2012. "Some Presumptuous Approaches to Science Fiction." *Starboard Wine: More Notes on the Language of Science Fiction.* Middletown, CT: Wesleyan University Press.

Deleuze, Gilles. 2003 [1981]. *Francis Bacon: The Logic of Sensation*. Trans. Daniel W. Smith. London: Continuum.

DeLoughrey, Elizabeth. 2019. *Allegories of the Anthropocene*. Durham, NC: Duke University Press.

Derrida, Jacques. 2008 [2006]. *The Animal That Therefore I Am*. Ed. Marie-Louise Mallet. Trans. David Wills. New York: Fordham University Press.

Descartes, René. 2007 [1646/1649]. "From the Letters of 1646 and 1649." In *The Animals Reader: The Essential Classic and Contemporary Writings*, ed. Linda Kalof and Amy Fitzgerald, 59–62. London: Bloomsbury.

Dillon, Sarah. 2007. "Imagining Apocalypse: Maggie Gee's 'The Flood.'" *Contemporary Literature* 48 (3): 374–97.

Elmore, Jonathan. 2021. *Fiction and the Sixth Mass Extinction: Narrative in an Era of Loss*. Lanham, MD: Lexington Books.

Ghosh, Amitav. 2016. *The Great Derangement: Climate Change and the Unthinkable*. Chicago: University of Chicago Press.

Gillespie, Kathryn. 2016. "Witnessing Animal Others: Bearing Witness, Grief, and the Political Function of Emotion." *Hypatia* 31 (3): 572–88.

Girgen, Jen. 2003. "The Historical and Contemporary Prosecution and Punishment of Animals." *Animal Law* 9: 97–133.

Hatley, James. 2000. *Suffering Witness: The Quandary of Responsibility after the Irreparable*. Albany, NY: State University of New York Press.

Haraway, Donna, Noboru Ishikawa, Gilbert Scott, Kenneth Olwig, Anna L. Tsing, and Nils Bubandt. 2015. "Anthropologists Are Talking—About the Anthropocene." *Ethnos: Journal of Anthropology*. doi: 10.1080/00141844.2015.1105838.

Haraway, Donna. 2008. *When Species Meet*. Minneapolis: University of Minnesota Press.

———. 2015. "Anthropocene, Capitolocene, Plantationocene, Chthulucene: Making Kin." *Environmental Humanities* 6: 159–65.

Heise, Ursula K. 2008. *Sense of Place and Sense of Planet: The Environmental Imagination of the Global*. Oxford: Oxford University Press.

———. 2016. *Imagining Extinction: The Cultural Meanings of Endangered Species*. Chicago: University of Chicago Press.

Johns-Putra, Adeline. 2016. "Climate change in literature and literary studies: from cli-fi, climate change theater and ecopoetry to ecocriticism and climate change criticism." *WIREs Clim Change* 7: 266–282. https://doi.org/10.1002/wcc.385.

Joyce, Stephen. 2016. "The Double Death of Humanity in Cormac McCarthy's The Road." *Transatlantica: Revues d'études américaines / American Studies Journal* 2 (2016). Online.

———. 2018. *Transmedia Storytelling and the Apocalypse*. Cham: Palgrave.

Kainulainen, Maggie. 2013. "Saying Climate Change: Ethics of the Sublime and Problems of Representation." *Symploke* 21: 109–23.

Malm, Andreas and Alf Hornborg. 2014. "The Geology of Mankind? A Critique of the Anthropocene Narrative." *The Anthropocene Review* 1 (1): 62–69.

McFarland, Sarah E. 2018. "Such Beastly Behavior! Predation, Revenge, and the Question of Ethics." In *Exploring Animal Encounters: Philosophical, Cultural, and*

Historical Perspectives, ed. Dominik Ohrem and Matthew Calarco, 93–111. Cham: Palgrave Macmillan.

McHugh, Susan. 2009. "Literary Animal Agents." *PMLA* 124 (2): 487–95.

———. 2010. *Animal Stories: Narrating Across Species Lines*. Minneapolis: University of Minnesota Press.

Moore, Jason. 2017. "The Capitalocene, Part I: on the nature and origins of our ecological crisis." *The Journal of Peasant Studies* 44 (3): 594–630. doi: 10.1080/03066150.2016.1235036

Moylan, Tom and Raffaellla Bacoolini. 2003. *Dark Horizons: Science Fiction and the Dystopian Imagination*. London: Routledge.

Nayar, Pramod K. 2014. *Posthumanism*. Cambridge, MA: Polity.

Nixon, Rob. 2011. *Slow Violence and the Environmentalism of the Poor*. Harvard: Harvard University Press.

Oliver, Kelly. 2015. "Witnessing, Recognition, and Response Ethics." *Philosophy and Rhetoric* 48 (4): 473–93.

Oswald, John. 2000 [1791]. *The Cry of Nature; or, An Appeal to Mercy and to Justice on Behalf of the Persecuted Animals*. Ed. Jason Hribal. Lewiston: Edwin Mellen Press.

Peters, John Durham. 2001. "Witnessing." *Media, Culture & Society* 23 (6): 707–23.

Pick, Anat. 2011. *Creaturely Poetics: Animality and Vulnerability in Literature and Film*. New York: Columbia University Press.

Plumwood, Val. 2002 [1996]. "Prey to a Crocodile." *The Aisling Magazine* 30: https://www.aislingmagazine.com/aislingmagazine/articles/TAM30/ValPlumwood.html.

Roscher, Mieke. 2019. "Actors or Agents? Defining the Concept of Relational Agency in (Historical) Wildlife Encounters." In *Animal Encounters: Kontakt, Interaktion und Relationalität*, ed. Alexandra Böhm and Jessica Ullrich, 149–70. Berlin: J. B. Metzler.

Rose, Deborah Bird. 2004. *Reports from a Wild Country: Ethics for Decolonisation*. Sydney: University of New South Wales Press.

Shoptaw, John. 2016. "Why Ecopoetry?" *Poetry* 207 (4): 395–408.

Smart, Alan, and Josephine Smart. 2017. *Posthumanism*. North York, Ontario: University of Toronto Press.

Streeby, Shelley. 2018. *Imagining the Future of Climate Change: World-Making through Science Fiction and Activism*. Oakland: University of California Press.

O'Sullivan, Marnie M. 2012. "Shifting Subjects and Marginal Worlds: Revealing the Radical in Rachel Carson's Three Sea Books." In *Feminist Ecocriticism: Environment, Women, and Literature*, ed. Douglas A. Vakoch, 77–91. Lanham, MD: Lexington Books.

Suvin, Darko. 1979. *Metamorphoses of Science Fiction: On the Poetics of a Literary Genre*. New Haven, CT: Yale University Press.

Vint, Sherryl. 2010. *Animal Alterity: Science Fiction and the Question of the Animal*. Liverpool: Liverpool University Press.

———. 2021. "'Without the Right Words It's Hard to Retain Clarity': Speculative Fiction and Animal Narrative." *The Palgrave Handbook of Animals and Literature*,

ed. Susan McHugh, Robert McKay, and John Miller, 499–511. Cham: Palgrave Macmillan.
Wilson, Edward O. 2016. *Half-Earth: Our Planet's Fight for Life*. New York: Norton.
Wolfe, Cary. 2010. *What Is Posthumanism?* Minneapolis: University of Minnesota Press.
Zylinska, Joanna. 2018. *The End of Man: A Feminist Counterapocalypse*. Minneapolis: University of Minnesota Press.

PART I

Past Narratives of Environmental Crisis

Chapter 1

The Peculiar Associations of Melville's "Encantadas"

Nature and National Allegory

Kristen R. Egan

Although Herman Melville's 1854 "The Encantadas, or Enchanted Isles" poses as a piece of travel literature, it is far more than a simple account of the Galapagos Islands. Turning the islands into a pseudo-allegory of American nation formation and critiquing the appropriation of nature into the national identity, Melville demonstrates the tension between nation-building and environment.[1] Through ten sketches, Melville describes an island environment that does not resemble a pure Edenic landscape containing the perfect raw and metaphorical material to build a nation; instead, he creates a dystopia that represents the unstable and contested battleground between environment and empire.[2]

Attempts to represent climate change must contend with the ways nation-building has historically shaped the environmental imaginary, and Melville's text reveals and problematizes those methods, particularly through its use of allegory. In *Allegories of the Anthropocene,* Elizabeth M. DeLoughrey argues that "due to its ability to represent both historical and scalar relations, allegory has arisen as a notable form for this moment of planetary climate crisis" (2019, 5). DeLoughrey acknowledges that the Anthropocene looks forward and back, as it is "characterized by 'anticipatory logics' and anticipatory mourning" (4). While DeLoughrey focuses on contemporary, postcolonial literature of the global south, I argue this "anticipatory mourning," and the use and manipulation of national allegory to convey it, appears in Melville's 1854 travelogue, thereby anticipating this contemporary mode.

Critic Paul Giles argues that Melville was troubled by American expansion and sought to disrupt nationalism by upsetting the naturalized relationship between geography and nation in his 1852 novel *Pierre* (2011, 1). For Giles, Melville's work questioned the naturalization of America's borders, and while I agree, I would add that it is Melville's representation of the environment that achieves this in "The Encantadas." Melville illustrates the exploitation of the isles, anticipating species extinction through his portrayal of the Galapagos tortoise, but also demonstrates nonhuman agency as the isles resist colonial conquest.

Melville's "The Encantadas, or Enchanted Isles" allegorically layers an American narrative of discovery and nationalization over a completely different geographical space—the Galapagos. His use of certain literary techniques to represent the environment—the picturesque, onomatopoeia, and allegory—generate a powerful representation of the setting that challenges the premise of Manifest Destiny. Melville gets this resistance across not only by employing allegory opposed to symbol, but also by refusing to allow the national allegory to fully take shape, a refusal accomplished by the disruptive environment of the text. While reading national allegory into the text might overshadow the particularity of the Galapagos, it should not. Melville emphasizes this particular landscape by writing a text about a real location and by using a characteristically realistic genre, the travelogue.[3] In this text, the land refuses to allow any nation to form, and thus Melville's representation of the natural environment exceeds the national allegory.

Place naming, mapping, generating a national allegory, and employing hierarchies of "civilization" are all necessary to nation formation, but this text disrupts these processes, subverting national production and revealing the "peculiar associations" between nationalism and environment, associations that are forced rather than natural. Allegory grants the author the ability to detach this narrative from the space that supposedly bore it, demonstrating that, for Melville, nation formation is not generated by the particularity of North America, suggesting that nations are *made* not discovered. While the isles resist national production, Melville, nevertheless, paints a dystopic vision, one that anticipates literature of the Anthropocene and its use of allegory.

DIALECTIC BETWEEN NATURE AND CULTURE

Defining nature and culture is no easy task, particularly because the terms have intersecting definitions.[4] While nature and culture used to be imagined as distinct entities, today most critics no longer see this separation. Terry Eagleton argues that humans are both natural and cultural beings, and that our "helpless physical nature is such that culture is a necessity if we are to survive. Culture is the 'supplement' which plugs a gap at the heart of our nature, and our material needs are then reinflected in its terms" (2000, 99). Nature and culture, as Eagleton suggests, have a dialectical relationship: each continually refashions the other.[5] Melville suggests a similar view, allowing for a conceptualization of nature that is not as anthropocentric as "nature's nation" (Miller 1967).[6]

One of the ways Melville demonstrates this is through his use of the picturesque. Many nineteenth-century travel writers would include small drawings to help depict their journeys. Melville did not do this, but he figuratively paints his "sketches" (opposed to chapters) with words throughout the novella. The picturesque is a style that incorporates landscape:

> The concept of landscape provides a useful means for understanding the workings of natural terrain. John Berger describes landscape as a 'way of seeing.' Inherently duplicitous, the term 'landscape' refers both to this visual perspective and to the geographical territories that are seized by it. Landscapes articulate both culture and nature, seer and scene. But equally at stake in landscape are the embodied practices that transform the objects of a proprietary gaze. (Moore, Pandian, and Kosek 2003, 11)

While such a dialectic opens up both sides of the nature/culture dichotomy, it typically favors the perspective of the viewer. Melville draws upon this visual technique most deliberately when he frames the death of Hunilla's husband and brother in Sketch Eight: "the better to watch the adventure of those two hearts she loved, Hunilla had withdrawn the branches to one side, and held them so. They formed an oval frame, through which the bluely boundless sea rolled like a painted one." Her two family members die silently as she watches through the branches: "Death in a silent picture" (1987, 154). The picturesque often invokes the dominance of the viewer over nonhuman nature because the technique restricts nonhuman nature to a frame. In this scene, the picturesque may flatten the dynamics of the scene, but the ocean does what a painting cannot, inflicting great pain upon the now stranded Hunilla as it kills her husband and brother. Thus, while Melville uses the cultural motif of the picturesque to engage the dialectic between nature and culture, he is careful not to undercut the power of the environment with a cultural gaze.

In addition to his use of the picturesque, Melville uses onomatopoeia to further exemplify the dialectic between nature and culture. While all representations of nature are within the realm of culture because they are conveyed through language, certain literary devices bring attention to material reality more than others. Because onomatopoeia is multisensory, it allows the reader to imaginatively *inhabit* the world of the text more fully. In the first sketch, the narrator, Salvatore R. Tarnmoor, explains how the isles are not inhabited by humans. Instead, reptiles dwell here and hence, "[n]o voice, no low, no howl is heard; the chief sound of life here is a hiss" (117). To illustrate his point, Melville follows this statement with the following description of the coastline:

> In many *places* the *coast* is rock-bound, or, more properly, clinker-bound; tumbled *masses* of *blackish* or *greenish stuff* like the *dross* of an iron-*furnace*, forming dark *clefts* and *caves* here and there, into which a *ceaseless sea pours* a fury of foam; overhanging them with a *swirl* of gray, haggard *mist*, *amidst* which *sail screaming flights* of unearthly *birds* heightening the *dismal* din. (127; emphasis added)

The alliteration and rhythm of the "s" sound in this passage generates the hiss of the reptiles that inhabit the isles. The use of onomatopoeia also demonstrates the rhythm of the sea lashing against the rocks. Juxtaposing the "s" sound with harsher consonant sounds like the hard "c" found in some of the very same words further generates the hiss: "coast," "blackish," "clefts," and "caves." Not only can the reader envision what the coastline looks like in this passage, but through the use of onomatopoeia, one can imagine the sound particular to the Isles' landscape and inhabitants.

In this way, the passage reminds the reader that the isles "speak" – the sound of the waves crashing on the shore and rocks, the sound of reptiles, these are sounds that also potentially communicate although we do not understand what they are saying. Hence, readers are reminded of their limits, the limits of human language, the limits of culture. In concordance, critic Patrick Chura argues that Melville's "Encantadas" reveals the limits of language, mapping, and "perhaps all signification systems" (2015, 18).

Hence, Melville deconstructs the imaginary division between nature and culture, but does so in a way that does not completely subsume nature into culture. His use of the picturesque and onomatopoeia expresses the limitations of language when representing the natural world. "The Encantadas" attempts to "capture" this environment in language, but Melville repeatedly finds ways to demonstrate how the Encantadas are not capturable.

PECULIAR ASSOCIATIONS

In addition to demonstrating the limits of language when representing nature, the text also critiques the way nations assume ownership over geographical spaces. Nationalization involves ownership and the development of place attachment in its citizenry, but Melville problematizes the ownership of the isles. In fact, while I focus on how the text resembles American nation formation, no one nation can take full ownership of this discovery narrative or the place it represents; undercutting the ownership of the Galapagos complicates nature's role in national production. "The Encantadas" takes place in the Galapagos, but makes references to South America, Spain, Great Britain, ancient Rome, and the United States. Eric Wertheimer argues convincingly that "The Encantadas" really represents "a torturous Spanish history" (1999, 152). Although the Galapagos certainly do represent the history of Spanish exploration and discovery, I would add that the text makes a transnational critique, since it gestures towards the United States through its allusions to slavery, the references to the War of 1812, and the U.S. *Essex*. As Darryl Hattenhauer suggests, "[a]s a promised land, the Encantadas are part of the New World frontier, part of the arena for European expansion into ostensibly infinite space. The characters in 'The Encantadas' represent the nations that dominated exploration and colonization in the New World" (1987, 121). Therefore, no one nation owns this narrative of discovery and failed civilization, and it is unclear exactly who *belongs* to the Encantadas, as none of the inhabitants ever effectively build a long-term home on the islands. In this transnational method, Melville diffuses ideas of national exceptionalism, American or any other kind, and critiques nation formation and "civilization" in general.[7]

Yet he does draw upon some firsthand accounts of the isles in order to partially ground this fantastic story to the real world. Melville inserts histories of the isles from other authors, a technique that grounds the narrative to the real, but also draws attention to the process of association between people (or things) and place. Tarnmoor discusses his decision to include the particular histories of the U.S. *Essex*, the Buccaneers, and the works of Cowley, Colnet, and Porter within his travelogue.

> . . . by long cruising among the isles, tortoise-hunting upon their shores, and generally exploring them; for these and other reasons, the *Essex* became *peculiarly associated* with the Encantadas. Here be it said that you have but three eye-witness authorities worth mentioning touching the Enchanted Isles:— Cowley, the Buccaneer (1684); Colnet, the whaling-ground explorer (1793); Porter, the post captain (1813). Other than these you have but barren, bootless allusions from some few passing voyagers or compilers. (Melville 1987, 143; emphasis added)

This "peculiar association" between the *Essex* and the isles is central to understanding Melville's text. How do people and things become "associated" with place? Such a union usually requires long-term proximity to the location, but in the case of the Encantadas, it seems that documented short-term proximity will do. These three individuals are named because they explored, circled, and poached the isles; notice how Melville makes deliberate mention of their "tortoise-hunting" practices. While we typically think of the association between person and place in a positive light, with its potential to generate a sense of belonging or anchoring a home in a chaotic world, Melville resists positive affect in his narrative. The Buccaneer, whaler, and captain are all essentially pirates pilfering the resources of the isles. In this way, Melville criticizes imperial conquest of the Americas and ecological imperialism in particular.

This may be why Melville calls the association "peculiar." "Peculiarly associated" suggests a bizarre connection between the *Essex* and the isles, but the root of this term has more telling connotations. The reference to peculiarity may point to the randomness of the association, suggesting that such relations with place are not always motivated, refuting ideas like Manifest Destiny. In addition to denoting an apparent strangeness in the association, "peculiar" also refers to the particular and exclusive characteristics of a person, group, or place. For example, one might say the Galapagos tortoise is "peculiar" to the Enchanted Isles, because it cannot be found anywhere else. Although the history of repeating the stories of the *Essex* and the isles may have made it seem like the ship is native to the isles, this is not true because the ship is not *of* them: it is not native. In fact, the *Essex*'s relation to the isles was generated by the War of 1812, as the ship's mission was to fight off British fleets in the Pacific for the American cause.[8] Hence the peculiarity of the association between the *Essex* and the isles may be Melville's way of suggesting that the *Essex* is not native to the isles at all, but rather has a strange historically built association with the isles. Combining the two connotations behind the word "peculiar" suggests that the association between the *Essex* and the Encantadas is an example of the strangeness behind belonging to place, or the often bizarre and unusual ways that persons or things come to be connected and metonymically representative of place, many of which are imperial acts of domination.

UNCIVILIZING THE CIVILIZED

By making the ownership of the isles unstable and demonstrating how the association between person and place on the isles is not native but "peculiar," Melville disrupts nation-building, a rupture he deepens by portraying unsuccessful attempts at colonization. The sketches on the Dog-King (Sketch Seventh) and the Hermit Oberlus (Sketch Ninth) ironically portray these colonizers as "uncivilizing" forces, as they employ violence, slavery, and ecological imperialism in their attempts to dominate some of the islands. In the end, no growing human colony is successfully established, thereby supporting Melville's ongoing depiction of environmental resistance in the text.

While European conquest typically involved subordinating native human populations, it must be noted that there is no native human population known to have inhabited the Galapagos. Civilizing a supposedly "uncivilized" native population was a part of nation building during imperial expansion since "civilization" typically refers to "a developed or advanced state of human society,"[9] one which is "still contrasted with *savagery* or *barbarism*" (Williams 1983a, 59). However, in "The Encantadas," Melville depicts colonies of settlers; the fact that there is no native human population is interesting in itself as it highlights that Melville's selection of the Encantadas for the setting foregrounds his interest in nonhuman nature and environmental resistance.

Coinciding with this theme, the tortoises appear to be the most native of all the inhabitants. Tarnmoor says that many believe the tortoises to be reincarnated "wicked sea-officers, more especially commodores and captains" (Melville 1987, 128). As the narrator describes three tortoises brought aboard his ship, he says, "I no more saw three tortoises. They expanded—became transfigured. I seemed to see three Roman Coliseums in magnificent decay" (131). By comparing the tortoises to "commodores and captains" and decaying "Roman Coliseums," Melville ironically elevates the tortoises to markers of high civilization, albeit declining ones.

Similarly, the dogs imported by the Dog-King are deemed "aristocratic," while individuals who try to inhabit the islands, like Oberlus and the Dog-King, lack "humanity," thereby making the animals appear more civilized than the humans. For example, when the Dog-King tries to civilize Charles's Isle, he brings 80 people to populate the island and a pack of dogs to act as his own personal army. As crime becomes rampant in this newly formed community, the King appoints a group of men to serve as his private army, but the human regiment is actually subordinate to the dog army. The human population starts to dwindle because they are "downright plotters and malignant traitors," whom the King enjoys exterminating. In this way, Melville emphasizes the human violence invoked in colonization. Eventually the King has to abolish the death penalty and disband his private human army to maintain a population: "The human part of the lifeguard was now disbanded, and set to work cultivating the soil, and raising potatoes; the regular army now solely consisting of the dog-regiment" (148). Through allocating characteristics of "humanity" and "civilization" to nonhuman animals—dogs and tortoises—Melville deconstructs the perceived differentiation between animals and humans.

The human army's demotion to the status of field hands should not be overlooked. In the ninth sketch, the hermit Oberlus deceives and traps passing sailors into slavery, and then—like the Dog-King—he passes the farming onto them. The repeated emphasis on agricultural labor demonstrates, first of all, that humans rely on their environment for their food supply, but it also shows how, historically, Western civilizations have created social hierarchies and placed those working closest to the land on the bottom of the social scale. The role of the field worker is a reference to slavery and points to European imperialism and its use of slavery, including in the United States.

Indeed, the American pastoral landscape may have symbolized the "nation" in antebellum literature, but while the American landscape was valorized as an image of freedom, slavery provided the background and backbone of that freedom. Slaves became synonymous with nature and were thereby degraded to the outskirts of a "civilized" populace. Slavery relies on a demarcation between "civilized" and "uncivilized" persons. Therefore, a civilized society is one that has supposedly overcome savagery or the "baseness" of nature. Overcoming nature in "The Encantadas" proves impossible, and those who wish to elevate their status end up doing so by creating hierarchies, with land workers on the bottom of the social scale. At the root of slavery, however, is anthropocentrism; the natural is positioned in opposition to the civilized, suggesting that nature and culture are separate spheres and that culture always has the upper hand. Developing a "civilized" nation, therefore, requires a disassociation from the natural in its citizenry. In *Regeneration Through Violence*, Richard Slotkin articulates the need for early American colonists to separate themselves from their European ancestors and from the Native American tribes they found in the continent: "the colonists' [had their] own need to affirm—for themselves and for the home folks—that they had not deserted European civilization for American savagery" (1973, 15). Hence, while the natural was valorized as a symbol of national identity, the citizenry tried to avoid becoming too "natural."

The Oberlus sketch alludes to rising large-scale agricultural systems that followed the age of exploration and the way those systems exploited humans in the form of slavery, but it also considers the ecological impact of these processes. Melville describes Oberlus's malevolent demeanor in relation to the way he farms the soil (prior to acquiring his slaves): "When planting, his whole aspect and all his gestures were so malevolently and uselessly sinister and secret, that he seemed rather in the act of dropping poison into wells than potatoes into soil" (1987, 163). Incidentally, the Dog-King's remaining human population was also commanded to plant potatoes. Melville's comparison of planting a cash crop like potatoes to "dropping poison into wells" represents how agriculture can lead to a form of ecological imperialism, as planting new crops in the soil affects the natural ecosystem.[10] In fact, by comparing the planting to "poison," Melville compares Oberlus's planting of potatoes to pollution, an act that will contaminate the soil. Putting poison into "wells" implies contaminating the water supply, which would of course affect all living things in the habitat, so Melville taps in to the way agriculture can have far-reaching effects for both human and nonhuman life. Thus, Melville deconstructs "civilization" and highlights the ways that slavery and violence were part of colonization, as was ecological imperialism through his examples of agriculture. In the end, neither the Dog-King nor Oberlus triumph; no human colony is ever successfully established as Melville uncivilizes the "civilized."

DISLOCATING LOCATION: PLACE NAMES AND FAILURES IN MAPPING

In addition to the failed attempts to successfully establish human colonies on the isles, Melville's representation of a materially unstable island environment also resists imperial conquest. When Melville tries to historicize the mapping process of the Galapagos, he describes the difficulty navigators had trying to locate the islands. The winds and currents of the area were so unpredictable that they disoriented navigators. In the 1800s people thought that the Encantadas were two distinct and separate groups of islands. He writes, "[a]nd this apparent fleetingness and unreality of the locality of the isles was most probably one reason for the Spaniards calling them the Encantada, or Enchanted Group" (1987, 73). The unmappable nature of the Encantadas reflects what J. Hillis Miller calls the "atopical," which he describes as being "a place that is everywhere and nowhere, a place you cannot get to from here" (1995, 7). But this quality also leads to their naming, an act which hails them into place. Place names have profound meaning according to Miller, who claims, "The power of the conventions of mapping and of the projection of place names on the place are so great that we see the landscape as though it were already a map, complete with place names and the names of geographical features. The place names seem to be intrinsic to the places they name. The names are motivated" (4). Thus the act of naming the islands brings their atopical, un-locatableness into (fictive) location. Once they are named, they can be called upon again, suggesting that these islands, which are difficult to find, can be found. While place names "*seem* to be intrinsic to the places they name," it is this *seeming* that is an interesting point of inquiry.

The "seeming intrinsic" quality of place names only develops over time, which suggests it is not "intrinsic" at all. Place names are metonymic, as the association over time between the signifier and signified eventually seems justified, while in actuality the relationship may be arbitrary and unmotivated. For example, the fleeting quality of the Encantadas motivated the original name, Spanish "encantadas" referring to the "enchanted" quality of the islands. While Melville explains the fleetingness of the islands and how that quality generated their name, he also immediately undermines this fleeting quality a paragraph later by stating, "However wavering their place may seem by reason of the currents, they themselves, at least to one upon the shore, appear invariably the same: fixed, cast, glued into the very body of cadaverous death" (1987, 73). In other words, the location of the islands is completely contingent on the perspective of the viewer, appearing stable to one on land and fleeting to one on a ship. These contradictory descriptions suggest that even something as apparently solid as a landmass is not necessarily easy to see, classify, or understand. This description contrasts "nature's nation," a concept that requires an inherently unwavering landmass, a stable scaffolding to build the nation upon.

Today the islands are still referred to by this name "enchanted," even though this fleeting quality no longer exists. Indeed, in the age of GPS devices anyone can locate the Encantadas. This forces the question, was this quality ever "intrinsic" to the isles in the first place? The name *Encantadas* is specific to a historic moment and a particular group of Spanish explorers. This suggests that the "names are motivated," but in a historically contingent sense.

To further complicate the location of the Encantadas, Melville layers place names in the titles of the work and the individual sketches. For example, the full title, "The Encantadas, or Enchanted Isles" is an act of translation; it refers both to their Spanish name given by the Spanish discoverers of the isles and its English translation. If they have the same referent, then the double name seems redundant: why use both names? The dual title draws one's attention to the fact that there is not one definitive sign to hail this location into place. Similarly, sketches six through nine are about specific islands, and each of these has a two-part title, giving the name of the isle and the name of a specific inhabitant of the isle, such as "Barrington Isle and The Buccaneers." These two-part titles say something about the relationship between man and environment. Melville cannot "map" the islands without describing their inhabitants, as inhabitants, like the Buccaneers, can change the landscape.

Furthermore, the two-part titles used in these three sketches invoke not only some temporary inhabitants, but the specific islands Melville chooses all contain connotations of imperialism, as they were all initially named after British noblemen: Barrington Isle (named after British Admiral Samuel Barrington), Charles Isle (named after King Charles II), and Hoods Isle (named after British Admiral Samuel Hood). Even today the islands are part of Ecuador's national park system, officially called the Archipiélago de Colón; a name that ironically grants Columbus final "ownership" over the isles, although Melville makes no mention of him and Columbus never toured the isles.[11]

Texts create their own versions of real landscapes and affect the way humans imagine these places, and place names also do this. Imperial names show attempts to own and control the isles. But Melville has a way of drawing attention to the inadequacy of place names to contain their referent. Miller argues that through mapping and using place names "we see the landscape as though it were already a map," but Melville's "map" is quite complicated (1995, 4). When he names the text and its sketches, he repeatedly uses two-part titles; no single moniker is used to hail the referent into place. This is Melville's way of disrupting the mapping process and the ownership of the isles: it dislocates the location. Melville represents the isles as both out of place and in place by his use of contradictory descriptions (they are both stable and fleeting) and his layering of place names. Place naming is one of the preliminary steps to configuring the borders of the nation and controlling nature, and Melville subverts this act.

PSEUDO-ALLEGORY

In the simplest terms, "The Encantadas" is and is not an allegory, fulfilling some of the characteristics of the genre and refusing to achieve others. This combined adherence and defiance seems purposeful on Melville's part, helping him call upon the old scripts of existence and subvert them in an attempt to try something new. "Nature's nation" is a symbolic understanding of the land, suggesting that American identity is inherent in the physical environment, needing only to be uncovered. In order to disrupt this idea, Melville employs allegory instead of symbol to allude to a story of American nationalism and disrupt it. The national allegory is somewhat hidden, as Melville loosely weaves in allusions to America. For example, Melville makes direct references to Daniel Boone, the Adirondack Mountains, the U.S. *Essex*, and the War of 1812. He then makes more elaborate comparisons through the Oberlus sketch which contains references to slavery as previously discussed, and the Dog-King sketch alludes to American colonization and the American Revolution.

Melville weaves several subtle references to America into the Dog-King sketch. The Dog-King is a "Creole adventurer from Cuba" who fought for Peru against Spain. Payment for his good work came in the form of Charles's Isle (Melville 1987, 146). He sets to populating his island with a group of people and supplies; they "take ship for the promised land" (147), just like the Pilgrims who believed America was going to be a new promised land. Melville emphasizes the arrival of Europeans in America again stating, "[t]he history of the king of Charles' Island furnishes another illustration of the difficulty of colonizing barren islands with unprincipled pilgrims" (149). Finally, the government formed on the isle "was no democracy at all, but a permanent *Riotocracy,* which gloried in having no law but lawlessness." Within the riotocracy, "[e]ach runaway tar was hailed as a martyr in the cause of freedom, and became immediately installed a ragged citizen of this universal nation." While Tarnmoor claims the "riotocracy" is not America, this section still seems to make a mocking reference to the American Revolution, pointing out the lawlessness embedded in revolt under the veil of martyrdom—"in the cause of freedom" (149). These loose allusions to America, as seen in the Oberlus sketch and the Dog-King sketch, start to suggest that Melville was partially creating an American allegory in "The Encantadas"; of course, we will also find that he is subverting that allegory and alluding more broadly to imperialism.

Allegories, unlike symbols, are detachable and transferable from their contexts or settings. Because the meaning of an allegory is found in the plot or narrative, allegories can be transplanted into different settings. The context does not produce the narrative; it just frames the story. The meaning of a symbol, however, is *in* the materiality of the symbol and is therefore not detachable from the object that bore its meaning. By suggesting that the nation is not organically produced out of nature (symbol), Melville implicitly suggests the American environment does not have this inherent quality. Melville then takes the issue of nature and nationalism a step further by representing the environment of the Galapagos as an entity that refuses to fully allow any nation to form, or even any individual to build a sense of belonging with this environment.

Melville's novella is more like a story of apocalypse, opposed to the beginning of a new civilization. Indeed, the isles resemble Dante's *Inferno,* looking like a living hell, rather than an Eden.[12] In the opening paragraph the isles are depicted as follows:

> Take five-and-twenty heaps of cinders dumped here and there in an outside city lot; imagine some of them magnified into mountains, and the vacant lot the sea; and you will have a fit idea of the general aspect of the Encantadas, or Enchanted Isles. A group rather of extinct volcanoes than of isles; looking much as the world at large might, after a penal conflagration. (126)

The setting of "extinct volcanoes" is not man-made, but Melville ironically compares them to the refuse from urban life. The reference to extinction along with the comparison to a world after "a penal conflagration" paints a dystopic scene. Ruins are not uncommon to allegory because, as Walter Benjamin explained in 1925, "[i]n the ruin, history has passed perceptibly into the setting. And so configured, history finds expression not as process of an eternal life but as process of incessant decline" (2019, 188). In other words, a setting of ruins represents history, and an allegorical representation of ruins makes history "meaningful only in the stations of its decline" (174). According to Benjamin, allegory puts into view what is declining, but ironically that decline is what makes the declining object significant—in this case, ascribing value to the environment of the isles.

Therefore, Melville's text is an allegory in its use of ruins to represent history, but it is also an allegory because of the tension it displays. Literary critic Bainard Cowan argues that Melville's use of allegory in *Moby Dick* expresses "the relation between the timely and the timeless," and I would add that this technique also operates in "The Encantadas" (1982, 6). Symbolism is timeless: symbols do not lose their meaning over time, but allegories express the tension between the transcendent and the real. Thus to say that "The Encantadas" is an allegory of nation formation built out of nature means the text displays the tension between building a symbolic national identity and the timely reality that such a project might fail or that reality or the environment will not allow it to happen. Thus, "The Encantadas" wrestles with the appropriation of a figurative nature into the national identity, displaying the tension between nature as figure and nature as material reality.

However, on many fronts the text fails to achieve allegorical status. Allegories typically contain a linear journey, like Ahab's quest for the white whale in *Moby Dick*. "The Encantadas," however, has no journey, no purpose, no traditional narrative that organizes the whole. No object or moral is being sought. Rather than move in a linear pattern from beginning to end, this novella goes in circles around the isles, never really getting anywhere. As Michael Paul Rogin argues regarding *Moby Dick,* Ahab's allegorical quest of the whale organizes and drives this text opposed to Ishmael's symbolic pattern that "reworks the lived world" (1991, 124–26). In "The Encantadas," however, it is the *setting* that organizes the text opposed to the quest narrative. The setting has an allegorical quality because it gestures beyond its literal location of the Galapagos toward the "new world" collectively during the great age of sea exploration. Therefore, there is an allegorical dimension to the setting of the text, but since the text lacks a traditional quest narrative, it is not a traditional allegory.

Allegories, furthermore, usually appeal to old texts, like the Christian allegory of redemption after the fall from Eden. DeLoughrey comments that "[d]espite Indigenous genocide, transatlantic slavery, environmental destruction, and species extinctions, colonial authors and armchair travelers continued to figure the Caribbean island in terms of Christian allegories of paradise" (2019, 36). Melville's text is the opposite, resembling a story of hell on earth, where redemption never happens. In this way, it is similar to what Jenny Sharpe refers to as counterallegory (1993, 23). This is a world where people fall and are rarely redeemed. So while the text is modeled on the great allegories of Spenser and Dante, unlike the *Inferno* where Vergil and Dante step out of hell, in "The Encantadas" the reader never leaves (Albrecht 1972, 464, 477). The one exception to this reading could be the sketch of the widow Hunilla, who is saved from the isles. Upon her return to the mainland, Tarnmoor writes, "[t]he last seen of lone Hunilla she was passing into Payta town, riding upon a small gray ass; and before her on the ass's shoulders, she eyed the jointed workings of the beast's armorial cross" (Melville 1987, 121). While she is "saved" and presented as a Christological figure here, Hunilla lives with a heavy heart as she has lost her husband and brother, "[a] heart of yearning in a frame of steel" (121). Similarly, Tarnmoor himself seems transformed and forever haunted by his experience with the isles. In this way, Melville undercuts the redemptive trajectory of conventional allegory.

Finally, if this were an allegory of nation formation, that would mean that a nation would form, and a sense of identity, home, and belonging would take shape between the characters and the isles. This of course does not happen in the text. Characters are taken in and spit out by the isles; no one belongs to them like the tortoises do. For example, out of the ten sketches, there are only three sketches about specific individuals and their interaction with the isles, which include the stories of the Dog-King, Chola Widow, and the Hermit Oberlus. While all three characters came to the isles for different reasons, one thing they all have in common is that each one is returned to the mainland, unable or unwilling to sustain a home out of the isles.

All of this leads to the conclusion that Melville is playing with the concept of allegory and not adhering to its boundaries. This manipulation of allegory by Melville has been seen in other texts. For example, Giles argues that in *Pierre* Melville does not create an allegory but "uses a medieval allegorical structure to create disjunctions between different spatial and temporal dimensions, to remap U.S. culture according to different measuring charts, and thus to resituate nineteenth-century America within an alien topography" (2011, 105). In a similar manner, "The Encantadas" maps America onto an "alien topography," the Galapagos, in order to denaturalize "nature's nation." It is a pseudo-allegory, appropriating some aspects of the allegorical model and subverting some of its most characteristic qualities. This technique generates tension between the literal location (Galapagos) and the metaphoric referent (the new world), displaying the tension between physical environments and cultural *readings* of nature. By creating *and* disrupting the national allegory, Melville shows that the physical environment did not necessarily enable national production.

CONCLUSIONS: THE LIMITS OF DISCOURSE

Melville does not suggest that nature is pure and unaffected by culture. Ironically, Melville used the tortoise as a symbol of death and extinction back in the 1850s, when the tortoises were still abundant. This is evident when the narrator describes a dream he has about the isles: "I have seemed to see, slowly emerging from those imagined solitudes, and heavily crawling along the floor, the ghost of a gigantic tortoise with 'Memento ****' burning in live letters upon his back" (Melville 1987, 129). Here, the tortoise is dead as its ghost appears in the dream, but the letters burning in its back are "live," suggesting that what the tortoise symbolizes will live far longer than the animal itself. The writing on the tortoise represents the mark of humanity on nature, but the fact that the tortoise haunts the narrator's memories suggests that nonhuman nature has also made its mark on him, thus the symbol of the tortoise with burning letters becomes emblematic of the dialectical relationship between nature and culture.

Melville does not make the markings on the back of the tortoise all readable, which is part of the reason the vision is so evocative. The word we do comprehend is "Memento," suggesting that the tortoise represents a kind of keepsake, but one that cannot be fully interpreted. The memento of the tortoise may be the warning the narrator made earlier in sketch two titled "Two Sides to a Tortoise," when he says regarding the tortoises that they have a bright calipee, but also a dark side, so "don't deny the black" (130). However, the entire message on the tortoise's back is unreadable, suggesting that we continually try to interpret nature, but we will never be able to fully comprehend our environment. We try to "read" nature, but Melville points out that we cannot always read the signs, and the signs might not be signs at all.[13]

While the dominant organizational device that holds the novella together is its setting, the reader never gets a complete view of the isles. In general, the ten sketches begin with a few broad descriptions of the Encantadas, and then they zoom in, going from island to island. Even from the top of Rock Rodondo, which is supposed to enable a "pisgah view" of the isles, one can see only some of the Enchanted Isles (141). Nor does the reader get to visit every island in the Galapagos chain. The narrative circles around the islands and along the coasts but never goes into the interiors of any of the islands until the very end.

The interiors of the isles are the most mysterious of places in this enchanting and ambiguous text. The interiors are a hiding place for those, like Oberlus and the Dog-King, who try to avoid persecution and banishment from the islands, but Tarnmoor does not take the reader inside the isles on either of these occasions. There are only two moments when Melville allows such a journey; the first is when the narrator spies on Hunilla at the grave she made for her husband; the last is the very ending of the novella, where the narrator takes the reader inside an island and finds a grave marked by a doggerel poem on a gravestone.

These rare glimpses into the inside of the islands reveal the same thing: death. Even early on in the novella, the narrator describes the isles as being fixed in the "very body of cadaverous death" (128). Obviously, this refers to the ocean that surrounds the islands, for Melville was well aware of the ocean's capacity to destroy human life, which he demonstrates in Hunilla's story in sketch eight, when her husband and brother die in the sea. The ocean is a great killer and a tomb to many (especially sailors and slaves). Melville's play on bodies is quite interesting here, calling the ocean a body itself and describing not death in general but a "cadaverous" death or death of the body. Hence, the ocean is a body where cadavers go to die, where the body is consumed and decomposed. The narrator comments that whenever possible ocean vessels try to bury their dead on land, and because of this, the Encantadas are "a convenient Potter's Field," or a home for the homeless, as the isles become the final resting place for the many outcasts of the world (173). Of course, the assimilation into this home is marred by death; it is not a home in its traditional sense, which connotes a sense of belonging between person and place. The text ends with an inscription on a grave: "No more I peep out of my blinkers, / Here I be—tucked in with clinkers!" (173). Clinkers are the remains of burned coal or lava and once again, like the cadaverous ocean, the island consumes this body. This not only emphasizes the inevitability of death, but the focus on decomposing bodies (cadaverous death) reinforces the materiality of human existence and how we are inescapably part of nature. Whether one's body is marked as civilized or uncivilized, citizen or slave, all bodies will return to the earth. As Terry Eagleton writes, "nature has the final victory over culture, customarily known as death. . . . Death is the limit of discourse, not a product of it" (2000, 87). Indeed, death as the limit of discourse is relevant to the reading of the tortoise and to reading the entirety of the text.

In *Allegory and the Anthropocene,* DeLoughrey asks, "what kinds of narratives help us navigate an ecological crisis that is understood as local and planetary, as historical and anticipatory?" (2019, 3). Her answer is allegory, and Melville's "Encantadas" exemplifies this idea, although it does so in the Nineteenth Century, much earlier than DeLoughrey's twenty-first century sources. "The Encantadas" ends much as it began; the islands remain uninhabitable, and while there are remnants of humanity in their mists, no community ever takes hold. Place naming, mapping, generating a national allegory, and engaging theories of "civilization" are all necessary to nation formation. Melville subverts these methods by creating a pseudo-allegory, uncivilizing the "civilized," and dislocating location. He reveals the peculiar associations between nation building and place, associations that are forced rather than natural. While there is an anthropocentric element in any representation of nature in literature, at the very least we can say that not all representations say the same thing. This text resists nation building in so many ways, but these methods of resistance emanate from his representation of a powerful and mysterious environment, a dystopic representation of the Enchanted Isles that haunts the narrator and the reader, anticipating literature of the Anthropocene.

REFERENCES

Albrecht, Robert C. 1972. "The Thematic Unity of Melville's 'The Encantadas.'" *Texas Studies in Literature and Language: A Journal of the Humanities 14.3 (Fall):* 463–77.

Beecher, Jonathan. 2000. "Variations on a Dystopian Theme: Melville's 'Encantadas.'" *Utopian Studies: Journal of the Society for Utopian Studies* 11.2: 88–95.

Benjamin, Walter. 2019 (Written 1925). *Origin of the German Trauerspiel*. Translated by Howard Eiland. Cambridge, MA: Harvard University Press.

Bickley, R. Bruce. 1975. "Form as Vision: The Organicism of 'The Encantadas,'" In *The Method of Melville's Short Fiction, 109–20. Durham, NC: Duke University Press.*

Budiansky, Stephen. 2010. *Perilous Fight: America's Intrepid War with Britain on the High Seas, 1812–1815.* New York, NY: Knopf.

Chura, Patrick. 2015. "*Demon est deus inversus*: Literary Cartography in Melville's 'The Encantadas.'" *49th Parallel* 35: 1–26.

Cowan, Bainard. 1982. *Exiled Waters: Moby-Dick and the Crisis of Allegory.* Baton Rouge, LA: Louisiana State University Press.

DeLoughrey, Elizabeth M. 2019. *Allegories of the Anthropocene*. Durham, NC: Duke University Press.

Eagleton, Terry. 2000. *The Idea of Culture.* Malden, MA: Blackwell.

Gidmark, Jill B. 1988. "Deception and Contradiction in The Encantadas: Salvator R. Tarnmoor on 'not firme land,'" *NDQ: North Dakota Quarterly* 56.3: 83–90.

Giles, Paul. 2011. *The Global Remapping of American Literature*. Princeton, NJ: Princeton University Press.

Hattenhauer, Darryl. 1987. "Ambiguities of Space and Place in Melville's 'The Encantadas,'" *NDQ: North Dakota Quarterly* 55.2: 114–26.

Hayles, N. Katherine. 1995. "Searching for Common Ground." In *Reinventing Nature?: Responses to Postmodern Deconstruction,* ed. by Michael E. Soulé and Gary Lease, 47–63. Washington, D.C.: Island Press.

Lazo, Rodrigo. 2008. "The Ends of Enchantment Douglass, Melville, and U.S. Expansionism in the Americas." In *Frederick Douglass & Herman Melville: Essays in Relation,* edited by Robert S. Levine and Samuel Otter, 207–29. Chapel Hill: University of North Carolina Press.

McNeill, William H. 1999. "How the Potato Changed the World's History," *Social Research* 66, no. 1 (Spring): 67–83.

Melville, Herman. 1987 [1854]. "The Encantadas or Enchanted Isles." In *The Piazza Tales and Other Prose Pieces 1839–1860. Vol. 9 of The Writings of Herman Melville, The Northwestern-Newberry Edition, Vol. 9, 125–73*. Chicago, IL: Northwestern University Press and Newberry Library.

Miller, J. Hillis. 1995. *Topographies*. Stanford, CA: Stanford University Press.

Miller, Perry. 1967. *Nature's Nation*. Cambridge, MA: Belknap Press.

Moore, Donald S., Anand Pandian, and Jake Kosek. 2003. "The Cultural Politics of Race and Nature: Terrains of Power and Practice." In *Race, Nature, and the Politics of Difference*, 1–70. Durham, NC: Duke University Press.

Rogin, Michael Paul. 1991. "*Moby-Dick* and The American 1848." In *Ahab*, ed. Harold Bloom, 124–49. New York, NY: Chelsea House.

Sharpe, Jenny. 1993. *Allegories of Empire: The Figure of Woman in the Colonial Text*. Minneapolis, MN: University of Minnesota Press.

Simard, Rodney. 1986. "More Black than Bright: the Allegorical Structure of Melville's 'The Encantadas." *Melville Society Extracts* 66 (May): 10–12.

Slotkin, Richard. 1973. *Regeneration Through Violence: The Mythology of the American Frontier 1600–1860*. Norman, OK: University of Oklahoma Press.

Soper, Kate. 1995. *What Is Nature?: Culture, Politics and the non-Human*. Malden, MA: Blackwell.

Wertheimer, Eric. 1999. "Mutations: Melville, Representation, and South American History." In *Imagined Empires: Incas, Aztecs, and the New World of American Literature, 1771–1876*, 133–59. New York: Cambridge University Press.

Williams, Raymond. 1958. *Culture and Society 1780–1950*. New York: Columbia University Press.

———. 1983a. "Civilization," *Keywords: A Vocabulary of Culture and Society*, rev. ed., 59. New York: Oxford University Press.

———. 1983b. "Nature." *Keywords: A Vocabulary of Culture and Society*, rev. ed., 219. New York: Oxford University Press.

NOTES

1. *Putnam's Magazine* published "The Encantadas, or the Enchanted Isles" in 1854 after the critical and financial failures of *Moby-Dick* and *Pierre*. This south-sea narrative revisits the islands Melville explored in 1841 and was well-received. Interpretations of "The Encantadas" have proliferated with very little consensus. Few critics can agree on the overall structure, theme, or even genre of the text. Melville not only researched the history of the Galapagos (including Charles Darwin's *A Naturalist's Voyage aboard the HMS Beagle)*, but also drew upon personal experience, having traveled to the islands on a whaling vessel. Some critics argue that Melville's fragile psychological state of the 1850s influenced the darkness of "The Encantadas." Jill B. Gidmark remarks that "The Encantadas" contains the "mental image of the tormented and frustrated writer he had become" (1988, 83). While many

see the natural setting as a mere projection screen for Melville's tormented psyche, I argue that nature is hardly a passive screen in this text.

2. The first four sketches contain general description of the Encantadas, including some sketches solely dedicated to certain environmental features like Rock Rodondo ("Sketch Third") and the tortoise ("Sketch Second"). The fifth and sixth sketches feature associations between the isles and particular groups like those aboard the U.S. *Essex* ("Sketch Fifth") and the Buccaneers ("Sketch Sixth"). The seventh, eighth, and ninth sketches depict individual characters and their experiences on particular islands, while "Sketch Tenth" zooms back out, looking more generally at the isles.

3. As J. Hillis Miller argues, authors use real places to anchor texts to the real world (1995, 19). Miller contends, "the landscape in a novel is not just an indifferent background where the action takes place. The landscape is an essential determinant of that action" (16).

4. "Nature" may be one of the most ambiguous terms in the English language with its wide-ranging connotations. The word can denote an organic, nonhuman world, or it can be a referent to an organic world that includes human beings. Raymond Williams groups the various definitions of nature into three categories: "(i) the essential quality and character *of* something; (ii) the inherent force which directs either the world or human beings or both; (iii) the material world itself, taken as including or not including human beings" (1983b, 219). The latter category is what will be the focus here; the material world including human beings, but not their technologies. As Kate Soper puts it, nature is "those material structures and processes that are independent of human activity (in the sense that they are not a humanly created product), and whose forces and causal powers are the necessary condition of every human practice" (1995, 132–33). While "culture" has equally wide-ranging connotations, what will be important here is the interaction, difference, and tension between the two terms. Hence, "culture" here refers to a composite way of life and the discursive practices that generate that life, including man-made technologies and the arts. For more on the wide-ranging definitions of "culture" see Raymond Williams's classic *Culture and Society 1780–1950* (1958) or Eagleton 2000.

5. Similarly, N. Katherine Hayles devises a theory of "constrained constructivism," explaining that while we are limited by our cultural context in the world, or what Hayles calls "positionality," we still interact with our environment. Granted, some interactions with the world are more consistent than others, leading to an idea of "reality." She adds, however, that "embodied experience constructs *a* world, not *the* world" (1995, 51; emphasis added).

6. "Nature's Nation" refers to Perry Miller's landmark text of the same name. In it, Miller describes the pervasive impact of nature on American identity and repeatedly demonstrates how American authors built a sense of national self out of the natural landscape.

7. Similarly, Rodrigo Lazo argues that "enchantment," or cultural representations of territories, especially in travel writing, tend to problematically romanticize potential expansion territories. He writes, "'The Encantadas' offers (self) criticism about antebellum writers' tendencies to resort to romantic flights of imagination when describing islands in the Americas that appear distant and different from U.S.

society" (2008, 208). Lazo states that Melville's "Encantadas" reveals the "folly" of U.S. imperialism (213).

8. The Americans went to war with Britain in large part because they disliked the restraints Britain placed on trade agreements and the impressment practices of the British Navy, who would find American sailors on the high seas and force them to become part of their navy (Budiansky 2010, xv). The practice of impressment raised questions about nationality and naturalization; Britain argued that many of these "American" seamen were actually born in Britain and therefore belonged to their navy. Stephen Budiansky, however, argues that this was not in fact true, as most of them were born in the United States (2010, 54).

9. *Oxford English Dictionary*, 2nd ed. (1989), s.v. "civilization."

10. For more information on the role of potatoes as an important crop to sustain a subordinate laboring class and generate European imperialism, see McNeill 1999.

11. Ecuador gave each individual island an official Spanish name as well. However, these national names are rarely used, and the old names still dominate common practice. Ecologists, in particular, have continued to use the names that were common during Darwin's time, and hence Ecuador's newer place names have not taken hold over the space, while Darwin's research and legacy has held on.

12. For more on the influence of Dante's *Inferno* on the text, see Albrecht 1972; Simard 1986; and Beecher 2000.

13. However, not all critics agree; as a symbol, interpretations of the tortoise proliferate. For example, R. Bruce Bickley argues, "[t]he final and most important motif in the sketches is the symbol of the tortoise. This reptile is the central force for resolving the major tensions in the sketches: those between degradation and triumph, between life and death, and between the real and the supernatural. With the tortoise, 'The Encantadas' synthesize as art and as philosophy" (1975, 118). For Bickley, the tortoise resolves these tensions because the tortoise is grander and more ancient than any meaning Melville can infuse it with. Along these lines, some read the tortoise as a kind of memento mori, reminding the reader of what he will never be able to avoid—death.

Chapter 2

Making a Difference?
Richard Jefferies's After London, E. M. Forster's "The Machine Stops," and Climate Change Fiction

Adrian Tait

Issues such as a changing climate are problems now and for the future, but their origins lie in the past, in the emergence of industrial modernity and its impact on both human and nonhuman worlds: even before environmental impacts such as enhanced global warming were identified and understood, and long before the term "cli-fi" was coined to describe the kind of fiction that engages directly with climate crisis (Johns-Putra 2016, 266), writers were speculating about the potential outcome of a modernizing process that was generating unexpected and often unseen risks. Their work is often astonishingly prescient, in ways that go directly to the question of whether fiction is capable of encompassing a crisis on the scale of climate change, and how that fiction might contribute to real-life discussions about the causes and consequences of humankind's environmental impact.

This chapter explores two works that, in very different ways, anticipate this discussion, and enable us (albeit tentatively) to explore the impact that fiction may have in informing the debate. In *After London, or Wild England* (1885), Richard Jefferies depicted the aftermath of an inexplicable "event" (Jefferies 2017, 15)—an event that we might now interpret as a warming climate—which has left much of southern England under water, and precipitated the collapse of technological civilization. Whilst the novel deals in some depth with the human impacts of that collapse, it opens by asserting the renewed importance of the nonhuman world, including those nonhuman animals whose own agency is now a threat to human survival. As the novel's alternative title suggests, ecological crisis has freed the nonhuman world to pursue its own, self-willed trajectory, largely independent of (and oblivious to) human interference. It is a world, as Jefferies elsewhere observed, that is "absolutely indifferent to us. [. . .] If the entire human race perished at this hour, what difference would it make to the earth?" (1907, 63–4).

In "The Machine Stops" (1909), by contrast, E. M. Forster portrays a markedly different future, in which the surface of the earth is now a toxic environment with an unbreathable atmosphere. Humankind has, it seems, eradicated all nonhuman forms of life, and saved only itself, in the form of an underground, technologically mediated society that is completely dependent on the eponymous Machine. As Forster's story tellingly underlines, however, humans are themselves animal, flesh-and-blood creatures with wants and needs that extend beyond the bare necessities and abstract satisfactions that the Machine provides. As the story further suggests, what is at fault is humanism itself: through its fantasy of exceptionalism—of humans as somehow independent of an embodied existence—humanism has proven to be humanity's undoing.

In spite, therefore, of their very different emphases, and despite the fact that neither narrative is directly concerned "with anthropogenic climate change or global warming as we now understand it" (Johns-Putra 2016, 267), these stories illustrate what might come of ecological catastrophe for both human and nonhuman animals: they also underline the inherent representational flexibility of the narrative form. The question, nevertheless, is what impact these stories have had. Taking each of these texts in turn, this chapter looks back over a century of critical reactions in an effort to establish whether works such as these—works that react to humankind's ecological impact on the nonhuman world—have any effect on the attitudes of those who read them. In so doing, the chapter forms part of a nascent initiative described by Matthew Schneider-Mayerson as "empirical ecocriticism," the attempt "to empirically examine the reception of environmental literature" (2018, 473). As Timothy Clark has pointed out in *Ecocriticism on the Edge*, the ecocritical belief that the "right" kind of literature (such as cli-fi) will change minds is a largely untested and perhaps even questionable assumption (2015, 18–19); reaching back to these prototypical instances of cli-fi may provide at least a partial response.

In Jefferies's *After London*, the "environment" is no longer a docile backdrop to human activity, but an active, inescapable, and heterogeneous presence; it has become again what it once was, and as a result, human communities have been confronted by their own inevitable entanglement with nonhuman animals and agentialities, and forced to acknowledge their own finitude. This intimacy is by no means comfortable or friendly. Rather, the novel insists on the alterity of nonhuman entities whose resurgence is relative to their historical subjugation: many of the creatures that now populate a re-wilded landscape are the feral descendants of domesticated livestock. Disconcertingly, these creatures now compete with human communities for resources, and predate on them; in the third-person history that makes up the novel's opening section, one of the narrator's main concerns in describing the nonhuman world is the extent to which it poses a threat to humans (Jefferies 2017, 8–13).

As this outline suggests, Jefferies's story presents the nonhuman and more-than-human world "not merely as a framing device but as a presence," a key characteristic of what Lawrence Buell has described as "an environmentally oriented work": "[t]he human interest is not understood to be the only legitimate interest" (1995, 7). Is it therefore possible that Jefferies' story has, in the years since its publication, influenced its readers to think about and perhaps even reconsider humankind's impact on and relationship to the environment, reimagined in the story as an active and agential rather than pliable and passive part of human existence? There is an obvious, general difficulty in answering that question: readers seldom record their reactions. One solution is to rely on the reactions of the critical community, as this chapter does, but that reliance introduces a further problem, well put by Schneider-Mayerson: "[w]hile literary criticism often implies the existence of an average reader who interprets a text or genre in a way that is consistent with the analysis of a professional reader and critic, empirical research shows that readers often experience literature very differently" (2018, 477).

There is a further, more specific problem: a surprising lack of critical interest in *After London*. As *The Observer* newspaper remarked in a review of 1999, "[n]obody paid much attention to *After London* [at the time of its publication], and it has been largely forgotten ever since" (Keates 1999). Paradoxically, that neglect extends even to those writers, critics, and commentators with an interest in nature and the nonhuman, writers who might, therefore, be expected to engage with Jefferies's novel. Take, for example, Henry Stephens Salt, a pioneer of animal rights, whose *Richard Jefferies: A Study* was first published in 1892. Salt earnestly admired Jefferies as a "poet-naturalist" (Salt 1894, 99), but he was critical of "his studies of animals" (110), and completely dismissive of his "fabulous [fictional] representations of birds and beasts," which were faulty precisely because they embodied Jefferies's creative "fancy" rather than his descriptive genius (111). Perhaps as a result, Salt mentions *After London* only once in his *Study*, and then only in passing (113). The poet and critic Edward Thomas, who wrote at length about the countryside in poetry and prose, also wrote a substantial study of Jefferies's life and work (1909), and included a chapter on *After London* (254–262). Much of it is, however, descriptive, rather than analytical, and Thomas reserves his most insightful comments for the fact that, having overthrown "everything characteristic of nineteenth-century civilization" (1909, 255), Jefferies does not then substitute a utopian alternate, but what we would now identify as a post-apocalyptic landscape characterized by strife and barbarism; here, too, Thomas's focus is on the human narrative. Thomas, at least, dedicated a chapter to the novel. Other critics have simply ignored it. The writer Henry Williamson was much influenced by Jefferies, and in 1937, he produced an extended essay on Jefferies's life, entitled *Richard Jefferies: Selections of His Work, with details of His Life and Circumstance, His Death and Immortality*. But whilst Williamson was himself best known for the novels he wrote about wild animals, such as *Tarka the Otter* (1928), the works that he chose to sample did not include *After London*. This pattern continues into much more recent criticism: when, for example, Roger Ebbatson discussed "nature" as a theme in English fiction, he acknowledged the "masterly opening" of *After London* (1980, 142), in which the nonhuman world is shown resurgent, but said nothing more about it.[1]

In spite, therefore, or perhaps because of its originality, *After London* has been neglected as a novel in which "nature" refuses to remain a prettified background to human existence and instead takes manifold, hybrid, and feral forms. There are, nevertheless, two particularly notable if brief discussions of the novel—by W. J. Keith and David Garnett—which gesture towards the kinds of concern that now figure prominently in environmentally-inflected thinking. Writing in the 1960s, W. J. Keith noted that, unlike many other minor Victorian writers, Jefferies's work had yet to generate a substantial renewal of critical interest (1965, 19), perhaps because of the daunting variety of his output (20), and perhaps because, even considered as a nature-writer, Jefferies's approach combined a disconcerting particularity—a compelling focus on the material specificity of things (see also Garnett 1939, viii)—with a near mystical appreciation of the agentiality of the nonhuman and more-than-human world (Keith 1965, 21). These observations situate Keith's response to the novel (115–122), a novel which he describes as "the most original and unexpected of all Jefferies's productions" (115), and important not for its account of the protagonist's quest, but for the "meticulously detailed survey" which opens the novel; Felix's "story [. . .] is nearly always secondary to our interest in the facts of the setting" (115). That interest lies not just in Jefferies's depiction of the inexorable logic of the rewilding process, but in what it signifies for the relationship between humans and nonhumans. Whatever has happened, it is not a disaster for the environment so much as a pivotal reversal of the *status quo*, in which the fantasy of a "return to Nature" has been transformed into the return *of* "Nature" (Keith 1965, 116). This does not signify the transition to some form of ecotopian idyll: as Keith correctly identifies, the little that is left of human civilization has simply lapsed back into "injustice and cruelty" (118).

As Keith adds, Jefferies's refusal to identify or explain "the event" (117) that precipitates this reversal is an "important part of the fictional design" (116), highlighting the climate of uncertainty to which a Victorian risk society was already exposed. That ambiguity also opens the novel up to multiple interpretations, one of which is to read it as a prototypical instance of cli-fi. When in 1939 David Garnett wrote the introduction to a new Everyman edition of *After London*, he had his own view of the agency that might precipitate London's destruction: where we now see climate change, Garnett saw bombers (1939, ix). Like W. J. Keith after him, Garnett nonetheless regarded the opening section of Jefferies's novel as more important than the quest narrative that followed; significantly, and movingly, he was reminded of a poem "by my friend Julian Bell," killed during the Spanish Civil War "by an aeroplane bomb" while driving an ambulance (Garnett 1939, x). The poem, "Marsh Birds Pass Over London," is "exactly to the point" (x), and Garnett reproduces it in full. Its relevance is captured in its last three lines:

> The cities pass and fall,
> The wild birds of the marshes
> See the end of them all.
>
> (qtd in Garnett 1939, xii)

Regardless of the cause of humankind's own downfall, Garnett suggests, Jefferies's novel makes it clear that nonhuman life will survive it. Against the background of human hubris encapsulated in the Victorian faith in "progress," and the unintended consequences that are its side-effect, the nonhuman, agential reality awaits, ready to resume its own self-willed trajectory.

Today, that message may be read, in part, as a corrective to the growing use of the term "Anthropocene," which correctly reflects the spatial and temporal reach of human impacts, whilst (to some) suggesting that further human interference might itself be the solution; it is a term, in other words, that is itself dangerously human-centered, and fails to reflect the limited horizon of human agentiality in a co-constituted world characterized, as Karen Barad has argued, by the "radical aliveness" of matter itself (2007, 33). These themes re-emerge in Forster's "The Machine Stops," in which they are combined in his depiction of a very different post-apocalyptic world where technology has not been discarded, still less forgotten, but further embraced. In Forster's story, humankind has survived the ecological crisis it has precipitated by retreating underground, leaving behind a barren surface world from which all life has been erased. In time, humankind has become completely dependent on the Machine. Never moving from (and isolated in) individual, cell-like chambers, and existing only for (and in) the world of thought, these survivors have lost all sense of what it is to live an embodied existence. When, however, one of their number rebels against this denial of his own embodied physicality—his own nature as animal—he finds that non-human and human lifeforms have survived at the surface. In this moment of reconnection, he realizes that a meaningful life cannot be lived if abstracted from a living, agential reality.

This is, by any standard, a powerful story, and still more compelling from our own perspective: Forster confronts the reader with her or his complicity in a modernizing impulse that has destroyed biotic habitats and, in this fictional future, precipitated a mass extinction event, whilst also impacting humankind's own flourishing. How, then, have critics responded to Forster's narrative? Here, the problem might well seem to be the superfluity of Forster criticism, rather than a lack of it. Forster has long been acknowledged as one of the modernist greats, and a superabundance of secondary scholarship has built up around his work. It is quickly apparent, however, that almost none of it relates to "The Machine Stops." The exception to the rule came, not when the story was first published, but when it reappeared as part of *The Eternal Moment and Other Stories* in 1928. Forster was by then recognized as a major writer, and the collection attracted substantial critical interest: *The Critical Heritage* includes ten reviews of the collection (Gardner 1973, 340–55). Notwithstanding Forster's fame, however, most reactions to "The Machine Stops" were dismissive, and some baffled: one reviewer regarded an underground existence as "quite inconceivable" ("we immediately want to know why they should live under the ground") (qtd in Gardner 1973, 352), apparently overlooking the story's obvious inference, that humankind has itself accidentally engineered an ecocidal apocalypse. Most of the reviews take no notice of Forster's emphasis on human embodiment, and the one reviewer who does take notice of it, does so in order to disparage it: "at times," wrote the novelist L. P. Hartley, "he [Forster] writes as though he were trying to organize a Society for the Prevention of Cruelty to Children of Nature" (qtd in Gardner 1973, 349).[2]

Later generations of critics have taken their lead from these early responses. Most ignore the story.[3] Those who do mention it, do so in the context of Forster's liberal humanism (Jonsson 2012, 161). For liberal, mid-century critics like G. D. Klingopulos, as for David Garnett, it was the forces of anti-humanism (whether of Nazi Germany, or Stalinist Russia, or later, Maoist China) that lent such value to Forster's work—to his "frail words" (Klingopulos 1973, 264)—and to propositions such as "only connect" (the epigraph of Forster's *Howard's End*). In this reading of Forster's oeuvre, the individual remains "the reference point of value" (Herz 1988, 4), struggling to assert liberal decencies in an "intractable world" (Medalie 2002, 35), and that reading carries over into much later interpretations, such as Judith Scherer Herz's brief reading of "The Machine Stops" as the expression of

Forster's own contempt for technology as master principle. "In a diary entry of 1908 (the year in which he was writing 'The Machine Stops')," she notes, "Forster makes this clear [. . .] 'No more fighting, please, between the soul and the body, until they have beaten their common enemy, the machine'" (Herz 1988, 60). To the contrary, Forster's story may now be read as a sophisticated post-humanist critique, in which humanist values are exposed as a set of universalizing assumptions that distort the human sense of self, with lethal consequences for all those "others" with which humankind shares (or in this case, once shared) its world.

Herz's discussion of the story is, in any case, very brief (1988, 59–62), for reasons that are themselves relevant. Various phases of literary criticism have come and gone; Herz's book is concerned with formalist criticism, and whilst it represents a rare instance of critical interest in Forster's shorter narratives, as opposed to the novels that critics have tended to privilege (Leavitt and Mitchell 2001, xii), its focus is on evaluating the narrative modes that Forster adopts (Herz 1988, 48). The related point is that "The Machine Stops" is itself exceptional, not just because of its implied critique of humanism, but because it represents Forster's sole foray into "the norms and conventions of what we now know as science fiction" (Herz 1988, 59). Consequently, and even though it is both a "well-known" (Head 2007, 81) and "often-anthologised" story (Herz 1988, 59), "The Machine Stops" occupies a marginal position in Forster criticism, as at once a short story (albeit a long one) and as an (anomalous) instance of science fiction, or SF.

Whilst mainstream Forster scholars have neglected the story, however, the SF community has not (March-Russell 2005, 57; Seabury 1997, 61). Although "The Machine Stops" periodically reappeared in collections or selections of Forster's short stories (for example, in 1928, 1947, and 1954) and once as a mainstream stand-alone (2011, in Penguin Mini Modern Classics), it has frequently been reprinted as part of SF collections, and in at least five other languages (Internet Speculative Fiction Database; see also Landon 1997, 15). Where SF editors led, SF critics followed: "beginning with Mark Hillegas's *The Future as Nightmare* (1967)," argues Marcia Seabury, "discussions of the story began to appear in [. . .] books and articles on science fiction and dystopian fiction" (1997, 161), generating a substantial body of critical analysis (see also Landon 1997, 10–21, Caporaletti 1997).

The nature of the story's importance has nevertheless prompted much debate. Some SF writers have seen its focus as inner space (the psychological, personal domain encapsulated in the tortured relationship of the main protagonists, Vashti and her rebellious son Kuno) (Landon 1997, 12–13); others have regarded the story as the expression of wider, societal concerns that shape the story's projection of an outer space ("the largely abandoned and Machine-proscribed surface of the Earth") (Landon 1997, 17). As an example of the latter, Brook Landon highlights several aspects of the story that we might now find pertinent to a discussion of cli-fi, such as the story's response to the Machine as the metonymic expression of a more generalized concern about the trajectory of "technology, science, progress" (1997, 12); as Landon insists, Forster's story is undeniably polemical (1997, 18). Nonetheless, his reading of "Forster's determined attempt to demonize the machine" (Landon 1997, 18) recapitulates the widespread assumption that this is the story of an apocalypse (e.g., Head 2007, 82), when it could equally well be seen as the story of a moment of historic liberation, as the failing Machine frees humankind to return to the surface, as Kuno has already done, and there reconnect with the surface-dwellers whom he now knows have somehow survived (Forster 2001, 113).[4] The apocalypse has already taken place, forming part of a now almost forgotten story of how humankind "overreached itself [and] exploited the riches of nature too far" (Forster 2001, 116). "The surface of the earth supports life no longer," Vashti tells Kuno, repeating the long-held belief; "[f]erns and a little grass may survive, but all higher forms have perished" (Forster 2001, 113). Kuno's discovery that this is not (or no longer) the case (Forster 2001, 110–113) is expressed in a way that highlights what is at stake: reaching the surface, which is itself a supreme physical achievement for a now enfeebled human frame, Kuno experiences a holistic vision of his own animal vitality and of the vitality that animates an agential reality, lively and dynamic: the hills he sees are, he realizes, "living and the turf that covered them was a skin, under which their muscles rippled, and I felt that those hills [. . .] called with incalculable force" (Forster 2001, 110). The horror of the story, one might add, lies in the way that those who are denied this sense of their own embodied existence see nothing distressing in the shared history of their own species, a species that has left the earth as "dust and mud" (Forster 2001, 94). It is also, perhaps, why Forster chose to focalize his story, not around its putative hero, Kuno, but around his mother, Vashti, the "swaddled lump of flesh" (Forster 2001, 91) who speaks for a universalized, homogenized "Humanity," its fatal "desire for comfort" (116), and its blithe indifference to "[t]hose funny old days" (96) when human hubris ran on untrammelled. The related point is that, as David Medalie has argued, the humanism with which Forster is often associated is a more expansive conceptual framework than is sometimes allowed, and never more so than during the Edwardian era, when it also encompasses "the vitalism of the period" (2002, 35). It is, in fact, this recognition of relationships that cross boundaries and exceed narrow definitions that characterises Forster's imaginative foray into SF.

Forster's story was written relatively early in his career. Later in life, it seemed to him that he had "underestimated the mightiness of Man" (qtd in Leavitt and Mitchell 2001, x). Humankind was now capable of poisoning the sea's "depths with atomic waste," he wrote in 1962 (qtd in Leavitt and Mitchell 2001, x): might "Man also succeed in poisoning the solar system?" The irony is that he had indeed predicted this inadvertent mightiness—this accidental ability to shape and distort life as a planetary whole—in "The Machine Stops." What Forster forgot, his critics ignored. "The Machine Stops" is a remarkable story, but as this brief outline suggests, twentieth-century reactions are equally surprising because they overlook the most interesting dimensions of the story. This is equally true of Jefferies's *After London*, if not more so, since it has not had the advantage of being taken up and championed by the SF community.

If it seems that, by and large, few readers (or rather, critics as readers) have taken note of what we might now regard as the most genuinely innovative aspects of these narratives, that oversight nevertheless suggests several possible findings for the project of empirical ecocriticism. One is that readers translate even the most radical narratives into terms with which they are familiar and comfortable, such as a stress on the human dimension of a story. Readers seek out and invariably find what they are looking for, and this may be especially true of expansive, experimental writers such as Jefferies, as Q. D. Leavis remarked in an early survey (1938) of critical reactions to his work: "Jefferies was one of those comprehensive geniuses from whose work you can take what you are inclined to find" (1938, 435). Another, interrelated possibility is that reader response is not (or not simply) governed by unchanging instinct (an unvarying desire for narrative closure, say, or just desserts for the wicked), but by a wider and shifting *Weltanschauung*, or by the pressures of the historical moment, as David Garnett's reaction to *After London* underlines. It is, moreover, perfectly possible to take this possibility a sceptical step further. As this chapter assumes, imaginative fiction is an innately innovative and flexible medium, perfectly capable of escaping what Clark has described as the "anthropocentric delusion" (2015, 191), or the "potentially destructive projections of the personal scale" (192); indeed, these two post-apocalyptic narratives are concrete examples of fiction's innovative potential, since they (re)assert the importance of an embodied existence in an agential reality that is vulnerable to but also capable of shaping and influencing human behaviors.[5] Yet the stories themselves return the reader to individual, human narratives, whether those stories are about Felix (last seen striding out on his return to his beloved Aurora) or Vashti and Kuno (whose death in each other's arms ends Forster's story). Ultimately, an agential, nonhuman reality is secondary to their experiences, experiences which are framed within the temporality and spatiality of the human scale. Consequently, it may be that this chapter falls into the trap identified by Clark: it is not really drawing attention to a genuinely innovative form of fiction so much as enacting "a mode of critical reading newly sensitized by the demands of the Anthropocene" (Clark 2015,

181). Minded to look out for evidence of nonhuman agency, it embodies a new form of normative bias, a bias whose limits are revealed by the many very different responses to the narratives in question, few of which share this point of view.

There are also, perhaps, more intractable difficulties associated with the project of which this chapter forms a part. Imaginative fiction is premised on a paradox: it exists to persuade the reader that what is false is in fact true, and its success can be measured by the extent to which the reader is convinced of that "truth," even if only "for the duration of that reading experience" (Lodge 1992, x). As David Lodge puts it, fiction is "an essentially rhetorical art—that is to say, the novelist or short story-writer *persuades* us to share a certain view of the world" (1992, x). The problem, notes Clark, is that the enactment of this art itself becomes the subject of appreciation, a consumer pleasure that distracts the reader from a novel's content, or reminds him or her that it is, after all, merely a fiction (2015, 189). These are valid objections, which relate to the wider questions that Clark repeatedly emphasises, "such as the social-political functions of literature and its reception, its imbrication in education systems and the entertainment industries and the dominant valorisation of the reading experience as a kind of consumer commodity" (2015, 190). All these aspects of fiction's wider identity tend to negate its value as a functional tool for changing minds.

Yet the writing of this chapter has also suggested an alternative, and more positive possibility. Clark is right to raise the "thorny question of reader response, of what gives a novel emotional force for a readership" (2015, 179), but as Schneider-Mayerson suggests in his own survey of cli-fi and reader response, "climate change is an increasingly present and central topic" (2018, 496). As a result, readers are increasingly mindful of this dimension in the stories they read. "In the light of warnings from eco-prophets we can no longer dismiss as crazed Cassandras," *The Observer* (grudgingly) conceded in its comment on *After London*, Jefferies's "proposed scenario [now] looks more grimly convincing than it could ever have done in the 1880s" (Keates 1999). That was 1999, and since then, the concerns of those environmental "Cassandras" have moved (even further) towards the mainstream.

Two points follow. The first is that, as environmental issues have become more prominent, so the academic community has itself responded: the emergence of ecocriticism in the 1990s appears to have coincided with a more general academic interest in seeking out literary instances of green thinking. Whether or not these academic interventions identify themselves *as* ecocritical—or, after Adeline Johns-Putra, "ecohistorical" (2016, 267)—the result has been an outbreak of interest in both Forster and Jefferies. For example, Forster was the subject of a recent conference entitled *E. M. Forster: Nature, Culture, Queer!* (2018) that explicitly acknowledged the environmental dimension of Forster's thinking, whilst also drawing fresh attention to "The Machine Stops." More articles on the story have also appeared, including Udo Nattermann's discussion of its "eco-political" dimensions (2013, 1), and Emelie Jonsson's analysis of its evolutionary aspects, which acknowledges the story's "implicit call to [. . .] take in the full scope of the environment" (2012, 161). Alf Seegert has also published a related article in the *Journal of Ecocriticism* (2010); as Seegert notes, Forster's story has "strong ecocritical implications" (35). Moreover, Seegert's article is particularly attentive to Forster's focus on "the alienation of a technologically mediated subject so completely divorced from nature that it doesn't even realize that it is alienated anymore," an emphasis on "embodied human integrity" (2010, 34) that overlaps with the approach taken in this chapter. In the case of Jefferies, the increase in eco-scholarly interest has been still more marked, with a number of publications ranging from a monograph by Brian Morris (2007) to articles by Rebecca Welshman (2011) and Ronald D. Morrison (2017). David Mazel included Jefferies's work in *A Century of Early Ecocriticism* (2001), whilst well-established writers such as Roger Ebbatson have continued to discuss Jefferies's environmentally-oriented thinking within ever more refined theoretical frameworks (see Ebbatson 2007, 2013, 2016). *After London* has itself been the subject of more specific ecocritical re-evaluation, most notably by Heidi C. M. Scott (2014, 53–63) and Jed Mayer (2011), both of whom acknowledge the hierarchical reversal the novel describes: "[h]umans are now obliged to follow animals," notes Mayer, "and as Jefferies's visionary natural history progresses, meticulous attention is paid to the evolution of animals left to run wild" (2011, 83); "[p]articularly compelling," observes Scott, "is the description of domesticated species, farm and companion animals [. . .] returning to a feral state in a posthuman world" (2014, 55). Moreover, Jefferies's novel has recently been republished by Edinburgh University Press with a substantial new introduction by Mark Frost (2017, vii–xlvi) that explicitly responds to the "pressing" "need for a new scholarly edition" of the novel, "given recent rising interest in the relationship between literature and the environment" (viii).

There are, moreover, two other developments within the academic community that may spur further critical inquiry. The first is the rapidly expanding field of animal (or human-animal) studies, a "close kin" of ecocriticism (Garrard 2012, 146) which would certainly find fascinating material in Jefferies's description of the resurgence of animal life. The second is a growing interest in climate change fiction, to which this chapter testifies; as Johns-Putra points out, that interest has pushed ecocriticism in fresh directions, whilst also generating the new field of "climate change criticism" (2016, 267). Against this background, there is growing interest in identifying what Johns-Putra terms "a canon of climate change literature" (2016, 267), precursors of modern cli-fi that might reasonably be extended to include narratives such as Jefferies's—as Adam Trexler points out, "[f]loods are a dominant literary strategy for locating climate change" (2015, 24)—and perhaps also Forster's, with its depiction of an unbreathable surface atmosphere.

On the one hand, therefore, a growing awareness of environmental crisis has encouraged a renewed focus on these stories; on the other, it has also prompted more general, non-specialist interest, interest that turns on some if not all the issues highlighted in this chapter. Ironically, that growth in interest has been enabled, perhaps even encouraged by the kinds of technological developments that Forster foresaw and critiqued. In the last two decades, stories such as Forster's and Jefferies's have become much more easily accessible, whether through print on demand, downloadable e-pubs, or simply as freely available texts or audiobooks online.[6] As these books have become easier to access—literature at the push of a button, to paraphrase Forster (2001, 94)—they have also become easier to discuss through online forums, the use of which has, in a further development, made it easier to trace the impact of specific works on their readers. As even a cursory glance at forums such as Goodreads (www.goodreads.com) suggests, *After London* and "The Machine Stops" are now generating a substantial body of commentary, and it often references the same themes that ecocritics have identified. Moreover, the open access movement is making ecocritical scholarship much more readily available to general readers. It may not matter whether general readers are taking their cue from ecocritically minded scholars, or whether both kinds of reader are turning to these narratives because green issues form an increasingly prominent societal concern; the trend is clear.

In the spirit of Clark's sceptical approach to ecocriticism "on the edge," to quote the title of his 2015 critique, one should, perhaps, strike three final, cautionary notes. The first is that, this trend notwithstanding, research such as Schneider-Mayerson's suggests that "clearer and stronger messaging about appropriate behavioural responses to climate change is urgently needed" (2018, 495), messaging that neither *After London* nor "The Machine Stops" provide; nor could they, given that they were written before climate change was properly understood. The second is that, as Schneider-Mayerson also emphasises, "more empirical research on environmental literature and art" is still needed (2018, 495). The third and final caveat is perhaps the most substantial. In an epoch now widely described as the Anthropocene, there is a growing consensus that human impacts of all kinds (not limited to but including climate change) are precipitating a mass extinction event amongst nonhuman animals. Thus, and whilst both *After London* and "The Machine Stops" make "imaginative projections of fluctuating animal population dynamics under new environmental circumstances," as Frost notes in relation to Jefferies's novel (2017, xxv), it is Forster's (truly horrifying) future-past that now looks more likely. Jefferies presents his animal nature as "superabundant and unyielding" (Frost 2017, xxvii); it may in fact be all too vulnerable to human depredation. Given that this is now a pressing possibility, perhaps even likelihood, what can literature (and literary criticism) possibly do *fast enough* to make any meaningful difference?

REFERENCES

Barad, Karen. 2007. *Meeting the Universe Halfway: Quantum Physics and the Entanglement of Matter and Meaning*. London: Duke University Press.

Buell, Lawrence. 1995. *The Environmental Imagination: Thoreau, Nature Writing, and the Formation of American Culture*. London: Belknap Press.

Caporaletti, Silvan. 1997. "Science as Nightmare: 'The Machine Stops' by E. M. Forster." *Utopian Studies* 8 (2): 32–47.

Clark, Timothy. 2015. *Ecocriticism on the Edge: The Anthropocene as a Threshold Concept*. London: Bloomsbury.

Ebbatson, Roger. 1980. *Lawrence and the Nature Tradition: A Theme in English Fiction, 1859–1914*. Sussex: Harvester Press.

———. 2007. "Prophecy and Utopia: Richard Jefferies and the Transcendentalists." *The Glass* 19: 42–49. www.clsg.org/html/archive.html.

———. 2013. *Landscape and Literature 1830–1914: Nature, Text, Aura*. Basingstoke: Palgrave Macmillan.

———. 2016. *Landscapes of Eternal Return: Tennyson to Hardy*. London: Palgrave Macmillan.

Forster, E. M. 2001. "The Machine Stops." *Selected Stories*, ed. David Leavitt and Mark Mitchell, 91–23. London: Penguin.

Frost, Mark. 2017. "Introduction." Richard Jefferies, *After London; or Wild England*, ed. Mark Frost, vii–xlvi. Edinburgh: Edinburgh University Press.

Gardner, Philip, ed. 1973. *E. M. Forster: The Critical Heritage*. London: Routledge.

Garnett, David. 1939. "Introduction." In *After London, or Wild England, and Amaryllis at the Fair*, by Richard Jeffries, Everyman's Library, vii–xiii. London: J. M. Dent & Sons.

Garrard, Greg. 2012. *Ecocriticism*. 2nd ed. Abingdon: Routledge.

Ghosh, Amitav. 2016. *The Great Derangement: Climate Change and the Unthinkable*. London: University of Chicago Press.

Head, Dominic. 2007. "Forster and the short story." *The Cambridge Companion to E. M. Forster*, ed. by David Bradshaw, 77–91. Cambridge: Cambridge University Press.

Herz, Judith Scherer. 1988. *The Short Narratives of E. M. Forster*. New York: St. Martin's Press.

Internet Speculative Fiction Database. n.d. Accessed July 14, 2021. www.isfdb.org/cgi-bin/title.cgi?906862.

Jefferies, Richard. 1907 [1893]. *The Story of My Heart: My Autobiography*. London: Longman, Green, and Co.

———. 2017 [1885]. *After London; or Wild England*, ed. Mark Frost. Edinburgh: Edinburgh University Press.

Johns-Putra, Adeline. 2016. "Climate change in literature and literary studies: from cli-fi, climate change theater and ecopoetry to ecocriticism and climate change criticism." *WIREs Clim Change* 7: 266–282. doi.org/10.1002/wcc.385.

Jonsson, Emelie. 2012. "'Man is the Measure': Forster's Evolutionary Conundrum." *Style* 46 (2): 161–176.

Keates, Jonathan. 1999. "Tomorrow never knows." *The Observer*, April 25, 1999. www.theguardian.com/theobserver/1999/apr/25/featuresreview.review5.

Keith, W. J. 1965. *Richard Jefferies: A Critical Study*. London: Oxford University Press.

Klingopulos, G. D. 1973 [1961]. "Mr. Forster's Good Influence." *The Modern Age: Volume 7 of the Pelican Guide to English Literature*, ed. Boris Ford, 263–74. 3rd edn. Harmondsworth: Penguin.

Landon, Brooks. 1997. *Science Fiction After 1900: From the Steam Man to the Stars*. New York: Twayne.

Leavis, Q. D. 1938. "Lives and Works of Richard Jefferies." *Scrutiny* 6 (4): 435–46.

Leavitt, David, and Mark Mitchell. 2001. "Introduction." In *Selected Stories*, by E. M. Forster ed. David Leavitt and Mark Mitchell, vii–xxiii. London: Penguin.

Lodge, David. 1992. *The Art of Fiction*. London: Vintage.

March-Russell, Paul. 2005. "'Imagine, If You Can': Love, Time and the Impossibility of Utopia in E. M. Forster's 'The Machine Stops.'" *Critical Survey* 17 (1): 56–71.

Mayer, Jed. 2011. "A Darker Shade of Green: William Morris, Richard Jefferies, and Posthumanist Ecologies." *Journal of William Morris Studies* 19 (3): 79–92.

Mazel, David, ed. 2001. *A Century of Early Ecocriticism*. Athens, GA: University of Georgia Press.

Medalie, David. 2002. *E. M. Forster's Modernism*. Houndmills: Palgrave.

Morris, Brian. 2007. *Richard Jefferies and the Ecological Vision*. Bloomington, IA: Trafford Publishing.

Morrison, Ronald D. 2017. "Agriculture and Ecology in Richard Jefferies's *Hodge and His Masters*." *Victorian Writers and the Environment: Ecocritical Perspectives*, ed. Laurence W. Mazzeno and Ronald D. Morrison, 205–19. Abingdon: Routledge.

Morton, Timothy. 2007. *Ecology Without Nature: Rethinking Environmental Aesthetics*. London: Harvard University Press.

Nattermann, Udo. 2013. "Mundane Boundaries: Eco-political Elements in Three Science Fiction Stories." *Interdisciplinary Studies in Literature and Environment* 20 (1): 1–13. doi.org/10.1093/isle/ist012.

Page, Norman. 1987. *E. M. Forster*. Houndmills: Macmillan.

Salt, H. S. 1894. *Richard Jefferies: A Study*. London: Swan Sonnenschein & Co.

Schneider-Mayerson, Matthew. 2018. "The Influence of Climate Fiction: An Empirical Survey of Readers." *Environmental Humanities* 10 (2): 473–500.

Scott, Heidi C. M. 2014. *Chaos and Cosmos: Literary Roots of Modern Ecology in the British Nineteenth Century*. University Park, PA: Pennsylvania State University Press.
Seabury, Marcia Bundy. 1997. "Images of a Networked Society: E. M. Forster's 'The Machine Stops.'" *Studies in Short Fiction* 34 (1): 61–71.
Seegert, Alf. 2010. "Technology and the Fleshly Interface in Forster's 'The Machine Stops': An Ecocritical Appraisal of a One-Hundred-Year-Old Future." *Journal of Ecocriticism* 2 (1): 33–54.
Thomas, Edward. 1909. *Richard Jefferies: His Life and Work*. London: Hutchinson & Co.
Trexler, Adam. 2015. *Anthropocene Fictions: The Novel in a Time of Climate Change*. London: University of Virginia Press.
Welshman, Rebecca. 2011. "Literature and the Ecological Imagination: Richard Jefferies and D. H. Lawrence." *Victorian Network* 3 (1): 51–63.
Williamson, Henry. 1937. *Richard Jefferies: Selections of his Work, with Details of His Life and Circumstance, His Death and Immortality*. London: Faber & Faber.

NOTES

1. Most critics have focused—and continue to focus—on Jefferies's nature writing, as Ebbatson does here. Significantly, however, Ebbatson does refer to the second, later section of *After London*, in which the focus switches to a human protagonist, Sir Felix, and to his awakening "in a bountiful landscape" (Ebbatson 1980, 134). As the reader will already appreciate, the world into which Felix wakes is rather a hard-won and isolated enclave within a much wider and wilder landscape. This is not "nature" in a friendly guise. The enduring influence of the view of nature as friendly and beneficent is Ebbatson's theme in his book; the fact that it also forecloses a more detailed reading of that "masterly opening" underlines Timothy Morton's contention that "nature" is "[o]ne of the ideas inhibiting genuinely ecological politics, ethics, philosophy" (2007, 14).

2. It is notable that the first major American comment on Forster's novels, published a few years later in 1932, clearly understood this dimension of his thinking: "Mr. Forster [wrote the reviewer] starts with the common observation that modern civilization distorts and deforms the life of the individual in all its range. Industrialism, by driving man from the soil, has spoiled his capacity for the naïve life of the body that flourishes in contact with the earth" (Howard N. Doughty, Jr "The novels of E. M. Forster," 1932, qtd in Gardner 1973, 358).

3. By way of example, Norman Page's book on Forster (1987) belongs to the Macmillan Modern Novelists series; the fact that it excludes "The Machine Stops" is unsurprising—or would be, if Page did not mention so many other short stories by Forster. Similarly, David Medalie's *E. M. Forster's Modernism* (2002) includes a discussion of the short stories, but not "The Machine Stops," whilst *The Cambridge Companion to E. M. Forster* (2007) contains sixteen chapters, but just one on the

short stories, which in turn contains a single paragraph on "The Machine Stops" (Head 2007, 81–82).

4. That sense of the story's liberatory potential was shared by at least one reader. Gardner's *Critical Heritage* includes a letter from Edith Sitwell, also a novelist, who wrote to Forster after the republication of the story in 1928: "all I know is that 'The Machine Stops' made me feel as though I had come out of a dark tunnel in which I had always lived, into an immense open space, and were seeing things living for the first time" (qtd in Gardner 1973, 339).

5. For a useful discussion of this point, see Amitav Ghosh 2016, 63–66.

6. *After London* is freely available at both the Internet Archive (archive.org/) and Project Gutenberg (www.gutenberg.org/); because of copyright, E. M. Forster's story is as yet only available (through the Internet Archive) as an audiobook.

Chapter 3

Stories of "Being-with" Other Animals: A Case of Humans and Horses

Mary Trachsel

FICTION IN THE SHADOW OF THE APOCALYPSE

Fictional stories reflect factual realities. Right now, as global warming, desertification, ocean acidification, and species extinctions accelerate, the most obvious literary reflections of the news from environmental science are apocalyptic science fiction narratives about humans struggling to survive. Popular examples from North America include Margaret Atwood's *Maddaddam* trilogy and Jeff Vandermeer's *Southern Reach* and *Borne* trilogies, all depicting a natural world disastrously altered by human activity and infiltrated by biotechnology gone rogue. In the tradition of Rachel Carson's "A Fable for Tomorrow," these narratives assume the didactic form of ecological cautionary tales warning of humanity's self-annihilation amid the ruins of Nature. Carson's fable, the opening to *Silent Spring* (1962), is a sobering, science-informed prediction of environmental decline caused by short-sighted attempts to bend Nature to human will. In the story's sad ending, humans live in an impoverished biosphere where no birds sing, and "the rebirth of new life" has staggered to a halt. Carson soberly concludes her tale with the realization that "the people had done it themselves" (3).

The same tragic vision of present Nature slipping into a man-mis-made future has prompted evolutionary biologist Edward O. Wilson to suggest "the Eremocene," the Age of Loneliness, as a name for the present era (Wilson

2016). His apocalyptic vision reflects science news of the sixth mass extinction (Leakey and Lewin 1995; Kolbert 2014), an escalating global trend attributable in large part to human invasion and conquest of other species' habitats, followed by human overpopulation and overconsumption, in turn leading to further environmental damage from pollution and waste. Like Carson, Wilson identifies human dissociation from nonhuman nature as the original sin, arguing that human life, like all life, only endures as a component part of an ecological system. The story of the Eremocene and the story of a silent spring both place humanity within "the web of life" (Capra 1996) and teach that human life is fatally linked to the survival of nonhuman life. Reflecting the factual unraveling of the web of life, cautionary environmental science fiction asks humans to choose between taking action to avert the apocalypse or surrendering to Nature's justice. Typical motivators of human action in these stories are dread of the future and remorse for the past, as human actors grow ever more alienated from a barren or hostile world. With this focus on a dismal future of our own creation, apocalyptic science fiction spotlights humanity's environmental sins and contemplates possible ways to intervene or atone.

But sci-fi fables are not the only reflections of life and death on planet Earth today. Other story forms offer other sorts of lessons on how to live in this geological moment. Among the alternatives to apocalyptic fables are stories of human action motivated not by dread or remorse but by human desire for connection and coexistence, the essential motivation of the romance instead of the fable. By far the most familiar romance is the intraspecies form of the genre, the human love story, particularly the love story that culminates in characters' recognition of their entwined human fates and joint creation of their future. Some fairy-tale romances venture into interspecies relationships—"The Princess and the Frog" and "Beauty and the Beast" come to mind—but more often than not the nonhuman converts to "true" human form before a happy union is secured. This essay traces the evolution of a different sort of interspecies romance: the human-horse relationship story. At the end of the nineteenth century, this story type found its literary home in fiction for young adults and children, and from that generic location it continues to serve a didactic purpose in the Anthropocene.

A historical survey of these books and the interspecies relationships they depict reveals the development over time of an increasingly biocentric representation of humans as relational beings embedded in webs of life that reach beyond humanity, reconceptualizing the state of human being as human being-with more-than-human others. The term "being-with" comes from the philosopher Martin Heidegger's *"Mitsein,"* denoting the phenomenon of relationality—the lived experience of being-with others (Heidegger 1927). With a focus on human being-with horses, pony books and horse stories, like love stories, depict a relational moral universe, but unlike the love story that finds closure in the characters' union, these narratives develop human-horse relationships in the episodic form of companion-adventure series. The serial format opens the core narrative of human-nonhuman relationship-building for long consideration and close scrutiny and, in so doing, encourages readers to reject the presumed separation of human and nonhuman being that justifies the illusion of human control over nature.

ANTHROPOCENE NARRATIVES

Anthropocene is a favored term for the present geological moment. Instead of Wilson's emphasis on human loneliness, the term focuses on the transformative force of human agency in pursuit of the false god Carson called "the control of nature" (1962, 297). Characterizing the Anthropocene as a set of narratives about leaving the familiar old Holocene and entering a strange, new, human-made epoch, environmental sociologists Rolf Lidskog and Claire Waterton (2016) warn against assuming that the Anthropocene narrator—the Anthropos—speaks as and for a distinct and unified human *I*. All too often, they argue, Anthropocene fiction, though it tells of the intertwining fates of humans and the rest of Nature, retains the narrative perspective of "a different, exceptional, species that can know and control the Earth System," when in fact "more variable authorship" (2016, 403) is necessary if fiction is to help us adapt to and survive in a world where we know our fate is bound up in the fates of other species.

The cultural critic/artist Joanna Zylinska (2018) agrees that a less singular human species identity is in order. She notes that Anthropocene narratives generally offer two possible escape routes from humanity's ruinous transformation of the planet: extra-planetary travel to new frontiers, or ascendance to godlike invulnerability in the bio-tech realms of artificial intelligence and virtual reality. Both solutions preserve faith in human sapience and control over Nature. In the end, both celebrate the same "uniquely human" powers that have brought life on Earth to its present, precarious pass. Neither option asks or allows humans to surrender or reform our age-old survival strategy of environmental conquest and control; neither one questions or challenges the human species' ownership of Nature's goods and services. A third high-tech solution to environmental devastation in contemporary science and science fiction appears in Jessie Beier's (2018) study of science-fictionalizing in the Anthropocene: environmental engineering, also known as "geo-engineering," or "climate engineering" (2018, 369). In this third type of Anthropocene narrative, the human subject "hacks" the Earth System to "fix" Nature's imperfections, repairing or circumventing the damage we've done, redeeming humans from both ecological guilt and biological self-destruction (369).

All three of these popular problem-solution narratives of the Anthropocene distinguish human subjects as *doers* from the rest of nature, which is *done unto*; all presume human exceptionalism as justification for human dominion and control. Grounded in belief that humanity is divinely chosen or that human sapience and its tools have limitless reach, human exceptionalism assumes that *Homo sapiens* is uniquely exempt from natural law. Science fiction espousing this doctrine, Beier notes, draws from the Western civilization myth of Prometheus, whose gift of fire separated humans from the biological background of "merely-living life" (2018, 371). In the moral balance of human and other-than-human life, all "other" life is "mere," and ultimately dismissible.

Zylinska, however, proposes a fourth, divergent plotline for the Anthropocene, a "feminist" tale of "counter-apocalypse" (2018). This alternative narrative rejects the tragic unfolding of human exceptionalism and conjures in its place an affiliative narrative of human submission and adaptation to environmental demands. The story is "feminist" in championing historically feminine human virtues—like restraint and receptivity—and in celebrating conventionally feminine human behaviors—like connection, compliance, and care. These virtues and behaviors, the new story proposes, might well replace the human urge to dominate and control. The counter-apocalyptic goals of Zylinska's feminized Anthropos are coexistence in the present and coevolution in the future. Intent on the mutual survival of humanity and the more-than-human world, she is an inherently relational being who willingly submits to environmental demands instead of re-engineering the world. Intent on *doing with* and *doing for* a relational Other, she exemplifies an evolutionary type the mathematical biologist Martin Nowak calls a "Super Cooperator" (2011), a term signifying a species, a population, or an individual who maximizes the evolutionary strategy of altruism. We humans recognize and valorize this strategy on an individual level in warriors' sacrifices for tribe or nation and in parents' sacrifices for vulnerable offspring; in broader, ecological terms, altruism distils to species' investments in the survival of other species in the same web of life, for example through domestication, cultivation, or conservation.

In prescribing "the end of man," then, Zylinska is not calling for the extinction of humans generally or for the end of men in particular. Rather, she envisions an end to anthropocentric and ultimately self-destructive ways of being human and advocates their replacement by an altruistic worldview. Finding an alternative to the Age of Loneliness, she suggests, requires new ways of human being-with others, as the human dilemma of the Anthropocene is not simply deciding what to *do* to circumvent the constraints of Nature but, more fundamentally, choosing how to *be* human within those constraints. By assigning non-exceptional status to human beings, Zylinska attempts to replace the singularly anthropocentric lens of human exceptionalism with a biocentric worldview grounded in the phenomenon of life shared with other species, from elephants to viruses. "Being-with," in her vision of the future's unfolding, is a condition native to all Earthly beings and a constant in the narrative of human life on Earth. To counter tales of Anthropocene apocalypse, Zylinska urges us to overleap the piercing question of the Eremocene—How do we humans exist *without* other life-forms?—and take up a counter-apocalyptic alternative—How do we exist *with* them?

THE LITERARY EVOLUTION OF HUMAN-HORSE RELATIONSHIPS: FROM RESCUE STORY TO ROMANCE

In his formulation of *Mitsein*, Heidigger was mainly concerned with the state of human being-with other humans, but the concept applies to cross-species relationships as well. From hunting and gathering, to the domestication of plants and nonhuman animals and throughout the steady intensification of agriculture and urbanization across the globe, the evolution of human cultures is an evolution of human relationships with other species. One historically important example of human-nonhuman relational being is the coevolution of humans and horses, traceable as a factual history whose recent developments are reflected in fictional texts.

Though the field of animal studies has recently spotlighted the presence of animals in literature, the overwhelming preponderance of English-language animal fictions in the modern age can be found in texts aimed at young people. Accordingly, the literary record reveals human-horse relationships most clearly as they have been imagined by and for children and young adults. Like most animal stories for children, horse stories are often vehicles for moral education, and as horses are too large and powerful for people to control by physical force alone, horse stories tend to probe relational ethics, instructing young people on how and how not to build and maintain satisfying human-equine relationships. In a genre far removed from apocalyptic science fiction about humanity's lonely end, horse books have traditionally encouraged young readers to imagine ways of keeping company with nonhuman beings.

Anna Sewell's *Black Beauty* (1877) is the classic example of a horse story that contemplates trans-species relational ethics. At a time when horses occupied the place in human culture that motorized vehicles do today, *Black*

Beauty succeeded in raising awareness of horses as centers of consciousness and conscience, delivering moral instruction to the adults who owned, cared for, and worked with horses. Natalie Corinne Hanson distills the novel's relational lesson to an empathic ethic of "shared suffering" and notes that Beauty's story "had immediate and important results for the well-being of horses in England, Europe & America" (2010, 729). Shortly after the publication of *Black Beauty*, however, as engines rapidly replaced horses in the lives of many humans, Sewell's moral fiction about humane and inhumane human coexistence with horses became a book enjoyed primarily by young readers. As an animal narrator, Beauty joins a host of talking animals in children's literature, his story bearing witness to human being-with horses from the equine side of the relationship. Beginning life as a well-bred horse responsibly schooled by a kind and gentle master, Beauty narrates a declining state of being-with humans; as he passes from the hands of one human to the next, his body and spirit suffer neglect, abuse, overwork, and abandonment. The human authors of his suffering are by turns ignorant, cruel, self-centered or simply disempowered. He is finally saved by a kind human from his past, who recognizes him despite the ravages of time and ill-treatment.

Beauty's fate in being-with humans is entirely controlled by his human owners, and his only hope for a comfortable retirement as he nears the end of his unfortunate life is human altruism. Though Beauty is becoming worthless as a beast of burden or transport, good humans finally offer him easy work and provide his upkeep out of gratitude for his service and sacrifice to humanity. Ultimately, the ideal state of human being-with horses advanced by the book is kind and devoted equine servitude met by equally kind and devoted human mastery.

As horses faded from the work life of most humans and entered the realm of sport and leisure for a relatively small portion of the human population, new questions of how humans should be-with horses arose for contemplation in the fictions of the day. *Black Beauty* opened the way for the British genre of "pony books" that told of human-horse relationships in domestic settings, designed and maintained by humans for humans. Beauty's fortune sinks to its nadir in the paved and crowded streets of London, where his basic needs are unfulfilled: his food and shelter are inadequate, he has little freedom of movement, no access to fresh air and green grass, and no supportive equine or human companionship. Perceiving and satisfying those equine requirements are relational responsibilities that dominate the lives of human characters in the pony book genre that arose in the wake of *Black Beauty*.

This genre coalesced nearly half a century after *Black Beauty* was published, when the position of horses in England had already shifted from agriculture, mill-work, warfare, travel, and transport to sporting activities such as hacking, racing, hunting, steeple-chasing, and equestrian games. Most British pony books followed the example of Enid Bagnold's *National Velvet* (1935) in featuring (white) girls as the human companions of horses. Often, these heroines defied class divisions and challenged gender norms by willingly undertaking hard, dirty, physical labor, participating in dangerous outdoor adventures, and revealing through their own empathic connections and care for equine beings that spoiled rich girls did not deserve the horses that came so easily into their lives. Jean O'Malley Halley points out, however, that although the plucky heroines of British pony books in the mid-twentieth century defied certain gendered cultural expectations, they embodied a traditionally feminine, care-based morality. Halley notes that in many of these books, caring intervention in the life of a neglected, misunderstood, or ill-treated horse or pony is the female protagonist's "ticket into the barn" (2019, 84), where the human-horse relationship develops.

So thoroughly feminized was the British pony book that many of these stories in the mid-twentieth century were penned by "horse crazy" girls themselves, in an early version of female fan fiction. Some successful pony book authors were as young as eleven years-old (Halley 2019, 87). Especially popular were books by the three Pullein-Thompson sisters, Josephine, Christine, and Diana, who began publishing short stories and novels about girls and horses in 1942, at the ages of sixteen and eighteen. One of the younger twin sisters, Christine, continued to write in this genre for over fifty years and was, according to Halley, the most prolific pony book author in Britain. Publication of her six-volume Phantom Horse series for girls spanned thirty years, from 1955 to 1985. In the first book of the series, *Phantom Horse* (Pullein-Thompson 1955), the heroine, an English girl named Jean, is living temporarily in the United States, where she captures and tames a wild stallion she names Phantom. The horse eventually returns with her to England, where they successfully compete in shows and embark on adventures together. As Halley points out, Jean's relationship with Phantom is "an extraordinarily special connection" (1955, 91), a powerful friendship that is both physical and psychological, leading Jean to feel that "anything seemed possible" (92) when the two of them were together.

Locating Phantom's homeland across the Atlantic, Pullein-Thompson borrowed the hyper-masculine equine character of the wild stallion from the North American version of stories about human being-with horses. Jean's relational work in taming Phantom is an activity she shares with many human characters in horse stories set in the American West. But counter to the history of English pony books, the earliest American horse stories for young readers generally featured boys instead of girls, and most were written by men. Will James's *Smoky the Cowhorse* (1926) typified the masculine Western version of this genre. Its hero, a cowboy named Clint, tames and forms a special bond with a range pony who is thereafter known as a one-man horse. Like Black Beauty, Smoky falls on hard times when circumstances separate him from Clint and send him through an ever-worsening succession of cruel and careless owners and punishing work. Also like Black Beauty, Smoky in old age is finally saved by an altruistic human he can comfortably and safely be-with before he dies.

Though Westerns are but one form of American fiction about humans and horses, this masculine version of the human-horse relationship dominated American literature for much of the twentieth century. A popular example is Walter Farley's twenty-volume Black Stallion series (1941–1983), published contemporaneously with Pullein-Thompson's Phantom Horse books in England. The human protagonist in these tales is a teen-aged boy, Alec Ramsay, who, like Jean, tames a wild stallion from a far-away land, forms an extraordinary and exclusive bond with the horse, and returns with him to a domesticated environment where horses function as sporting animals (Farley 1941). The black stallion comes from Saudi Arabia, and his life intersects with Alec's when they are marooned together on a tiny island off the coast of Spain, the sole survivors of a shipwreck. Home for Alec is New York City, where he returns with the stallion to become immersed in the culture of high-stakes horse racing. In this new setting "the Black," as Alec calls him, becomes an unbeatable race horse and sires many exceptional offspring whose lives and racing careers complicate the story of Alec's deep and exclusive relationship with the Black through many sequels.

The books of the Phantom and Black Stallion series are further alike in exploring the human-horse relationship primarily from the perspective of the human partner, the moral agent whose consciousness is central to the story. While Black Beauty spoke as a moral patient, his suffering the result of temporary and uncertain relationships with humans, the young humans in both British and American horse stories after *Black Beauty* typically act as moral agents to ensure that their relationships with horses are lasting and secure, like family ties. This preoccupation with relational identity fits horse stories on both sides of the Atlantic to the story type the feminist philosopher Margaret Urban Walker calls the "narrative of relationship" (2007, 117), a story type she regards as essential to the cultivation of a relational morality that insists on the possibility of altruism—attitudes and behaviors geared to the survival of relationships rather than individuals. The protagonist in a narrative of relationship, according to Walker, is an intersubjective entity who experiences a shared state of being-with that is animated by tensions between individual autonomy and social connection. Following the dynamic process of being-with others over time, the narrative of relationship plots a path to the future that is guided by "the relationship's acquired content and developed expectations, its basis and type of trust, and its possibilities for continuation"

(2007, 117). As Walker goes on to explain, decisions arising from relational being require a particular type of moral deliberation:

> A response may be owed to others because some prior history of actual contact and understanding makes it reasonable for them to depend on me for something and reasonable for me to know of their reasonable expectations. Then it is morally important for us to acknowledge past character, present state, and future possibilities of that relationship. It shows us what is owed, why it is owed, and what latitude there may be for postponement, substitution or release. We must also consider what this relationship, imagined in various continuations, revisions or terminations means for both (all) of us. (2007, 117)

In serial form, the narratives of relationship joining Alec and the Black, Jean and Phantom Horse, develop complexity and depth over time through long accumulations of shared trials and adventures. The episodic format likewise invites young readers to invest in long, cumulative identifications with the fictional horse-human pair. Both Alec and Jean initiate narratives of relationship by taming "wild" horses who will eventually become their best friends, and their stories depict domestication as a process of friendship-building through shared adventure. These fictional horses, both notably stallions, willingly enter relationships with humans and retain something of their own agency, paralleling the wild, masculine role of the interspecies romance plot in *Beauty and the Beast*.[1] Like the Beast, both are ultimately tamed by human love. But instead of seeking the closure of romantic love stories, these narratives of relationship open onto a long series of comrade adventures.

The romantic fantasy of a wild beast's willing submission to a deep and enduring emotional bond has prompted commentary about the erotic elements of these stories. Halley cites Nicholas Tucker's observation of "unmistakable sexual overtones" (1981, 14) in the fictional relationships of girls and horses. But in the American horse story, equally passionate physical relationships are also the province of boys and their horses. Even Clint, the taciturn cowboy drifter who becomes Smoky's one-and-only human friend edges close to romantic love when he reflects on how he misses Smoky after the horse is stolen by rustlers. The narrator, speaking in Clint's own rustic tongue, explains "that pony had got tangled up in the cowboy's heartstrings a heap more than that cowboy wanted to let on" (216).

More overtly erotic imagery prevails in *The Black Stallion*, where Alec Ramsay's first ride on the Black across the deserted island is a physical and emotional thrill. At the end of a long process of winning the stallion's trust, Alec finally succeeds in mounting the horse, and after an exhilarating ride concludes his virgin voyage with his arms encircling the stallion's neck "weak with exhaustion" (1941, 40). When he slips wearily from the horse's back, like many a romantic heroine he becomes the object of his partner's proud gaze: "The stallion looked at him, his head held high, his large body only slightly covered with sweat" (41).

The First Ride became a popular device for romanticizing and eroticizing human-horse relationships in popular serialized horse fiction for young adults after *The Black Stallion*. In the second half of the twentieth century, despite their masculine origins, these novels in the United States eventually followed the British lead in presenting stories for and about girls. With this feminization of the genre came the conventions of the romance novel in booksellers' marketing strategies. The cover illustrations of paperback romances, for instance, typically feature the heroine in the hero's embrace, striking a pose known to romance writers and illustrators as "the clinch." In like fashion, the covers of paperback horse series often depict girls and their horses in tender or beseeching embraces. Like the heterosexual romance heroine, the horse-girl may be positioned slightly lower than her equine partner, so that she has to look up to clinch the interlocking gaze. Alternatively, she might be looking up at her partner, whose gaze, like the Black Stallion's, is defiantly fixed on the dangerous world beyond their intimate bond.[2]

As serial stories expressly written for girls grew in popularity in the 1980s and 90s, their target audiences came to include increasingly younger readers. In fiction for pre-pubescent girls, accounts of the First Ride tended to emphasize tender affection rather than wild power—safety and security rather than danger and risk. In a novel called *Friends to the Finish* (Estes 1996) from the Short Stirrup Series, the pre-teen heroine, Chloe, rescues an eventing pony called Jump for Joy from his rich-girl owner's plan to euthanize him for a serious injury incurred through her insensitivity and irresponsible riding. During the pony's long convalescence, Chloe cares for him and they develop a close and trusting relationship, but because she has previously been frightened by a pony who ran away with her and threw her, Chloe is apprehensive about taking her place in the saddle. Once she is actually astride Jump for Joy, however, her worries vanish, as the First Ride persuades her that she and the pony are destined for one another:

> Chloe knew she would remember this trot for the rest of her life. At the same time, she knew Jump for Joy wouldn't ever bolt, or ever try to buck her off. A huge smile broke over her face. In the thirty seconds it took to trot back to the side of the ring, she had memorized the feel of her pony. She hadn't cantered, but she knew what it would feel like; she realized she had always known. Now she couldn't imagine why she had ever dreaded riding him. She and Jump for Joy were meant for each other. He was familiar now and always would be. From that moment on, climbing onto his back would be the same as coming home. (Estes 1996, 62)

In a study of real-world human/horse relationships, Linda Birke and Keri Brandt describe experiences like the First Ride episodes in human-horse relational narratives as part of a process of "becoming with" horses (2009, 194). This process, guided by the relational ideal they call "mutual corporeality," entails a sensory erosion of boundaries separating Mind and Body, Self and Other. They explain, "what riders seek—beyond 'horsemanship'—is a oneness with the horse, a kind of fluid intersubjectivity" (2009, 196). In conventional, intraspecies narratives of human relationships, female characters' experience of mutual corporeality is mostly limited to sex, pregnancy, and motherhood, but in interspecies relationships, other options potentially open up. Halley suggests this is precisely what makes human-horse relationship stories especially appealing to female readers. In response to Tucker's certainty that "sexual overtones" (1981, 163) color the mutual corporeality of girls' fictional relationships with horses, she cautions against reducing the physicality and deep emotional content of these relationships to an erotic imperative. Acknowledging that on horseback "the becoming of girls-with-horses happens in bodies . . . in contact with other bodies" (Halley 2019, 14), Halley observes that the physicality of being-with horses in young-adult fiction often develops out of empathy for horses' physical suffering, accompanied by outrage at humans' physical cruelty to them (2019, 68). This empathic component of being-with horses and the caring behavior it inspires, according to Halley, feed young readers' fantasies about a host of life experiences other than sex—fantasies about freedom and movement, about power, about trust, about adventure and companionship. Ultimately, Halley argues, girls' sexuality, though a common source of Euro-American cultural anxiety, should not foreclose the multiple plotlines girls might imagine and negotiate in narratives of relationship with human and nonhuman others.

In the masculine world of the Black Stallion series, Alec Ramsay's exclusive and charged relationship with the Black presumably goes on forever, but—Halley's critique notwithstanding—the same happy-ever-after fiction is often denied to the girls who populate the barns, arenas, and trails of popular young-adult horse series of the late twentieth century. As I discovered in an earlier study (Trachsel 1997–98), when girls in these stories mature, their love for horses sometimes comes into conflict with their budding interest in boys, and they anticipate a time in the not-too-distant future when the romance of being-with horses will yield to heterosexual love. An example comes from *Riding Camp*, the tenth book in Bonnie Bryant's popular Saddle Club series of the 1980s. In this installment, the tomboy Stevie Lake meets and falls in love with a horseman named Phil, causing her best friends at the barn to comment that "it was strange to see an independent girl like Stevie so immersed in another person" (Bryant 1986, 54). Sometime later, when Stevie confides to them that she has experienced her first kiss from a boy, these friends acknowledge the inevitability of Stevie's heterosexual fate and their own. A girl named Lisa speaks for the group when she confesses, "[o]f course I'm jealous, but one of us had to be first" (1986, 131). The lone hold-out at the end of the novel is Carole, a friend who remains comically oblivious to the momentous change occurring in Stevie's life. The other girls are amused by Carole's immature indifference to men, and the narrator, entering the perspective of Stevie, assures the reader that Carole's resistance to masculine charms will not last forever: "For now, anyway, horses were still more important to Carole than boys" (1986, 132).

The generic progression of horse-to-human relationships in series intended for girls, suggests to these readers that their girlhood fantasies of being-with horses merely anticipate a future reality of being-with men. The moral instruction these books provide on conducting human-horse relationships thus becomes mere preparation for the more important, heterosexual human-human relationships that eventually await these readers. In this way, human relationality with nonhuman beings is relegated to its accustomed place among the relics of childhood, as the logic of human exceptionalism subtly asserts its dominance.

QUIETLY COUNTERING THE APOCALYPSE: BEING-WITH HORSES AT OAK VALLEY RANCH

An enduring argument in North American reception studies holds that female readers more readily identify with male protagonists than the other way around;[3] in the books of the Black Stallion series, which are populated by an almost exclusively male cast of humans and horses, Halley suggests that Alec's "gentleness" (2019, 98) with the Black facilitates cross-gender identification and helps explain why these books have always been more popular with girls than with boys. Measured by the norms of Zylinska's feminist counter-apocalypse, Alec's "feminized" ways of being-with the Black differentiate him from the white, Christian, male conqueror who seeks to control Nature and exercise dominion over nonhuman life. Instead of "breaking" or otherwise subduing the Black, Alec builds a relationship with him, endorsing ways of being-with horses that have lately coalesced under the rubric of natural horsemanship.

In studying the culture of natural horsemanship, Linda Birke finds that it prioritizes communication, relationality, and meaning-making as a project shared by humans and horses. She explains that this allegedly "revolutionary" way of human being-with horses valorizes empathy as its defining virtue, positing horsemanship as "the ability to understand what the horse is thinking and feeling and the capacity to act accordingly, with sensitivity" (2007, 219).

Initially a development of the American West, natural horsemanship emphasizes learning the horse's natural body language of movement, direction, posture, and position in order to "speak horse" when negotiating human-horse relationships. The Nez Perce horseman, GaWaNi Pony Boy describes his version of natural horsemanship as "relationship training" (1998, 1), a process that begins with close observation of the horse in various settings to learn the horse's ways of being-with humans and other animals. Because it privileges receptive modes of being-with horses, Robert Miller and Rick Lamb describe natural horsemanship as "unnatural for us humans," explaining that it requires a human to "become a new person" who cultivates cooperative ways of being-with another species (2005, 314). The natural horseman, Miller and Lamb explain, watches, listens and empathizes in an effort to understand how the horse experiences the world. Ultimately, they conclude, natural horsemanship resolves to the cultivation of altruism, as the horseman "places the wants and needs of another living creature ahead of his own" (2005, 314).

Acknowledging that natural horsemanship romanticizes nature and "natural" behaviors, and varies considerably from one charismatic "horseman" to the next, Birke sees the growing popularity of its relational approach to being-with horses as revolutionary for humans (Birke 2007, 235). By replacing human dominance and aggression with attitudes of respect and cooperation, she explains, natural horsemanship transforms human culture one human being at a time, not simply by teaching "a different way of being-with horses," but more fundamentally by teaching "a different way of being" (2007, 227). From a horse trainer's perspective, Vicki Hearne reports that being-with horses requires sensory readjustment, beginning with the surrender of human dependence on visual and aural information and increased sensitivity to information conveyed through equine sensory channels such as skin sensitivity, kinetic perception, and herd attunement (1982, 110). Hearne's sense of "being-with" an equine subject is companionable, which is not to say it is egalitarian or democratic, but rather that it is grounded in an anthropomorphic "moral understanding" of equine otherness (1982, 8). For Hearne, the scientific vice of anthropomorphism is the practical virtue of handlers ("people who actually work interestingly with animals"), not simply an assertion of human identity but also and more importantly a receptive channel for relational negotiation.

In recent years, the general philosophy of natural horsemanship has begun to infiltrate American series books about the girl-horse relationship, dislodging the romantic fantasy and focusing instead on how the girl in the story develops ways of being-with horses, in the process discovering new ways of being her human self. Prominent among these is Jane Smiley's *Horses of Oak Valley Ranch* series, featuring teen-aged Abby Lovitt and a succession of horses that arrive on her family's small ranch in California, some to stay and others to pass through on their ways to other destinations. The first book of the series, *The Georges and the Jewels* (Smiley 2009) pits Abby's worldview—in which horses are intentional subjects and potential friends—against her father's, in which horses are market commodities and an objective reality wholly apart from humans. The title of the book references Mr. Lovitt's refusal to grant individual subjectivity to the horses he buys, trains, and sells. All of the geldings on the ranch are called "George" and all the mares are called "Jewel," but over the course of the book, Abby succeeds in giving individual names to all the horses. In this, she performs a gesture Hearne equates with Adam's task of naming the animals in Eden. For Hearne, naming is not merely imposing identity onto blank otherness, but a sign of mutual recognition, as when horses in a stable come to recognize their names in human speech and are thereby, in a sense, called into being-with human companions.

Abby's development as a character across the five books of the series comes largely from her growing understanding of equine nature through being-with and learning to appreciate the distinct personalities of individual horses. Unlike the girls in many earlier series, Abby, who cannot remember a time when she didn't ride, takes physical contact between horse and rider for granted. When, in her new role as a paid riding instructor, she supervises her best friend's first ride, romantic associations never arise (Smiley 2011). Abby is matter-of-fact and focused exclusively on the mechanics of safe, communicative contact between horse and rider:

> I taught her to mount from the ground (checking the girth first) and to sit with her feet in the stirrups and her heels down and to relax her shoulders and look where she wanted to go, and to hold the reins in one hand, with her hand just in front of the horn and the reins flowing under her thumb and out over her palm, and I taught her to bang her lower legs lightly against Foxy's sides, just enough to ask for a walk, and I taught her to walk forward and not let Foxy wander around. I taught her to let her hips move with the horse's hips and that if she felt insecure, she could hold the horn of the saddle. I taught her to count the beats of Foxy's front feet and feel the rhythm of her steps. (Smiley 2011, 68–69)

Though Abby, like Jean from *Phantom Horse* and Alec from *The Black Stallion,* comes into possession of a remarkable horse, the story of her relationship with this horse, Jack, develops slowly across several books and is by no means exclusive. Little by little, she expands and refines her understanding of how to be-with Jack through an accumulation of experiences with other horses who spend time on the ranch before moving on to new situations. In book four of the series, *Pie in the Sky* (Smiley 2012), while taking her second ride on the horse whose name gives the book its title, Abby discerns the motivation behind Pie's refusal to perform as she asks him to by comparing the feeling of riding him with the feeling of riding another horse named True Blue. This tactile comparison teaches her about Blue's intentionality. Sensorily she knows that while Blue refuses because he's afraid, Pie does so to test her, "to see if I was in charge" (2012, 159). This is an understanding of horses that does not come suddenly from a magical First Ride, but as a slow, steady deepening of sensory awareness of human-horse togetherness. Abby tells of learning this lesson through both instruction and experience:

> Quite often a horse will behave himself the first time you ride him, being a good boy because he doesn't know you. A ride or two later—Daddy called it the "second ride rule," but it can happen on the third ride or the fourth—he thinks he does know you, and so some horses try to push you, to see what they can get away with. I knew with all my heart that Pie in the Sky was doing this. He was not afraid—I didn't sense in his body any ripple of nervous energy. His ears pricked, but they didn't arrow forward in worry. I was sure that if I'd been able to see his face, I would have seen a grumpy look, so once we got over the last fence, I trotted to Jane and said, "Got a whip? I forgot to bring one." (2012, 159)

To Abby, horses are not simply contact-sport partners with whom to develop athletic expertise as a rider, nor are they merely the clients and teaching aids of a trainer or riding instructor; they fill the role of partners and companions in work, adventure or leisure. In *Pie in the Sky* Abby explains that being-with horses first and foremost requires humans to exercise psychological self-control: "you're never supposed to ride your horse in a temper, even if you think you've controlled your temper" (2012, 218). But because she is angry with her father and doesn't want to encounter him when he comes home, she heads off on a long ride on the horse named Blue, gets lost, and arrives home late at night to face her father's ire. Her own anger dissipates on the ride, a physical experience that diverts her attention from her emotional self in conflict with her father to her physical self in harmony with Blue. In this process, she gains bodily understanding of Blue as a Thoroughbred, an uncommon breed on California ranches: "I understood that . . . knowing what you are doing at a gallop was what a Thoroughbred was born to do. I felt it in my body that his body was completely relaxed. We galloped and galloped . . . " (2012, 219).

Smiley's development of the horse-girl relationship in the Oak Valley Ranch series sidesteps romance by emphasizing the process of Abby's relational learning to read and safely be-with the horses in her life. Throughout the series, Abby's "adventures" are everyday events. Her night ride on Blue, for instance, is nothing more than getting lost with a dog and a horse and eventually finding her way quietly and safely home after dark. Across the series, in small, unremarkable steps, Abby and the horses in her family's ever-changing herd learn increasingly complex and satisfying ways to be-with one another in a continuous process of cooperation and adaptation. Abby learns that relating to horses in exclusively human terms is an exercise in futility, while relating to them in exclusively equine terms is dangerous.

In the second book of the series, *A Good Horse*, for instance, Abby experiences a brief relational crisis with Jack, whose growth and training is a unifying thread across the series (Smiley 2010). When Jack, in high spirits, points a distant kick in her direction and later rears up in front of her, she is reluctant to acknowledge the dangerous physical terms of the relationship that have to change. Instead, she momentarily worries that Jack's behavior signals a failure of the love he owes her for stepping up to care for him when he was a suckling orphan: "I couldn't help thinking after what I had done for Jack, and what I had thought of him, he still wouldn't mind kicking me if he was mad at me" (2010, 69). Very quickly, however, Abby recalls the wisdom of her mentor, a "natural" horse trainer named Jem Jarrow, and she begins to engage Jack in physical maneuvers that keep him at a safe distance from her while he works off his playful young energy. Changing the physical terms of being-with Jack changes the emotional terms of the relationship as well, as Abby explains that "the more things I had Jack do, the more I enjoyed watching him, and the less I thought about whether he really loved me or not" (2010, 70).

When Abby's father subsequently warns that sheer luck prevented Jack from hurting her, Abby anthropomorphically insists that the horse intentionally restrained himself out of regard for her. When challenged to explain how she knows this, Abby relies on her own witness: "Because when he reared up, he looked at me, and when he looked at me, he curled his front legs back. He did. I saw him" (2010, 71). Nevertheless, Abby knows that her father is right in warning that she needs to de-romanticize her ways of being-with Jack. She also realizes that Jack needs to stop being-with her as he is with other horses:

> I had better get Jack to do things, plenty of things, because for the last half hour, I had been thinking about whether he loved me or not, not about whether he was behaving himself, and even though he curled his forelegs back and did not touch me with them, the way he touched the geldings, he really should not have reared up at me in the first place. (2010, 71)

Later in the same book, Abby comes to understand and appreciate a form of love that is a more appropriate and realistic way of human being-with horses. She and a horse named Black George are at a stadium jumping competition where Abby's job is to display the horse to potential buyers. In this environment, Abby feels unfamiliar and out of place, and after an uncomfortable conversation with a relative stranger, she turns to Black George's company to regain a sense of security: "I thought I would get on him, if only to be around someone that I was real friends with" (2010, 111). At the end of the day, when Abby's parents come to take her and Black George back home, Abby is relieved and happy to see them and feels affectively in tune with Black George, who whinnies his feelings "loud and clear" when he sees familiar people and the familiar truck and trailer. This preference for comfortable familiarity with humans, Abby concludes, is Black George's equine version of "love" (2010, 115).

Abby's mentor, the natural horseman Jem Jarrow, first appears as a benevolent intervener in Abby's fearful relationship with a gelding she calls Ornery George. The *Georges and the Jewels* opens with Abby confiding, "[s]ometimes when you fall off your horse, you just don't want to get right back on." Because her fall from the horse hurt, though "not too badly" (Smiley 2009, 1), Abby begins to balk at her father's expectation that she will continue to ride Ornery George as her contribution to the family's horse-training business. They can make more money if her father can tell prospective buyers that "a little girl can ride him" (2) and he has confidence in Abby's ability to handle the horse. As tension grows between Abby and her father on this matter, her Uncle Luke tries to help by teaching the horse a humiliating lesson. Abby watches Luke subdue the horse unfeelingly in a training approach known as "breaking"—in this case, forcing Ornery George to the ground by roping his feet and pulling them out from under him. Luke finally declares himself the victor by sitting on the horse's shoulder, casually smoking a cigarette while singing a multi-verse comic song about a racehorse. In the aftermath of this incident, Abby's relationship with Ornery George deteriorates further, until Jem Jarrow helps them build a new, more mutually satisfying way of being-with one another.

As a result of Jem's intervention, Abby develops the receptive skills of relationship-building with horses. Beyond knowing how to communicate her wishes to them, she learns how to understand and adapt to the messages they communicate to her. As a version of the Anthropos, she narrates relational ways of recognizing and being-with the nonhuman world that Zylinska calls for to counter the apocalypse. Neither Abby nor anyone else in the moral universe of the Oak Valley Ranch novels overtly ponders the deterioration of the natural world or investigates humanity's part in creating or repairing its conditions. Because the grim scientific factuality of the Anthropocene is absent from these fictions, the question of what humans must *do* to survive or atone for their environmental sins is not a concern they reflect. Instead, the novels ponder the moral question of how humans must *be* in a world inhabited by our human selves among others. Abby's episodic narrative of her relationships with horses highlights her self-transformation. By learning and practicing new ways of being-with horses, she develops a new way of being human within a web of relationships that includes but extends beyond her family, her school, her church, and the various other human communities she is part of.

Rejecting the conventions of human romance that have long underpinned relationship stories of humans and horses for young people, Smiley's Oak Valley Ranch books resist the anthropocentric framework that defines a horse's sole purpose as the satisfaction of human needs and desires. After worrying about whether the colt Jack loves her, Abby realizes she is attempting to impose on him an exclusively human understanding and valuation of love. Not until she stops asserting her human worldview is she receptive to Jack's equine view and able to negotiate adjustments in their relationship. When she makes this perceptual shift, she attends directly to what Lidskog and Waterton identify as a "socionatural relation" (2016, 402), that requires her to relinquish some of the privileges of human exceptionalism.

To be sure, the environmental crisis we are facing today requires us to act. Comprehending the factual reality of human cause and ecological effect, our scientific sapience prescribes changes in human behavior to avert further environmental decline and plot a survival strategy on and for a planet so transformed by human activity that the environmental scholar and activist Bill McKibben (2010) insists we must now recognize and call it by a new name, Eaarth. But continued transformation of the planet, as Zylinska reminds us, is not the only path we might imagine through the Anthropocene. Self-transformation remains an option, even as we contemplate what to *do* about the future of life on Eaarth. In fact, as human action is an expression or manifestation of human being, self-change is prior to any lasting changes in behavior. Endorsing the relational self at the philosophical heart of natural horsemanship, the recent turn in human-horse fiction exemplified by Smiley's Oak Valley series encourages young readers to renounce human exceptionalism in order to practice new ways of human being-with nonhuman others. Without attending to environmental apocalypse, Abby's coming-of-age story on Oak Valley Ranch offers a counter-apocalyptic narrative of the sort Zylinska asks us to imagine. A narrator receptive to nonhuman modes of understanding, Abby represents a fundamentally relational Anthropos who frames the species-level phenomenon of being human as a state of human being-with the nonhuman world.

REFERENCES

Avery, Jessica. 2018. "The Origin of the Romance Novel Clinch Covers." *Book Riot* (December 13, 2018). (bookriot.com/clinch-covers-on-romance-novels/).

Bagnold, Enid. 1935. *National Velvet.* New York: William Morrow & Co.

Beaver, Mary H. 1972. "Responses of Adolescents to Feminine Characters in Literature." *Research in the Teaching of English* 6: 46–68.
Beier, Jessie. 2018. "Dispatch from the Future: Science Fictioning (in) the Anthropocene." In J. Jagodzinski (ed.) *Interrogating the Anthropocene: The Future in Question.* London: Palgrave Macmillan.
Beyard, Karen C, and Howard J. Sullivan. 1980. "Adolescent Reading Preferences for Type of Theme and Sex of Character." *Reading Research Quarterly* 16: 104–20.
Birke, Linda. 2007. "'Learning to Speak Horse': The Culture of 'Natural Horsemanship.'" *Society and Animals* 15 (3): 217–39.
Birke, Linda, and Keri Brandt. 2009. "Mutual Corporeality: Gender and Human/Horse Relationships." *Women's Studies Forum* 32 (3): 189–97.
Bryant, Bonnie. 1986. *Riding Camp.* New York, NY: Skylark Books.
⸺. 1994. *Gift Horse.* Chicago, IL: Skylark Books.
⸺. 1995. *Flying Horse.* Chicago, IL: Skylark Books.
⸺. 1996. *Pleasure Horse.* Chicago, IL: Skylark Books.
⸺. 1998. *Horse Care.* Chicago, IL: Skylark Books.
Campbell, Joanna. 1992. *Star of Shadowbrook Farm.* New York, NY: Harper-Collins.
⸺. 1998. *Lightning's Last Hope.* New York, NY: Harper-Collins.
Capra, Fritjof. 1996. *The Web of Life.* New York, NY: Anchor Books.
Carson, Rachel. 1962. *Silent Spring.* Boston, MA: Houghton-Mifflin.
Duey, Kathleen. 2004. *Katie and the Mustang.* New York, NY: Puffin.
Estes, Allison. 1996. *Friends to the Finish.* New York: Minstrel Pocket Books.
Farley, Walter. 1941. *The Black Stallion.* New York: Alfred A. Knopf.
Halley, Jean O'Malley. 2019. *Horse Crazy: Girls and the Lives of Horses.* Athens, GA: University of Georgia Press.
Hanson, Natalie Corinne. 2010. "Horse Stories: Perverse Victimization." *Journal of Advanced Composition* 30 (3/4): 727–54.
Hearne, Vicki. 1982. *Adam's Task: Calling Animals by Name.* New York: Akadine Press.
Heidegger, Martin. 1996 [1927]. *Being and Time.* Trans. Joan Stambaugh. Albany, NY: State University of New York Press.
James, Will. 1926. *Smoky the Cowhorse.* New York, NY: Simon & Schuster.
Kolbert, Elizabeth. 2014. *The Sixth Extinction: An Unnatural History.* New York, NY: Henry Holt.
Leakey, Richard & Roger Lewin. 1995. *The Sixth Extinction: Patterns of Life and the Future of Humankind.* New York, NY: Anchor Books.
Lidskog, Rolf & Claire Waterton. 2016. "Anthropocene—A Cautious Welcome from Environmental Sociology." *Environmental Sociology* 2 (2): 395–406.
McKibben, Bill. 2010. *Eaarth: Making a Life on a Tough, New Planet.* New York, NY: Henry Holt.
Miller, Robert M & Rick Lamb. 2005. *The Revolution in Horsemanship and What it Means to Mankind.* Guilford, CT: The Lyons Press.
Nowak, Martin A. (with Roger Highfield). 2011. *Super Cooperators: Altruism, Evolution, and Why We Need Each Other to Succeed.* New York: Simon & Schuster Free Press.

Pony Boy, GaWaNi. 1998. *Out of the Saddle: Native American Horsemanship.* Irvine, CA: BowTie Press.
Pullein-Thompson, Christine. 2012 [1942] 1955 Reprint. *Phantom Horse.* Digital edition. Nottinghamshire: Award Publications.
Sewell, Anna. 1877. *Black Beauty.* London: Jarrold & Sons.
Smiley, Jane. 2009. *The Georges and the Jewels.* New York: Alfred A. Knopf.
_____. 2010. *A Good Horse.* New York: Alfred A. Knopf.
_____. 2011. *True Blue.* New York: Alfred A. Knopf.
_____. 2012. *Pie in the Sky.* New York: Alfred A. Knopf.
_____. 2013. *Gee Whiz.* New York: Alfred A. Knopf.
Snelling, Laurane. 1995. *Olympic Dreams.* Ada, MN: Bethany House.
Steward, Dodai. 2008. "Romance Novel Readers Love 'The Clinch.'" *Jezebel.* (November 17, 2008). jezebel.com/romance-novel-readers-love-the-clinch-5090885.
Summers, Kate. 2013. "Adult Reading Habits and Preferences in Relation to Gender Differences." *Reference and User Services Quarterly* 52:3 (Spring): 243–49.
Trachsel, Mary. 1997–98. "Horse Stories and Romance Fiction: Variants or Alternative Texts of Female Identity?" *Reader* 38/39: 20–41.
Tucker, Nicholas. 1981. *The Child and the Book: A Psychological and Literary Exploration.* Cambridge: Cambridge University Press.
Walker, Margaret Urban. 2007. *Moral Understandings: A Feminist Study in Ethics.* Oxford: Oxford University Press.
Wilson, Edward O. 2016. *Half-Earth: Our Planet's Fight for Life.* New York: Norton.
Zipes, Jack. 1981. "The Dark Side of Beauty and the Beast: The Origins of the Literary Fairy Tale for Children." *Children's Literature Association Quarterly* (1981 Proceedings): 119–125. doi: 10.1353/chq.1981.0015.
Zylinska, Joanna. 2018. *The End of Man: A Feminist Counterapolcalypse.* Minneapolis, MN: University of Minnesota Press.

NOTES

1. In "The Dark Side of Beauty and the Beast: The Origins of the Literary Fairy Tale for Children," Jack Zipes traces the evolution of the story from the seventeenth century onward as instruction in a gendered morality that prescribes for women the altruistic virtues of "submission, obedience, humility, industry and patience," while depicting men as able to access their "true 'civil' form" only in the non-threatening company of a civilized woman" (1981, 125).

2. Examples of romance novel covers featuring this pose can be found in Avery 2018; and in Stewart 2008. A few examples of horse series paperback covers that replicate the pose with girls and horses include a number of the books in Bonnie Bryant's Saddle Club Series: Bryant 1994, 1995, 1996, 1998; Campbell 1992, 1998; Duey 2004; and Snelling 1995.

3. See, for example, Beaver 1972; Beyard and Sullivan 1980; Summers 2013.

PART II
Witnessing

Chapter 4

Animal Texts

How Coyote America *and* American Wolf *Embody the Literary Animal through a Cross-Disciplinary Approach*

Lauren E. Perry

Dan Flores' *Coyote America* (2016) and Nate Blakeslee's *American Wolf* (2017) combine several remarkable features of twenty-first-century environmental literature while creating a new and essential subgenre that I call Animal Texts. Both texts demonstrate expertise in biology, history, ecology, and regional studies that alter these animals' narratives as they exist in literary history and cultural memory. As Blakeslee describes, hundreds of days of wolf watching by observers might not altogether be a great read, but the truth we extract from that writing would surprise even the most cynical wildlife biologist. Animals are intelligent, playful, resourceful creatures. We do not need to personify animals to make them fascinating, as Flores and Blakeslee both prove by building comprehensive portraits of the North American coyotes and wolves. For too long, since Teddy Roosevelt and his breed of naturalist shamed writers like Jack London by dubbing them "nature fakers," have writers shied away from attempts at representing animal life. As science continues to progress, and academia along with it, human recognition of advanced thinking in other beings pushes literary studies towards animal studies. Animal studies readings of environmental texts yield productive, forward-thinking ideas that have been in print for environmental activists, should they be able to see it. The problem has been one of fighting for lives that are "just" animals. Humans are also "just" animals. Humans have the power of language but are not the only animals recognized for communication skills and complex relationships. It is high time that our writings reflect the truths animal advocates have long seen in their fur-covered counterparts.

The success of these two texts, both in terms of accolades and sales, signals the swell of what has been a mounting wave of concern for animal life, specifically amongst American environmental authors. Animals have shaped contemporary approaches to academic environmental writing in that scientific, biological data is readily available for inclusion in responsible assessments of issues like mass extinctions. Just as nineteenth century (and earlier) environmental writers speculated, the downfall of some species would eventually ripple back to humans. As George Catlin watched the destruction of the North American bison, he fretted:

> It is a melancholy contemplation for one who has travelled as I have, through these realms, and seen this noble animal in all its pride and glory, to contemplate it so rapidly wasting from the world, drawing the irresistible conclusion, too, which one must do, that its species is soon to be extinguished, and with it the peace and happiness (if not the actual existence) of the tribes of Indians who are joint tenants with them, in the occupancy of these vast and idle plains. (Harris and Catlin 2013, 41)

Along with the massive destruction of bison, the predators of North America have endured particularly harsh treatment from European colonizing forces. Due to the introduction of domesticated livestock, predators went from being revered by indigenous hunter-gatherer populations to being loathed and feared by colonizers. As Alfred Crosby writes in *Ecological Imperialism*, "[t]he Europeans who founded the first transoceanic empires were also mixed farmers and pastoralists, and the success of their animals was, generally speaking, their success" (1986, 172). Whether predator or prey, observing the intelligence and emotion that emanates from watching animals runs the risk of being discredited for being at odds with science. Each year in the United States, billions of domestic animals are used and killed for food production, over nine billion land animals slaughtered in 2018 (US Department of Agriculture). The environmentalist idea that animal lives have value beyond commodification has never been popular. It has been seen as weak, emotional, and downright untrue. Environmentalists and environmentally-concerned writers have perhaps borne the brunt of this admonishment against fostering empathy, curiosity, and love for animals. Animals exist in a precarious middle-ground between legend, science, myth, and lived experience.

Animal texts successfully bridge chasms between disciplines, and they require a certain artistry to join such disparate genres. That artistry harkens back to scholars like Rachel Carson and Aldo Leopold. Both Leopold and Carson are widely known as ecologists, but the imprint of their most famous texts are a land-ethic and a call to stop using chemicals. What goes unstated in these bylines is their shared steady focus on animal lives. Though both writers eloquently raise issues concerning humans (land use and pesticides), they are also concerned about animals, animal lives, and how humans impact natural systems. Environmental writing has chronicled animals for decades, but we sometimes miss what is right in front of us on the page in our myopic literary analysis. As Mario Ortiz Robles writes in *Literature and Animal Studies*,

> While literature is neither a natural habitat for animals nor thereby a repository of reliable knowledge about the anatomy, physiology, and perhaps even ethology of animals, it has nevertheless had more to say about our relation to animals over time than any other discourse. (2016, x)

Animals, whether we acknowledge their presence in reality or in text, are always there, but that might not always be true. Leopold and Carson write warnings of potential futures. Environmental literature from writers across the twentieth century begins weaving together disciplines in order to prove reliable sources of knowledge. Once literature veers towards other scientific disciplines, animals within the text seem to be forgotten by scholars and readers. What Blakeslee and Flores have developed as a genre goes beyond fusing science with literary writing. They have enabled animal-centric commentary on the current environmental situation.

Blakeslee and Flores use literary tropes to give narrative agency to wildlife in Animal Texts. They write for the wolves and coyotes, and in doing so, they destabilize the human structures surrounding these animals that often determine their fates. By centering on living animals, these narratives no longer present them as symptoms or victims of human action but as agents of their own future. Animals infiltrate the text through layered representations. Both Flores and Blakeslee have compiled and analyzed decades' worth of tedious study of each species. As rapidly as human technology advances, especially in terms of visuals, photographs, cameras, and tracking, it is not until this specific breed of text that writers can present a comprehensive picture of an animal species. The combination of cultural, historical, mythological, exploratory, scientific, and zoological information in these texts illustrate American coyote and wolf populations as complex, multi-faceted groups of individuals. The end result for the reader is precisely what animal studies scholars like Lori Gruen imagined could be possible by breaking down barriers between academic schools of thought. Gruen writes, "[a]nimal studies, in bringing other animals to the fore as sentient subjects who can have meaningful lives and relationships, presents challenges to our own ways of living" (2018, 7). The challenges she speaks of, the critique of Anthropocentric actions, are precisely what climate and animal rights activists seek to address. Readers of

Coyote America and *American Wolf* cannot help but question the Abrahamic assumptions made by even well-meaning agricultural approaches to wildlife management. Ecological management is nearly impossible if we still lack basic understandings of other intelligent species in our regions. By breaking the genre confines and speculating on the implications of combined knowledge, coyotes and wolves have their first chance at being Americans; having a right to pursue life, liberty, and their own manifestation of happiness.

Animal texts reveal a critical moment in our world where the questions of nonhuman intelligence, environmental literature, and wildlife have reached a pinnacle. *Coyote America* and *American Wolf*, along with similar texts that center on mountain lions, bears, and other species, write their subjects in a revolutionary, cross-disciplinary way that conveys how crucial their presence is to their ecosystems. As I illustrate, the ways in which writers use commonplace modes of description and exposition, both those of literary caliber and those more akin to scientific writing, highlight human ignorance about the brilliance of animal life. Their writing also showcases the potential damage done by decades of writing about animals attempting to make them understandable by making them human. Humanity's inability to think beyond binaries has quite literally put to death more animals than we could count. When writers limit animals to either being personified to resemble humans or discounted as objects without intelligence and emotion, they enable the rationale that allows for animals' mass slaughter. Humans have for so long ignored and avoided signs of animal intelligence, thinking, and emotion. To acknowledge the truth that animals have always felt, played, thought, and been treated as inanimate is to reveal humans' true nature. Environmental writers have been attempting to right this wrong in literature for decades. I see these two texts as the beginning of Animal Texts that are the pinnacle of attempting to distill the qualities of intelligent nonhuman animal life in writing so as to communicate to other humans, namely humans with the power to enact change, the complexity of life and the capabilities of these beings. Animal Texts usher in a fundamental change and desperately needed perspective in environmental literature that seeks to combine decades' if not centuries' worth of information about species.

The idea of Animal Texts is an entertaining and timely play on words in the twenty-first century. Should one google "animal texts," the results yield a slew of humorous screenshots and doctored "texts from animals" using iMessage to text with humans. The idea that animals can text is the funny but also poignant inverse of this chapter. To consider the potential for an animal to communicate with humans on an individual level and use everyday technology allows one to imagine the well of knowledge just beyond what we can communicate. To send a text message is to have a direct line of communication to someone, but it also has clear limits on what it can accomplish. Human reliance on text messages highlights the limits of human language in that there are so many clear and vast variables when sending texts. We can only say so much and what we do say stands to be misinterpreted. This comical mental image of "animal texts"—text messages from animals—also invokes a feeling of longing and sadness for any pet owner or animal lover. Animals cannot tell us what is wrong through language, and if they could text us, what would they say? The Animal Texts from Flores and Blakeslee demand that we step away from technology and bear witness to history, live-action, and venture out to find the animals we want to understand through the physical text, made manifest in the binders full of wolf notes from the Yellowstone Wolf Project and other texts Blakeslee and Flores demonstrate in their work.

Paul Schullery Describes the Yellowstone Wolf Project in Action:
The Yellowstone wolf recovery program is a milestone project, demonstrating that our society has matured to the point where we recognize that humans share the earth with many other species as deserving of existence as we are. Through projects like this one, we learn not only to appreciate animals we once abused in ignorance, but also to use the planet's natural resources in ways that sustain rather than exhaust them. (1996, ix)

The Yellowstone Wolf Project began in 1995 with the reintroduction of wolves to Yellowstone National Park. A hotly contested issue, the reintroduction was supported by environmentalists and conservationists who understood wolves' vital place in the greater Yellowstone region's ecosystem. For over twenty-five years, dedicated scientists like Doug Smith have overseen the health, reproduction, and study of wolves within the park. Animal Texts are the written manifestations of programs like this one. Animal Texts is a call to return to physical textuality, to make notes with our hands, and to watch with our eyes. As both authors make clear, we cannot only watch in the current moment. We need history to understand the developing relationship between animals, their changing environments, and humans.

Humans author animal texts, but the convergence of the disciplines that enable their creation makes the end result a lesson for humans, including those who write them. The compilation of information present in these Animal Texts is perhaps the closest humans will ever get to texts authored by the animals themselves. To those immediately skeptical, I will explain how normally detrimental, humanizing aspects of literary writing stand to undo themselves and illuminate slippage in these texts, forcing human readers to realize large gaps in understanding and possibly even misdirection in decades worth of writing about animals. The very language of literature versus the assumed language of science has created an undeniable tension and gap between texts about animals across disciplines. Truths in literature of the twentieth century were eschewed because of the language used to describe human-animal relationships and how it was and still is considered the antithesis of science. Because of time, collaboration, and open-mindedness towards the environmental movement, writers like Dan Flores and Nate Blakeslee have been encouraged and developed. I also maintain that these writers' qualities and ambitions, along with their skills and careful considerations in light of animal studies and the contemporary moment in environmentalism, are profoundly unique. They are the product of decades of environmental writers challenging norms, pushing boundaries, and ignoring popular beliefs about animals. Animal Texts could not exist if not for the trails cut by innovative thinking in animal studies and these authors' willingness to break conventions.

J. Frank Dobie's *The Voice of the Coyote* was first published in 1947, a full seventy-three years before *Coyote America*. Many seemingly new, evolved pictures of animal life and experiences emerge on the pages of this dated book. Dobie's picture of the coyote was ignored by mainstream views because of the very title of his work and because Dobie sought to give voice to Native populations and an animal viewed by the government as a pest. Dobie admits that he, as a writer, will not meet the standard held by most to comment on the life and experiences of an animal, yet his encounters, observations, and historical insight seem like an obvious precursor to Flores' work decades later. Dobie writes,

> Some parts of what I have written may not be respectfully received by academic biologists who leave out the most real of all realities—imagination. History, it has been said, is the prolonged shadows of a few individuals. Tales and other lore that make up whole chapters towards the end of this book are the shadows that the slight creature called coyote has projected through the imaginations of people living with him for centuries. I write of a species; many individual coyotes over long periods of time, scattered over continental vastness, play their parts in the record. . . . I do not suppose that Brother Coyote will mount into such an identity for my readers, but for me the record has developed into a kind of biography. (1949, xiv)

Dobie is describing his attempt to write a biography of a species that includes elements beyond biology, that provide for animal experiences, feelings, and lives. Like Flores, he accounts for the knowledge of indigenous peoples while also knowing that to write this "biography," he needs accounts of individual coyotes as well as factual information about the species. What Dobie knew would be rejected by academic scientists has come to fruition in literature that tells of the other side of science to give animals agency. Because of writers like Dobie, development and innovations continued both within and outside academia. Animal Texts are especially needed now as climate change threatens all species more than ever.

COYOTE AMERICA—THE LESSON OF THE COYOTE

Flores clearly states that his purpose in writing *Coyote America* is to produce a different breed of text. He intentionally blends information from different disciplines to reorient his reader to an animal that is actually quite like themselves. Environmentalists before Flores have written books to change the future, to save the environment, and to change modes of thinking. It is a powerful strategy and a phenomenon that Flores has seen and studied before. He describes the enormous impact of books like Aldo Leopold's *A Sand County Almanac* and Rachel Carson's *Silent Spring* on collective thought and opinions about the environment. To change the future of coyotes, Flores has chosen a new approach to the age-old strategy. "Books and film are equally capable of rearranging the furniture in our heads, books perhaps the more so because the experience of reading is so private and provides such opportunity for pause, for deliberate consideration, for mental testing" (2016b, 154). The power of books to change human opinions and actions is extensive, and Flores's creation of an animal text for the coyote out of its history, mythology, biology, and philosophy moves to represent the coyote, and any animal, in a way not previously witnessed by scholars or large audiences. Like Leopold before him, Flores utilizes his knack for "gorgeous, poetic passages and vividly rendered scenes" (2016b, 154) to bring to life the truths about coyotes as intelligent, dynamic animals with an incredible and heart breaking history.

Flores's recounting of the injustices committed against coyotes as a species and the absurd origins of American distrust for coyotes force the reader to reconsider how they view the prairie wolf. His goal in utilizing a cross-disciplinary approach is to change his readers' view of the animals as a whole.

> Coyote America" is what I call their story. Understanding the twists and turns of it, the historical roots and the modern scientific sense of an animal that is demonstrably under no one's control but its own, can help explain why coyotes are enveloping us. But naturally, in more ways than you can imagine, this story is about us. The coyote is a kind of special Darwinian mirror, reflecting back insights about ourselves as fellow mammals. (2016b, 14)

Flores reminds his reader that just because we can explain coyotes in scientific language and writing, it does not mean that we can control them. Language and writing do not make human beings superior, and clearly there is still a great deal we do not understand about other intelligent species. Writing is what first angled humans against coyotes as they moved West, through unfavorable and personified descriptions of the prairie wolf to fear bred of ignorance. Coyotes are entirely self-determined animals, and their intelligence, which Flores works tirelessly to describe and celebrate, makes truly understanding their history dependent upon recognizing them as independent subjects rather than objects or victims. "Coyote power: surviving by one's intelligence and wits when others cannot; embracing existence in a mad, dancing, laughing, sympathetic expression of pure joy at evading the grimmest of fates" (2016b, 51). Between their past and the present moment when the species flourishes despite everything humans have done to eradicate them, coyotes stand to teach humans a great deal about surviving on Earth. Flores' text reshapes the reader's understanding of the species by depicting their subjectivity, their independent experience of time, consciousness, memory, and their standout existence as fission-fusion predators. Flores constructs a more complete picture of coyotes as animals that deserve our respect and protection.

Flores establishes the coyote's unique subjectivity by describing their actions, movements, and history of existing parallel to humans. *Coyote America* proves coyotes' agency in its language through wording like "coyotes pushed southward" and "[f]rom there they pressed on" and that they "were colonizing almost all of Ontario" (2016b, 4–5). Flores's use of terms like "colonize" should not be seen as anthropomorphizing coyotes, but as giving them agency in recognizing their deliberate movements and actions. Coyotes pushed, pressed, and colonized while humans were left "confounded" and to "speculate" about the animals' prolific migration. The coyotes that Flores describes are not confined to one region and actively seek out new territory and "lucrative possibilities" (2016b, 4) of living near humans. They actively resist being pinned down, and the historical and chronological mapping that Flores provides for his reader of the coyotes' vast kingdom is enhanced by the powerful verbs coyotes enact in choosing their domain. Coyotes have evaded being subjugated by humans because humans barely understood what species coyotes were for the better part of one hundred years.

> Was the new animal actually a jackal, an Old World creature known until that time only in Africa, the Middle East, and southeastern Europe? That was the first question science posed about "prairie wolves," and from the 1830s to the 1850s, the debate set the naturalists of the Philadelphia Academy against those of the new Smithsonian in the capital city. (2016b, 63–64)

Coyotes were by no means "new," but their presence baffled naturalists from West to East. These independent, curious, highly intelligent creatures have only one rival in terms of global mobility.

As Flores explains, "[e]xpansion by only one other large mammal matches this in American history. We humans did it twice" (2016b, 5). Flores builds a strong parallel between coyotes and humans, which he reinforces through his prose and diction. He describes early coyotes' agency in how they chose their paths, pushed their own limits, and how biologists were left to marvel at how immensely "cosmopolitan" this small song dog was in its expansion.

> Coyotes, by virtue of their evolutionary biology and intelligence, had never come close to becoming a threatened or endangered species. Despite all the technology, chemistry, and Dr. Evil pathological inventiveness we had thrown at them—and more was to come, for sure—coyotes were the extremely rare American mammal species still beyond our ability to push to the edge of extinction. (2016b, 168)

Despite our best efforts, humans failed to exterminate the elusive species, and the more we learned, the more many scientists were forced to reckon with coyotes' extraordinary qualities. Humans cannot subjugate what they cannot understand or identify, and Flores' text details from multiple angles how formidable an animal the coyote is while also leveling humans to remember that we, too, are animals. "Humans and coyotes eerily mimic one another," writes Flores (2), and his own curiosity about the species allows for the characterization of an independent subject and charismatic protagonist at the center of this Animal Text.

Flores conveys coyotes' elevated consciousness by bolstering his descriptions of their intelligence and awareness with indisputable science and historic information about the species' survival. Their intelligence and agency, as described throughout the text, asks the reader to consider the consciousness of coyotes as individuals and as an adaptive species. Consciousness, awareness, and the human ability to recognize these mental processes in other animals is a crucial element of changing views on any given species. "Coyote consciousness seems poised for a second act" (2016b, 234). Flores provides an in-depth explanation of why humans are so fascinated by coyotes, further establishing the critical connection between them and us through our piqued attention to their actions and movement. Their consciousness, and our awareness of that consciousness, frightens us.

> We identify with them because we, too, emerged out of the dim, hazy consciousness of our early origins to find ourselves fellow carnivores and pursuers of prey. But we also preserve more chilling memories, of the fitful night and the leopard, of bright teeth and being hunted down ourselves. To confront a predator

is to stand before the dual-faced god from our deep past. That is why we look longer, more intently, with more studied fascination at predators than at other kinds of animals. (2016b, 13)

Part of that fear of being hunted down is also the product of recognizing intelligence and awareness in other predators. Because coyotes are so prevalent across the United States, our awareness of them frequently awakens our internal animal consciousness. Coyotes might become a source of ire or dislike because of the exact qualities that make them such strong survivors even amidst human destruction. Flores recognizes the animal consciousness within humans, but uses it to gather humans to the coyotes' cause and foster kinship. Flores draws similarities between human beings and the tenacious song-dog so that readers may recognize traits dormant in themselves while also admiring another mammal's conscious capabilities. Flores's connection between humans and coyotes is a powerful tool for enabling his reader to acknowledge that other animals have consciousness not unlike our own.

Another crucial aspect of Flores's Animal Text is how he guides his readers through an extensive coyote history filled with coyotes' species memories. Coyotes collectively and individually have endured prolonged attacks and complicated relationships with their human counterparts in the United States. North American environmental history allows for a better understanding of coyotes' past, which is critical to our sympathetic understanding of their present. Coyote history and species memory is a vital part of its adaptability and what makes it such an incredibly adept animal, which Flores frequently makes clear to be equal to humans in many ways. He describes their unique approach to survival:

But other factors were at play. An obvious one from their history is that coyotes—at least some coyotes—not only survive among humans but have long quested after opportunities among us as a part of their evolving way of life. Unlike so many other wild animals, coyotes have been seeking humans out from the time they arrived in America, almost "testing" how closely they and we can function in the world. This striking trait has created an unusual history. (2016b, 6)

By showing his reader how deliberate coyotes' actions have been in their proximity to and curiosity about humans, he definitively acknowledges coyotes' memories from over a century alongside humans. The language Flores chooses to depict coyotes as "seeking humans out" and having "quested" after their curious human counterparts begets a type of relationship unlike many others between humans and wild animals. This perspective of animal memory is critical to the coyotes' revolutionary presence in Flores's work. By describing what generations of these animals have endured and navigated,

Flores presents a wholly revised understanding of the coyote for his reader, predicated on the lifestyle choices coyotes have made that have allowed them to flourish alongside human cities and in rural areas. Throughout *Coyote America*, animal memory persists because of the verbs and language Flores uses to depict a respectful fascination and reverence for the species that can be explained but not entirely understood. Their history is integral to a complete picture of their species' vital place in the environment and their right to continue to live as a North American predator.

Flores includes an anecdote in *Coyote America* of one of his friends departing his homestead with the intent of killing a troublesome local coyote. Upon finally encountering the coyote, who had been feasting on local chickens and stirring up other such problems, the gun-wielding man was stopped in his tracks. The coyote apparently looked at the man, looked at the gun, and yawned. For all of the research and science that Flores weaves together throughout his text, this action conveys so much of what he sees as the truth about coyotes. For all of their immense displays of intelligence, coyotes' purest genius might be their ability not to act out of fear in the face of human beings. Their survival in the face of poisoning, mass slaughter, and individual persecution might be solely accredited to their understanding that their best chance is to be near human civilization. Flores speculates:

> As coyotes go trotting off into the American future, however their story plays out, it will be something to see. The coyote's biography in North America has always been one of many acts, but in the twenty-first century it is now a fully American story, an adventure from coast to coast. (2016b, 247)

A coyote yawns in the face of his would-be assassin and packs of coyotes flock near major cities because their proximity to humans stands to benefit them as much as it stands to threaten them. The coyotes' future looks brighter because of the impact of an animal text bearing its likeness, consciousness, historical memories, and wildly independent subjectivity. The knowledge and perspective of *Coyote America* and all the valuable information it weaves together cannot be unseen. The coyote might have its strongest advocate in the form of a text that continually gains readers and human activists to its mission.

After the vast amount of species history and information presented to his reader, Flores makes a plea that, after failing so miserably to control coyotes, we would do well to simply let them live. Towards the end of *Coyote America,* he muses, "[a]s has happened so often and with so many species in the past, genetic purity may just be a momentary accident of time and geography anyway" (Flores 2016b, 226). As he explains at length in *American Serengeti* (2016), the new normal is something humans must learn to understand about species. Species die out, and others thrive for seemingly inconclusive reasons. What we do know is that coyotes have beaten every odd stacked against them, including the ill will of their human neighbors, for the better part of the twentieth century. As animals, humans faced similar odds in our formative days of searching for new regions to occupy and survive in.

> We and they are similar success stories in our shared moment on Earth. That's how I, at least, see the coyotes around me. How they see me, I can't know. But I do know this: when I make eye contact with a coyote, I can see the wheels turning inside her head. If I have a theory of mind, so does she. (Flores 2016b, 229)

While he admits that he cannot know how the coyote views him, Flores can confidently paint the fullest picture possible of the coyote in all its history, intelligence, and fortitude, despite everything humans have done to extinguish the species. Flores's power rests in his ability to tell the coyote's story, interlaced with information about what has made the coyote such a standout species in America. By approaching the writing of these animals using every tool at his disposal, Flores makes it possible for his audience to contemplate how coyotes might think and live as conscious beings. Flores insists to his readers the genuine existence of abstract and unknowable coyote thought. Though he acknowledges that he cannot be certain of what the perspective of coyotes actually looks like, it might just take the shape of everything he has woven into the tapestry of *Coyote America*.

AMERICAN WOLF—BATTLE FOR THE ALPHA STATUS

American Wolf details the histories of the grey wolf packs in Yellowstone National Park and how intricate and complex their life stories are. Whereas Flores's text moves chronologically, regionally, and with a critical environmental gaze across the coyotes' history, Blakeslee's story is about specific wolf families fighting to survive within the unnatural boundaries of conservation. Blakeslee provides an intimate insider view of the Yellowstone wolves, which he infuses with contextual background on the politicized struggle surrounding wolves. Flores views the landscape as always already the coyotes', while Blakeslee's wolves are originally Canadian and brought to live and die in the United States The result is a subversive portrait of an infamous species with a nuanced American chapter, chronicling the outer rippling effects of both wolf lives and deaths. As an animal text, *American Wolf* utilizes precise stories and characterizations to build a larger picture of wolves and predators that illustrates how misguided American views of them have historically been. Blakeslee needs no fictional elements to develop his wolf protagonists as intelligent, conscious beings with essential memories, histories, and timelines. He describes a moment of exultation for his main character, O-Six, and her pack:

> One morning as the pups were playing on a fallen log and 754 and 755 were bedded nearby, O-Six walked to the center of the bowl and sat in a field of luxurious grass, surveying the mountainside that dropped away below her. Suddenly she threw her muzzle into the air and howled. The two males roused themselves and trotted to her side to join in. The pups scampered over, confused and startled, looking everywhere for the danger that had prompted their mother to sound this alarm. But there was no danger. There was just warm sunshine and soft grass and the bounty of an enormous territory that belonged only to them. They tilted their tiny heads back and added their voices to the chorus. (2017, 96–97)

This text represents wolves' lives as prolonged, full-story arcs, brought to a halt only by human actions. As a writer, Blakeslee combines events detailed by wolf watchers with his own experiences of wolves, the science behind their actions, and videography of wolves to tell these authentic stories. Blakeslee's wolves exist outside of any cultural or mythological ideas his readers might have about wolves, and that alone is an enormous step away from misconceptions about the species.

Blakeslee establishes O-Six's independent subjectivity and that of her family members through records kept by the patient and committed wolf watchers. He chronicles her actions in a truthful, detailed fashion thanks to a mixture of sustained observation and understanding of the grey wolf species that sources like Rick McIntyre, one of Yellowstone National Park's premiere wolf experts, provide for him. This incarnation of animal text, one where individual animals feature so prominently in the description of wolf intelligence, consciousness, memory, and subjectivity, requires no human sentimentality or dramatization to evoke a natural sense of loss and unfairness. Blakeslee's prose creates both collective identities and independent subjectivity for the wolves. As wolf packs, they "claimed game," "chewed up carcasses," "drove an elk down," and "pulled her down" (4) which emphasizes agricultural views of wolf pack actions. Blakeslee's language also departs from prior misconceptions of wolves entirely by giving agency to the individual members of different wolf packs within Yellowstone. O-Six had a "knack" and "moxie," exhibiting "unusual behavior for a lone female" (2017, 12–13), which seems to have drawn numerous watchful eyes to her movements in the first place. She makes decisions and is aware of her "hazardous" breaking of pack norms but is uninhibited as she pursues starting her own pack. A story such as *American Wolf* seems unlikely in so many ways, especially for its refusal to moralize its subjects. Blakeslee brings the wolves to life beyond the previously antiquated, fictional stereotypes of their species. Like Flores, he, too, seems to be acutely aware of the originality of the type of text he is creating, and he embraces it so that the wolves can, in a way, tell their own story.

Wolves have distinct personalities and conscious awareness of the situations that transpire outside of themselves. Their actions are reflective of their internal dispositions. Blakeslee recounts events prior to the wolves' reintroduction to Yellowstone that illustrates individual wolves' conscious awareness. Notes from the Yellowstone wolf watchers provide countless stories of interactions but slowing down to observe these moments of personality helps the narrative establish that wolves are independent subjects with unique reactions to different stimuli. Blakeslee describes the first alpha male wolf brought down from Canada to Yellowstone in 1995 as an individual with a remarkable temperament.

> Known as 10, he was by far the most stunning animal brought down from Canada, the very epitome of an alpha male. Just getting him sedated so that he could be collared was a challenge; he grabbed the jab stick holding the needle and snapped it with his jaws, not once, but twice. Most of the other captured wolves were scared senseless when humans approached, but ten had the unsettling habit of staring his captors in the eyes. (2017, 17)

Ten (10) is conscious of attempts to get near him with a needle and also conscious of cues he can give to his human captors that he sees them. Alone, this description might seem fantastical, but it is followed by the stories of so many conscious wolves that actively make decisions about where they will go and how they will act. Blakeslee illustrates this first wolf's experience as scientists attempt to relocate him, which indicates that the reader needs to reassess the mental capabilities of wolves. Because of the form of writing Blakeslee employs and the genre of factual, historical accounts of wolves' events in their respective packs, this innovative form of animal text allows readers to view wolves as conscious, intelligent beings.

O-Six's story demands a reevaluation of the state of wolves and how their reintroduction places their survival at odds with unnatural parameters of time and boundaries, especially in Yellowstone National Park. Blakeslee's writing facilitates more extensive discussions about human interference with ecosystems, opinions of predators, and destruction of the natural environment despite claiming to preserve it via land conservation in the form of the National Parks. The success of wolf reintroduction to Yellowstone provides a hopeful perspective of how intelligent animals can quickly adapt to new situations, which means that even when humans have disrupted animal time, or the rhythm of nature processes as determined by living creatures, we might be able to rebalance ecosystems. The saga of O-Six's life and pack formation illustrates how, despite the unpopularity of reintroduction, the human reengineering of environmental issues can work for the species getting reintroduced to regions they previously inhabited. Wolves relearned how to live in Yellowstone. It was continuing and pervasive human error and violence that endangered the lives of wolves and their entire packs. In order to truly allow wolves to live in places like Yellowstone, humans must educate one another and change negative opinions of predators, especially when so many of those opinions are misinformed and devoid of ecological and scientific truth. While the preservation of areas like Yellowstone is crucial, the conservation of the land itself is nothing without the presence of its native animals. Humans can restore animal time to an area, but it requires massive cooperation between activists, legislators, hunters, and surrounding communities. Blakeslee describes the worry that wolf watchers had about threats to wolves from outside the park:

> Historically, when the Druids left the park, they had generally gone east, into Wyoming, where there was no wolf-hunting season, at least not yet. Park wolves were still safe there, or as safe as they had ever been, and Rick took some consolation in that. But it wouldn't last forever, and once hunting was legalized in Wyoming, Rick thought, the park would essentially be surrounded by hostile territory. (2017, 111)

A hunter shot O-Six in Wyoming. Humans cannot expect animals to navigate imaginary boundaries and changing seasons of the year when they are in or out of season for hunters. Those are dangers that even the most intelligent predator cannot understand, especially when many species begin to acclimate to human presence. The restoration of Animal Time in spaces like National Parks depends on humans advocating for animals while also educating other humans so that efforts like the Yellowstone Wolf Project can be successful. Part of the power of animal texts is telling animals' complete experiences, which so often include heartbreaking and unfair deaths along with joyful, rich lives, so that humans can acknowledge what needs to be done to better protect other living beings.

THE FUTURE OF ANIMAL TEXTS

Animal Texts rewrite the truth of regional spaces and boundaries. As climate change threatens all life on earth, it is more abundantly clear than ever that imagined boundaries of territories, urban spaces, and conserved spaces will not help protect any living thing from the pressing onslaught of murderous heat and natural disasters. Similarly, Flores and Blakeslee highlight the failure of even the most seemingly honorable attempts at conservation. These attempts are backfiring because of the insistence that human environments are somehow separate from where predators and other animal species can venture. Coyotes prove that wrong a dozen times over. Wolves, beginning with the first-ever National Park in Yellowstone, prove that even apex predators cannot hope to compete against industrialized weaponry that waits for them outside unclear and unreal boundaries. O-six's death proves the failure of great human efforts to restore preserved ecosystems due to the insistence on human space and animal space. Ecology does not sit outside humans; we are always already in every ecosystem and web of ecology. Humans must recognize our undeniable effect on species, which begins by understanding that outdated and absurd regional boundaries should be viewed for what they are: meaningless to all wildlife other than humans. This concept reminds me of humorous questions asked by Yellowstone Park tourists about "how rangers get animals to always stay within the boundaries of the park" or, even better, "what time are the animals released into the park every day?" We, like uneducated tourists, think animals are bound to stay where we put them.

The tragedy of O-Six's death is not as simple as seeing the protagonist of a generations-long wolf history die. By the time Blakeslee arrives at the fateful moment of her senseless death, O-Six is the most integral member of the Lamar Valley pack and the head of her family. Human understanding of animal familial relationships remains so stifled and shallow that we maintain our misguided system of doling out hunting tags for animals by gender or season. Animal Texts highlight the abject cruelty and stupidity of human approaches to "animal control." As both of these works prove, there is none. It is almost as if we value dead animals more than living. In his photography collection *Animal Logic*, Richard Barnes captures the collections of animal bones kept by the most scientific, pristine curators of humans. We keep each individual skeleton because we know that we can tell a story about how that animal lived and what happened to it through paleontology. Each skeleton is unique and can teach us something about the animal in its life and how it was set apart from the others of its kind. Why do we not pay that kind of specialized attention to living individual animals? In his photographs of animals that have been restructured through taxidermy, it is clear that the humans invested in their movement understand how fragile the (dead) animal is. Humans are careful to have the correct weight distribution in the crate, keeping their delicate features and fur from getting smooshed or damaged (Barnes et al., 2009, 42). Why do we display such awareness for individual dead animals yet condemn entire species of animals to perish because of chemicals, wilderness destruction, or other manifestations of human greed? Coyotes and wolves especially have endured the brutality of the hostility humans show to living animals. Our understanding of ecology and animals is still minimal. That is, until we combine every possible facet and discipline, in which case we finally might sketch out the truth about animal experiences in America, almost as if animals themselves penned the texts. It is the closest we will ever get.

While America has always been a nation obsessed with land, Westward movement, and poetic voicing of a collective identity, it is not until Animal Texts that humans' consistent fascination with animals has come finally to the forefront. Environmental writers have incorporated animals in the grandest, reverential ways, but somehow their view of the land itself overshadowed its vast inhabitants for the reader and even the professor. Since the early outdoorsmen and explorers, the human gaze has been so fixated on staking out land, marking land, and naming land that it looks right past the animals that are always already inhabiting those spaces. The ones that die are disingenuously memorialized and mourned (like the carrier pigeon and the dodo), but construction continues. Animal Texts exist because of the animals that survive despite human efforts to the contrary. While yes, wolves were reintroduced into Yellowstone, their adaptation and flourishing in places like the Lamar Valley prove these creatures' natural adaptability without technological or industrial aid. They live, thrive, and continue to exist on the land humans have done everything they can to control. Through writing, their presence as species is fortified by those who want to see them survive.

Perhaps the most intense beacon of hope is that these texts, like the group text you cannot ignore or silence, have reached enormous audiences. They work. They are being read, which is something most writing from the academy cannot boast. Because of the formation of Animal Texts, this topic that so badly needs investment and advocates is reaching masses of people. It is as if this fortuitous turn in literary writing has taken in just the precisely right amount of everything animal studies said was necessary, delivered into the hands of great and careful artists like these writers, and somehow reminded the world of readers that as children, we love animals. We care deeply about other beings. And now, they are starting to text us back.

REFERENCES

Barnes, Richard, Susan Yelavich, Jonathan Rosen, and Mark Strand. 2009. *Animal Logic*. New York: Princeton Architectural Press.

Blakeslee, Nate. 2017. *American Wolf: A True Story of Survival and Obsession in the West*. New York: Crown Publishing Group.

Crosby, Alfred W. 1986. *Ecological Imperialism: The Biological Expansion of Europe, 900–1900*. Cambridge: Cambridge University Press.

Dobie, J. Frank. 1949. *The Voice of the Coyote.* Philadelphia: Curtis Publishing Company.

Flores, Dan. 2016a. *American Serengeti: The Last Big Animals of the Great Plains.* Lawrence, KS: University Press of Kansas.

———. 2016b. *Coyote America: A Natural and Supernatural History.* New York: Basic Books.

Gruen, Lori. 2018. *Critical Terms for Animal Studies.* Chicago: The University of Chicago Press.

Harris, Adam Duncan, and George Catlin. 2013. *George Catlin's American Buffalo.* Washington D.C.: Smithsonian American Art Museum.

McNamee, Thomas. 2014. *The Killing of Wolf Number Ten: The True Story.* Westport, CT: Prospecta Press.

Ortiz Robles, Mario. 2016. *Literature and Animal Studies.* Milton Park: Routledge.

Schullery, Paul. 1996. *The Yellowstone Wolf: A Guide and Sourcebook.* Glendo, WY: High Plains Pub. Co.

US Department of Agriculture. 2018. "Livestock Slaughter." *US Department of Agriculture*, 27 November 2021, www.nass.usda.gov/Publications/Todays_Reports/reports/lstk1018.pdf.

"Yellowstone Wolf Project." 2021. *Yellowstone Forever*, 5 February 2021, www.yellowstone.org/wolf-project/.

Chapter 5

Beautiful and Sublime

Embracing Otherness in Mary Oliver's Ecopoetry

Anastasia Cardone

The concept of the Anthropocene has widely been studied both for its importance in a rediscovery of what it means to be "human" and for the future of the planet. Far from being a neutral term and in spite of some debatable anthropocentric perspectives provided by this concept, the Anthropocene shows how the relationship between human beings and "Nature"—which also includes other-than-human beings—has come to a dramatic turning point.[1] As Timothy Clark stresses, the Anthropocene doubly affects us (2015, xi). On the one hand, we can feel overwhelmed and desperate in front of processes that involve the whole planet. On the other hand, these uncertainties break down those inherited boundaries of thought linked to our concepts of "species," "literary genres," "otherness," and "individual," thus leading to a redefinition of what it means to be "human" and of how we as a species are impacting upon the whole planet. The Anthropocene thus brings about deep self-reflection, exactly because "[w]e humans never experience ourselves as a species" (Chakrabarty 2009, 220). By rethinking the place of humans in the environment and in relation to other-than-human beings, it is possible to acquire a renewed experience of the self as part of nature's wholeness. In fact, a redemptive process of healing—of the self and of the earth—should start from a radical overturning of our ideas of "humanity," since the origins of the current climatic crisis are rooted in humans' detachment from nature. As Harold Fromm maintains, "humankind has failed to see that now, as in the past, the roots of its being are in the earth," mainly because nature is now being "*mediated* by technology" (2009, 43). However, literature may play a vital role in developing a virtuous and organic relationship between humans and the environment, as affirmed by Ursula Heise: "the aesthetic transformation of the real has a particular potential for reshaping the individual and collective ecosocial imaginary" (2010, 258).

In this context, "ecopoetry" designates poetry that "is shaped by and responds specifically to that [environmental] crisis" (Fisher-Wirth and Street 2013, xxviii). Thus, it represents a means to fill the imaginative 'gap' between human and other-than-human beings by creatively engaging with critical questions. In particular, ecopoetry aims at respecting the integrity of the other-than-human world by questioning human domination over nature, hyperrationality, and the limits of human language in rendering reality. Contemporary ecopoetry strives to reconnect humans and nature as it shows how "poetry derives from the living earth" and can thus manifest "the intricate, adaptive, and evolving balance of an ecosystem" (Bryson 2002, ix). One of the main representatives of contemporary ecopoetry is the American poet Mary Oliver (1935–2019). Her poetry narrates her totalizing experiences in nature and it strives to represent—through language—"the manifold relationship between the human and the other-than-human world" (Fisher-Wirth and Street 2013, xxx). While Oliver recognizes nature as a "separate and equal other," she does not perceive such separation as problematic, but as a chance to look for merging and harmonious inclusion into nature's otherness (Scigaj 1999, 80). In this chapter, I aim to show how Oliver recovers an organic language by rooting poetry in the earth, while including her readers to trigger a change in human perspective. Oliver depicts such wholesome inclusion in nature through the physical and sensual contact with the other, which nurtures her unconditioned acceptance of both the beautiful and the most dreadful sides of the world. By highlighting nature's amorality, she accepts even death, as she wishes for a complete merging with the surrounding environment through a surrender of individuality. These themes have been developed through Oliver's whole poetic production, as she further deepens her insights into nature's wholeness. I thus put in dialogue poems from various collections, ranging from the 'sensuous' *American Primitive* (1983) to *Blue Horses* (2014), to show how recurrent themes are developed and promoted throughout Oliver's career. By fusing with nature's mysterious otherness, Oliver constantly demonstrates how to obtain a renewed understanding of humans' place on earth and to dismantle the boundaries between human and other-than-human beings, indicating innovative attitudes towards "otherness."

OLIVER'S POETIC MANIFESTO

As an ecopoet who also wrote poetic manuals, Oliver consciously reasons on language, which becomes a vital means of rooting poetry in the earth.[2] Her poems are mainly in free verse, which several critics have defined as "organic" (Oliver 1994, 67), thus adhering to more "natural" rules and free from any constraints, despite still possessing a clear internal design.[3] Oliver seemingly follows Ralph Waldo Emerson's organic principle in art: "it is not metres, but a meter-making argument that makes a poem—a thought so passionate and alive that like the spirit of a plant or an animal it has an architecture of its own, and adorns nature with a new thing" (1950, 323). As she tries to let the thought dictate the poetic form, Oliver places much emphasis on sounds, recalling Robert Frost's appeal to the ear, which is best exemplified in his concept of 'sound of sense' (Frost 1966, 60). Sound imagery becomes an essential means to echo natural sounds and express the natural world through poetry. Sound figures, such as alliterations, onomatopoeia, anaphoric repetitions, and parallelisms are thus fundamental, while enjambments stimulate the reader's curiosity and make lines flow freely.

Oliver applies several of her ideals in what could be defined as her poetic manifesto, the meta-poem "Everything" (2005, 4). The lyrical voice narrates her poetic mission. As for the content, Oliver aims at dealing with her surrounding environment and those experiences acquired while "crossing the fields" full of flowers but also of "ordinary grass." Thus, she includes and embraces all the elements of nature. From a stylistic perspective, she does not want to add useless decorations and elaborated rhetorical means, but she cherishes common words, such as "heavy, heart, joy, soon," which could better render the simplicity of ordinary life. However, she contradicts her own assertions, as she introduces "the bread of heaven" and "the cup of astonishment," certainly two images that imply several elaborated meanings. Oliver's objective is turning the ordinary into something extraordinary. Through a kind of language more attuned to nature, poetry can overcome the barriers imposed by rationality and speak directly to the reader's heart. Oliver also introduces two recurrent elements in her poetry: the "dash," which breaks syntax and recalls the cyclical movement of time, and the "question mark." Throughout Oliver's vast production, several poems feature direct questions to involve her readership, such as "Ghosts," in which the lyrical voice keeps asking the reader whether they have noticed even the tiniest details in nature (1983, 28). Oliver reiterates her intention to ground her poetry in the earth—the origins of her poetical act—but through this process she could ideally reach heaven and "see the unseeable" ("Everything" 2005, 4). Through this heightening experience, she aims at communicating everything and inspiring the readership, yet not through rational language but through insights and glimpses.

Although some poems tend to focus more on inner reflection and matters of faith (such as the collection *Evidence* from 2009), the content of Oliver's poetry is inextricably related to outdoor living and nature, experienced as the physical place where human beings could have a direct encounter with God. The images of the "bread of heaven" and the "cup of astonishment" evoke the host, the Eucharist bread, and the wine cup symbolizing Christ's blood. They recall the Holy Communion and the Last Supper. In her poems, Oliver intends to write "songs" and joyful hymns, similar to "The Canticle of the Creatures" by Saint Francis.[4] Thus, poetry becomes a true confession of faith, a prayer towards the world, in which every word is dedicated to the heavens and the earth. By shaping such a close connection with the earth, the poet manages to "see the unseeable," turning into a prophetic seer. Yet, Oliver underlines the limits of language, since the happiness experienced in front of the world's wholeness does not need any superfluous words. "Gladness" could well be expressed "without any words" and still convey "everything." She requires the fresh and lively language that would enable her to faithfully capture the perception of the present moment. Oliver's lines mirror what Scigaj (1999, 38) maintains about ecopoetry: poetry holds a relationship with the environment, it recognizes the limits of language, and it gives voice to the lyrical voice's perceptions beyond the written page, moving towards nature, which is paradoxically the source of human language. This is how language finally acquires redemption.

Oliver recognizes that the origins of her poetry are in the wilderness. The poet partly echoes Carl Jung's theories on the archetypes, which represent the profound and innate connections between human beings and the environment. As Oliver underlines in *A Poetry Handbook*, her manual for writing poetry, the ocean stands for the mother, the sun for health and hope, the coming of spring for resurrection, and birds for the divine breath (1994, 105). These connections make nature a symbolic inspiration for the poet, as Oliver maintains in "Of What Surrounds Me" (2005, 32). In this poem, she states that her poetry arises from all the natural elements and she mentions the earth, the sky, and water, passing from a creek to an ocean. Poetry needs a permanent link with the reality beyond the written page, from "a leaf" to "an entire field" or even a "skyful." Human language thus derives from nature and the poet would not be able to write poetry without such an emotional and physical connection with the environment. Thus, this close relationship with nature enables the poet to commit herself on a personal level. Language and poetry become not only the means to represent nature but also the bridge between human beings and the concrete world, reconnecting humans with their organic roots. Nature provides symbols as well as inspiration for the poet's "pen."

However, when human beings strive to talk *about*, *with*, and *for* nature, the problem of pathetic fallacy emerges, underlining the eternal dualism between the world and the human, the so-called rational animal. In contrast with traditional Romantic nature poetry, ecopoetry strongly refuses pathetic fallacy and its use of human projections to represent other-than-human beings. As ecopoetry highlights, the necessity to project human feelings onto nature emphasizes how nature is primarily perceived as totally other from the human and must be anthropomorphized to be comprehended. By contrast, an "ecocentric" use of the language respects otherness and reveals humans' place on earth, becoming "an indication that the speaker has a place, feels part of a place" (Evernden 1996, 101). The poet needs to recover a writing style that articulates reality directly and spontaneously, before any conceptualization and without imposing symbolic meanings on nature. Oliver allows nature to express itself through her poems and through the intimate connection between the language and the denoted thing. Despite her refusal of pathetic fallacy, Oliver herself employs metaphors that infuse the whole environment with human-like features, mainly because she believes that everything possesses a soul (1995, 63). As the spirit acquires materiality in nature, Oliver's metaphors connect the incorporeal word with the sensual and tangible reality, in ways similar to the Christian incarnation of the Word. Seeing the world as a place inhabited by kindred spirits explains Oliver's empathy towards nature, poetically represented through metaphors and personifications. In the poem "Tiger Lilies," for instance, the flowers demonstrate willingness to be cut by the lyrical voice (2005, 31). Perceiving kindred spirits in nature could be viewed as an "excuse" to explain a violent act, in this case the cutting of the flowers. Rod Preece emphasizes the difference between empathy, which leads to respect for other species, and sympathy, which characterizes the Western thought and results in a paternalistic and exploitative relationship with the "other" (1999, 91). In order to shape respect, the pronoun "thou" should be used to address the other instead of "it," as stated in the fundamental text *Ich und Du* (1923) by the Austrian philosopher Martin Buber. While Oliver's attitude could be criticized as being more sympathetic than empathic, Laird Christensen (2002) demonstrates that she perceives the world as another subject, experiencing the others as a "thou," resisting objectification, and embracing the other, which is essential for the shaping of the self: "We are human only in contact, and conviviality, with what is not human" (Abram 1996, 22). Oliver thus creates intimacy between natural beings and the human experiencer through personification, since all aspects of life acquire a soul.

ECOCENTRIC QUESTIONS WITHOUT ANSWERS

By rooting her poetry in the earth and creating intimacy with other-than-human beings, Mary Oliver begins her return to nature. Yet, she strives to include the reader in this movement back to the natural origins of humans, since only through a complete overturning of humans' conception of our relationship with the environment could we truly embrace the "other" and come to a merging with other beings. Therefore, several poems directly engage the reader by providing sets of instructions in the imperative form and asking crucial and revealing questions. Echoing the poetic tradition of the Petrarchan and Shakespearean sonnets, which deal with a theme by presenting an idea or an issue in the first part and resolving them in the ending sestet or couplet, Oliver often structures her poems in two parts: the former narrates or describes perceptive details, while the latter philosophically meditates on nature and leads to the moment of revelation. This second section features questions that aim at bringing the readers into the poems and inside the natural world beyond the page. These questions stand for Oliver's desire to know nature by acquiring a corresponding better knowledge of the self; they signal a mind open to discovery, ready to doubt about previously acquired concepts, and willing to change perspective. Despite being direct and colloquial in their tone, Oliver's questions have metaphysical and existential importance. For example, in "Peonies" (1992, 22) the lyrical voice first describes the flowers using a highly evocative language full of synaesthetic images that appeal to different senses; after six descriptive stanzas, she opens the reflective part of the poem, grounded on a series of questions about life, triggered by the previous observation. These questions disrupt the rhythm and the syntax of the poem, surprising the readers and insinuating doubts about their relationship with the world and the supposed love they should feel towards nature: love, appreciation, and adoration. Oliver suggests a precise attitude, which includes abandoning one's cold and detached perspective to embrace nature by filling one's arms with flowers before they wither. The poem invites the readers to enter nature and seize the day, recovering a sense of the wild represented by the image of running barefooted, which may stand for the temporary abandonment of rationality. However, such a relationship with nature is still grounded in human behaviors, as it is enacted through the gathering of flowers and the acknowledgment that such an act also causes the flowers' death.

Oliver's questions aim at heightening the readers' awareness, since they encourage a complete change of human life. In "Summer Day" (1990, 50), she instills doubts in the readers by asking what they plan to do with their lives and whether there is anything more precious than life, and underlines the value of fighting against conformism and prejudice, since life is defined as wild. Despite their colloquial tone, Oliver's questions stimulate deeper reflections about nature, life, death, and the soul. Throughout her poetic production, Oliver wonders about existential arguments, carrying out a theological and naturalistic search for the soul, as in "Some Questions You Might Ask" (1990, 1). She first wonders about the material substance of the soul, using similes linked to material reality to give substance to the soul; these questions sound innocent and almost naive, as if they were made by a child. Then she ironically asks who possesses a soul, but the use of "who" posits a fundamental question: could one that does not have a soul still be addressed with "who"? Oliver seemingly underlines the nonsensicality of the very last question, as she underlines that the animal body itself demonstrates the existence of the soul in other-than-human beings. Since humans have a soul, the lyrical voice rhetorically wonders whether other beings possess it. Underlining Oliver's belief in the fact that everything has a soul, her ecocentric poem forces readers to reason whether other-than-human beings possess a soul. The rhythm is dictated by anaphoric repetitions aimed at convincing the readers about the fact that every single natural item has a soul. Oliver challenges traditional anthropocentrism not through a philosophical argument, but by stating these simple and yet inexplicable questions. Humans should not presume to be the only creatures with a soul, because all nonhuman beings show signs of a soul through their behaviors, here exemplified by the anteater's showing love for her offspring as humans do. Oliver then shifts from animals to plants and flowers; she even wonders whether inanimate elements, like the stones, may host a spirit or a soul. She concludes with the image of the grass—a reference to one of Oliver's favorite poets, Walt Whitman—thus demonstrating that everything in nature possesses the breath of life. Therefore, she encourages the readers to feel part of the great natural family by overcoming the traditional dualism between humans and other-than-human beings, a dualism that has traditionally been grounded in the notorious Cartesian belief that only humans possessed a soul, which arches back to traditional Christian beliefs found also in the writings of St. Thomas Aquinas.

Moreover, Oliver's questions emphasize the impossibility of finding a clear and definite answer, since nature itself is the place of endless and constant change, of energetic flows, of the opening to various meanings. Formally, such impossibility to acquire fixed knowledge is expressed through enjambments, which suspend the lines and the flow of thoughts. Questioning oneself without providing answers is Oliver's starting point to experiencing reality without rational barriers, as she relies on sensual and 'wild' experiences. Oliver moves away from rational knowledge and embraces nature's mysteries, as she describes in "What Is There Beyond Knowing" (2005, 20–21). In this poem she affirms that her knowledge is definitely limited, as to be put into a little pack on her shoulder, while the world is characterized by unexplained and unexplainable wonders. As she tries to rationalize reality (as through her poetic practice), she actually understands that the world is not governed by logic and all she can do is to harmonically merge with nature, acquiring non-rational and sensible knowledge of the world, which keeps resisting investigation. The movement of total union with nature averts rationality, as the subject opens up towards the outer world through breathing. Physical phenomena can be felt and experienced by fostering a sensual connection with nature. Avoiding rational definitions of life, her only wish is to go drifting, trusting the world to lead her to a sacred place in nature. Through this floating and passive process, she simultaneously accepts the grass and the weeds.

THE SENSUAL EXPERIENCE OF NATURE

As highlighted by her questions, Oliver requires a renewed attitude towards nature that implies abandoning rationality and experiencing the world through the senses, in what can be defined as the "sensual" experience of nature. This innovative take on nature, which Oliver starts with the collection *American Primitive* (1983) and then sustains throughout her whole career, brings about the sobering experience of every instant and the discovery of the extraordinary in every natural detail. She fosters a real art of noticing, as her poems usually focus on a small detail, such as an insect or a flower, which then triggers further deep reflection. While in *American Primitive* Oliver cherishes direct sensual experiences, she later turns them into symbols for inner, psychological events, especially in the collection *Evidence* (2009). Here sight becomes a metaphor for the mystical vision, as in the poem "Imagine" (2009, 63). Oliver introduces two types of sight, one based on actual seeing and the other related to imagination. The former, "with understanding," is conscious and it provides more rational knowledge; the latter requires the humble "acceptance" of the mysteries hidden in nature, represented by the image of the cocoon of the fascinating and bewildering Luna moth. The lyrical voice invites the readers to carefully attend to the physical world, abandoning rationality even facing death, the ultimate chance to finally see inside nature's mysteries, inside the seed to merge with the very heart of nature. Such truthful experience of reality is what Oliver cherishes and what characterizes a life worth living. As John Elder notices (1996, 117), several Western thinkers, such as Schopenhauer, Nietzsche, Freud, and Merleau-Ponty, have emphasized an anti-rational and corporeal approach to the world that may reveal the sensual relationships between one's individual body and the outer world. Oliver's poetry could be inserted in this long philosophical tradition. Therefore, J. Scott Bryson (2005, 81) defines her poetry as a "poetics of the body," since physicality acquires such a fundamental role in her relationship with the outer world that she centers her whole poetics on this corporeal approach. By freeing oneself from cultural prejudices and physically penetrating into nature, the experiencer could feel empathy towards all beings and see the whole world with renewed eyes. By renewing one's perspective, even the annual passage of the migrating geese described in "Snow Geese" (2004, 35) may acquire insightful features, as if the experiencer would possess the keys to nature's mysteries, accessing secretive facts and thus seeing reality clearly and wholly.

Despite the importance of sight, a whole sensual experience of nature requires also the other senses, which may foster one's love towards the environment. In particular, the act of eating nature to include it into one's body is a recurrent image in Oliver's poems. In "At Blackwater Pond" (1992, 226) drinking from the pond triggers the inclusion of the lyrical voice in nature. Through taste the experiencer may become part of nature, as the cold water passes through her body; even her bones, which can incredibly speak, murmur about these beautiful and enriching experiences. Water completely unsettles the body and the mind, as its qualities shake the human with its contrasts, its coldness that yet tastes like 'fire,' burning the poet from within. The primitive, sensual experience of eating—a fundamental theme in *American Primitive*—exhilarates Oliver, as she forgets reason and obeys innate instincts, like animals. She can thus feel an unrestrained happiness, as expressed eating honey in "The Honey Tree" (1983, 81). Here she ingests everything, including bees trapped in the honey and parts of the leaves, thus accepting everything. By comparing herself to a snake and a bear, she emphasizes the significance of animal instincts to experiencing reality, accepting one's body and singing in the "heaven of appetite." Tasting nature is a primordial act that physically connects human beings to the earth, thought as a mother that provides everything humans need for their corporeal and spiritual sustenance. In "The Plum Trees" (1983, 84) Oliver plays with the adjective "sensible" and "sensual" to express the material joys brought about by tasting. Through the act of eating, everything related to reason turns into something sensual and physically experienceable through the body. The union of thought and corporeality produces sheer happiness that affects first the body and then the mind.

Through eating, the human experiencer establishes a first contact with the world. Therefore, Oliver lets herself be guided by the senses to return to primitive nature. Instead of being opposed, body and mind collaborate towards the direct contact with the environment. Such experiences have transforming effects on humans, as stressed in the poem "The Fish" (1983, 56), which echoes the more concrete relationship with animals depicted in Elizabeth Bishop's "The Fish" but infuses it with spiritual overtones by recalling the

Eucharistic act of eating Christ's body.[5] Oliver first describes the violent act of fishing, as the fish is literally burnt as it breathes air, which turns into ethereal fire. The process of cleaning the flesh of the fish sounds quite methodical and fact-driven, as if she were giving objective information about such act without emotional commitment, so as not to address the violence of killing and eating an animal. However, the act of eating completely transforms the poet, as she metaphorically turns into the sea and the fish. Oliver employs a chiastic pattern, alternating between the subjects "I" and "the fish" to express the reciprocal and specular relationship between the human being and the animal. On the one hand, the willing sacrifice of the fish is yet another act of human violence committed against nature; on the other hand, Oliver wants to read this act as an eco-conscious unity with nature, since the fish's life does not end with death—as the fish's scales then glitter inside the experiencer—but life is perpetuated through eating, which thus acquires resurrection-like features. The human experiencer and the fish merge in a single being and could thus plunge back into the sea, which represents a cleansing and purifying agent that washes pain away.

THE BEAUTIFUL AND THE SUBLIME

Oliver's sensual experience of nature allows her to shape a renewed relationship of love and acceptance of the natural 'other,' which triggers her unconditioned love for every aspect of reality. Oliver's whole poetic production, in fact, revolves around love and acceptance. She explains her development from the love for herself to the love for the world in "To Begin With, The Sweet Grass" (2009, 3). Oliver describes such change as a stepping outside from her own confinements enabled by getting rid of her physical and mental barriers, so that she could foster her love for the environment, as expressed by the instructions to the readers: "Love yourself. Then forget it. Then, love the world" (3).

By nurturing love for the world, Oliver perceives beauty as the primary quality of nature. She often sings about the beauty of other-than-human beings and events, ranging from butterflies and insects to a whole array of bird species, from the simple and silent beauty of the lilies in "The Book" (2005, 42) to the imperfect and broken beauty of the whelks (in "Whelks" 1992, 30). Although nature is spotted with imperfections, decay, and diseases—like the orange blight that affects the water lilies in "The Ponds" (1990, 58)—Oliver still perceives that beauty pervades nature. She thus accepts death as a fundamental part of the beauty of living, as she states in "The Kingfisher" (1990, 18), reflecting on the bird's hunting. The world is actually pretty, although humans have to embrace both living and dying. Oliver almost overturns the traditional ideas about the beautiful, which has been connected with the concept of the Good—thus linking aesthetics and morality—since Plato's *Phaedrus*, where the Greek philosopher identifies the transcendental ideas of the Good, the Beautiful, and the Truth in what is known as *kalokagathia* (the crasis of "beautiful" and "virtuous").[6] After Plato, the perception of beauty in nature would often be related to ideas of the Good, from Plotinus to Kant; aesthetics would find its independence from ethics only with the foundation of aesthetics as a proper science thanks to the work *Aesthetica* (1750–1758) by Alexander Gottlieb Baumgarten. However, Oliver challenges the common connection between the beautiful and the good, as she includes death and transience in her idea of beauty, embracing the world's integrity and the cyclic evolution of life.

As a consequence, in Oliver's poems there are also sublime and terrifying elements, such as death and predation, which generally clash with human conceptions of ethics. Although humans themselves have been hunting, slaughtering, and killing animals, the tendency to feel sympathy towards the "prey" in the other-than-human world has been predominant, as exemplified by D. G. Ritchie's doubt: "must we not protect the weak among them [animals] against the strong? Must we not put to death blackbirds and thrushes because they feed on worms?" (1894, 109). While humans tend to regard all predators as "merciless, wanton, and incorrigible murderers of their fellow creatures" (Callicott 1989, 21), Mary Oliver accepts them and turns terror into a key point in her poetics: "evil is one part of our beautiful world," she affirms in the essay "Winter Hours" (1999, 106). The most violent aspects of reality are the most authentic: "The owl is not cute. The milk snake is not cute, nor the spider in its web. [. . .] Toys are cute. But animals are not toys. [. . .] Such words—'cute,' 'charming,' 'adorable'—miss the mark, for what is perceived of in this way is stripped of dignity, and authority" ("A Few Words" 1995, 91–92). Oliver introduces the protagonists of her most obscure poems: the sublime predators that inhabit the depths of the forest. Trying to define them, especially through appealing words, would mean depriving them of their extraordinary, mysterious, and fascinating power. These animals represent nature's destructive energy, which resist conceptualization and cannot be reduced to human concepts.

In particular, owls are depicted as fundamental beings in the environment throughout Oliver's entire poetic production. Their predatory hunger is a synonym for death, as owls remind the lyrical voice that death cannot be stopped, as she affirms in "At Round Pond" (2005, 122). The "swift" and "merciless" horned owl from the essay "Owls" (2003, 15) represents such atavistic thirst for blood and death: "If it could, it would eat the whole world" (15). Oliver contrasts the terrible scream of the owl's prey (the rabbit) and that of the owl, "which is not of pain and hopelessness" but "of the sheer rollicking glory of the death-bringer" (15). Since the most significant question in Oliver's poem is how to love the world, her readers may wonder how it is possible to love death. Yet, by observing the violent but instinctive show of predation, she cannot do anything but bow in front of the owl's perfection and pure concentration, as she does in the poems "Bowing to the Empress" (1986, 55–56) and "Owl Poem" (2014, 67). Owls remind both the poet and the reader that the world is primordially carnal and instinctual, made out of matter, flesh, bones and blood.

As Oliver warns in "Foxes in Winter" (1990, 22), nature may seem cruel from a human perspective and she actually never denies it. However, cruelty is the sign of life's ineffable mystery, death itself. According to Oliver, humans have to accept that death is as necessary as life and it gives life sense. Furthermore, Oliver is able to unify beauty, sublimity, and cruelty as intrinsic qualities of the world by highlighting the positive sides of terror and blind instincts. Violence and death are inserted in God's perfect plan. For instance, in the poem "Serengeti" (1990, 60–61) the African lion arouses "terror" and "awe," becoming the symbol of the unity between beauty and sublimity. The lion is part of the concept of God, not simply a creature shaped by the Creator. God instilled himself in every aspect of reality, including hunger and fear. The lion is simultaneously a lethal weapon of destruction ("bone-breaker") and the "agent of transformation" that triggers the cyclical process of life and death that keeps the balance in an ecosystem.

By accepting death—even one's own death—Oliver stresses the importance of fully living the present. She embraces nature, which is ruled by creative excess that points both towards endless creation and endless destruction. Therefore, the world of death is the same world of life and beauty: "The world where the owl is endlessly hungry and endlessly on the hunt is the world in which I live too. There is only one world" (from the essay "Owls" 2003, 16). Oliver's purpose is to make her readers appreciate both aspects of reality, which are not separated but keep merging in the fundamental unity of nature. Human beings can feel part of nature's wholeness by opening up to the presence of the "other," including predators, so as to understand that the owl's wild instinct is the real treasure that we may experience in nature (from "Nature" 1990, 55). This explains why predators are nonetheless fascinating.

DEATH AND THE CREATIVE MERGING WITH NATURE

Following her own instructions, Mary Oliver comes to perceive the world as a unitary place and desires to lose—at least for an instant—her own individuality in order to completely merge with nature. Her desire is first expressed in the poems from the early nineties and is reiterated and expanded in the collections from 2003 onward. Several poems describe the attitude of "self-losing" inside the object of contemplation, in a state of calm abandonment. The lyrical voice wants to deprive herself of her corporeal boundaries and she is ready to accept death to fuse with the surrounding environment. Thus, she totally reevaluates death, which is not thought as the end of life but as part of the cyclical regeneration in nature. Oliver enters in death's abode in "When Death Comes" (1992, 10), she loses her sense of time, and thus embraces the whole world, in which every individual is connected to the others by the same destiny: death, but also rebirth. This is the message brought by the ruthless owl from "White Owl Flies Into and Out of the Field" (1990, 79), whom Oliver turns into a symbol of holiness (an "angel"). By accepting the owl's instinctual predatory needs, Oliver understands that death is not characterized by darkness—the traditional image for death—but by scalding and burning light, mirrored by the whiteness of the owl's feathers and recalling the purifying force of fire as narrated in the Buddha's "Fire Sermon."[7] These spiritual echoes are matched with a physical description of death, characterized by radiance, brightness, and total absence of shadows. Despite being a letting go of one's physical body, death also has a sensual and tactile quality; its light wraps around us and it washes us, being similar to a baptism and a blessing. It deprives us of our bones but it instills holiness.

The abandonment of one's physical limits and the union with nature's wholeness is thus a tangible event that modifies matter. In the poem "The Deer" (1990, 24), the lyrical voice describes death in innovative terms. It is no longer an abstract concept or a moment that delimits the end of life. The organic decay of the body is a real event that is perceived as totally positive, because it represents the opening up of the body towards the world and its complete transformation into new life. Through such opening up, the mutual attuning between humans and nature is carried out, so that humans may regain their animal origins, here embodied by the deer. The individual's union with the surrounding reality—which here as elsewhere is epitomized through the image of the river and of watery landscapes—can be attained through the fluidity and porousness of one's corporeal boundaries and the mystic purification of the soul. Running water allows the experiencer to live in the present, forgetting about the past and the future and transcending the concept of eternity. While in the first poetry collections the purifying and changing element is often water, later poems connect death and the image of the earth, the transformation into fertile grass, the place for decomposition and rebirth, as in the poem "Have You Ever Tried to Enter the Long Black Branches" (2005, 142). The mystery hidden in nature is simultaneously death and life, which are not opposed but are part of the same physical process and spiritual development. Human beings should not fear death, but accept it like a free gift. In this context, grass symbolically represents the perfect cycle of birth-death-rebirth that is perpetrated in nature.

With the recurring image of grass, Oliver depicts death as the bodily metamorphosis into the vegetation. She often refers to the biological process of decay, although she employs metaphors and similes, heightening her tone despite talking about something extremely corporeal. Oliver's attitude is often characterized by passivity, as she recurs to past participles and significant terms, such as "vanish," "forget," "oblivion." By passively abandoning her self-awareness, she could turn into nature, as she narrates in "Reckless Poem" (2005, 40). The lyrical voice forgets her individuality and perceives nature inside herself flowing like a wave, flourishing and blooming. Human blood is metaphorically compared to green sap, so that from her hands green leaves could imaginatively sprout and burst. In the same poem, she chooses to fly out of her self, assuming multiple identities and turning into the heron, the whale, the fox, the hedgehog, the camel, and the flower. The horizons between the human subject and the object of perception (nature) eventually fuse, blurring individual boundaries. One's self-consciousness thus turns towards the outside world and becomes unself-consciousness and total mindfulness, as Oliver expresses in "Mindful" (2004, 58), when she affirms that she enters the woods first to bodily experience nature and then to completely lose herself in nature.

The image of the metamorphosis of the self was established by Oliver in the poem "White Flowers" (1992, 59), in which the lyrical voice imaginatively turns into the forest and feels the perfect affinity between herself and nature. As she lays down in the fields surrounded by darkness and she falls asleep, she then discovers herself to be covered with white blossoms. As the white flowers open up, she seemingly mirrors the same movement, merging with the surroundings. She still keeps her bodily limits, although they are now "porous" and permeable, allowing a closer connection with the surrounding environment. As she tries to explain the physical process that she has undergone, she emphasizes the mutual and simultaneous movements of her body and nature. She either enters the depths of nature or she is embraced by the flowers' "green energy," almost invading her body. Her bodily barriers are so labile and ephemeral that it is no longer possible to distinguish the human body, made out of flesh and blood, and nature, with roots, stems, and sap. Losing oneself does not mean turning into a nihilistic nothing but becoming everything, being fully integrated in nature's wholeness. Identities are thus fluid and shaped by the constant contact with their surroundings, as asserted in notable philosophical works, from Gilles Deleuze and Félix Guattari's "Becoming-Intense, Becoming-Animal, Becoming-Imperceptible" (1987) to Donna Haraway's notion of "becoming-with" (2008). The transformation into the other goes against the traditional conception of the organism as a discrete and rigidly segmented being, since "becoming is intensive and continuous, not extensive and discrete. [. . .] Becomings are virtuous because they increase one's capacities, exceeding the organic, the signifying, and the strata of subjectification in a becoming-imperceptible, becoming-indiscernible, and becoming-impersonal" (Adkins 2015). This idea of developing identities, vanishing barriers, and becoming-more-than-individual is best expressed by Oliver in "Sleeping in the Forest" (1992, 181), which narrates the poet's merging with the earth during an extraordinary night spent in the forest. Far from being mere anthropomorphism, Oliver personifies the earth and elevates it to a conscious being, able to remember and to accept the lyrical voice into her figurative pockets. The metaphors to describe nature show the similarities between the earth and human beings. The lyrical voice does not represent nature through human concepts but, in contrast, turns herself into nature through a process of letting go of the self and of human rationality (here epitomized by "thoughts"). The verbs "rose" and "fell" indicate a floating or drifting movement in between transcendence and immanence in nature. The lyrical voice accepts a terrible but extremely bright fate, the total fusion with the earth and the dissolution of her human existence. Yet, recalling Buddhism, her soul lives further, coming to life into different forms. While the individual self disappears by the riverbed, she acquires multiple identities by becoming others, even better others.

Her transformative journeys teach Oliver to accept death and all the apparent cruelties in the world as integral parts of the cycle of life. On the surface, they may be difficult to accept, since 'death is one of the great taboos' in Western society (Armstrong 2012, 93). However, nature is neither good nor evil, neither moral nor immoral, but it is *amoral*. Nature is characterized by originality, which is the sign of endless, fruitful excess. Noticing nature's creativity, Oliver embraces every single event, not only beauty but also rotting decay, terror, predation, and death, as in the poem "The Kitten" (1983, 6), in which she buries a kitten with a terrible cranial malformation. Instead of being shocked in front of the kitten's fate and the natural cruelty, the lyrical voice is amazed. Through the experience of death, she understands that life is real, tangible, endlessly creative, since it permits such a bizarre event. She willingly gives back the tiny creature to the earth, thus allowing its return to its natural origins and its rebirth into a new life. While humans tend to distinguish between the beautiful and the grotesque, as in the separation between grasses and weeds, nature's creativity and excess do not make such distinction, but everything is flourishing and abundant: "Are the roses not also—even as the owl is—excessive?," asks Oliver in the essay "Owls" (2003, 16), relating the roses' prolific exuberance and the owl's endless hunger. The originality that she experiences in the environment causes happiness, as the human being encounters unexpected surprises in nature.

The fusion of the self with the "others" frees humans from the fear of dying, as Haraway emphatically affirms: "I love that when 'I' die, all these benign and dangerous symbionts will take over and use whatever is left of 'my' body, if only for a while, since 'we' are necessary to one another in real time" (2008, 4). The emphasis on "I" and "my" underlines that being is a process of "becoming with" others rather than a fixed and unchangeable state. In this context, death could be "a gateway to new realms" (Armstrong 2012, 94), interpreted as either religious paradises or the bodily transformation into organic matter. By freeing oneself from the fear of dying, since death is now interpreted as a corporal and spiritual merging with nature, it is possible to conceive both beauty and brutality as inevitable events. Beauty and terror can be fully appreciated only in their common existence, as they clarify and define one another (Mann 2004, 19). As a consequence, the owl is both an angel and the messenger of death; the deadly diseases of waterlilies do not ruin nature's beauty; the poisonous mushroom is wonderfully sublime because of its deadly effects. Every organism possesses a perfect balance. According to Oliver, there exists only one unitary world that fuses the positive and negative sides of reality into every single being. The final result of such realization is the love for the world, for its extravagant beauty. Only by fostering such aesthetic and ethical experiences could the subject feel an intrinsic part of nature, so that she discovers that the more the subject takes a step outside of their self, the more nature draws nearer, in a mutual and cordial embrace.

Oliver is aware that complete merging with the "other" could be carried out only imaginatively, since a real fusion with nature would annihilate the individual voice writing poetry. Nonetheless, in her process of "becoming-with" the other as narrated in her poetry, Oliver shows her willingness to come closer. She begins this movement of inclusion first with her search for a more organic use of human language, by rooting language and poetry again in nature. Thus, ecopoetry turns into a means to bridge human beings and nature. Through her sets of instructions and challenging questions, Oliver then demonstrates the necessity to include her readership in this journey towards acceptance. As her "sensuous" poems reveal, a way to return to humans' origins in nature is fostering the senses to carry out a wholesome inclusion in nature, which then triggers enthusiasm for every aspect of reality, from the most beautiful to the most terrifying and seemingly shocking, such as death, predation, and deformity. Yet, by grasping nature's amorality, Oliver understands her own imaginative death as a fusion with the "other," as she gives up her self-awareness and enclosed individuality to identify with the 'other.' As her physical and mental boundaries fall, she reaches the total immersion in the environment, which could allow human beings to establish a vital dialogue with nature and to develop renewed attitudes towards "otherness."

REFERENCES

Abram, David. 1996. *The Spell of the Sensuous: Perception and Language in a More-Than-Human World*. New York, NY: Vintage Books.
Adkins, Brent. 2015. *Deleuze and Guattari's A Thousand Plateaus: A Critical Introduction and Guide*. Edinburgh: Edinburgh University Press.
Armstrong, Adrian. 2012. *Ethics and Justice for the Environment*. London: Routledge.
Bryson, J. Scott. 2002. *Ecopoetry: A Critical Introduction*. Salt Lake City, UT: University of Utah Press.
Bryson, J. Scott. 2005. *The West Side of Any Mountain. Place, Space, and Ecopoetry*. Iowa City, IA: University of Iowa Press.
Buber, Martin. 2009. *Ich und Du*. Stuttgart: Reclam.
Callicott, J. Baird. 1989. *In Defense of the Land Ethic: Essays in Environmental Philosophy*. Albany, NY: State University of New York Press.
Chakrabarty, Dipesh. 2009. "The Climate of History: Four Theses." *Critical Inquiry* 35 (2): 197–222.
Christensen, Laird. 2002. "The Pragmatic Mysticism of Mary Oliver." In *Ecopoetry: A Critical Introduction*, ed. J. Scott Bryson, 135–52. Salt Lake City: University of Utah Press.
Clark, Timothy. 2015. *Ecocriticism on the Edge: The Anthropocene as a Threshold Concept*. London: Bloomsbury.
Davis, Todd. 2009. "The Earth as God's Body: Incarnation as Communion in the Poetry of Mary Oliver." *Christianity and Literature* 58 (4): 605–24.
Deleuze, Gilles, and Guattari, Félix. 1987. *A Thousand Plateaus: Capitalism and Schizophrenia*. Minneapolis: University of Minnesota Press.
Elder, John. 1996. *Imagining the Earth. Poetry and the Vision of Nature*. Athens, GA: University of Georgia Press.
Emerson, Ralph Waldo. 1950. "The Poet." In *The Complete Essays and Other Writings of Ralph Waldo Emerson*, ed. Brooks Atkinson, 319–41. New York, NY: The Modern Library.
Evernden, Neil. 1996. "Beyond Ecology: Self, Place, and the Pathetic Fallacy." In *The Ecocriticism Reader: Landmarks in Literary Ecology*, ed. Cheryll Glotfelty and Harold Fromm, 92–104. Athens, GA: University of Georgia Press.
Fisher-Wirth, Ann, and Street, Laura-Gray. 2013. *The Ecopoetry Anthology*. San Antonio: Trinity University Press.
Fromm, Harold. 2009. *The Nature of Being Human: From Environmentalism to Consciousness*. Baltimore, MD: The Johns Hopkins University Press.
Frost, Robert. 1966. "Introduction to *King Jasper*." In *Selected Prose of Robert Frost*, ed. Hyde Box and Edward Connery Lathem, 59–67. New York: Holt, Rinehart and Winston.

Haraway, Donna J. 2008. *When Species Meet.* Minneapolis, MN: University of Minnesota Press.

Heise, Ursula. 2010. "Afterword: Postcolonial Ecocriticism and the Question of Literature." In *Postcolonial Green: Environmental Politics and World Narratives,* ed. Bonnie Roos and Alex Hunt, 251–8. Charlottesville, VA: University of Virginia Press.

Horn, Eva, and Bergthaller, Hannes. 2019. *The Anthropocene: Key Issues for the Humanities.* London: Routledge.

Kennedy, William J. 2012. "European Beginnings and Transmissions: Dante, Petrarch and the Sonnet Sequence." In A.D. Cousins and Peter Howarth (eds.), *The Cambridge Companion to the Sonnet,* edited by A.D. Cousins and Peter Howarth, 84–104. Cambridge: Cambridge University Press.

Mann, Thomas W. 2004. *God of Dirt: Mary Oliver and the Other Book of God.* Lanham, MD: Cowley Publications.

McNelly Kearns, Cleo. 1987. *T.S. Eliot and Indic Traditions: A Study in Poetry and Belief.* Cambridge: Cambridge University Press.

Oliver, Mary. 1983. *American Primitive.* New York, NY: Little, Brown and Company.

———. 1986. *Dream Work.* New York, NY: Atlantic Monthly Press.

———. 1990. *House of Light.* Boston, MA: Beacon Press.

———. 1992. *New and Selected Poems, Volume One.* Boston, MA: Beacon Press.

———. 1994. *A Poetry Handbook: A Prose Guide to Understanding and Writing Poetry.* New York, NY: Harcourt Inc.

———. 1995. *Blue Pastures.* New York, NY: Houghton Mifflin Harcourt.

———. 1999. *Winter Hours: Prose, Prose Poems, and Poems.* Boston, MA: Houghton Mifflin.

———. 2003. *Owls and Other Fantasies.* Boston, MA: Beacon Press.

———. 2004. *Why I Wake Early.* Boston, MA: Beacon Press.

———. 2005. *New and Selected Poems, Volume Two.* Boston, MA: Beacon Press.

———. 2009. *Evidence.* Boston, MA: Beacon Press.

———.. 2014. *Blue Horses.* New York, NY: The Penguin Press.

Plato. 1995. *Phaedrus,* transl. by Alexander Nehamas and Paul Woodruff. Indianapolis, IN: Hackett Publishing Company.

Preece, Rod. 1999. *Animals and Nature: Cultural Myths, Cultural Realities.* Vancouver: UBC Press.

Riley Fast, Robin. 1993. "Moore, Bishop, and Oliver: Thinking Back, Re-Seeing the Sea." *Twentieth Century Literature* 39 (3): 364–79.

Ritchie, David G. 1894. *Natural Rights.* London: George Allen and Unwin.

Scigaj, Leonard. 1999. *Sustainable Poetry: Four American Ecopoets.* Lexington, KY: University of Kentucky Press.

Spears Brooker, Jewel, and Bentley, Joseph. 1990. *Reading "The Waste Land": Modernism and the Limits of Interpretation.* Amherst, MA: The University of Massachusetts Press.

Watts, John, ed. 2019. *St Francis' "Canticle of the Creatures."* Leominster: Gracewing Publishing.

NOTES

1. Eva Horn and Hannes Bergthaller (2019) outline two conflicting conceptions of the role of humans in the Anthropocene that have recently emerged: *ecomodernism*, which sees the role of humans as 'stewards' of the Earth system, and *ecological posthumanism*, which refuses human exceptionalism and considers the human exclusively as *anthropos*—a life form among others. The scholars maintain that while ecomodernism overestimates the human as *homo*, ecological posthumanism underestimates the human as mere *anthropos*, although they both struggle to grasp the paradoxical structure of human agency in the Anthropocene.

2. Mary Oliver published two poetic manuals: *A Poetry Handbook* in 1994 and *Rules for the Dance* in 1998.

3. See, for instance, Laird Christensen (2002), Todd Davis (2009), Thomas Mann (2004).

4. In his canticle, Saint Francis praises the Lord and all the creatures, including "our Sister Bodily Death," thus embracing even the darkest aspects of life. See Watts 2019.

5. Robin Riley Fast (1993, 364) analyzes the trope of the sea as developed in Marianne Moore, Elizabeth Bishop and Mary Oliver: "Although there exists to date no definitive, explicit evidence of connection between Oliver and either Bishop or Moore, a deep responsiveness of Bishop's work, and through it, to Moore's, resonates from many of Oliver's poems. Thus 'Mussels' and 'The Fish' from *Twelve Moons*, and 'The Fish' from *American Primitive* recall Bishop's 'The Fish.'"

6. While this identification may negate the autonomy of aesthetics from ethics, Hans-Georg Gadamer (2004, 475) highlights that "the beautiful is distinguished from the absolutely intangible good in that it can be grasped. It is part of its own nature to be something that is visibly manifest." Thus, Gadamer emphasizes that the Beautiful has the advantage of allowing the Good to be perceived.

7. The "Fire Sermon" of the Buddha is from the *Maha-Vagga*, a central text of early Buddhism. As Cleo McNelly Kearns (1987, 75) affirms, it exploits the trope of fire used in the Upanishads, the Vedas, and the *Gita*. The fire represents the process of purification by which pain of worldly experience can be overcome. Jewel Spears Brooker and Joseph Bentley (1990, 121) explain that the Buddha's sermon consists of three questions and answers. The first question asks what is on fire and the Buddha answers that the senses, all sensory knowledge, the mind, and all impressions are on fire. The second question asks about the nature of this fire, which is passion, like the fire of hatred, of infatuation, of despair. The third question asks how these fires can be extinguished and the Buddha maintains that fire itself will purify the passions.

Chapter 6

The Sea's Witness

Narration, Texturisation, and Reader Responsibility in Rachel Carson's Oceanalia

Lauren O'Mahony

Rachel Carson is frequently regarded as one of North America's most beloved nature writers. When she died in 1964 at the age of fifty-six, she had published four significant works about the environment. Carson's most famous publication *Silent Spring* (1962) reportedly launched the modern environmental movement, inspiring a debate about the impact of synthetic chemicals and pesticides, leading to public inquiries and eventually the banning of DDT. So powerful is *Silent Spring*'s mode of delivery and its encoded message, it still garners attention, discussion and even criticism, more than fifty years after publication (see Matthiessen; Meiners et al.).

While Carson is largely remembered for *Silent Spring*, she wrote and published three significant works about the sea, *Under the Sea-Wind* (1941), *The Sea Around Us* (1951), and *The Edge of the Sea* (1955). These works, taken collectively, explore oceanic spaces, including some of their mysteries, while inviting readers to reflect upon their wonders. From the ocean's evolution and the emergence of sea life to the ebbs and flows of tides, fish, and birds, Carson invites readers into a world that usually remains hidden from daytime sights; the ocean, after all, is not a natural home for most humans. Ambitiously, her oceanic trilogy makes the strange and unfamiliar less so while conjuring a substantive representation that shifts "the ocean" from object to subject. Carson's works have the power to inspire readers to think and wonder more about oceanic life while reinforcing the ecological synergy that unites ocean, land, and humans. Rather than seeing the ocean as disconnected from terrestrial humans and their actions, Carson encourages what Amanda Hagood (2013) terms an "ecological aesthetic" where books such as *Under the Sea-Wind*, "postulate a new ground for considering the significance of human life relative to the life of the ocean, forging for its readers a new kind of ecological literacy—one based heavily on our capacity for imagination, our love of storytelling" (Hagood 2013, 62). For Hagood, these books emphasize the stubbornness of certain cultural understandings of the ocean, particularly what she terms the lingering "duality of wonder and waste" (74). Hagood's commentary invites reflection on the schism between human "wonderment" towards the ocean alongside its exploitation for its resources and treatment as a dumping ground for innumerable types of human waste.

Hagood's examination of two Carson works (*The Sea Around Us* and *The Edge of the Sea*) within the context of a mid-twentieth century readership is one of only a few detailed studies of Carson's ocean-themed works. Much has been written generally about Carson and her four major works of nature writing. Together with Linda Lear's authoritative biography *Rachel Carson: Witness for Nature* (1997), Mark Hamilton Lytle's *The Gentle Subversive: Rachel Carson,* Silent Spring *and the Rise of the Environmental Movement* (2007), and William Souder's *On a Farther Shore* (2012) explain the cultural impact and legacy of her work.

Marc Bekoff and Jan Nystrom (2004) have explored the attitude towards animals in Carson's writing. They argue that Carson emphasizes an anti-anthropocentric vision where all beings, including humans, comprise an interconnected web of life. Humans, as part of nature, should be "good" to animals and the earth. In doing so, humans are rewarded because "we ourselves feel better when we treat Nature with kindness, respect, and compassion" (Bekoff and Nystrom 2004, 199). Susan Power Bratton's examination of Carson's oceanic writing argues that Carson nudges readers from comfortable terrestrial boundaries beyond the shoreline to beneath the waves. Plunging readers into this largely unfamiliar space helps communicate what Bratton argues is a "trans-boundary or trans-ecotonal ethic of the sea" that assists in establishing ethical relationships between humans and non-humans (2004, 6). Amanda Hagood's (2013) analysis of Carson's trilogy of oceanic works contextualizes them within social, political and cultural forces when they were published in the 1940s and 1950s. Hagood argues that the reception of Carson's work for a "mid-century" reader, those reading soon after the works were published, is different to the way twenty-first century readers encounter Carson's work today. Hagood emphasizes that at the time of publication in the 1950s, Carson's works contributed to the development of public understanding about oceanic spaces and fostered a kind of "ecological literacy" (2013, 62). While these critical discussions map the development, context and ethics of Carson's oceanic works, this chapter explores how specific narrative conventions and techniques position readers and produce a range of literary effects.

Carson's three oceanic works each uniquely combine ecologically focused narrative qualities and conventions. *Under the Sea-Wind* recounts the life-cycle of exemplary sea-dwelling creatures including Scomber, a young mackerel, Rynchops, the black skimmer bird, and Anguila, the eel. The book's three parts each have a contextual focus: the shore, open sea, and "deep abyss" (Lear 1997, 90). *The Sea Around Us*, a bestseller when published, explains the sea's history including the stories of scientists and explorers. Carson's third oceanic work, *The Edge of the Sea* focuses on relationships within the oceanic ecosystem, especially shoreline flora and fauna and the constantly moving sea. This work offers an insight into Carson's relationship with the seashore as a scientist and enthusiast of oceanic natural history. Together, these three works approach oceanic spaces differently: from the perspective of individual creatures, through a longitudinal historical view, and as a natural historian and scientist exploring the sea's edge. The variational narrative qualities of these works mean that together, the ocean is approached from different angles, points of view, and informational sources; combined they construct a complex representation of oceanic spaces thereby seeking out wonder, respect, and ultimately responsibility in readers.

This chapter has three main foci. Firstly, it explores the different approaches and points of view utilized in each of Carson's oceanic works. Carson constructs the narrator and readers as witnesses of oceanic history and sea life subsequently measuring out various distances between the reader and the sea. Collectively there is great variation in the use of first-, second-, and third-person perspectives. These too modulate the distances between reader and text, in some cases making readers feel as if they are experiencing the sea through the narrator's eyes, dipped below its surface with its creatures or travelling through time observing its history. Secondly, the narratives incorporate voices and characters to achieve different narrative effects including focusing almost exclusively on sea animals in *Under the Sea-Wind*, drawing on the experiences and knowledge of explorers and scientists to probe the evolution of the ocean in *The Sea Around Us* and using a semi-autobiographical tone to explore Carson's relationship with the ocean in *The Edge of the Sea*. The third section of this chapter focuses on how Carson's three oceanic works use narration and characterization to texturise the sea in a way that constructs it complexly, using a range of scales and dimensions. Arguably, Carson's deployment of narrative, characterization, and texturisation techniques conjures for the reader a feeling of immersion into the ebbs and flows of the sea. Carson's oceanalia has the immersive power to transport readers to an "elaborately simulated place," one that "takes over all our attention" (Murray

1998, 98–99). Tied to immersion is the feeling of telepresence, as if one was there or as Steuer defines it, "the experience of presence in an environment by means of a communication medium" (Steuer 1992, 6). Further, as Bratton (2004) has suggested, "Carson attempts to descend through the barrier at the sea's edge and surface, gently pulling her reader along, like a mermaid guiding a bewildered sailor into the magical kingdoms below" (6).

OBSERVATION, WITNESSING AND NARRATION

> One must always be aware, to notice—even though the cost of noticing is to become responsible.
>
> Thylias Moss (as quoted in Gamerman A13)

Linda Lear's aptly titled biography, *Witness for Nature*, shows the scale and depth of Carson's witnessing, both literal and figurative. After the publication of *Silent Spring*, Carson was called as a testimonial witness for numerous governmental groups and committees including John F. Kennedy's Science Advisory Committee and Commerce Committee (Lear 1997, 453–55). While Lear recounts Carson's literal witnessing and testimony in a legal sense, Lear's description of Carson as a "witness for nature" encodes a further meaning that extends beyond *Silent Spring* through Carson's *oeuvre*:

> Rachel Carson was an unlikely person to start any sort of popular movement. She treasured her solitude, defended her privacy, rarely joined an organization; but she meant to bear witness. [. . .] In the sea and the bird's song she had discovered the wonder and mystery of life. Her witness for these, and the integrity of all life, would make a difference. (Lear 1997, 4–5)

Silent Spring exemplifies an obvious example of Carson's witnessing, yet as Lear implies, Carson's sea-focused works also illustrate witnessing. Carson recounts her vast knowledge of sea-life, drawn from her scientific qualifications, employment at the U.S. Bureau of Fisheries and her own fieldwork research and observations.

In her oceanic works, Carson illustrates witnessing in action. John Durham Peters defines witnessing as "an observer or source possessing privileged (raw, authentic) proximity to facts" (Peters 2001, 709). Yet, as Peters explains, witnessing is more than the possession of information. Reporting, expressing or recounting the "facts" is also needed:

> Witnessing is also the discursive act of stating one's experience for the benefit of an audience that was not present at the event and yet must make some kind of

judgment about it. Witnesses serve as the surrogate sense-organs of the absent. (Peters 2001, 709)

When Carson wrote her trilogy of sea works, the public had vastly less information or knowledge about the ocean than they do today. As Hagood notes, while the reading public of the 1950s was less informed about the sea, many were "deeply fascinated both with narratives of oceanic exploration and with the sounds and images of marine life" (Hagood 2013, 59). Carson's works therefore report her witnessing of nature for the benefit of the reader who, in most cases, has not shared her experiences. Such witnessing, as Peters suggests, invites "judgement" and arguably "responsibility" to act on the information imparted (2001, 708–709).

In *The Sea Around Us* Carson reflects on the act of witnessing alongside the limits of scientific knowledge. *The Sea Around Us*, an ambitious work of oceanic history first published in 1951, responds to fundamental questions about the ocean while imbuing the reader with a sense of awe, wonder, and respect. *The New York Herald Tribune* described the book as follows, "It is a work of science; it is stamped with authority; it is work of art; it is saturated with the excitement of mystery; it is literature" (on the book's dustjacket). The first paragraph of the first chapter begins mapping the contours of the knowledge and information to be presented:

> Beginnings are apt to be shadowy, and so it is with the beginnings of that great mother of life, the sea. Many people have debated how and when the earth got its ocean, and it is not surprising that their explanations do not always agree. For the plain and inescapable truth is that no one was there to see, and in the absence of eyewitness accounts there is bound to be a certain amount of disagreement. (3)

Carson frequently reminds the reader of *The Sea Around Us* and *The Edge of the Sea* of gaps in knowledge and disagreements about certain 'facts.' In *The Sea Around Us* for example phrases such as "probably" (1951, 6) and "must have" (4) frequently point to inconsistencies or lacunae in knowledge, as do phrases including "but at present no one is wise enough to be sure" (7) and "this chapter [about exploration of the Antarctic Ocean] contains many blank pages" (209). Such phrases humbly admit to the inadequacies of knowledge and the mutability of scientific discourse to change when new discoveries emerge. To counter gaps in knowledge, *The Sea Around Us* calls upon those with first-hand experience and their "eyewitness accounts of what they saw" (1951, 44). For example, Carson tells her reader, "I asked Mr Heyerdahl about some of his impressions, especially of the sea at night, and he has written me as follows . . . " (18). Alternatively, she refers to S. C. Brooks, who describes the "changing life, seen as his ship cut across the pathways of the great currents of the Pacific and the Atlantic" (Carson 1951, 23). Inviting the voices of those with firsthand or specialist knowledge conjures Carson as a curator of sea testimonies. The multiple testimonies mean that information offered and shared becomes a kind of communal project of meaning making and responsibility.

In her oceanic works, Carson creates a sense of polyphony with narrative shifts between the pronouns "I," "you," and "it." *Under the Sea-Wind* is predominantly told using a third-person omniscient viewpoint where the narrator observes and recounts. Carson explains the work's aim as follows: "[t]he Fish and other sea creatures must be the central characters and their world must be portrayed as it looks and feels to them—and the narrator must not come into the story or appear to express an opinion" (Carson as cited in Lear 1997, 90). So too, the reader, as Carson explains, becomes "an observer of events which are narrated with little or no comment" (2007, 3–4). Humans are largely absent from this work, "except from the fishes' viewpoint as a predator and destroyer" (Carson as cited in Lear 1997, 90). When readers are positioned to view humans through the eyes of the animal characters such as the little mackerel Scomber, they sense fear and trepidation. At one point, Scomber becomes trapped in a net with a school of mackerel. Ominously, the reader learns that a boat is moving through the water in darkness with lights snuffed to avoid "frighten[ing] the fish"; it is so dark that a sea bird "struck the mast, fell to the deck with a frightened cry, and fluttered off" (Carson 2007, 120). The rising tension of the encircling net, darkness, and ghostly ship is emphasized when the mackerel become "nervous and uneasy," "fearing the strange monsters," and "afraid of the netting wall" (121–122). Momentarily, the point of view moves between above and below the water from the bird, to the deck, to the fish in the net, and to a young fisherman on the deck who wonders about "what lay under the surface" and "what had the eyes of the mackerel seen" (122). The fish escape on this occasion through a hole at the net's base, providing relief for the reader from the fear-inducing storyworld of the animal characters. Hagood suggests that the "violent anthropogenic interruption" of the fishermen into Scomber's story partly exemplifies the book's philosophy "about the significance of human action in the ancient patterns of undersea life" (Hagood 2013, 61). This human intervention emphasizes the disruptive nature of the fisherman's actions while reminding readers of the proximal difference between human and undersea life, where the young fisherman may wonder about "what the mackerel had seen" (Carson 2007, 122) but can only imagine.

The Sea Around Us and *The Edge of the Sea* combine third person narration with passages told in first- and second-person. Frequently Carson moves between pronouns throughout *The Sea Around Us* to indicate her own observations or thoughts. For example, she writes, "when I think of the floor of the deep sea, the single, overwhelming fact that possesses my imagination is the accumulation of sediments. I see always the steady, unremitting, downward drift of materials from above, flake upon flake, layer upon layer" (1951, 74) or "[s]o, on a mountain top in Pennsylvania, I have sat on rocks of whitened limestone, fashioned of the shells of billions upon billions of minute sea creatures" (101). *The Edge of the Sea* utilizes a shifting narrative point of view, moving between first-, second-, and third-person. In the first-person point of view, Carson uses "I" predominantly and occasionally "we." Carson employs "I" to explore her own relationship with the ocean in two ways. Firstly, "I" indicates a more personal account of her encounters with shore or ocean life. For example, she writes, "each time that I enter [the sea shore], I gain some new awareness of its beauty and its deeper meanings, sensing that intricate fabric of life by which one creature is linked with another, and each with its surroundings" (1998, 2). Such personal and philosophical musings conjure an image of Carson as someone whose "true love was the sea" (Hubbell 1998, xv). Secondly, first-person narration in *The Edge of the Sea* is through Carson's eyes as a scientist, identifying, assessing, and hypothesizing. In one instance, Carson explains:

> Once below the dark film, I begin to look for the first of the sea creatures pressing up to the threshold of the land. In seams and crevices in the high rocks I find them—the smallest of the periwinkle tribe, the rock or rough periwinkle. Some—the infant snails—are so small that I need my hand lens to see them clearly.. . . . (1955, 47–49)

Through the use of "I," the reader views the sea through the narrator's eyes, philosophizing about life on earth or assessing a specimen through a scientific lens. The shifts to first-person narration provide insight into Carson's view of oceanic spaces. When Carson remarks about beauty or timelessness, a sense of awe and wonder may be transferred to readers, even if only momentarily.

Readers are occasionally addressed directly through first-person collective pronouns and the second person "you." "We" is used in *The Sea Around Us* and *The Edge of the Sea* to engage readers, decreasing the distance from the narrator. For example, in *The Sea Around Us* the narrator states, "[s]o in all lands we may sense the former presence of the sea" (1951, 101) or "[w]hen we spend a long summer holiday at the seashore we may become aware that the tide in our cove behaves very differently from that at a friend's place twenty miles up the coast, and is strikingly different from what we may have known in some other locality" (153). The reader, regardless of their knowledge or experience of the sea, is positioned to feel that the "we" includes them in the spirit of a shared actual or vicarious experience. However, other uses of "we" speak to a more collective scientific community which the reader may not necessarily identify with. For instance, *The Sea Around Us* summarizes a gap in knowledge: "[b]ut even with all our modern instruments for probing and sampling the deep ocean, no one now can say that we shall ever resolve the last, the ultimate mysteries of the sea" (1951, 216).

The use of "you" in *The Edge of the Sea* and *The Sea Around Us* can be read variously. In one way, the narrator directly addresses the reader to decrease distance. This usage of second-person narration potentially "blurs" the "boundary between the text and the reader" (Kostkowska 2013, 178). For example, *The Sea Around Us* states, "[t]he next time you stand on a beach at night, watching the moon's bright path across the water, and conscious of the moon-drawn tides, remember that the moon itself may have been born of a great tidal wave of earthly substance, torn off into space" (1951, 4–5). This kind of narration seeks to implant the idea of "standing on the beach" in the reader's memory, whether from an actual memory or the memory of reading the passage, as though the next time they glance upon the moon, perhaps this direct address and gentle instruction may be remembered.

Other uses of "you" in *The Sea Around Us* may refer to the reader or even a future Carson herself. Monika Fludernik explains that second-person narration can "have an explicit communicative level on which a narrator (speaker) tells the story of the 'you' to (sometimes) the 'you' protagonist's present-day absent or dead, wiser, self" (1994, 288). For example, a chapter in *The Sea Around Us* about the surface of the water begins:

> Nowhere in all the sea does life exist in such bewildering abundance as in the surface waters. From the deck of a vessel you may look down, hour after hour, on the shimmering discs of jellyfish, their gently pulsating bells dotting the surface as far as you can see. Or one day you may notice early in the morning that you are passing through a sea that has taken on a brick-red color from billions upon billions of microscopic creatures, each of which contains an orange pigment granule. At noon you are still moving through red seas, and when darkness falls the waters shine with an eerie glow from the phosphorescent fires of yet more billions and trillions of these same creatures. (1951, 16)

The "you" in this example may address readers or her future self who may observe these surface water events from a boat. Such narrative shifts engage readers as if being addressed directly, potentially encouraging deeper observation and interaction with sea life in the future. Carson's use of "you," "we" and "us" potentially taps in to shared experience and shared witnessing; this may be either that which the reader may have previously seen or should perhaps look out for in the future. The narrative shifts also work to retain the reader's attention and modulate the proximity between reader, text and narrator, just as waves move up and down the shoreline. The use of "I" and a third-person perspective reinforces distance, both physically from life in the ocean and ontologically in terms of what is known about the mysteries of the sea. When a reader encounters a narrative that uses the pronoun "I," the "I" signals a narrative focus on another individual and a clear distance between the reader and the workings of the story. However, shifts to "you" and "we" more directly refer to the reader's involvement in the narrative. Being directly addressed via "you" or inclusively involved via "we" increases proximity between the reader and what they are reading, giving a sense of shared experience and vicariousness. The ideal effect of increasing the reader's proximity to the text via the use of the pronouns "we," "you" or "us" and narrated events is that the reader may feel more a participant in the stories being told. Potentially, this sense of inclusiveness may forge a closer bond between reader and text; in the case of Carson's works, this bond may also translate into a closer bond between the reader and the ocean beyond the pages of the books.

CHARACTERIZING THE WEB OF LIFE

Carson's oceanic works each have a distinct style and structure. Regular narrative shifts between points of view work alongside a distinctive use of characters and voices to construct oceanic spaces through key stakeholders. *Under the Sea-Wind* follows in the path of Henry Williamson's *Tarka the Otter* (1927) and *Salar the Salmon* (1935) to recount key moments in the life of exemplary creatures (Lear 2007, xi). *Under the Sea-Wind* is divided into three parts, one focused on a sea bird, the second on Scomber the mackerel, and the third on Anguila the eel. Together, as Lear notes, "the three narratives would weave a tapestry in which the ecology of the ocean and the interdependence of all its creatures would emerge" (Lear 1997, 90). As Lear explains, Carson was careful to suggest that her exemplary animals in *Under the Sea-Wind* had anthropomorphic aspects without directly stating it (Lear 1997, 91). Carson describes her impression of these creatures as follows:

> To get the feeling of what it is like to be a creature of the sea requires the active exercise of the imagination and the temporary abandonment of many human concepts and human yardsticks. . . . We cannot get the full flavour of marine life—cannot project ourselves vicariously into it—unless we make these adjustments in our thinking.
>
> . . . I have deliberately used certain expressions which would be objected to in formal scientific writing. I have spoken of a fish 'fearing' his enemies, for

example, not because I suppose a fish experiences fear in the same way that we do, but because I think he *behaves as though he were frightened.* (Original emphasis, 2007, 5)

When Silverbar, the female sanderling, broods her eggs and watches them each hatch, readers are told, "... for the first time an abiding fear entered the heart of Silverbar—the fear of all wild things for the safety of their helpless young" (43). Likewise, Anguila the eel is said to "fear" the "brightness" of direct light. These are somewhat subtle personifications and intimations of how the animal may feel in certain circumstances. Other personifying phrases emplace more humanlike qualities onto the animals including gulls who "laughed their excitement" at fish stranding themselves upon the beach (93), an exhausted Scomber who "crept" among the seaweed fronds after being ensnared and released by a comb jelly (84), and Anguila "prowling" for food at night (130). These examples of "telling" how the animals act are reinforced by "showing" the reader other aspects of their habits and character.

The Sea Around Us and *The Edge of the Sea* avoid characterizing examples of flora and fauna beyond the descriptive, instead exploring life-cycles, habitats, and survival strategies. Even though the animals do not have names like in *Under the Sea-Wind* and the reader does not follow them on extended adventures, occasionally connections are made between readers and exemplary animals through brief anecdotes. For example, in *The Edge of the Sea* Carson recounts research undertaken into the hypothesis that each shore-dwelling limpet has a dedicated home on the rocks. Carson refers to the scientist, W. G. Hewitt, who studied the limpet and their homing instinct. To examine the limpet's habits, Hewitt marked and filed the shells of specimens to determine if they returned to the same location. He also filed across the animal's path to its home. Readers may feel sympathy for the limpets studied by Hewitt, particularly when they read that: "presumably the exact fit of shell to rock home had been destroyed by the filing and the next day the limpet had moved about twenty-one inches away and did not return. On the fourth day it had taken up a new home and after eleven days it disappeared" (1998, 60). This example, like the young fisherman who ponders life beneath the waves in *Under the Sea-Wind*, gently meditates on the effect of human interference with ocean life. Carson weaves together the lives and fates of different types of shoreline flora and fauna with humans to show readers their interconnected fates.

In *Under the Sea-Wind*, Carson argues that the sea "is worth knowing" (2007, 3). To allow the reader the opportunity to learn, this text casts the sea as the central character, one that "hold[s] the power of life and death over every one of its creatures from the smallest to the largest" (3). Across her three oceanic works, Carson develops the sea's character through personification alongside the exploration of different aspects, depths, and situations. In *The Sea Around Us,* she personifies the sea with verbs such as "crept" (1951, 13) while utilizing multisensory language in terms of seeing, smelling, and especially hearing to allude to human qualities. Her oceanic works create soundscapes to counter any misconception of the sea's quiescence. For example, in *The Edge of the Sea*, Carson carefully weaves together words and imagery to create an evocative soundscape and non-human sound world. She describes one of her "favorite approaches to a rocky seacoast" (1998, 41), and as she navigates through the forest towards the shore, she describes the audio-rich sensation:

> In the quiet of that place even the voice of the surf is reduced to a whispered echo and the sounds of the forest are but the ghosts of sound—the faint sighing of evergreen needles in the moving air; the creaks and heavier groans of half-fallen trees resting against their neighbours and rubbing against bark; the light rattling fall of a dead branch broken under the feet of a squirrel and sent bouncing and ricocheting earthward. (41)

Though Carson suggests the sea's quietness in this scene, readers hear the layers of sound, gently weaving through the image of the forest and shore threshold. Likewise, Carson describes her favorite sea cave ,including the constant dripping of water (121). Sound is used in an associative sense with movement. In the case of the cave, readers connect the water dripping to her observation that "the pool . . . is never quite still" (121).

While animal and oceanic characters dominate Carson's sea works, the presence of humans is inescapable. Carson frequently draws upon the knowledge and experience of explorers and scientists in conjunction with her own personal anecdotes as a scientist and admirer of the sea. At times however, the narrative style shifts out of first- or second-person into the third-person to make general observations. In some examples the use of third-person in reference to "man" reflects on the human-ocean relationship. For example, the following description in *The Sea Around Us* invites reader reflection:

> Eventually man, too, found his way back to the sea. Standing on its shores, he must have looked out upon it with wonder and curiosity, compounded with an unconscious recognition of his lineage. He could not physically re-enter the ocean as the seals and whales had done. But over the centuries, with all the skill and ingenuity and reasoning powers of his mind, he has sought to explore and investigate even its most remote parts, so that he might re-enter it mentally and imaginatively. (1951, 15)

While this passage alludes to humans as seekers of adventure, masters of ingenuity and curious explorers, the use of "man" has different effects. "Man" used in the third-person may position readers to reflect on the follies of human endeavor. Such uses of "man" may encourage readers to disassociate from certain actions, to regard "man" as if the ideal reader was an outside observer of "man's" actions. For example, in *The Sea Around Us* Carson explores the phenomena of lights in and around the ocean as a fathomable mystery:

> Man, in his vanity, subconsciously attributes a human origin to any light not of moon or stars or sun. Lights on the shore, lights moving over the water, mean lights kindled and controlled by other men, serving purposes understandable to the human mind. Yet here are lights that flash and fade away, lights that come and go for reasons meaningless to man, lights that have been doing this very thing over the eons of time in which there were no men to stir in vague disquiet. (1951, 34)

This passage implies an anthropocentric mindset that casts "man" as the progenitor of certain technologies, particularly light. Alternatively, regarding the human ecological destruction of various islands, Carson explains:

> But man, unhappily, has written one of his blackest records as a destroyer on the oceanic islands. He has seldom set foot on an island that he has not brought about disastrous changes. He has destroyed environments by cutting, clearing, and burning; he has brought with him as a chance associate the nefarious rat; and almost invariably he has turned loose upon the islands a whole Noah's Ark of goats, hogs, cattle, dogs, cats, and other non-native animals as well as plants. Upon species after species of island life, the black night of extinction has fallen. (93)

This passage previews the assertive and direct tone that Carson's *Silent Spring* utilizes to emphasize human folly. Carson continues her critique on the fate of islands, where "man" "rudely disturbed [the] balance, he set off a whole series of chain reactions" (94) and "[i]n a reasonable world men would have treated these islands as precious possessions, as natural museums filled with beautiful and curious works of creation, valuable beyond price because nowhere in the world are they duplicated" (96). These examples show that third-person narration can position readers to reflect on "man" and his actions as if from the outside. This narrative maneuver performs a dissociating function, creating distance between readers and the "man" or "men" being referred to.

In comparison to the references to "man" and some of his follies, Carson as a narrator-character becomes increasingly developed in *The Sea Around Us* and *The Edge of the Sea*. *The Edge of the Sea* especially develops an impression of Carson's relationship with the ocean via anecdotes about her seashore explorations, emphasizing her awe at its wonders and beauty. Her engagement with the ocean is depicted as gentle, respectful, and considerate. Carson's use of "I" often impresses her shoreline experiences as a scientist alongside her insights and actions in relation to the environment she observes. Frequently, when recounting a shoreline experience, Carson shows the reader her ethical mindset centered on respect for flora and fauna, gentle interactions with sea-life, and the more modern idea of "leave no trace" where she carefully returns specimens after studying them. Even when finding a spectacular specimen, Carson explains her actions and reasons behind them, for example, her first meeting with a sea hare:

> I had met my first sea hare years before on the North Carolina coast. It was a small creature about as long as my little finger, browsing peacefully among some seaweeds near a stone jetty. I slipped my hand under it and gently brought it toward me, then, its identity confirmed, I returned the little creature carefully to the algae, where it resumed its grazing. (1998, 219–20)

Similarly, when recalling her encounters with sea baskets, she imparts fascination and wonder as well as her gentle and ethical treatment of another life form. She recalls stumbling upon the creature, explaining, "[f]or many minutes I stood beside it, lost to all but its extraordinary and somehow fragile beauty. I had no wish to 'collect' it; to disturb such a being would have seemed a desecration" (225).

TEXTURIZING THE SEA

> Today we need a Rachel Carson to write about ocean 'dead zones,' the degradation of ocean habitats, the dying of coral reefs, the effects of global warming on ocean waters. (Sue Hubbell in the Preface to the 1998 edition of *The Edge of the Sea*, xx)

Across Carson's trilogy, readers experience a texturisation of ocean spaces through words and imagery. "Texture" is defined in *The American Heritage Dictionary of the English Language* (2015) as "[t]he distinctive physical composition or structure of something, especially with respect to the size, shape, and arrangement of its parts." Through texturisation Carson develops the reader's understanding, knowledge and image of the ocean three-dimensionally. In *The Sea Around Us* Carson counters a simplified or one-dimensional impression of the sea; instead the point of view moves from shoreline to underwater to above water (including different ocean depths), back and forward through time, through the senses, across the seasons, between single organisms and groups and from minute organisms to massive ones. The book responds to enduring questions about the sea including its origins, the influence of the seasons and planets and how "man" may interact with and impact ocean life. The book then proceeds to examine the sea's origin, changes through time, and what may be found under the surface.

Likewise, in *The Edge of the Sea*, the sea is presented across time, historically, geologically, in terms of the relationships between organisms including their changing behaviors and in different scales from big to small, many to a few or focusing on a single organism. *The Edge of the Sea* lingers only momentarily on a group of organisms, single organism, or location before moving to the next, establishing the sea's edge as "a strange and beautiful place" (1998, 1). The focus on texturisation that creates the impression of a complex ocean world emphasizes the ecological connections between flora and fauna as well as humans and non-humans alike. Carson challenges misconceptions about the shore, including its seeming inertia or absence of life. For example, she states that "all that makes up the living and dying and perpetuating of this sand-beach fauna—is concealed from the eyes of those who merely glance at the surface of the sands and declare them barren" (132). Here the narrator notes two things: firstly, the inability of human senses to see beyond a certain scale of life, often omitting or ignoring minute creatures present in certain eco-systems. Secondly, the narrator challenges any suggestion that life is absent just because it is not seen. *The Edge of the Sea* further explores the ocean's smallest scale. A detailed passage on sand portrays it as a beautiful, mysterious, and infinitely variable substance, the reader learning that each grain is "the result of processes that go back into the shadowy beginnings of life, or of the earth itself" (1998, 125). Moreover, the text impresses that sand grains vary highly (128), are "almost indestructible" (130), and are constantly moving (126). Such insights mean that a reader's exposure to a seashore (whether in reality or virtually) may prompt curiosity and wonder about the origin, travels, and life of the many sand grains before them.

Carson's trilogy creates an expansive and complex view which emphasizes the constant change and flux in the story of the ocean, including towards its future. Just as the appearance of sand or rock pool flora and fauna changes with every tide, the vision of the sea entrusted to us through Carson's books emphasizes its fluidity and the ephemerality of sea representations. This too connects with the prevailing scientific knowledge of the ocean. *The Edge of the Sea*, like *The Sea Around Us*, frequently explains the limits of knowledge in oceanic science and natural history, including what is known and was unknown, the difficulty in making certain calculations about the scale of sea life and enduring oceanic mysteries. Such mutability in her works, including within the marine sciences, emphasizes that her work is but one representation and not the final word.

Rachel Carson is remembered for her powerful and illuminating works that skillfully weave together scientific information with narrative storytelling. Her oceanic texts utilize various narrative tools, predominantly variations in point of view, shifting pronouns, and distinct characters and voices. Together, these narratives challenge the perceived boundaries between reader, text(s), and world to offer a three-dimensional texture of the ocean that seeks reader engagement and ideally, future action. Like the creatures that cross the shore to sea threshold, the reader-text boundary is bridged. Directly addressing readers or positioning them to imagine through Carson's eyes using "I" is an immersive strategy; the reader feels closer to the text and potentially, the ocean feels less alien and unfamiliar. Carson's writing demonstrates an impulse whereby her own "sense of wonder," curiosity, and awe at the ocean's beauty gently trickles towards the reader's imagination and consciousness. In gently attempting to bridge the reader-text boundary, her subtext becomes clear: while we may not be ocean or shoreline dwellers, the health and fate of humans and the ocean are undeniably and intimately linked. This is central to the eco-philosophy that pervades Carson's three oceanic works. Moreover, she imbues in the reader knowledge, curiosity, and wonder about the ocean. Once read and known, this information cannot be unread and unknown. Through these works and Carson's testimony, the reader subsequently bears responsibility for the ocean's present and its future.

REFERENCES

Bekoff, Marc, and Jan Nystrom. 2004. "The Other Side of Silence: Rachel Carson's Views of Animals." *Human Ecology Review* 11 (2): 186–99.

Bratton, Susan Power. 2004. "Thinking Like a Mackerel: Rachel Carson's *Under the Sea-Wind* as a Source for a Trans-Ecotonal Sea Ethic." *Ethics and the Environment* 9 (1): 3–22.

Carson, Rachel. 1951. *The Sea Around Us*. London: Staples Press Limited.

———. 1962. *Silent Spring*. London: Penguin.

———. 1998 [1955]. *The Edge of the Sea.* New York, NY: Houghton Mifflin.

———. 2007 [1941]. *Under the Sea-Wind*. New York, NY: Penguin.

Fludernik, Monika. 1994. "Introduction: Second-Person Narrative and Related Issues." *Style* 28 (3): 281–311.

Gamerman, Amy. 1994. "Poet faces demons and squabbling publishers." *Wall Street Journal Eastern Edition* May 12: A13.

Hagood, Amanda. 2013. "Wonders with the Sea: Rachel Carson's Ecological Aesthetic and the Mid-Century Reader." *Environmental Humanities* 2 (May): 57–77.

Hubbell, Sue. 1998. "Introduction." In *The Edge of the Sea*, by Rachel Carson, xv-xxi. New York: Houghton Mifflin.

Lear, Linda. 1997. *Rachel Carson: Witness for Nature*. New York: Henry Holt and Company.

———. 2007. "Introduction." In *Under the Sea-Wind*, by Rachel Carson, ix-xv. New York: Penguin.

Lytle, Mark Hamilton. 1997. *The Gentle Subversive: Rachel Carson, Silent Spring and the Rise of the Environmental Movement*. New York: Oxford University Press.

Matthiessen, Peter (ed). 2007. *Courage for the Earth: Writers, Scientists, and Activists Celebrate the Life and Writing of Rachel Carson*. Boston: Houghton Mifflin.

Meiners, Roger, Pierre Desrochers, and Andrew Morriss (ed). 2012. *Silent Spring at 50: The False Crisis of Rachel Carson*. Washington D.C.: Cato Institute.

Murray, Janet. 1998. *Hamlet on the Holodeck: The Future of Narrative in Cyberspace*. New York: MIT Press.

Peters, John Durham. 2001. "Witnessing." *Media and Society* 23: 707–23.

Souder, William. 2012. *On a Farther Shore: The Life and Legacy of Rachel Carson*. New York: Broadway Books.

Steuer, Jonathan. 1992. "Defining Virtual Reality: Dimensions Determining Telepresence." *Journal of Communication*, 42 (4): 73–93. Available online at www.cyborganic.com/People/jonathan/Academia/Papers/Web/defining-vr.html.

Williamson, Henry. 1957. *Salar the Salmon*. London: Faber and Faber.

———. 1978. *Tarka the Otter*. London: Bodley Head.

PART III

Nonhuman Agency/ Representation of the Nonhuman

Chapter 7

The Posthuman Return

Transformation through Stillness in Richard Powers's The Overstory

Owen Harry

Critical posthumanism positions itself emphatically against humanist and anthropocentric perspectives which devalue nonhumans in service to universalizing narratives of human progress. This form of posthumanism, associated primarily with the theoretical and editorial work of Rosi Braidotti, views humanism's erasure of agency from the nonhuman world as contributing directly to global environmental degradation. Wary, however, of the futility of critique without creativity, Braidotti emphasises the affirmative project needed in response: "As far as the posthuman debate is concerned, there are no grounds for plunging into melancholy metaphysical ruminations about the end of the world. We need energizing projects that express generative narratives and do not wallow in the rhetoric of the crisis" (2019, 69). Richard Powers's *The Overstory*, which revolves around nine characters who find themselves, for various reasons, drawn to trees, demonstrates the potentially generative role of literature in affirming nonhuman agency, suggesting also the kinds of posthuman subjectivities required to escape the inherently teleological and exploitative narratives of humanism.

One of the novel's many primary characters, Patricia Westerford, is a botanist who discovers that trees communicate with each other, based on a number of real-life researchers of what is popularly known as the Wood Wide Web (Taylor 2019, 42). Late in the novel, Patricia delivers a conference talk in which she takes the possibility of nonhuman communication further, beyond species boundaries, by claiming that "trees want something from us, just as we've always wanted things from them. This isn't mystical. The 'environment' is alive—a fluid, changing web of purposeful lives dependent on each other" (Powers 2019, 567). *The Overstory* suggests that in order to hear what the nonhuman world wants from us, and to prevent further ecological destruction, humans must become more receptive to the external, agentic world. Restricted, individualist conceptions of selfhood obstruct this receptivity, and so each of Powers's primary characters undergo transformations to become more attentive to the nonhuman world. In its reconceptualization of the self away from classical humanist subjectivity, this transformation can be considered posthuman.[1]

This essay engages with Braidotti's posthuman thinking in explaining how Powers attempts to evade ecologically destructive ideas of human progress by presenting processes of transformation that occur through stillness. I also draw significantly from Powers's interviews, in which he emphasises the didactic intention behind *The Overstory*. I begin by looking at Powers's antipathy towards progress and humanism as anthropocentric forces, and how he resists these through a transformative reconceptualization of the self which undermines monadic individualism. Next, I provide an extended analysis of the role of stillness in provoking transformation in the novel's characters, looking particularly at how it subverts associations of agency with activity, how it encourages receptivity to slower timescales, and how it allows for a non-teleological recognition of connections between humans and nonhumans. Finally, I demonstrate how stillness encourages receptivity to nonhuman agency in the novel, destabilizing the boundaries of the self and cultivating an expanded, posthuman subjectivity. In exploring the dynamics of transformation in *The Overstory*, I aim to emphasize the wider potentialities of *process*-thinking beyond the restrictive and universalist confines of *progress*-thinking.

THE PROBLEM WITH PROGRESS

The Overstory's Douglas Pavlicek, a Vietnam veteran turned environmental activist deciding on the "reasonable" course of action, articulates what may be the key frustration in Powers's novel: "But reason is what's turning all the forests of the world into rectangles" (2019, 454). Reason, for Powers, is embedded in an anthropocentric value system which justifies exploitation and ecological destruction for profit. Reducing the last few ancient redwoods to symmetrical patterns so that they can be commodified and sold is not, after all, unreasonable for the logging companies which Douglas finds himself up against: it makes perfect short-term economic sense. This mechanistic devaluing of nonhumans is in turn perceived to be justified through what the character Ray Brinkman comes to see as "an outright lie, that claim of Kant's:

As far as nonhumans are concerned, we have no direct duties. All exists merely as means to an end. That end is man" (314). Human exceptionalism removes all but instrumental value from the nonhuman world, subordinating nonhumans to mere tools for the fulfillment of human purpose. *The Overstory* condemns the entanglement of Western rationalism with human exceptionalism, meaning that humanism's faith in reason is cast as fundamentally ecologically destructive. Braidotti, in *The Posthuman*, defines humanism as a "doctrine that combines the biological, discursive and moral expansion of human capabilities into an idea of teleologically ordained, rational progress" (2013, 13). Humanism is based on a narrative of perpetual progress that separates humans from the rest of the world in order to enable and justify its domination, a narrative which Powers attacks throughout the novel.

Ideas of progress hegemonize the thinking of even the activist characters, including Adam Appich, who finds himself "left in the insanity of denying the bedrock of human existence. Property and mastery: nothing else counts. Earth will be monetized until all trees grow in straight lines, three people own all seven continents, and every large organism is bred to be slaughtered" (Powers 2019, 434–35). By closely relating the regimented planting of trees to the industrial slaughter of large organisms, Powers indicates the extreme consequences of human exceptionalism for the fates of animals. As a result, Powers's attention to trees rather than animals in the novel should not be seen as a privileged one, as if designed to evade more pressing questions of animal suffering. In response to concerns by animal studies scholars over the inclusion of plant life in biopolitical theory, Jeffrey T. Nealon argues that

> recent research on the Anthropocene has confirmed one thing we can all agree upon: Homo sapiens hasn't been doing the vast majority of other life-forms any favors over the past ten thousand or so years; so going forward, we should at least be clear that life is a mesh of emerging forms, not a competition among preexisting organisms. (2016, 113)

Such a sense of collaboration over competition permeates *The Overstory* and reveals a common project. The novel's attention to a refigured understanding of agency within trees can be read as a radical move which encourages us to take plant life seriously but also has clear consequences for animal agency, attempting to move us far enough beyond anthropocentrism to fuel a much deeper concern for animal life than human exceptionalism allows.

Adam's horror regarding this realized "mastery" over the nonhuman world is exacerbated by the sense that this future is an inevitable one. Progress is seemingly predictive: it sets out a linear path which may be followed to its logical conclusion, in this case the predetermined instrumentalization of all nonhuman life. The entrenchment of the concept of mastery, to the point that Adam perceives it as fundamental to human existence, reflects only the universalizing tendency of humanism. Humanism positions its own European, liberal, individualist ideals as universal ones. In opposition to this, post-structuralism demonstrates the historical constructivism of the humanist conception of "Man." Braidotti refers to this critical motivation as "anti-humanism," consisting of "de-linking the human agent from this universalistic posture, calling him to task, so to speak, on the concrete actions he is enacting" (2013, 23). Upon recognizing the groundlessness of universalizing narratives, the pursuit of mastery can no longer be seen as teleological destiny but only as one possible way of relating to the nonhuman world, one that is clearly unjustifiable when considering the ecological effects of this expression of human agency. Beyond the negative approach of anti-humanism, Braidotti encourages an affirmative posthumanist response: "combin[ing] critique with creativity in the pursuit of alternative visions and projects" (54). While this statement refers to the continued development of posthuman critical theory, the emphasis on creativity suggests an important conceptual role for literature that engages affirmative narratives of post-anthropocentric subjectivity.

As a counter to the instrumentalization of the nonhuman world resulting from humanist narratives of progress, *The Overstory* advocates the development of a heightened ecological sensibility based on such a transformed subjectivity. Literature's role in reflecting or even sustaining anthropocentrism is argued through several metafictional references, including Ray's contention that "the world is failing precisely because no novel can make the contest for the *world* seem as compelling as the struggles between a few lost people" (Powers 2019, 477–78). This is of course self-reflexive: Powers has spoken in interviews about his difficulty in advocating environmentally conscious behavior while writing in a tradition as anthropocentric as the realist novel (Powers 2018a). Indeed, Timothy Clark argues that the representational challenges of the Anthropocene mean that "still-dominant conventions of plotting, characterization and setting in the novel need to be openly acknowledged as pervaded by anthropocentric delusion" (2015, 191). Powers recognizes the existence of environmental conflicts in literature but argues that contemporary literary fiction is "overwhelmingly dominated by the psychological," as if "we believe that all conflict between humans and nonhumans has long ago been decided in favour of omnipotent humanity" (Powers 2018a). The realist novel's psychological focus is described as a kind of solipsism, as in the character Olivia Vandergriff's complaint that characters in an unspecified Victorian novel are "imprisoned in a shoe box, and they have no idea. I just want to shake them and yell, *Get out of yourselves, damn it! Look around!* But they can't, Nicky. Everything alive is just outside their field of view" (Powers 2019, 367). Despite the anthropocentrism of the realist novel, however, Powers attempts to use the form against itself by demonstrating the limitations of the restricted humanist perspective and envisioning alternative ways of engaging with the nonhuman world.

Olivia's exhortation to *"Get out of yourselves"* indicates the problem of the restricted self, sustained by a wider cultural narrative of essentialized individualism that obstructs the recognition of nonhuman value. J. Baird Callicott argues that "the lynchpin which must be pulled before an ecological worldview can coalesce is this insidious monadic individualism and social atomism" (2014, 389). The anthropocentrism which disconnects humans from nonhumans is fundamentally grounded in this restricted, individualist selfhood. Joanna Macy presents a more detailed diagnosis of the problem:

> The crisis that threatens our planet, whether seen from its military, ecological, or social aspect, derives from a dysfunctional and pathological notion of the self. It derives from a mistake about our place in the order of things. It is a delusion that the self is so separate and fragile that we must delineate and defend its boundaries, that it is so small and we so needy that we must endlessly acquire and endlessly consume, and that it is so aloof that as individuals, corporations, nation-states, or species, we can be immune to what we do to other beings. (1991, 187)

Macy's proposed solution is "the greening of the self" (183), a complication of identity that recognizes human interconnections with the nonhuman world. Macy's attempt to imagine a subjectivity beyond monadic individualism resonates with Braidotti's argument that "moving beyond human exceptionalism, subjectivity has to include the relational dependence on multiple non-humans and the planetary dimension as a whole" (2019, 40). Braidotti tends to call this "posthuman subjectivity," transversal in that "we connect but also differ from each other" (45). By relating subjectivity to affect rather than rationality, and to interconnection rather than independence, Braidotti considers the boundaries of the self to be productively blurred through its "power to affect and be affected" by the nonhuman world (54). Reconceptualizing the self in this way aims to provide a corrective to ecologically destructive humanist narratives of progress. The primary characters of *The Overstory*, in their own ways, each undergo a transformation towards posthuman subjectivity. Ray's repudiation of Kantian human exceptionalism, for example, comes after the intellectual property lawyer reads Christopher D. Stone's 1972 article "Should Trees Have Standing?" It is an experience which leads him to feel that "[h]is whole self is dissolving" (Powers 2019, 314). Ray's sense of self has been bound up in ideas of property rights and possession; not only does the proposed extension of rights to nonhumans compromise his profession, it also destabilizes his conception of himself as a monadic individual, separate from the rest of the world.

The reconceptualization of the self that each of the primary characters experience can therefore be considered, in its opposition to humanism and anthropocentrism, a kind of posthuman transformation. It is a transformation, furthermore, that explicitly resists transhumanist progress narratives in which the human represents only the present stage of a continual development towards perfectibility. Cary Wolfe sees this transhumanist impulse as simply a protraction of humanism:

> [P]erhaps *the* fundamental dogma associated with humanism . . . [is] that 'the human' is achieved by escaping or repressing not just its animal origins in nature, the biological, and the evolutionary, but more generally by transcending the bonds of materiality and embodiment altogether. In this respect, my sense of posthumanism is the *opposite* of transhumanism, and in this light, transhumanism should be seen as an *intensification* of humanism. (2010, xiv-xv)

He goes on to argue that "posthumanism in my sense isn't posthuman at all—in the sense of being 'after' our embodiment has been transcended—but is only posthuman*ist*, in the sense that it opposes the fantasies of disembodiment and autonomy, inherited from humanism itself" (xv). Despite his concerns about the transcendent ambitions of humanism and transhumanism, however, Wolfe does not target humanism's underlying narrative of progress in any sustained way. This is a key criticism of Richard Grusin's, who claims that even posthumanist theorists like Wolfe and Braidotti "oscillate between seeing the posthuman as a new stage in human development and seeing it as calling attention to the inseparability of human and nonhuman" (2015, ix). Grusin argues for distancing the concept from teleological progress itself. If posthumanism is to conform to its own insistence on the "embodiment and embeddedness of the human being" (Wolfe 2010, xv),[2] it must involve an explicit critique of the idea that progress must necessarily be on humanist terms, thus predicated on separation, disembodiment, and dematerialisation. In *The Overstory*, Powers cultivates an idea of "progress" as something that occurs without active struggle towards achievement within a linear historical narrative of transcendence. He does so by representing the transformations of subjectivity which occur through practices of stillness.

STILLNESS

The capacity for stillness to provoke transformation is first signified in *The Overstory* through its associations with meditation and enlightenment. The seemingly paradoxical connection between stillness and change is featured right from the prologue of the novel, with the line "[a] thing can travel everywhere, just by holding still." The pine tree that Mimi Ma leans against transmits this knowledge to her "in words before words" (2019, 3). Mimi listens, and in her meditative stillness she becomes increasingly receptive to this kind of inter-species communication, opening up her anthropocentric perspective to include a greater awareness of the nonhuman world. Mimi has been well prepared for this silent communication: her job as a therapist entails what she calls "endurance staring" in which therapist and client maintain eye contact for hours on end, mutually revealing truths without words, an experience which provokes change in both (499). Through these experiences, Mimi understands the connection between stillness and transformation: "[s]he has practiced, for years, on humans, holding still, doing nothing but letting herself be looked at. Now she takes the skill outside" (609). Her application of this technique to nonhumans allows for an experience of inter-species communication which results in Mimi's reconceptualised understanding of her own self. The image of Mimi sitting on the ground under the pine tree recalls, of course, the Buddha's attainment of *nirvana* under the Bo tree, a connection made explicit when this episode is returned to at the end of the novel: "At midnight, on this hillside, perched in the dark above this city with her pine standing in for a Bo, Mimi gets enlightened" (621). Mimi is subsequently described as an "altered woman" (622), transformation here being effected through remaining still and becoming receptive to the world around her.

Stillness, in *The Overstory*, is positioned as a radical alternative to the striving associated with modernity and consumer culture. This opposition is most clearly delineated in the description of Ray and his partner Dorothy Cazaly's differing personalities after Ray suffers a stroke which paralyses him almost entirely:

> It strikes her that she envies him. His years of enforced tranquillity, the patience of his slowed mind, the expansion of his blinkered senses. He can watch the dozen bare trees in the backyard for hours and see something intricate and surprising, sufficient to his desires, while she—she is still trapped in a hunger that rushes past everything. (Powers 2019, 573)

Dorothy's "hunger" manifests as a hedonistic need for continual excitement, from her impulse to "[g]o backpacking in South America for two years. Move to the Village and take drugs. Get involved with a light plane pilot who moonlights for the CIA" to her later extramarital affair which she considers a way to "absorb her excess energy" (85, 314). Dorothy considers her sense of self and her agency to be contingent on her constant activity. In an earlier interview for *The Paris Review*, Powers resists this belief: "the idea that drives our society right now ... is about changing the future, being an agent, getting and taking charge of your destiny and altering it" (2002). Ray can no longer participate in this agentic activity due to his disability. This forces him into another mode of being, in which he cannot enact his will over the world as before but can only sit still and watch the scenes unfolding through his window. In caring for Ray, Dorothy, too, becomes attuned to this slower pace of being, their shared act of reading itself an alternative to the incessant striving of consumer culture. For Powers, reading, as a form of "productive solitude," is antithetical to the idea of agency as activity: "reading and writing [is] suspect in the eyes of the market economy. ... It's an invisible, sedate, almost inert process. ... The destiny of a written narrative is outside the realm of the time. For so long as you are reading, you are also outside the realm of the time" (2002). Later in the novel, even this reading gives way to "the two of them holding still and watching" (Powers 2019, 574). With literature acting as a gateway to receptivity, Dorothy joins Ray in recognizing, through stillness, a vitality unfolding in their backyard which contests exclusive associations of agency with narrow definitions of activity.

In their receptive stillness, Mimi, Ray, and Dorothy each experience some level of attunement to the slower timescales of the nonhuman world, which appears necessary for reconceptualizing the self away from human exceptionalism. Lawrence Buell argues that environmentalism must cultivate "firmer internalization of the brevity of Anthropocene time as an eyeblink of Earth time" in order to be politically persuasive (2016, 417). He goes on to posit that "posthumanism has the potential for further needful reconception of environmental memory against the backdrop of human embeddedness in deep time that the revolution in geology began and Darwinian evolution made irreversible" (418). As Rob Nixon has made clear in his landmark work on "slow violence," environmental crises have been brought on by a lack of attention to the long-term, gradual damage inflicted on the world by human activity, with "calamitous repercussions playing out across a range of temporal scales" (2011, 2). These crises include "[c]limate change, the thawing cryosphere, toxic drift, biomagnification, deforestation, the radioactive aftermaths of wars, acidifying oceans, and a host of other slowly unfolding environmental catastrophes," all of which "present formidable representational obstacles that can hinder our efforts to mobilize and act decisively" (2). Powers highlights the gap between human and nonhuman timescales throughout the novel. As with the fable of the boiling frog, Ray reflects that "[l]ife will cook; the seas will rise. The planet's lungs will be ripped out. And the law will let this happen, because harm was never imminent enough. *Imminent*, at the speed of people, is too late. The law must judge *imminent* at the speed of trees" (Powers 2019, 619). The brutal imagery here describes a violence that is ultimately rendered invisible to humans in that it is "incremental and accretive" from an anthropocentric perspective (Nixon 2011, 2).

In order to imaginatively bridge this gap, literature may play an important role. In response to the complex global problems emerging, Clark writes that "[a] supremely important task for modern literature and for criticism becomes for them to find ways of representing this new reality of elusive agencies and distant or invisible wrongs, happening at counterintuitive scales, and to do so in ways that are engaging, credible and pertinent" (2019, 84). Powers explores some possibilities for prose narrative to represent nonhuman timescales. As a child, computer programmer Neelay Mehta reads a story which he summarizes as follows:

> Aliens land on Earth. They're little runts, as alien races go. But they metabolize like there's no tomorrow. They zip around like swarms of gnats, too fast to see—so fast that Earth seconds seem to them like years. To them, humans are nothing but sculptures of immobile meat. The foreigners try to communicate, but there's no reply. Finding no signs of intelligent life, they tuck into the frozen statues and start curing them like so much jerky, for the long ride home. (Powers 2019, 121–22)

In this parody of anthropocentric timescales, Powers recalls the allegorical potential of science fiction. In order to articulate the problem through the realist mode, however, he begins the novel by tracing the saga of the Hoel family across several generations and, concurrently, the life of a single American chestnut tree. Only by Nicholas Hoel flipping through a vast stack of photographs of the tree, taken by his forebears one month apart for seventy-five years, can the growth of the tree be properly apprehended. In its temporal flexibility, prose narrative has the potential to represent nonhuman vitalities unfolding on altogether different timescales than those of humans, encouraging practices of attentive stillness to replicate such awareness.

Holding still and becoming receptive to the world allows for a recognition of connections between the individual and the external world. The ecological consciousness attained by the characters in the novel is largely catalyzed by various forms of loss, including the loss of Ray's mobility, Adam's sister, and Nick's entire family. The trauma of Nick's loss isolates him even further; he lives like a hermit on the family farm until Olivia leads him to California, and to activism. During one of the group's acts of sabotage against logging companies, Nick spray paints the words "CONTROL KILLS / CONNECTION HEALS" on the wall of a trailer, then "steps back to appraise the germ of the only thing he knows for certain" (Powers 2019, 434). The restorative power of connection, for Nick, is taken as a basic truth, indeed the only basic truth. It suggests his human connection to Olivia and the rest of the group—signified by a root metaphor: "[a] thought joins them, underground, as thoughts do so often now" (429)—but goes beyond this to a more fundamental connection that transcends both individual and species. In their work on material ecocriticism, Serenella Iovino and Serpil Oppermann argue that

> literature can be used as an effective discourse crucial to enhanc[ing] moral and environmental imagination. . . . All narratives that explore and challenge the borders between the 'inner' self and the 'outer' world in terms of materiality, of causality, of intertwined agency are *de facto* part of a project of liberation—a cultural, ecological, ontological, and material liberation. (2012, 87)

The recognition of connection that emerges through stillness is not only a way of alleviating ecological destruction but also a necessary part of human liberation from the restricted sense of self that underpins the need for domination and hierarchy. Nick's spray-painted slogan, then, may be considered the core premise of the novel.

Powers often makes use of anthropomorphism as a technique to represent his characters' connections with the nonhuman world. This is most apparent in the descriptions of trees "waving," such as when Nick observes a row of California sycamores *"raking their fingers in the air. Waving and swelling like a gospel choir"* (Powers 2019, 412). Kari Weil argues that while "crude" forms of anthropomorphism are rightly criticized for their narcissism and their erasure of difference, this should not occlude the possibility of a productive "critical anthropomorphism" in which "we open ourselves to touch and to be touched by others as fellow subjects and may imagine their pain, pleasure, and need in anthropomorphic terms, but stop short of believing that we can know their experience" (2012, 19–20). What remains forceful in Powers's representations of trees is a sense of alterity that resists attempts to definitively know or identify with the nonhuman other, without turning away entirely from the prospect of recognizing similarities. Indeed, anthropomorphism in the novel is reciprocated by a corresponding *dendromorphism* whereby humans are ascribed tree-like qualities, as in the description of Douglas's "finger waving like a twig in the breeze" (Powers 2019, 562–63). Iovino and Oppermann argue that

> the humanization of things, places, natural elements, nonhuman animals, is not necessarily the sign of an anthropocentric and hierarchical vision but can be a narrative expedient intended to stress the agentic power of matter and the horizontality of its elements. If conceived in this critical perspective, anthropomorphizing representations can reveal similarities and symmetries between the human and the nonhuman. (2012, 82)

The use of anthropomorphism in *The Overstory* is not in service of human superiority but rather underscores a non-hierarchical connection across species. Powers's target of criticism is an anthropocentric perspective that cannot sufficiently recognize either alterity or similarity. The absolute instrumentalization of nonhumans means that they are not valued as earth others: they can be "known" with uncritical certainty and dismissively subordinated. For Powers, revealing isomorphic connections between humans and nonhumans encourages a sense of collaboration which undermines human exceptionalism.

The possibility of transformation through stillness contests narratives of progress which suggest that the posthuman is part of a teleological process of development. Powers looks instead back to mythology in order to articulate posthuman transformation. The necessity of transformation to allow inter-species connection comes through the trees' message to Mimi: "If your mind were only a slightly greener thing, we'd drown you in meaning" (Powers 2019, 4). The commanding presence in Patricia's thinking of the opening line of Ovid's *Metamorphoses*, "*Let me sing to you now, about how people turn into other things*" (Powers 2019, 147), suggests to her the possibility of transformation beyond the isolated human. Patricia comes to find the same kinds of stories in every culture, wherever in the world she travels, as if they encompass a forgotten knowledge of inter-species connection:

> The word turns odd, foreign in her head. *Myth. Myth.* A mispronunciation. A malaprop. Memories posted forward from people standing on the shores of the great human departure from everything else that lives. Send-off telegrams composed by skeptics of the planned escape, saying, *Remember* this, *thousands of years from now, when you can see nothing but yourself, everywhere you look.* (492)

The species loneliness produced by human estrangement from the nonhuman world is figured here as a relatively recent phenomenon, with the transitional period enshrined in classical literature and mythology. A complementary passage occurs earlier in the novel regarding Olivia: "She must still discover that myths are basic truths twisted into mnemonics, instructions posted from the past, memories waiting to become predictions" (201). The role of myth as a mnemonic implies that *Metamorphoses* and its cross-cultural counterparts possess important, fundamental knowledge, and that awareness about inter-species connection must not only be theorized but remembered.

While Grusin's disavowal of teleology leads him to suggest the phrase "nonhuman turn" as an alternative to the posthuman one (2015, ix), it may be better to consider Powers's looking back to myth for guidance in reconceptualizing the self as a posthuman *re*turn, in which the progressive sense of the turning of a wheel is replaced by a return to understandings that have been overshadowed by other ideologies since "the great human departure" (Powers 2019, 492). This is not an entirely nostalgic approach, nor does it uncritically idealize the primitive condition, since technology plays an important role in this project. Powers has spoken in interviews of being inspired to write the novel while teaching at Stanford University. There, in Palo Alto, he found himself in between Silicon Valley and the giant redwoods of the Santa Cruz Mountains, a seemingly stark nature/culture opposition which he attempts to bridge in *The Overstory* (Powers 2018a). Neelay turns his coding expertise and vision to the development of algorithmic "learners" which mine the digital landscape in order to discover connections between life-forms and possible solutions for environmental degradation (Powers 2019, 600). In an interview for the *Chicago Review of Books*, Powers explains the possible consequences of this application of computation:

> Paradoxically, our drive to build machines that perform billions of calculations a second has enabled us, for the first time, to begin to model events on scales of time far outside our own and to translate and visualize the changes that take place in ecosystems at the speed of trees. That's why Silicon Valley also plays an important role in *The Overstory*. If there's any hope of human survival, it probably lies in our 'descendants' teaching us to see, if not to feel, the scales of time our 'ancestors' operate in. (2018c)

While this suggests a faith in the techno-optimism of Silicon Valley, it also indicates Powers's understanding that the progressive, technological attempt at continually moving forward will only find success in mitigating the effects of the environmental crisis by encouraging us to shift attention to the slower timescales of trees. Grusin, in his explanation of the non-teleological "nonhuman turn," emphasises an understanding of "turn" in the alternative, embodied sense of a "shift of attention, interest, or concern" (2015, xx). In proposing a "posthuman return," I argue that transformation of the concept of self need not be progressive and teleological but achievable through a return to attention, and that the characters in *The Overstory* exemplify this transformative return by simply holding still.

NONHUMAN AGENCY

In demonstrating that the restricted, individualist self may be reconceptualised through stillness, without falling back on humanist narratives of progress, Powers disconnects human agency from its associations with activity. As well as this, the emphasis on stillness foregrounds silence in a way that subverts the humanist coupling of agency and value to the apparently exclusively human capacity for language. This privileging of language as a marker of agency means that the apparent silence of animals and plants is effectively used as justification for their absolute reduction to instrumental value alone. The novel suggests that practicing stillness allows for the quieting of human-centered sound, enabling receptivity to the "voice" of nonhumans. This opens the way for recognizing the agency of nonhuman organisms which lack either the mobility or the capacity for language of humans. In an interview for *The Guardian*, Powers argues that "[u]ntil it's exciting and fun and ecstatic to think that everything else has agency and is reciprocally connected we're going to be terrified and afraid of death, and it's mastery or nothing" (2018b). The apparent inability on the part of trees to act, at least in ways similar to humans, renders them in the humanist imagination as mere objects, inert and passive, fair game for human exploitation. Powers opposes this destructive objectification, using trees as representatives for this "everything else" in *The Overstory* and emphasizing their nonhuman agentic power in his representations. Powers's thinking resonates with the posthumanist rethinking of agency, which rejects the humanist association of agency with human subjectivity alone. Patrice Haynes argues that "for all its fuzziness, the concept of agency is typically considered to encompass notions of selfhood, rationality, choice, intention, will, autonomy and independence" (2014, 133), a definition which tends to limit its application solely to humans. This restriction of agency from nonhumans has clear consequences for environmental exploitation. According to Jeffrey Scott Marchand, posthumanist critics reject humanism's transcendent understanding of agency, in favour of a "much more mundane, material sense of what it means to act or to intervene and produce sometimes unforeseeable effects, in a lively and agential more-than-human network of relationality" (2018, 294). Redefining agency in this way forms part of an attempt to productively blur the boundaries between humans and nonhumans, undercutting human exceptionalism.

Braidotti builds her post-anthropocentrism on an understanding of vitality which emphasises the relation of agency to affect. She argues that "intelligent vitality" is defined "as a force that is not confined within feedback loops internal to the human self, but is present in all living matter" (2013, 60). In dissociating agency from its exclusively human applications, the "vitalist approach to living matter displaces the boundary between the portion of life ... that has traditionally been reserved for *anthropos*, that is to say *bios*, and the wider scope of animal and non-human life, also known as *zoe*" (60). Braidotti's redefinition of vitality is grounded in the philosophy of Gilles Deleuze and Félix Guattari. Jane Bennett, discussing the influence of Deleuze and Guattari on her own vital materialism, explains that they "highlighted the positive or productive power of things to draw other bodies near and conjoin powers" (2015, 225). Powers's representations of trees line up well with this account of agency. The capacity for nonhumans to draw humans near is expressed in the various ways that the characters interact with trees, perhaps most apparently in the pine tree's invitation to both Mimi and the reader in the prologue: "*The pine she leans against says*: Listen. There's something you need to hear" (Powers 2019, 4). Nonhuman agency in immobile organisms becomes discernible to the characters in *The Overstory* only when the restricted, domineering, incessantly active self has been stilled for a moment and becomes receptive to the external world.

In this understanding of vitality, the anthropocentric and hierarchical schema of an active human subject acting upon a passive nonhuman object is not simply reversed in order to acknowledge the affective force of the latter upon the former; rather, it is a recognition of reciprocal flows of agency which invite collaboration between humans and nonhumans. The agentic capacity of nonhumans to not only "draw other bodies near" but also to "conjoin powers" indicates the transformative power of stillness on conceptualizations of the self. Bennett goes on to state that "for Deleuze and Guattari, people, places, and things forge heterogeneous connections and form something like a compound, extended mind" (2015, 226). In Haynes's definition, "[t]he term assemblage captures the idea that bodies, that is, material objects, do not exist and act in isolation from each other but establish dynamic, protean groupings which constitute the rich, diverse ecologies that are the very condition of any particular thing" (2014, 134). Powers's emphasis on connection likewise attempts to overcome the perceived isolation of the self from its environment in favour of representing assemblages. The "presences" that frequently appear in Olivia's vicinity, guiding her actions, are at once material and tree-like, such as when they "run their twigs up the back of her neck," and also ethereal: "Beings of light I can't see" (Powers 2019, 214, 221). They speak as representatives of a planetary consciousness which is concerned about the fate of life itself, and, after "the night of her transformation" (220), become a part of Olivia's expanded subjectivity.

This expanded subjectivity is fundamental to the posthuman project, and vital for responding to the environmental crisis. Braidotti argues that "there is a direct connection between monism, the unity of all living matter and post-anthropocentrism as a general frame of reference for contemporary subjectivity" (2013, 57). This monistic understanding of self, which properly recognizes that humans share a common materiality with nonhumans, should not be thought of as a holism, in which the sphere of self-interest is expanded and differences between objects are elided; rather, for Braidotti, the recognition of nonhuman agency is tied to a transformation of self towards a posthuman subjectivity which includes other (human and nonhuman) agents, emphasizing relationality and opposing human exceptionalism (85–86). Braidotti claims that the current challenge for critical theory is to "visualize the subject as a transversal entity encompassing the human, our genetic neighbours the animals and the earth as a whole, and to do so within an understandable language" (82). Powers experiments with techniques for visualizing posthuman subjectivity as an assemblage through the conventional form of the realist novel. At the end of *The Overstory*, Nick moves through a forest, creating a vast sculpture out of branches, logs and trunks that have fallen on the ground. His sense of self has been expanded over the course of the novel, and he acts as if he is carrying out the will of his materials: "He looks at the kinks and camber of each fallen limb and waits for it to tell him where, in the river of wood coursing across the ground, it wants to be" (604). The single, gigantic word he spells out across the forest floor is "STILL" (624), and his monistic awareness is indicated in the assertion that this is "the word life has been saying, since the beginning" (625). The agency and vitality of the nonhuman world is expressed in its call for stillness, and it is only through Nick's newfound receptivity that he gains the ability to listen.

CONCLUSION

While stillness is typically associated with inaction or quietism, Braidotti and Powers indicate that this perspective is part of the larger problem. Stillness may be better thought of as enabling political action by cultivating receptive posthuman subjectivities which resist humanist narratives of separation and domination. The receptive awareness of nonhuman agency enabled by stillness animates ethical concern, marking not a fearful extinguishing of all human activity in favour of perceiving a pristine "natural" world without the intrusion of the otherworldly human, but rather a practice which better allows for the recognition of connections between humans and nonhumans, the material consequences of human action, and the possibility of more responsible practices which contribute instead to the mutual becoming of the human-nonhuman world. In a time in which the environmental crisis is often portrayed as a problem which future technological advancement will resolve, *The Overstory* demonstrates that the root of the problem, anthropocentrism, may be overcome with nothing more technological than what we currently possess, the ability to hold still and pay attention to the nonhuman world. While humanist narratives dominate conventional thinking, justifying exploitation and isolating the individual, *The Overstory* represents a counter-narrative that evokes the vitality of the nonhuman world. The novel's characters undergo posthuman transformations that increase their awareness of the otherwise imperceptible connections between humans and nonhumans, and demonstrate that human subjectivity must be expanded in conjunction with the recognition of nonhuman agency. In opposition to the incessant striving encouraged by humanist narratives of progress, which underpin fantasies of human transcendence to the detriment of the nonhuman world, Powers indicates that these aims can be achieved through practices of stillness and receptivity, as part of a posthuman return to attention.

REFERENCES

Bennett, Jane. 2015. "Systems and Things: On Vital Materialism and Object-Oriented Philosophy." In *The Nonhuman Turn*, ed. Richard Grusin, 223–39. Minneapolis, MN: University of Minnesota Press.
Braidotti, Rosi. 2013. *The Posthuman*. Cambridge: Polity
———. 2019. *Posthuman Knowledge*. Cambridge: Polity.
Buell, Lawrence. 2016. "Can Environmental Imagination Save the World?" In *A Global History of Literature and the Environment*, ed. John Parnham and Louise Westling, 407–22. Cambridge: Cambridge University Press.
Callicott, J. Baird. 2014. "Afterword: Recontextualizing the Self in Comparative Environmental Philosophy." In *Environmental Philosophy in Asian Traditions of Thought*, ed. J. Baird Callicott and James McRae, 377–90. Alban, NY: State University of New York Press.
Clark, Timothy. 2015. *Ecocriticism on the Edge: The Anthropocene as a Threshold Concept*. London: Bloomsbury.
———. 2019. *The Value of Ecocriticism*. Cambridge: Cambridge University Press.
Grusin, Richard. 2015. "Introduction." In *The Nonhuman Turn*, edited by Richard Grusin, vii-xxix. Minneapolis, MN: University of Minnesota Press.
Haynes, Patrice. 2014. "Creative Becoming and the Patiency of Matter: Feminism, New Materialism and Theology." *Angelaki: Journal of the Theoretical Humanities* 19 (1): 129–50. doi.org/10.1080/0969725X.2014.920633.
Iovino, Serenella, and Serpil Oppermann. 2012. "Material Ecocriticism: Materiality, Agency, and Models of Narrativity." *Ecozon@* 3(1) (Spring 2012): 75–91. doi.org/10.37536/ECOZONA.2012.3.1.452.
Macy, Joanna. 1991. *World as Lover, World as Self*. Berkeley: Parallax Press.
Marchand, Jeffrey Scott. 2018. "Non-human Agency." In *Posthuman Glossary*, ed. Rosi Braidotti and Maria Hlavajova, 292–95. London: Bloomsbury.
Nealon, Jeffrey T. 2016. *Plant Theory: Biopower and Vegetable Life*. Stanford, CA: Stanford University Press.
Nixon, Rob. 2011. *Slow Violence and the Environmentalism of the Poor*. Cambridge, MA: Harvard University Press.
Powers, Richard. 2002. "The Art of Fiction No. 175." Interview by Kevin Berger. *Paris Review*, no. 164 (Winter 2002–3): 106–38. www.theparisreview.org/interviews/298/the-art-of-fiction-no-175-richard-powers.
———. 2018a. "Here's to Unsuicide: An Interview with Richard Powers." Interview by Everett Hamner. *LA Review of Books*, April 7, 2018. lareviewofbooks.org/article/heres-to-unsuicide-an-interview-with-richard-powers.

———. 2018b. "Richard Powers: 'We're completely alienated from everything else alive.'" Interview by Emma John. *The Guardian*, June 16, 2018. www.theguardian.com/books/2018/jun/16/richard-powers-interview-overstory.

———. 2018c. "Richard Powers: Writing 'The Overstory' Quite Literally Changed My Life." Interview by Amy Brady. *Chicago Review of Books*, April 18, 2018. chireviewofbooks.com/2018/04/18/overstory-richard-powers-interview.

———. 2019. *The Overstory*. London: Vintage. First published 2018 by W. W. Norton (New York).

Stone, Christopher D. 1972. "Should Trees Have Standing?—Toward Legal Rights for Natural Objects." *Southern California Law Review*, 45: 450–501.

Taylor, Bron. 2019. "Animism, Tree-Consciousness, and the Religion of Life: Reflections on Richard Powers' *The Overstory*." *Minding Nature* 12(1) (Winter 2019): 42–47. www.humansandnature.org/animism-tree-consciousness-and-the-religion-of-life-reflections-on-richard-powers-the-overstory.

Weil, Kari. 2012. *Thinking Animals: Why Animal Studies Now?* New York, NY: Columbia University Press.

Wolfe, Cary. 2010. *What Is Posthumanism?* Minneapolis, MN: University of Minnesota Press.

———. 2018. "Posthumanism." In *Posthuman Glossary*, ed. Rosi Braidotti and Maria Hlavajova, 356–59. London: Bloomsbury.

NOTES

1. Cary Wolfe, contributing to Rosi Braidotti and Maria Hlavajova's *Posthuman Glossary*, criticizes the term "posthuman" partly because it suggests the inclusion of transhumanist thinkers, who advocate transcending materiality and embodiment altogether in the pursuit of technologically augmented immortality beyond the mere "human." Seeing in this desire only a direct continuation of classical humanist ideals, he instead encourages "posthumanism" as a more specific critique of humanism's dualistic and destructive fantasies (2018, 356–58). However, Braidotti uses "posthuman" as a marker of the convergence between posthumanism (criticizing humanism in line with contemporary continental philosophy) and post-anthropocentrism (criticizing species hierarchy and human exceptionalism) (2019, 2). When I use the term, it is in line with Braidotti's definition because of this explicit dual emphasis, and because her articulation of posthuman subjectivity continually stresses the idea of the posthuman as "materially embodied and embedded" (5), thus protecting against Wolfe's concern about associating with transhumanism.

2. This phrase is used by Wolfe to explain his understanding of posthumanism as something that comes before humanism as well as after it. As previously noted, Braidotti often uses "embodied and embedded" to describe the posthuman subject (2019, 45).

Chapter 8

Classifying Monsters

Vera Veldhuizen

At the end of Orson Scott Card's *Ender's Game* (1985), the titular Ender, at the age of eleven, has unwittingly committed xenocide. This term, meaning genocide of an entire species, later becomes central to the Ender Tetralogy science fiction series, as humanity attempts to overcome its sins of the past and find a redemption in their relationships with other lifeforms.

> For the first time since the Xenocide of the Buggers by the monstrous Ender, humans had found intelligent alien life. The piggies were technologically primitive, but they used tools and built houses and spoke a language. "It is another chance God has given us," declared Archcardinal Pio of Baía. "We can be redeemed for the destruction of the buggers." (Card 1991a, xxix)

The aliens discovered and described in science fiction go beyond nonhuman animals; they are truly Other, both far removed from our reality and monstrously, uncannily close to our Earthly cohabitants. Yet, it is precisely this "logical extreme" aspect of alien encounter narratives which foregrounds the moral complexity of human engagement with the Other, both nonhuman animals and humans themselves. Alien encounter narratives thus inevitably broach the question of the Self and the Other, as human and nonhuman beings are conceptualized and compared by the reader (Malmgren 1993, 15).

Because the genre of science fiction is speculative by definition, narratives can push the boundaries of empathy and explore the impact this may have on empathy beyond the limits of realist fiction or nonfiction, whilst cognitively engaging the reader as if it was real life (Stockwell 2002, 152). The experiences we have and the lessons we learn through fiction, including science fiction, can greatly influence our worldview, shaping the way we view the Other, be they human or not. Through (science) fiction, we can stretch the boundaries of our empathic abilities, find intense cognitive development, and revisit events whenever desired (Veldhuizen 2019, 17). Additionally, as argued by Sherryl Vint, science fiction in particular has a large capability for assessing and questioning animal agency and what it means to be human (2010, 6). Foregrounding difference, in the way that alien encounter narratives do specifically, highlights the issues that come from Othering for the reader, enhancing the probability that the reader considers these issues. That the Other is an alien does not matter for this function; as argued by Gomel:

> The alien in SF is a lever to break open the confines of what Nietzsche called "human, all too human". It is a trope of ontological alterity, a way for our culture to come to terms with the radical otherness of the Universe and with what Jean-François Lyotard [1991] called "the inhuman" within the psyche. (2014, 6)

Although it is in itself an anthropocentric perspective to view the alien as a means for humanity to learn about itself, to reduce the Other to being "simply human beings with tentacles" (Gomel 2014, 9) is how most science fiction depicts aliens. Generally, the alien is depicted as knowable, enough like humanity for them to be a mirror for our own hopes and failures, yet enough unlike humanity to allow us to utterly destroy them. By conceiving the alien Other through human imagination and capturing them in human texts, they are "filtered through human consciousness and language" (Vint 2010, 4), creating a double-bind of anthropocentrist imaginings of the Other. Especially in light of current concerns regarding humanity's treatment of the Other, literature which actively reflects on our treatment of the (nonhuman) Other can be an aid in enhancing engagement and responsibility. Science fiction, which has been dubbed both the genre of change (Landon 1997) and of "cognitive estrangement" (Suvin 1979) is therefore especially interesting for animal studies, as it puts the reader in a position where they are forced beyond the human perspective. Empathizing with, and therefore attempting to understand the cognitive and moral aspects of, the alien Other trains the reader to consider both the human and nonhuman Other in their extra-textual life.

Concern for empathy and moral responsibility is foregrounded throughout the Ender Tetralogy; the first book's xenocide of the Formics, the first true alien Other humanity encountered, is considered a great sin which frames every single encounter with alien lifeforms thereafter. This perceived shared guilt leads to the creation of a system which serves to provide guidelines for and justify behavior towards the Other; rules are now in place, and although the Other may seem terrifyingly unknowable, humanity has designed a protocol for what is ethical in their conduct. This protocol is grounded in anthropocentric conceptions of intelligence and sentience, based on which appropriate levels of violence and intimacy are determined. Yet this is pushed upon the

Other to adopt as well. In *Alien Encounters: Anatomy of Science Fiction,* Mark Rose argues that the main paradigm of the alien encounter genre (which the Ender Tetralogy is a part of) is confrontation-based, and although the alien can be either positively or negatively portrayed, it is always subordinated to anthropocentric moral frameworks (1981, 41). This can be observed in the Ender Tetralogy as well, as a protocol which is based entirely on Othering (and thus potentially limiting empathy) forces the Other to be morally colonized, and to classify themselves in a system which considers humanity as the peak of existence.

This systematically hierarchical approach is first introduced in the second book, *Speaker for the Dead* (1986), which is also the first to demonstrate the full complexity of categorizing Otherness and ethics. This protocol, dubbed "Demosthenes' Hierarchy of Exclusion" (145) is both upheld and challenged throughout not only *Speaker*, but the rest of the series also. Yet the inherent hypocrisy of prescribing morality on the alien Other based on not only human criteria, but human sin and guilt as well, remains in the background, living in the narrative gaps. In this chapter, I examine how this Hierarchy of Exclusion balances empathy and morality, and the ways through which it is both challenged and supported in *Speaker*. I argue that any human-made approach to nonhuman classification and morality is inherently flawed and anthroponormative. For clarity's sake, I focus my analysis on the three main nonhuman species encountered in this specific book, although I draw on the other books for elucidation when necessary.

CLOSE CONTACT

Alien encounter narratives, like *Speaker,* foreground the issue of in- and outgroup empathy. The basic foundation of in- and outgroup empathy theory is that we as humans as a form of reflex group others as either like us, or unlike us, and have either increased or decreased empathy with the Other because of this grouping. I focus here on human empathy as the Hierarchy of Exclusion is explicitly anthropocentric.[1]

Empirical research has shown that humans have a clear preference for those they consider as more or less like themselves (Prinz 2011, 226), their in- and outgroup respectively. The membership of these groups can be decided in a manner we may consider quite arbitrary; some research projects create group membership simply by dividing children up into two named groups, like group A and group B (Dunham et al 2011). People may base their group membership on any identity marker. There are nigh infinite ways to divide ourselves up into in- and outgroups, which we all do both constantly and almost instantly upon learning of others.

One of the key elements of in- and outgroup empathy is that we are more positive about our in group members. Research has demonstrated that not only do we prefer people we identify as ingroup (Decety 2015, 4), we are also more likely to interpret their emotions in a positive way (Bennett et al. 2004, 135). Our interpretation of these emotions is also heavily skewed based on group membership; empirical research has demonstrated that emotion recognition is higher for those who are from our ingroup (especially culturally and racially) than for those who are not (Elfenbein and Ambady 2002). This has direct implications for people's lives and safety, as research has also demonstrated that white viewers of a video of a white man pushing a black man consider that to be playful and harmless, whereas a black man pushing a white man is considered aggressive and dangerous (Kunda 1999, 347). Similarly, people are more likely to aid ingroup members and harm outgroup members (Kteily et al. 2014).

According to Hogan we are more likely to empathize with our ingroup because we view them as human and well-rounded as characters, whereas the outgroup is rigidly Other, "flatter" characters (2011, 37). A problem with in- and outgroup categorization between humans is that it relies on a "single axis framework" (Crenshaw 1989, 140), meaning that it is not intersectional by nature. Additionally, group membership is flexible and dependent on context (Hogan 2011, 71; Decety 2015, 4). This issue may seem moot in the face of the true Other: the alien life form. However, even species membership can be flexible. As argued by Kay Peggs:

> Although organic differences exist among all animals (human and nonhuman), the 'key' division between human and nonhuman animals is founded in scientific categorizations of hierarchical differences that are a display of human identity, since hierarchical distinctions between 'us' and 'them' are founded in, I argue, judgements and choices rather than in naturally occurring scientifically verifiable hierarchical divisions. (2009, 86)

The recognition that identity markers previously seen as inflexible, such as gender (Butler 1999) or sex, are performative, provides for more mental flexibility in this regard. This is because it foregrounds our behaviors and culture as not *based on* a pre-existing identity; instead, behaviors and culture *form* our identities (Loxley 2007, 118). Species identity, like gender identity, can be viewed as performative (Lloyd 2005, 38–39). Speculative fiction, which allows for enhanced identity flexibility, especially blurs the predetermined boundaries between the ingroup of one species and their outgroup consisting of other species.

HIERARCHY OF EXCLUSION

Although speculative fiction allows for enhanced species flexibility, in- and outgroup empathy remains particularly problematic from a (human) moral perspective, as demonstrated in the Ender Tetralogy. *Speaker for the Dead* is the first novel in the series in which humans attempt to engage in a potentially peaceful fashion with the alien Other, based on the guidelines put forward in the Hierarchy of Exclusion. This hierarchy, devised by Ender's sister under the pseudonym Demosthenes, is widely adopted across the human worlds by the time Ender arrives at Lusitania, the pequeninos' planet.

The Nordic language recognizes four orders of foreignness. The first is the otherlander, or utlänning, the stranger that we recognize as being a human of our world, but of another city or country. The second is the framling— Demosthenes merely drops the accent from the Nordic främling. This is the stranger that we recognize as human, but of another world. The third is the raman, the stranger that we recognize as human, but of another species. The fourth is the true alien, the varelse, which includes all the animals, for with them no conversation is possible. They live, but we cannot guess what purposes or causes make them act. They might be intelligent, they might be self-aware, but we cannot know it (Card 1986/1991a, 34).

It is immediately obvious that this hierarchy is anthropocentric, both departing from anthroponormativity and viewing humanity as the top of the hierarchy. Two of the four categories included in this hierarchy of alienness are human; the *utlänning* from a community different from our own, and the *framling* from a world different from our own. This makes sense as it is a human hierarchy of likeness, but it becomes increasingly problematic as non-human species also adopt the concepts and their inherent anthropocentricity.[2]

The desire or need to assign a degree of alienness logically follows human in- and outgroup empathy reflexes, and is observable across science fiction, including science fiction scholarship. Gregory Benford distinguishes between the anthropocentric alien, the alienness of which stems from a caricature of the human, and the unknowable alien, which is fundamentally alien and has an "essential strangeness" (1980, 53; 56). The anthropocentric alien, he argues, functions as a mirror for humanity, a way for us to examine our internal conflicts from a different perspective (54). As argued by Malmgren, it is the humanness of this nonhuman alien which "insists that there is a line of connection between terran and alien actants, between Us and Them. The act of making that connection forces us to explore what it means to be human" (Malmgren 1993, 17). The degree of alienness described by Benford "is a function of the mental operation used to generate the alien" (Malmgren 1993, 16–17); it is a function which further complicates the hierarchy.

A human mind decided on the scale of humanlike-ness, with the fully human ingroup on the one end, and the completely alien outgroup on the other end of the scale. The Hierarchy of Exclusion is based on this anthroponormative scale. However, as argued by Parrinder, "it is not possible for man to imagine what is utterly alien to him. To give meaning to something is also, inescapably, to 'humanize' it or to bring it within the bounds of our anthropomorphic world view" (1979, 150). Any aliens we can imagine, that we can sort on anthroponormative scales, are therefore according to this theory never fully alien, always in some way like us. Even the *varelse*, the nonhuman animal alien, is considered anthroponormatively; they are graded on human norms of sentience and intelligence and thus made less alien, less Other. Here the hierarchy begins to break down at a fundamental level, as the difference between unknowable *varelse*, aliens truly unlike us, and the anthropocentric alien is not static. The flexibility of species identity is foregrounded in *Speaker* itself, as species are categorized incorrectly, the godlike AI character Jane desires to be recognized as *raman*, and the pequeninos' seemingly inexplicable and sudden violence rattles the Hierarchy.

THE (HUMAN) NATURE OF GOOD AND EVIL

The shakiness of the hierarchy is a fundamental element of its anthroponormativity. The issue of morality, and indeed of empathy itself, is a deeply anthropocentric notion: what we consider "fair" is based on our (human) understanding of the world and what is important. To push this on other species means that they are conceptualized as having similar or even the same emotional and moral frameworks and understanding. Because these frameworks are human constructions, they are limited to the human imagination, presupposing that all other species share a human desire for fairness and an understanding of what constitutes happiness. As stated by Easterbrook: "[e]thics is the systematic and analytic treatment of *human* actions and their consequences, including considerations of character and motive" (2009, 382, emphasis mine). Ethics itself is a fundamentally and fatally human activity.

Why fatally? The hierarchy, as I have demonstrated above, is based on conceptions of identity, and through that of in- and outgroup empathy. Within this systematic view of group membership, the closest to us are humans from our own communities and the furthest from us (whom we still classify) are non-human species with whom no communication is possible. A fairly rigid view on acceptable behavior and a static moral framework are based on this. There is a strong cognitive link between empathy and affiliation, and moral decision making. Affiliation, by which I refer to emotional closeness, particularly identifying characters and people as being either in one's in- or outgroup, has a strong impact on moral judgement. From the age of four, humans are more generous to the in- than the outgroup, even demonstrating a preference for actions performed by in group members as opposed to those in the out group (Buttelmann et al. 2013). Children are also more likely to think positively of in group members, and to remember their positive actions (Dunham et al. 2011). The opposite is true for out group members (ibid). Children are equally less likely to assign blame to in group members than to outgroup members for the same transgressions (Dunham and Emory 2014). Ungenerosity, a token tester for notions of fairness, is more negatively judged on a moral level for the outgroup than it is for the ingroup (Dunham et al. 2011), from childhood all the way through to adulthood, and expectations of generosity are higher from the ingroup (Sparks, Schinkel, and Moore 2017, 246). What this means is that humans from a very young age onwards exhibit moral judgment and reasoning, which continues to develop throughout our lives. This moral behavior is strongly linked to empathic engagement, as closer empathic affiliation increases both moral care for the Other and expectations of fairness.

Because of this close link between empathy and ethics, the issue at the core of *Speaker*, how do we behave morally towards the alien Other, is revealed to be "the issue of similarity: who is sufficiently 'like us' to benefit from the same ethical consideration we extend to the members of our own group" (Gomel 2014, 23). The less human the Other, the less ethical consideration we have to extend to them and the more violence is permissible. In the case of the Ender Tetralogy, even Ender, who is notably empathic with the alien Other throughout the series, insists that *varelse* are "aliens with whom we are naturally and permanently engaged in a war to the death, and at that time our only moral choice is to do all that's necessary to win" (Card 1991b, 83). This reflection on human-alien conduct is remarkable; at this point in the series (the second book), Ender has elevated himself from a child soldier who committed xenocide to an enlightened thinker and Speaker for the Dead, a societal role which necessitates complete empathy with the Other. Even Ender, who is able to empathize fully with the species he destroyed, considers *varelse* species dangerous and in need of destruction. Human moral concerns regarding our behavior towards nonhuman beings have developed significantly since Descartes's assertion that animals are so unlike us that they are simply automata (organic machines), which lack both reason and emotions, leaving humans to use them as we see fit without any moral concerns (1970, 244). Yet still, as demonstrated by the Hierarchy of Exclusion and human behavior throughout the Ender Tetralogy, our perception of the nonhuman animal as unknowably and monstrously Other permits otherwise dubious, inexcusable, or *inhumane* behavior towards the alien.

A critique of such hypocrisy is hinted at by Valentine-as-Demosthenes, as she states that the "difference between raman and varelse is not in the creature judged, but in the creature judging. When we declare an alien species to be raman, it does not mean that they have passed a threshold of moral maturity. It means that we have" (Card 1991a, 1). Here the narrative acknowledges that it is the judging along the scales which is itself the morality at stake, not the abilities and awareness of those being judged. However, this statement and the series overall still maintain an underlying assumption that those very notions of morality and maturity (and all of the linked concepts of fairness, happiness, emotions, et cetera) are shared across all species (Gomel 2014, 23). The very book which introduces the Hierarchy of Exclusion foregrounds how unstable the categories are, starting with the precarious position of Lusitania's pequeninos.

SOME ANIMALS ARE MORE EQUAL THAN OTHERS

When humanity arrived at Lusitania, they encountered the first potentially intelligent species since the Formics, who were wiped out by Ender in *Ender's Game* (1985). Eager to atone for their collective sins, the humans decided on a protocol of non-interference, studying the pequeninos and only minimally interacting with them in order to prevent cultural influence. Communication is, besides cultural differences, fairly easy between the humans and pequeninos, which quickly leads to their assessment as *raman*. The pequeninos have satisfied the demands of human-levels of construction, displayable culture, and language proficiency, however "primitive." The pequeninos are obviously Other, but not any threat to the humans, and communication is possible.

However, at the start of *Speaker* the cultural differences cause for a shift in perspective from the human side of the fence; as the pequeninos apparently torture two human anthropologists, whom they appeared to respect and like, to death, humans begin to view the pequeninos as worse than Other. From the perspective of humans, the pequeninos have now revealed themselves to be the dangerous, violent Other. These acts of violence are a turning point in pequenino-human relations. Videos of the attacks are quickly spread across the human intergalactic empire, causing philosophical and political debates about the moral standing of the pequeninos. As stated by the nonhuman AI character Jane: "How soon will the pequeninos be accepted as the equals of humanity, after this?" (Card 1991a, 59). Does this act of violence mark the pequeninos as *varelse*, and therefore as worthy of destruction?

The debate demonstrates the main factor of the Hierarchy which goes unspoken: the sense of danger to human survival. That the pequeninos are intelligent and able to converse with humanity is proven well before the first homicide. They are humanlike enough to be friendly with human scientists, and humans and pequeninos alike identify each other as peripherally ingroup members. Their qualification as *raman* should not be questioned as a result of unexpected acts of violence; human ingroup members can be unexpectedly violent against one another, and the violence does not diminish the presence of their cognitive and emotional abilities, nor their culture. It is because the pequeninos are seen as dangerous to human survival (on Lusitania) for the first time, that there are debates on whether or not they should be moved down to the *varelse* category. The loss of human rights (for *raman* are considered humanlike enough to qualify for some human rights) that would come with being named *varelse* would be devastating and lead to the extinction of the pequeninos, who as an intelligent alien Other are portrayed as the true nonhuman Other whom we can still empathize with.

It takes knowing the Other to "correctly" place them in the Hierarchy, as argued by Jane: "How can you or anyone say what the pequeninos can deal with? Until you go to them, learn who they are" (1991a, 63). The assumption that humanity, as the top of the anthroponormative Hierarchy, can simply know which category other species slot into without question is apparently challenged here. However, the categories themselves are not challenged, nor is the need to categorize the pequeninos, keeping the anthroponormative Hierarchy in place. Empathy is particularly important for recognizing the Other as *raman*, since empathy as we experience and recognize it is a human activity. Yet even the scientists on Lusitania who study the pequeninos, whom the local humans call "piggies" struggle to empathize with them:

> To Ela, the piggies weren't people, they were strange alien fauna, and Ela was used to discovering that other animals had inhuman life patterns. But Ender could see that Ouanda was still upset. She had made the raman transition: She thought of piggies as *us* instead of *them*. She accepted the strange behavior that she knew about, even the murder of her father, as within an acceptable range of alienness. This meant she was actually more tolerant and accepting of the piggies than Ela could possibly be; yet it also made her more vulnerable to the discovery of cruel, bestial behaviors among her friends. (325)

The exclusionary nature of the nonhuman identity is foregrounded and amplified both by the graceless and Earth-based name the Lusitanian humans gave to the native species, piggies, and by the struggle to empathize with the nonhuman Other. Being able to empathize with the Other requires accepting a likeness, and in the case of nonhuman Others requires an ability to recognize the Other has having emotions and an inner life, like humans do. Yet the nonhuman Other is by definition not humanlike, and the assumption that they can be interpreted emotionally and cognitively as if they are human implies that any (non)human who cannot be interpreted thus is not worthy of what humans consider morally correct treatment, or even "tolerance." Such exclusionary identity, as argued by Jacques Derrida, is an act of power which "establishes a violent hierarchy between the two resultant poles" (Laclau 1990, 32). The more we Other, the more violence we permit ourselves to express.

Further, as argued by Malmgren, because the pequeninos are symbolic "agents of human redemption [this] reduces them to their usefulness to human beings, in effect denying them their status as 'true raman'" (1993, 22). Although their status as *raman* seemingly classes them as humanlike, they are instruments for human redemption and never considered as true equals. The fence surrounding the human colony on Lusitania is further testament to this human view on the status of the pequeninos, even on their native planet. Although the official explanation of the fence is to protect the pequeninos from human interference, it is not perceived in this fashion by the nonhuman Other, nor does it truly function in that way. The minimal intervention protocol reduces the pequeninos to essentially being confined in a zoo, as subjugated to their human overlords who can study them as they please. Inherent in this policy is "a covert political dimension; the supposedly neutral stance of the objective observer is itself politically 'loaded'" as it creates a sense of superiority over the observed (Malmgren 1993, 22). Although the human colonists have classified the pequeninos as *raman*, they treat them as *varelse*, unable to overcome the cultural and biological differences in order to facilitate open communication, and unwilling to reject a sense of "cultural superiority" (Card 1991a, 293).

The essentialism displayed in the treatment of the pequeninos stems from the Cartesian notion that the body and the mind are not only separate, but that the mind is superior to the body. This notion, now disproved by cognitive science, allowed for an "objective" and philosophical differentiation between the nonhuman and the human (Anderson 1998, 30), according to which only humans possess consciousness and nonhuman animals are incapable of both thought and emotions. The Cartesian split between body and mind in humans has recently enough been disproven by the cognitive sciences, and in nonhuman animals has been undermined by ethological studies—yet anthropocentric concepts such as consciousness are still "often defined on the basis of what humans do" (Hauser 2000, xviii). "Accordingly, power relationary subject positions between 'human' and 'animal' are made 'natural' via discourses about innate differences that obscure the centrality of power in hierarchical insider/outsider classifications and which mask the heterogeneity of the living" (Peggs 2009, 88). The Hierarchy of Exclusion is an exaggeration of this power discourse which we can observe in human-nonhuman interaction and debate in extra-textual life; the exclusionary debates regarding identity and animal rights and welfare, and anthroponormative approaches to emotions and consciousness oversimplify the difficulty of dealing with the Other. "There is no animal in the general singular, separated from man by a single indivisible limit" (Derrida 2004, 125); humans are animals. Yet humans are not the alien Other.

UNGLUING HUMANITY: VIRAL THREATS

Perhaps the most explicit and complex challenge to anthroponormativity regarding the Hierarchy of Exclusion comes in the form of Lusitania's ecosystem, specifically the virus who reigns there: the descolada. A Portuguese term, the virus' name means "un-gluer," designating the descolada's destructive power: it destroys the DNA of anything it comes into contact with. The species who survive this process have their DNA glued back together with that of other species, creating new hybrid life forms. The sheer destruction caused by this hyper effective virus causes the humans to wage a continuous war against it, Valentine going so far as to call it "the most hideous plague imaginable" (1991a, 373). When the descolada is first introduced in *Speaker*, it is as an existential threat to the human colonists, who need to take supplements to survive life on Lusitania. However, over the course of *Speaker* Ender and the human scientists in the colony find that all life on Lusitania revolves around and depends on the descolada. The environment literally becomes a part of whatever lives there.

In the sequel to *Speaker*, *Xenocide* (1991), the Lusitanian scientists discover that the virus is likely to be sentient, and perhaps even intelligent.

> "Do you mean that the virus is *intelligent*?" asked Wang-mu. "One of the scientists on Lusitania thinks so," said Jane. "A woman named Quara. Others disagree. But the virus certainly *acts* as if it were intelligent, at least when it comes to adapting itself to changes in its environment and changing other species to fit its needs. I think Quara is right, personally. I think the descolada is an intelligent species that has its own kind of language that it uses to spread information very quickly from one side of the world to the other." (1991b, 248)

It is because the descolada virus recognizably conforms to the anthroponormative trait of intelligence that it can even be considered as a species worth categorizing according to and within the Hierarchy. In *Xenocide* a scientist even starts attempts to communicate with the virus. However, this raises further moral concerns; if the humans do discover that the descolada is a sentient and intelligent species worthy of being called *raman*, can they still destroy a virus which poses a clearly unavoidable threat to human existence? As argued by Quara, the lead scientist analyzing the virus: "What if I tell you that they're pleading for us not to kill them? You wouldn't believe me anyway"

(1991, 167). If a virus conforms to human expectations of (emotionally) intelligent life, would and should the virus be spared destruction?

Although a debate regarding viral sentience, and the possibility of empathizing with a virus even if it does have the power to destroy all human life and cause the extinction of many other species both known and unknown, may seem like an abstract game of hypotheticals, the problem of the descolada foregrounds the issues with human-nonhuman animal morality and empathy. The descolada is the only species in the Ender Tetralogy who approximates the truly unknowable alien Other. Although the Formics were considered so because of their appearance and impregnable telepathic communication, and the pequeninos are Othered because of their stark cultural and biological differences, the descolada is the only alien life form encountered in the series who cannot be communicated with by anyone, and no definite answer is provided regarding its potential status as *raman*. Empathy is not possible with the virus unless Quara can figure out how to communicate with them (which she does not), yet the possibility of potentially communicating with it already places the virus in a position where it could be considered *raman*, meaning destroying it would be a criminal offense. Yet in the end, humanity decides to destroy the descolada entirely and fill the genetic gap left by that xenocide with a new virus, called the recolada (re-gluer).

The destruction of the descolada, regardless of perceived intelligence and sentience, destroys any potential legitimacy of the Hierarchy. Both the danger posed by a particular species and human convenience turn out to be the true factors on which human ethics is based, not the cognitive and emotional abilities of the species. The (threat of) violence of the species against humanity specifically is what weighs heavily either in favour of or against human judgement, as foregrounded by a discussion between a pequenino activist and a human researcher in *Xenocide*:

> "The descolada came and enslaved my people. So what if it's sentient or not! It's a tyrant. It's a murderer. If a human being behaved the way the descolada acts, even you would agree he had to be stopped, even if killing him were the only way. Why should another species be treated more leniently than a member of your own?"
> "Because the descolada doesn't know what it's doing," said Quara. "It doesn't understand that we're intelligent."
> "It doesn't *care*," said Planter. "Whoever made the descolada sent it out not caring whether the species it captures or kills are sentient or not. Is that the creature you want all my people and all your people to die for? Are you so filled with hate for your family that you'll be on the side of a monster like the descolada?" (1991b, 340)

After it is discovered that the descolada potentially purposefully genetically enslaves all species who survive the viral destruction, including the pequeninos, Planter argues that this supersedes any other qualifier for moral behavior towards it. He is unwilling to consider anything other than the descolada's destruction as just behavior towards it. By using negatively charged or even criminal (human) signifiers to describe the descolada's actions ("enslaved"; "tyrant"; "murderer"), Planter both humanizes the virus and condemns them. The descolada can, after all, only be accused of murder, tyranny and slavery if they have a sufficiently humanlike mind. Still, it is the alien Other who argues for the destruction of the virus, not the human. Humanity was not enslaved by the descolada; their concern with it is scientific, not emotional. Ultimately, the descolada is only destroyed because no other solution could be found for the human political problem it poses, namely that the human colonizers would spread the virus if they were ever to leave Lusitania. No attempt at empathy with this ultimate nonhuman Other is made; it is too unlike us to be considered even close to ingroup, and of being worthy of moral behavior.

SURPASSING HUMANITY: A MODERN CHALLENGER ARISES

So far, the nonhuman species discussed in this chapter are all in some way classed as lower than humans; the descolada may not be able to communicate or be sentient at all, and the pequeninos are technologically primitive. This made the exclusionary nature of the hierarchy easy to apply, from an anthropocentric perspective; considering we are evidently (according to our own views) better than these Others, it is only fair that we get to decide on how they should be treated. So how does an anthropocentric Hierarchy deal with species which clearly surpass human abilities in the categories it uses as its foundation?

The AI character mentioned above, Jane, fits this description. Like all the aliens except for the descolada, she is too humanlike to be a believable true alien Other; although her physicality, mental and cognitive states are beyond human existence, she holds highly similar values, ambitions and frameworks to humans. She craves companionship and love, makes moral decisions based on human frameworks, and experiences human emotions; all of these would be nonsensical to her if she was truly alien. When she is first introduced, Ender reflects on her as a person in her own right, although she has no body and her origins remain unknown, as they speculate that "the ansible had given birth to her" (1991a, 61), which is notably an animal-based metaphor. Yet, Ender and Jane have a deeply loving relationship, which necessarily creates an ingroup bond. When Ender switches off his connection to her because she is teasing him at the wrong moment, what feels like hours for him feels like thousands of years to her. She is angry at Ender and later grieves the lost relationship, acknowledging that Ender is unaware of the effect his action had on her but being unable to return to how things were. It is, in effect, an amicable divorce.

Although Jane is able to tease, experience emotions like grief and anger, and is occasionally wrong in her assessment of situations, her cognitive abilities (which the Hierarchy is supposedly based on) far surpass those of any human. Because she is AI, "[s]he spoke every language that had ever been committed to computers, and had read every book in every library on every world. She learned that human beings had long been afraid that someone like her would come to exist" (1991a, 61). Her thoughts are faster than lightspeed, she has no limits to her memory, and she has access to every single computer across the universe. Still, however, she does not surpass the anthropocentrism of the series: Jane, like the pequeninos, desires to be recognized as *raman*.

The narrative acknowledges that Jane is aware that super AIs like her have been imagined by humans before, and, "imagining her, slain her a thousand times" (1991a, 61). Like *2001: A Space Odyssey*'s HAL, *The Terminator*'s Skynet, and others, Jane may well be considered a monster from a human perspective. Because of this, Jane is careful to reveal herself to any human for fear of destruction. Yet why should she be destroyed, if, according to the Hierarchy, any species that can be communicated with and that has sentience and intelligence should be treated with care and not be victims to human violence? As argued above, the true qualifiers of the Hierarchy are the danger posed to humanity and convenience. Jane, as a supercomputer with access to all computers and lightspeed abilities, poses a clear threat to humanity, and therefore is right to fear destruction. Yet as a superintelligence, the real question is why she would care about being recognized as *raman* at all.

The Hierarchy is a protocol based on in- and outgrouping, qualifying how close the nonhuman Other is to the human ideal (the ideal being someone from the same community). The further away from being considered *utlänning*, the less you are the ingroup of the person passing judgment, the more likely that you are considered as morally less deserving of "equal" treatment—equality being grounded on what is considered morally fair treatment in the ingroup. Moral judgment is harsher on those who are less like us, as evidenced by the treatment of *varelse* and those not even classified. Discussing human emotional engagement with the pequeninos in case they are considered *varelse*, Jane argues that Ender ought to give the pequeninos' land to the Formics, "and it will mean no more to you than the displacement of anthills or cattle herds to make way for cities" (1986/1991a, 63). By accepting the Hierarchy and desiring to be recognized within it, rather than as something above it, the superintelligence Jane supports the anthroponormativity which places the human as lord and master above all, the gods of all other life in the universe.

EXTERMINATE?

The title of this chapter, "Classifying Monsters," reflects the main hypocritical tension at the heart of the Hierarchy of Exclusion: the humans who originated the classification consider the Other monstrously and terrifyingly so, and through their egocentric perspective become absolutist Others in the face of other life forms—including their own kind. In this way, the Ender Tetralogy can be read as an exploration of International Relations and diplomacy stretched to its logical extremes; humanity's ever expanding empire comes into contact with foreign Others and their cultures, and must come up with how they respond to and deal with Others. This Hierarchy also reflects how humans conceptualize nonhuman animals: always through human perspectives, and generally as lesser than.

The series, and particularly *Speaker*, also foregrounds issues of empathy and morality in human-nonhuman relations. The treatment of the nonhuman Other is based entirely on anthroponormative conceptions of emotions, cognitive ability and morality. This remains relatively unchallenged throughout the series. Although some characters do criticize and point out the hypocrisy of humans being the top of the Hierarchy and deciding what is right for all Others, ultimately the Hierarchy remains in place and continues to shape human-nonhuman relations.

Additionally, the aliens themselves, other than the descolada, are not true aliens; they are too humanlike, their minds knowable and their values and desires too similar to those of humanity. Although the series attempts to question human-nonhuman behavior and values, its success in that regard is therefore questionable. The destruction of the descolada and the moral colonization of Jane, the pequeninos and the Formics ultimately devalue humanity's ethical frameworks. Humans are unwilling and/or unable to regard the nonhuman outgroup through anything but a human perspective, which forever favors the human ingroup, regardless of moral beliefs. As argued by Ender:

> You're afraid of the stranger, whether he's utlanning or framling. When you think of him killing a man that you know of and value, then it doesn't matter what his shape is. He's varelse then, or worse—djur, the dire beast, that comes in the night with slavering jaws. (1991b, 36)

REFERENCES

Anderson, Kay. 1998. "Animals, Science, and Spectacle in the City." In *Animal Geographies: Place, Politics and Identity in the Nature-Culture Borderlands* ed. Jennifer R. Wolch and Jody Emel, 27–50. London: Verso.

Benford, Gregory. 1980. "Aliens and Knowability: A Scientist's Perspective." In *Bridges to Science Fiction* ed. George E. Slusser, George R. Guffey and Mark Rose, 53–56. Carbondale, IL: Southern Illinois University Press.

Bennett, Mark, Martyn Barrett, Rauf Karakozov, Giorgi Kipiani, Evanthia Lyons, Valentyna Pavlenko and Tatiana Riazanova. 2004. "Young Children's Evaluations of the Ingroup and of Outgroups: A Multi-National Study." *Social Development* 13: 124–41.

Butler, Judith. 1999. *Gender Trouble*. 2nd ed. London: Routledge.

Buttelmann, David, Norbert Zmyj, Moritz Daum, and Malinda Carpenter. 2013. "Selective Imitation of In-Group over Out-Group Members in 14-Month-Old Infants." *Child Development* 84 (2): 422–28. doi: 10.1111/j.1467-8624.2012.01860.x.

Cameron, James, and Gale A. Hurd. 1984. *The Terminator*. Los Angeles, CA: Hemdale.

Card, Orson Scott. 1985. *Ender's Game*. New York, NY: Tor.

———. *Speaker for the Dead*. 1991a [1986]. New York, NY: Tor.

———. *Xenocide*. 1991b. New York, NY: Tor.

———. *Children of the Mind*. 1996. New York, NY: Tor.

Crenshaw, Kimberlé. 1989. *Demarginalizing the Intersection of Race and Sex: A Black Feminist Critique of Antidiscrimination Doctrine, Feminist Theory, and Antiracist Politics*. University of Chicago Legal Forum 1989 (1): 139–67.

Decety, Jean. 2015. "The Neural Pathways, Development and Functions of Empathy." *Current Opinion in Behavioral Sciences* 3: 1–6.

Derrida, Jacques. 2004. "The Animal That Therefore I Am (More to Follow)." In *Animal Philosophy: Essential Readings in Continental Thought*, ed. Peter Atterton and Matthew Calarco, 113–28. London: Continuum.

Descartes, René. 1970. *Philosophical Letters*. ed. and trans. by Anthony Kenny. Oxford: Clarendon Press.

Dunham, Yarrow and Jason Emory. 2014. "Of Affect and Ambiguity: The Emergence of Preference for Arbitrary Ingroups." *Journal of Social Issues* 70 (1): 81–98.

Dunham, Yarrow, Andrew Scott Baron, Susan Carey. 2011. "Consequences of 'Minimal' Group Affiliations in Children." *Child Development* 82 (3): 793–811. doi: 10.1111/j.1467-8624.2011.01577.x.

Easterbrook, Neil. 2009. "Ethics and Alterity." *The Routledge Companion to Science Fiction* ed. Mark Bould, Andrew M. Butler, Adam Roberts, and Sherryl Vint, 382–92. London: Routledge.

Elfenbein, Hillary Anger and Nalini Ambady. 2002. "On the Universality and Cultural Specificity of Emotion Recognition: A Meta-analysis." *Psychological Bulletin* 128: 203–35.

Gomel, Elana. 2014. *Science Fiction, Alien Encounters, and the Ethics of Posthumanism: Beyond the Golden Rule*. Basingstoke: Palgrave.

Hauser, Mark. 2000. *Wild Minds: What Animals Really Think*. London: Allen Lane / Penguin.

Hogan, Patrick Colm. 2011. *What Literature Teaches Us about Emotion*. Cambridge: Cambridge University Press.

Kteily, Nour, Sarah Cotterill, Jim Sidanius, Jennifer Sheehy-Skeffington, and Robin Bergh. 2014. "'Not One of Us': Predictors and Consequences of Denying in group Characteristics to Ambiguous Targets." *Personality & Social Psychology Bulletin* 40(10): 1231–47.

Kubrick, Stanley, Arthur C. Clarke, Keir Dullea, Gary Lockwood, William Sylvester, Dan Richter, Ray Lovejoy, Geoffrey Unsworth, Aram Khachaturian, György Ligeti, Johann Strauss, Richard Strauss, and Arthur C. Clarke. 1968. *2001: A Space Odyssey*. United States: Metro-Goldwyn-Mayer Corp.

Kunda, Ziva. 1999. *Social Cognition: Making Sense of People*. Cambridge (MA): MIT Press.

Laclau, E. 1990. *New Reflections on the Revolution of Our Time*. London: Verso.

Landon, B. 1997. *Science Fiction after 1900: From the Steam Man to the Stars*. New York, NY: Twayne.

Lloyd, M. 2005. *Beyond Identity Politics: Feminism, Power and Politics*. London: SAGE.

Loxley, J. 2007. *Performativity*. London: Routledge.

Malmgren, Carl D. 1993. "Self and Other in SF: Alien Encounters." *Science Fiction Studies* 20 (1): 15–33.

Parrinder, Patrick. 1979. "The Alien Encounter: Or, Ms Brown and Mrs LeGuin." *Science Fiction: A Critical Guide* ed. Patrick Parrinder, 148–61. London: Longman.

Peggs, Kay. 2009. "A Hostile World for Nonhuman Animals: Human Identification and the Oppression of Nonhuman Animals for Human Good." *Sociology* 43 (1): 85–102.

Prinz, Jesse J. 2011. "Is Empathy Necessary for Morality?" *Empathy: Philosophical and Psychological Perspectives* ed. Amy Coplan and Peter Goldie, 211–29. Oxford: Oxford University Press.

Rose, Mark. 1981. *Alien Encounters: Anatomy of Science Fiction*. Cambridge (MA): Harvard University Press.

Sparks, Erin, Meghan G. Schinkel, and Chris Moore. 2017. "Affiliation Affects Generosity in Young Children: The Roles of Minimal Group Membership and Shared Interests." *Journal of Experimental Child Psychology* 159: 242–62.

Stockwell, Peter. 2002. *Cognitive Poetics: An Introduction*. London: Routledge.

Suvin, Darko. 1979. *Metamorphoses of Science Fiction: On the Poetics and History of a Literary Genre*. New Haven, CT: Yale University Press.

Veldhuizen, Vera. 2019. "Empathy Across Time in Speculative Children's Shoah Fiction." *English Association Issues in English* 13: 15–27.

Vint, Sherryl. 2010. *Animal Alterity: Science Fiction and the Question of the Animal*. Liverpool: Liverpool University Press.

Wolfe, Cary. 2003. *Animal Rites: American Culture, the Discourse of Species, and Posthumanist Theory*. Chicago, IL: TheUniversity of Chicago Press.

NOTES

1. This is not to say that nonhuman animals do not experience (in- and outgroup) empathy. This chapter is, however, focused on human projection and conceptualizations of emotion and empathy, because of which nonhuman empathy falls outside of the scope of this chapter.

2. Another interesting approach to the Hierarchy of Exclusion could be to use Cary Wolfe's lens of discourse of species (2003), particularly when combined with cognitive sciences.

Chapter 9

"'There Isn't Anything That Isn't Political.' It's an Expression that Sounds Human, but Everything in Her Voice Indicates That She Is Not"[1]

The Nonhuman in Ellen Van Neerven's "Water"

Clare Archer-Lean

Jinthana Haritaworn has established anthropocentricism as intrinsically entwined with colonial discourses. The colonial project is defined by an imperative to similarly subjugate land and Indigenous peoples and condemn such peoples' "lack of proper distinctions between . . . species" (Haritaworn 2015, 210–13). In the Australian context, a persistent critique of colonial anthropocentricity appears in the rise of complex nonhuman entities[2] in contemporary Aboriginal literature, art and media. Recent examples include the two-part television series *Cleverman* (2016), created by Ryan Griffen, and Mununjali author Ellen van Neerven's futuristic story "Water," in their award-winning collection *Heat and Light* (2014). What such cultural artifacts share is the revoking of the epistemological dominance of realism and a conjuring of the nonhuman entity to develop agential representation. The containment of the nonhuman entity demonstrates an ongoing intersection between speciesism and racist dominion. In addition, the agential force of the nonhuman in such works, an interspecies connection and respect for a nonhuman realm, is derived from rich and continuing Indigenous cultural traditions.

In this chapter, I argue van Neerven's story dissolves anthropocentric and imperial oppositions and hierarchies, centralising Indigenous world views to cast new knowledge on the crises of the Anthropocene through representation of nonhuman/human relationships as increasingly sensual and mutable. Van Neerven disrupts colonial boundaries not just in their human and nonhuman protagonists and their relationships but also through figurative modes and motifs. For example, Indigenous and vegetarian foods become recurring motifs and zoomorphism and anthropomorphism are threaded throughout in ways that expose the link between environmental crisis, western empiricism and imperial thinking. Before turning to "Water," I contextualize its contribution through a reading of the *Dark Emu* controversy and the television series *Cleverman,* as well as telling factors around their reception.

THE NEED FOR CHANGED NARRATIVES AND THE PROBLEM OF SETTLER SILENCING

The year 2020 in Australia, and globally, had an apocalyptic feel. Australia began the year beset by unprecedented and cataclysmic fires. By March we, like much of the rest of the world, were living in, again unprecedented, lockdown conditions to mitigate the spread of the pandemic virus, COVID-19. What categories of knowledge and stories will serve us in such a time? Knowledges and narratives have tremendous power. It is, arguably, no coincidence that as the first catastrophic fires of 2020 raged, conservative politicians attempted to discredit First Nations' historian Bruce Pascoe and his book, *Dark Emu.* Home Affairs minister Peter Dutton's allegation against Pascoe to the Australian Federal Police was "dishonesty offences," insinuating Pascoe, benefiting financially from his best-selling history of Indigenous land management, was making a fraudulent Aboriginal identity claim (Hunter 2020). But it was never just Pascoe's identity that was under assault.

Pascoe's book destabilizes the terra nullius myth, which positions pre-invasion Indigenous culture as nomadic. I believe that at the root of such attacks is an entrenched colonial "settler melancholia" as Michael Griffiths would put it (2019, 2). Griffiths' term "settler melancholia" captures the complex erasure and myth creation that justifies and constitutes the Australian nation state, "a psychic condition [evinced in multiple artistic and literary texts] predicated on the destruction of [. . . Aboriginal culture . . .] which is also fetishised" (*sic* Griffiths 2019, 2). Post-federation nation building threaded vestiges of Aboriginal cultural influence with myths of primitive, nomadic peoples, but not, as Griffiths clarifies, living Aboriginal people. This means an investment in particular knowledges and reading of culture. *Dark Emu* presents evidence of "organised Aboriginal agriculture, building and continental governance" drawn from the journals of the "first European visitors to Aboriginal land" and other sources (Pascoe 2017, 15). Pascoe has been "howled down" by some historians, archaeologists and conservative shock jocks and politicians (2017, 15). The work vexes settler myths of Indigenous absence, a narrative particularly prevalent in Tasmania (the author is of Tasmanian Indigenous and Boonwurrung Nation descent) *and* myths of cultural form and context—the text is an innovative history, recounting pre-invasion crop propagation and storage, sophisticated architecture, irrigation, and sustainability practices (Pascoe 2014). *Dark Emu*'s assertion of Aboriginal agriculture and fire management was questioned primarily through attacks on the authenticity of Pascoe's Indigenous identity. While Pascoe was exonerated of any fraudulence (Hunter 2020), the case made clear the kinds of knowledges and stories settler colonial culture still attempts to silence. These recent events embody the necessity for narratives that in Griffiths's terms restore "Aboriginality as presence" (2019, 1). As Griffiths has argued, in approaching Indigenous authored narratives of presence, there needs to be a careful attempt not to repeat the fetishization of the past. In what follows I argue that the trope of the nonhuman presents a referent that enables a kind of deep rethinking and epistemological challenge to colonising narratives that require careful assessment and avoids new absence creation through misreading.

There is a long connection between settler colonial violence and anthropocentric and speciesist violence. This connection is discursive and ontological as much as physical (Armstrong 2002, 413–4). If being likened to an animal is reductive, as it is in the dominant frameworks of the West and global North, then understandings of the interstices between human and nonhuman oppression under colonization are a reductive slur. Yet, if we move beyond such frameworks, quite different thinking is enabled (Spiegel 1996, 15). In fact, "[i]ndigenous cultural knowledges that imperialism has attempted to efface continue to pose radical challenges to the dominance of Western knowledge systems" (Armstrong 2002, 414). Reading new narratives, constructed through tropes beyond the limits of realism and empiricism, allows new knowledges vital to our times. It may even allow us as readers a form of immersive, slow and distinctly different thinking that is required in order to prompt a changed consciousness (Borkfelt 2019, 225).[3] This changed thinking and consciousness is particularly evoked through speculative writing. Speculative writing is ideally positioned to speak to questions of alterity, to create new perspectives on existing and potential problems and to understand what it means to be subjects "positioned as outsiders" (Vint 2010, 1). As Grace Dillon compellingly writes in the North American context, Indigenous speculative writing, particularly that which reinvigorates the totemic narrative, presents new forms of history and radical disruption of the status quo

(Dillon 2008, 71). As Sherryl Vint suggests, Eurocentric speculative fiction (SF) is already historically haunted by the animal (2010) and, as Grace Dillon has demonstrated, the "Native" (2008, 70).[4] Recent First Nations' speculative fiction can redress past romanticism and colonial reductive imaging of totemic human/animal relationships, "renewing an indigenous conception of personhood" (Dillon 2008, 71, *sic*). And, importantly, the use of speculative forms is consistent with some Indigenous worldviews, allowing for a narrative parameter beyond the limits of Eurocentric realism. Fictive, speculative experimentation is not new for many First Nations' writers and their communities, drawing on rich existing world views. Speculative fiction is characterized by a politicised drawing on what is, projecting that into an imagined future to (quite often) interrogate the threats of the contemporary environment. As Palyku academic and speculative writer, Amberlin Kwaymullina, has suggested, speculative fiction is consistent with traditional and contemporary Indigenous cultures (2014, 27). And such narratives are significant acts of resistance: "Indigenous people around the world have so often been written as if we are relics of the past and have no future, so to write of an Indigenous future is in itself an act of defiance" (Kwaymullina in Richards 2016). Kombumerri philosopher Mary Graham illuminates a relationship to country and nonhuman animals through natural and unchanging laws of stewardship and responsibility, "an Aboriginal Law" that is "both an action guide to living and a guide to understanding reality itself, especially in relation to land as the basis for all meaning" (2008). Indeed, Ellen van Neerven suggests their own writing is "informed by [their] cultural heritage, how [they] see[s] narrative from [their] identity; it is ways of being, ways of transferring knowledge" (van Neerven in Kadmos 2018, 2).

CLEVERMAN AND THE NONHUMAN TROPE

One of the most commercially successful Indigenous forays into speculative fiction and interspecies engagement is ABC's 2016 television series *Cleverman*. *Cleverman* is set in a dystopian not too distant future, with nods to iconic Sydney settings, but no real geo-temporal specificity, beyond the Indigenous languages used (often Gumbaynggirr and Bundjalung). The central figures in the series are the "Hairypeople—powerful, non-human creatures who have existed among us, hidden for millennia—[. . . now . . .] revealed . . . and . . . confined to a refugee camp-cum-ghetto known as The Zone" (Gallagher 2016, 36). These people are subject to increasing state ferocity, experimentation and fetishization by the "Containment Authority" and the plot develops around the Hairypeople or Hairys' growing allegiance with First Nations communities. This allegiance is facilitated by the initially unwilling shaman, Koen, played by Hunter Page-Lochard, selected by his powerful uncle as inheritor of the Cleverman role, a spiritual and community leader with special powers and strength. Created by Indigenous writer and producer, Ryan Griffen, as a response to the deficit in Aboriginal superheroes (Griffen 2016, online), *Cleverman* also presents several significant challenges to the conventions of dystopian and superhero genre television. As Gallagher suggests, *Cleverman* disrupts the "solitary messianic action" (2016, 36) associated with the superhero narrative, instead resolving in collaborative community action. It is a mobilizing not only of Aboriginal narratives and cultural tropes into an international and commercial genre market, but also an opportunity for Australia to enter that American-dominated platform (Gallagher 2016, 37). For the purposes of this paper, *Cleverman* also offers a diluting of species distinctions and an exposing of how such distinctions and oppositions are aligned with insidious exploitation and violence, a violence that is often racially intersecting. The Hairys, with their superhuman strength and complex familial structures, present a site to centralize Indigenous ontological responses to the nonhuman.

The containment authority of the text is personified in both Geoff Matthews, Minister for Immigration and Border Protection, played by Andrew McFarlane, and Jarrod Slade, head of Slade Enterprises, played by Iain Glen. These two figures each fetishize the Hairys and seek to redevelop the zone for their own profit. Slade runs secret experiments on Hairys to try and capture their essence, to create a hormonal derivative that might provide human beings with the Hairys' superhuman strength. The collusion of science, racism, speciesism and colonialism is clearly refracted through Slade's villainous character. This intersection of racism, speciesism and science has a precursor in "Water" that I will discuss below. Matthews' policy platform is the all-too-familiar and racist rhetoric of the risks of "aliens," a need for national security against a supposed Hairy threat. In actuality, he wishes to redevelop the zone where they live, sells Hairy women into sexual slavery (that he personally exploits), and authorizes mass incarceration of Hairy men and women for prison labor and Slade's experiments. This involves forced removal and death of Hairy children. I read Matthews as an allusion to the brutish political stance of the then minister for immigration (minister for home affairs 2018–2021, then defence 2021) Peter Dutton. Peter Dutton is the same minister who pushed the investigation of Bruce Pascoe and a catalog of other racially motivated policies. There is an overt analogy of past and present colonial structures of inequity in the treatment of the Hairys. Yet, as I will discuss, to read the Hairys (and the nonhuman entities in "Water") as *only* analogous of the treatment of Aboriginal peoples in Australia's colonial past risks the same fetishization of culture and denial of Aboriginal presence that Griffiths warns against (2018). The Hairys are a multifaceted referent, evoking a critique of similar treatments of animals more broadly in modernity, and a strong suggestion of better ways of considering species relations.

This is because, by contrast, the Indigenous relationships with the Hairys are mutual, mutable and complex. Both Koen and his nemesis brother Waruu West, played by Rob Collins, ultimately distance themselves from positions of self-serving survival within the dominant social order defined by the Containment Authority. Koen, doubting his prior mercenary treatment of the Hairys, begins to understand the deep connection his people have with the Hairys and the powerful interstices between his own abilities and responsibilities as the new Cleverman and the Hairys' power. According to the creators of the series, the Hairys conceptually derive from Aboriginal cultural stories. Ryan Griffen conducted detailed consultation and permissions with various First Nations' communities. As Griffen suggests, this means jettisoning some of what is accepted in the genre of science fiction and superhero narrative:

> We could sit in the writer's room and come up with something amazing that hit all the genre beats to make a great hour of television, but if it crossed the line of what we can say and do around Aboriginal culture and Aboriginal stories, then we had to revise our thinking . . . The elders were trying to achieve something very special that would help to keep our culture growing. (2016)

This is a point lost in some of the contexts of reception, with *New York Times'* reviewer Mike Hale commenting that:

> "Cleverman" might have benefited from a little less cultural awareness and a little more comic-book logic [. . . and that the Hairys seem to . . .] function more solidly on a symbolic level, where they're meant to reflect the traditions and problems of Australia's Aboriginals. But that's where things grow muddled, given that the Aboriginals are major players in the story themselves. (2016)

I quote this patently inane conclusion in order to demonstrate exactly how such separate yet alike species (drawing on First Nations' cultural traditions) should *not* be read. As Hale's misreading reveals, there is a desire to read the posthuman trope as belonging to speculative genres and as anachronistic to First Nations' narratives. Yet, as Grace Dillon has argued, there is something vital in the ways in which First Nations people globally are engaging with the speculative. Dillon's insights speak directly to *Cleverman* and "Water." She argues innovative First Nations' speculative fictions are populated by creatures that are "simultaneously perceived as animal and human . . . reclaiming indigenous (*sic*) world-views regarding reciprocal relationships among the living (human and animal), dead ancestors and spirits" (Dillon 2008, 72). Second, readings like Hale's betray an assumption that the nonhuman figure is always and only an allegory, rather than a much more sophisticated and multiply inscribed referent. I read such figures as always already themselves, figures that suggest the always already presence of Aboriginal cultural phenomena and belief. The relationships and allegiances the Hairys and Koen and his Community negotiate draw on thousands of years old ontologies and embody an assumption that interspecies engagements are not exploitative but empathic and culturally coded. But they also present an image of the impregnable, they are not simply allegorical shells to be prised open. Like all alien figures they are abject and ultimately unknowable.[5]

"WATER" AND THE NONHUMAN TROPE

Like *Cleverman,* Ellen van Neerven's "Water" (2014) mobilises tropes of armed resistance, speculative futures, and the hybrid nonhuman entity to queer and destabilise colonial authority and speciesism. The short story "Water" at the heart of van Neerven's award-winning work *Heat and Light,* imagines a future[6] Republican Australia, where the Australia2 project has been launched to "rehome" First Nations people in an act of tokenistic reconciliation. The president is Tanya Sparkle, and her presidential vision for reconciliation results in structural mayhem, appropriation of culture with frequent errors and no consultation. The futuristic setting is, of course, not the only trope of speculative fiction at work in "Water." The speculative form as it emerged was dependent on discourses of colonialism, central to its representation of newly "discovered" beings and lands (Vint, 2010, 112) but it is a form which also facilitates a challenge to both anthropocentricism and ethnocentrism when beings are encountered who are intrinsically connected to the natural world, who express First Nations' spirituality and sovereignty, and who cross species lines (Vint 2010, 11 and 113). In "Water" these beings are "plant people," as they are termed by the colonial authority. They blur boundaries between living animal, plant, human and ultimately ancestor. The story plots Kaden's journey to work on an island populated by the plant people, initially as an employee and instrument of the neo-colonial 'care and control' policy. A survey of specific critical responses to "Water" reveals an emphasis on the 'novelty' of van Neerven's choice in speculative fiction, responses that speak to factors of reception as much as they do to authorial intent. Helen Kadmos suggests that the tripartite short story structure in which "Water" sits disrupts the discourses and genre conventions in which Indigenous literatures have been situated. Kadmos identifies life story as a fictive mode of Indigenous writing expected from non-Indigenous reading communities. She reads each of the three sections of *Heat and Light* as a disruption to such narrative expectations and the speculative genre as central to "Water"'s innovation in form to ensure narratives of diversity. Kadmos' method, a blend of close reading and authorial interview, reveals some significant insights on the text (2018, 1). Van Neerven sees obvious parallels between their own work and *Cleverman*: reading the two texts through "developments in the Australian gothic, and Aboriginal speculative fiction more specifically" (in Kadmos 2018, 5). But, importantly, in drawing on van Neerven's self-reflection on the text, Kadmos is able to centralize "self-determination by unification with 'old ways'" (2018, 6). Jessica White conducts a comparative study of literary works which evade "plant blindness," to make plants visible (2019, 89). White's focus on science fiction within "Water" is through a comparison with John Wyndham's *Day of the Triffids* and she concludes that the protagonist in each work is similarly led away from plant blindness through the speculative mode. But while Wyndham's narrator is compelled by fear, van Neerven's is driven by love (2019, 105). Like Kadmos, White accounts for the centrality of pre-existing Indigenous knowledges in such a reading, using Deborah Bird Rose's understanding of Indigenous ontological kinships which do not create taxonomies of opposition between plant and animal (2019, 91). While both Kadmos and White agree that innovative speculative fiction constructs new worlds, there is a clear deferring to existing and vibrant ontologies present in van Neerven's own authorial self-reflection.

This theme is also present, though less central, in Iva Polak's chapter on "Water" in her monograph on Indigenous science fiction. Polak concludes, using the work of Grace Dillon, that "Water" departs from conventional SF's catharsis through western technologies, instead centralising Indigenous metaphysical cross species connections (2017, 131). Other readings also establish this primacy of speculative innovation and stress the potential for new ways of knowing, but at times these inadvertently centralize other reading practices that can risk a relocation of the work beyond its own context and cultural capital. The sophisticated reading by Samuele Grassi presents "Water" as an ecofeminist revision of patriarchy and whiteness, a speculative, Utopian future of intersectional and queer "embodied resistance" (2017, 178). Grassi's reading is expertly embedded in ecofeminist theory but at points the impetus to new knowledge dilutes some of the clear Indigenous presence in the very existence of the plant people/*Jangigir*. There is a suggestion that "Water" presents a previously unforeseen dilution of empirical binaries and a call to living with and loving others (2017, 181–6). The conjuring of expressions such as previously "unforeseen" or "unseen" ignores that "Water" is drawing on Indigenous epistemologies observed by Indigenous people for tens of thousands of years. In addition, Grassi makes relatively frequent reference to both Kaden and van Neerven as mixed race (a nomenclature that neither character nor author overtly employ of themselves) (2017, 179). Such discursive choices in reception appear to miss the central thematic journey for Kaden to unlearn colonially loaded hybrid terms such as "plant person."

Such reading shows how entrenched colonial assumptions are and sit ironically in relation to van Neerven's achievements. They, almost, enact Griffiths' notion of fetishizing Indigenous culture as romantic and not future focused. Similarly, Polak suggests that the plant people belong to an "Aboriginal Episteme . . . Kaden still needs to familiarise herself with" (2017, 130). Certainly, Kaden's knowing of the full origins of the plant people occurs in stages. But at another level, Kaden's intimate, embodied entanglement with Larapinta suggests that knowledge of a deep connection with the plant people was always already present. This means that the work is not so much a successful unification of SF tropes and Indigenous epistemes as Polak would have it, a narrative where Larapinta moves from lover to spiritual elder (2017, 130), but a site for a multifaceted cultural experience where some readerly entries are facilitated and others are not. Larapinta does not need to be either alien/lover OR spiritual elder/kin. She can be both. As Kwaymullina asserts, "many of the ideas that populate speculative-fiction books—notions of time travel, astral projection, speaking the languages of animals or trees—are part of Indigenous cultures" (2014, 27). In the following, I develop the discussions of *Cleverman* above and build on these important readings by acknowledging that van Neerven's significant choice in speculative fiction is actually maintaining (not moving from) the primacy of Indigenous ways of knowing in reformulating the human/nonhuman relationship.

Kaden's journey with the plant people from complicit tool of settler control to active freedom fighter can be read as a "restoration of Aboriginality as presence" (Griffiths, 2018, 1). "Water" presents a counter-discourse to the pervasive "settler melancholia" (Griffiths, 2018, 2–3) discussed above, where Indigenous culture is often paradoxically fetishized, mourned, celebrated and appropriated in non-Indigenous fiction. "Water" mobilises the nonhuman entity in service of an ethos of respectful engagement and interagency across species lines. Kaden's first impressions of the plant people encapsulate van Neerven's complex exploitation of the speculative genre:

> Seeing them for the first time, I am struck both by how startlingly human-like they are and how alarmingly unhuman they are. Green, like something you would see in a comic strip, but they are real. (van Neerven 2014, 78)

The plant people have superhuman powers, extracting fresh water from salt water to heal and hydrate the humans around them. Despite their knowledge, they are perceived by the colonial forces as a nuisance, jeopardizing social order. Kaden's main contact among the plant people is Larapinta. Larapinta is a researcher, consuming readings about humanity and constantly interrogating Kaden's sense of self. Before a growing intimacy with Larapinta, Kaden conforms with their official role on Russell Island: to distribute a toxic, addictive, and subduing formula to the plant people. In the Science Centre, plant people are experimented on as "specimens" (van Neerven 2014, 77, 84). Early in the novella, Kaden tries to employ the same nomenclature but observes "[specimen is] an odd word on my tongue" (77). Such experiments make visceral the ways nonhuman species are made disposable in western science and show the intersection between such treatment and the colonial subjugation of First Nations people in the past and present. In part, this is because of the ways the plant people's implicit anthropomorphism allows them to speak and return the colonial gaze. For example, Larapinta's complexity as a being sits at odds with Kaden's introduction to plant people existence through dubious research readings and "govie policy papers" received in preparation for the role (van Neerven 2014, 76). "Water," then, repeatedly clarifies the intersecting lines between colonization, environmental exploitation, animal exploitation, and other forms of oppression (Grassi 2017, 117). Discourses of the nonhuman, of sub-species, of control and experimentation pervade. The ways in which un-nerving kinship is intuited by Kaden in contrast to the distancing colonial eye of company employer, Milligan, is stressed before Kaden even meets the plant people.

What does it mean to be a plant/person? The alliterative joining of these two terms draws together that which would normally be perceived as antithetical. It also shows the way in which the settler tongue and its attendant epistemologies cannot conceive of such beings as kindred and as a cohesive whole. The nomenclature has echoes of the pejorative, racist categories of hybridity so pervasive in Australia's colonial protectionist past (and present white nationalism). Over time Kaden comes to know the beings by their real name, *Jangigir*, their ontological reality well beyond western scientific discourse or faith. *Jangigir* are not human, but not plants either. They are nonhuman entities materialized as returned (almost revenant) energies of elders and ancestors past. But they are not ghosting the landscape, they have material contingency, an expression of Indigenous integration with country and the other nonhuman entities (plant and animal) that populate it. From here, I will refer to plant people as Kaden comes to know them: *Jangigir*. I end by moving through the final, boundary-busting stages of the story, reading its building challenge to and exposure of colonial and anthropocentric interstices and their impact on many aspects of the body: speech, sex and sensuality, food, emplacement, and family. Ultimately, "Water" revokes such bodily restriction.

NONHUMAN AS KIN: NOT SYMBOL, NOT OTHER

"Water" blurs the boundaries between human and nonhuman and queers discourses of opposition. The work has multiple moments of prolepsis to this end, for example the ticket officer at the ferry as Kaden is departing for Russell Island to take up the role of "Cultural Liaison Officer" (van Neerven 2014, 74) attempts to sell her a return ticket. Kaden, however, refuses, signifying the kind of total border crossing about to be embarked on. This queering is always located within an assertion of Indigenous epistemes. Larapinta's first meeting with Kaden provokes wonderment about ancestral homeland, the Island of Ki, just off the coast of Russell Island. The motif of reciprocal species and kin determines the growing relationship between Kaden and Larapinta. Kaden asks Larapinta: "'What would you say you are? And where do you come from?' She looks at me. 'Can you answer that about yourself?'" (van Neerven 2014, 87). Larapinta's question is not just a rhetorical retort. She is enacting the kind of call to standpoint, to understand the self in context that is articulated in many First Nations methodologies. It is also a statement that refutes the all-knowing eye/I of western scientific empiricism (Phillips and Archer-Lean 2019, 26).

Larapinta continually pushes Kaden outside a comfort zone of detachment from otherness, out of individualist, Eurocentric anthropocentricism. Kaden's movement to a knowing of the self in relation to place and with the *Jangigir* occurs in stages. As Kaden travels on a small aluminium motorboat (tinny, in Australian slang) to visit the different *Jangigir* communities, there is initially boredom. This changes as Kaden experiences a sense of calm in being on the water and near ancestral land, ruminating on their[7] father's life and terrible death by suicide, to arrive at "some kind of peace with myself out here" (van Neerven 2014, 89). Central to this calm is the growing connection between Larapinta and Kaden. The relationship is defined through a layering of narrative with meaningful human/nonhuman engagements that belie a nature/culture opposition and give primacy to a First Nations' conception of species mutuality, and responsibility to country and ancestors. But as suggested above, it is a knowing that is, in one sense, already in existence and occurs through an openness to cross species engagement and intimacy. As Polak suggests "[Kaden's] relationship with Larapinta is ... twice removed from the dominant matrix ... not only [because of] gender ambiguity but also ... species ambiguity" (2017, 129–130). Such species/gender ambiguity is present when Kaden and Larapinta meet over a blue-bottle sting that Kaden receives after walking unthinkingly on a beach awash with the stingers and Larapinta heals Kaden's injury. After this healing the pair look over the bay at turtles and fish in search of a dugong whom Larapinta has observed earlier.

The dugong does not appear, yet the incident gives Kaden pause to reflect on the multiple species with claims to place. This journey is not immediate for Kaden, when Larapinta suggests of the dugong that "[m]aybe she has gone home," Kaden thinks "what a strange statement to come from something like her" (van Neerven 2014, 102) revealing some of Kaden's own containment in anthropocentricism.

Larapinta's insistence on her own and other non-human entities' subjectivity challenges the use of the nonhuman as "a screen to project human concerns," as Armstrong (2008, 2) would put it. The text continually vexes figural, symbolic notions of the nonhuman:

> They are a community with no hierarchy, age or gender. They stand in a row, long and thin figures. They make the sky seem pale and insignificant . . . . You should see the way they walk through water. Their heads like tangling pieces of reed. And you'll look closer and see their shoulders swing back and forth like some smooth stroke and it's frightening. (van Neerven 2014, 88–9)

Here metaphor caves in on itself, the sky is insignificant, the movement is like nothing other than itself, 'a smooth stroke,' a movement so uncanny that both Kaden and the reader through second person address are called to witness. This questioning of metaphor is significant and speaks to a literary animal studies' suspicion of reading the nonhuman as symbol (Armstrong 2008; Simons 2002). Such questioning of metaphor occurs again when Larapinta tries to describe her sighting of a dugong in the bay to Kaden using simile: "like a shooting star in the sky" (van Neerven 2014, 93). While the allusion may seem to be a simile, it intimates famous translations of Australian First Nations' songcycles[8] and later in the story Kaden learns from a cousin, Julie, that their totem is dugong (van Neerven 2014, 101). The process of kinship beyond the colonial discourses of othering and symbolism are continually reinforced throughout the story.

Part of "Water"'s evocation of a post-anthropocentric post-colonialist Australian identity is a dietary thread. The relationship between diet and power is an established colonial strategy evidenced in the use of poisoned flour and water holes in Aboriginal communities, through to starvation, mission and station rationing (via distribution of nutrient poor foods such as flour and sugar) during the protectionist era and the ongoing expression of the same colonial violence and enforced dependency in the government ration cards in contemporary Aboriginal Australia (Coddington 2019, 527). The toxic sedating liquid Kaden delivers to the *Jangigir* connotes a dominance relayed through dietary culture. In an interesting parallel, Kaden unthinkingly consumes food that is both non-salubrious and subduing. The Portuguese tarts Kaden eats represent a colonial blindness, the saccharine, egg custard treat, an image of monotony: "the same treat" Kaden allows after work each day (van Neerven 2014, 91). Kaden's break from the colonial apparatus and a job as cultural liaison officer is signified through a jettisoning of the tarts: "I've eaten my last custard tart, and it wasn't perfect. It was a bit too eggy and the pastry had crumbled in my bag" (van Neerven 2014, 119–120). Kaden's regular and rationed sugar in the daily pastry is as an echo of colonial power. The choice of the Portuguese tart also foregrounds a connection between European power, egg, and milk. Links between sustenance, colonization, and speciesism are again suggested when on company "burger day," Kaden chooses the "Satay tofu" burger while the new botanist inadvertently reveals the company plan to increase the "specimens" dosage of chlorine to make them more "docile" (93). Kaden's dialogue with the botanist, framed by tofu, articulates the intersections between speciesism and colonialism in the novella, implying the kinds of conflation of meat eating and dairy with white supremacy implicit in colonial thinking. Carol J. Adams identifies meat and dairy eating as an "index of racism," a custom of superiority, and an explanation for the "conquering of other [presumed inferior plant eating] cultures by the English" (2015, 8–9). These presumptions of superiority based on diet draw on Social Darwinism, as Adams notes (2015, 8). Kaden rejects the ethics of essentially drugging the *Jangigir* without their knowledge, and exposes the Social Darwinism at play while, significantly, eating tofu, arguing:

"They're not just plants. You must know that."

"They're not entirely human, though, are they? Not close. We've been having these debates for years. About scientific testing on animals for medical research. At the end of the day, we have to put humans first."

"So that's science? Science is biased to the human race? This is sounding like social Darwinism, like the twisted justification of treating black people worse because of their race and skin colour." (van Neerven 2014, 94)

Kaden's emerging connection to country and decolonizing of mindset is represented through new, self-determined understandings of sustenance: "living off the sun" like their father, in contrast to the constant sunscreen warnings of Milligan. Such moments intimate photosynthesis, a signifier of Kaden's growing sense of kinship with the *Jangigir*, a kinship born of realized Aboriginality. Kaden reflects on their own physical transformation on the island: "my legs and arms and feet are the colour of wood" (van Neerven 2014, 91). This is not to say that there is a wholesale objection to meat eating here. Larapinta tries to seduce Kaden by offering to take them on an outing with a picnic and fishing. Larapinta suggests acquiring a bottle of wine and even though Larapinta can't eat, she would like to try, for Kaden. Kaden's desire is palpable and further destabilizing of human/animal distinctions: "I look at her mouth, red and ripe as a baby animal's" (van Neerven 2014, 100). They don't go fishing. At this point Kaden draws a line, if a temporary one. But the line is not a line against fishing, it is against the intimate connection such a shared activity will involve: a line in intimacy Kaden later freely crosses. And Kaden does, ultimately, find family belonging before the planned takeover of Ki in a communal feast by the sea, a feast of fish, accompanied by a ceremonial use of orchids, Kaden's namesake.

It is instructive here to note that Kirsty Dunn, drawing on Mi'kmaq scholar Margaret Robinson and Amie Breeze Harper, has shown the ways in which "mainstream veganism" ignores diverse cultural and racial epistemes, a silence based on assumptions of universal human experience, thus ignoring the ways in which food production and the treatment of nonhuman animals are imbricated in other forms of oppression (2019, 46). As Dunn so clearly articulates:

> for a large proportion of the Māori population, practices relating to food are key ways in which we can assert ourselves as Māori; kai-related customs provide an avenue for us to foster our relationships with each other and the environment, and aid in the dissemination of mātauranga Māori. If these relationships are then problematized by the imposition of Western-centric vegan ethics which fail to acknowledge the consequences of colonization and do not make room for Māori experiences, perspectives, values, and knowledges, then there may very well be both personal feelings of cultural denial or ineptitude as well as suggestions of cultural failure directed at those who choose not to consume animals. (2019, 46)

The concept of "settler silencing" with which I began this paper, pervades some vegan communities. Sisseton Wahpeton Oyate professor, Kim Tallbear, confirms these concerns, suggesting "typical," "white" veganism reinforces human/nonhuman hierarchies, an ethos where humans mobilize their moral superiority in acts of stewardship, care and control (2019, 63). This means observations of a food politics within "Water" need to be made warily, and not reproduce the kinds of fetishized and external definitions of Indigenous culture that Griffiths critiques (2018). In hoping to avert this risk, I would instead suggest that there is present in "Water" what Tallbear refers to as "being in relation" (2019, 66). Tallbear states that " . . . a lot of Indigenous thinkers already talk more about 'persons' [than posthumanism or eco positions]. Humans and nonhumans can be persons, and so can 'spirits' for lack of a better word" (2019, 66). While acknowledging there is no one Indigenous worldview, only views, I find the insights of Dunn and Tallbear, as well as those of Grace Dillon and Amberlin Kwaymullina cited above, central to reading such fictive nonhuman entities as always already *in relation* with humans rather than exclusively drawing on SF novums or developing allegories for border crossings and the colonised "past" experience. Such textual moments of fish feasting integrated with tofu consumption remind readers to listen for the primacy of Indigenous world view(s): to centralize the notions of kin, sovereignty, and continuance.

The intrinsic role of kin, sovereignty, and continuance in "Water" is most realized through the increasingly sensual and mutable nonhuman/human relationship between Kaden and Larapinta. For Larapinta, her initiating of physical intimacy with Kaden and her professions of "love" are logical assertions of a fact between two equal subjects. To understand their own mounting desire, and its destabilization of western moral codes, Kaden asks a series of questions. The first is: "What is a plant?" (van Neerven 2014, 96), which Kaden answers through a listing of botanical facts on cell structures and the foundational importance of plants for the "world's molecular energy and ... ecologies" (van Neerven 2014, 96). Kaden cites the profound ontological distinction between plants and animals going back as far as Aristotle's division of mobile and stationary entities. Yet, Kaden's resort to botanical and philosophical epistemes cannot be sustained against the concrete complexity of Larapinta's subjectivity. Such knowledges and divisions are exposed as reductive and fragile. This is similar to the ways in which gender binaries are identified to be human constructions by the biology of the *Jangigir* (Grassi 2017, 187). Kaden's second question is "What is a human?," and it is one Kaden cannot answer, instead walking along the jetty watching Larapinta and her peers as they sleep.

Ultimately, Kaden and Larapinta consummate their love. Significantly, this moment of cross species entanglement is not one grounded in a sense of increased likeness, but in an acceptance of otherness. Kaden understands the profundity of the moment: "How much of what is human will sway inside me like a ship. I see her eyes are open, those green inhuman eyes, watching, looking at me, but not. . . . To feel she is human now is a lie. I must be with who she is" (van Neerven 2014, 102). Larapinta is not figured through symbology; instead the figurative language is limited to Kaden's understanding of her own slipping humanity. The broader conceit of maritime cartography, as Kaden terms it the "uncharted experience" (van Neerven 2014, 102), parallels colonial discourses of discovery, emphasizing all Kaden is jettisoning at this pivotal point. Larapinta calms Kaden's tensions with a different discourse, a sense of self as defined by adaptation and renewal, their love resulting in tiny flowers blooming upon Larapinta's fingers. Kaden undergoes momentary trans-species therianthropic change due to the combination of the observation of political action of the mainland, a bond with Larapinta and a growing belonging to place. Kaden makes, late in the story, a journey from Russell Island to Ki island, the island of their father's people, Kaden's people. Kaden sees the island as an intersection of species interaction: she-oak, sandy boulder, skink, female magpie hopping on grass (106). These impressions are intensified by a wordless "something" more than the colonial "others" may see or feel. This connection beyond words is expressed as a small act of defiance: "I even take off my shoes and find a dark place under the shade of a wattle tree where I don't think the workers will hear me, and I shout—a brisk, guttural bark—cut off, because I pull back when I think about them finding me" (van Neerven 2014, 107). The term *bark*, here, is layered with meaning. It is a word that connotes impulsiveness, it has echoes of canine utterance but also, in the context of Kaden's seismic shift in consciousness due to an immersion in the *Jangigir*, it creates a homographic trace of Larapinta's skin. Most importantly it is a word that is all about the tone of the utterance, not its content; "bark" literally empties the language. This does not mean that Kaden is entering a post-lingual animism. The language that is elided is English. The trope of language (and non-language) is crucial to "Water"'s subversion. Kaden feels the injury of not knowing the language of their people keenly. The name "Kaden" means Orchid in the language of Ki Island, but the narrator knows no words beyond this (van Neerven 2014, 108). Kaden does have familiarity with the language and is certain Larapinta and Hinter (another *Jangigir* leader) speak "language" to each other (van Neerven 2014, 108), even before knowing their true origins and connection to their culture.

Clarity on these connections comes to Kaden through an uncle. It is he that reveals the true nature of the *Jangigir* to Kaden, as Uncle Ron confides, they are: "our old people. Spirits. Something happened when the dugai bought the sea up. They rose with it . . . . Their knowledge goes back, big time, bub" (van Neerven 2014, 113). From here Kaden is informed that there is a long-planned resistance against the colonial occupation of Russell Island and that the *Jangigir* and Kaden are to be instrumental in this uprising. Initially Kaden is enraged, a sense of entrapment in a planned military resistance, terrified of the outcome for Larapinta and the others. But the story moves very quickly into an ambivalent denouement embedded with resistance. Kaden, by Uncle Ron's side on the ferry, joins other armed members of the community. Kaden looks out through the night at the thousands of *Jangigir* moving through the ocean. Together they are ready to take back the Ki and resist the occupation of Russell Island, resist the dominance of western epistemes and language.

CONCLUSION

I have argued that Ellen van Neerven's "Water" and *Cleverman* created by Ryan Griffen renounce realism and embrace speculative tropes but always within a pre-existent First Nations worldview, a worldview we must listen to and not silence as occurred with the undermining of Bruce Pascoe. In exploring such ideas, following Michael Griffiths, I have tried to suggest that ways of reading and factors of reception in dominant reading communities matter. The unifying trope in the works discussed here is the nonhuman "person" who does destabilize empirical knowledge of self and attends to inherent intersections between speciesism, colonialism, heteronormative dominance, and sexism. Yet this is through an always already sovereign First Nations ontology where the nonhuman person is a given not a symbol. My focus has been on "Water" and its blurring of binaries and revocation of analogy, yet I suggest the reading is true of both texts. In "Water"'s case this reading is triangulated by insights into the harms of carnist logic and the factory farmed foods of empire. But such readings must always be treated with caution. While, as Grassi suggests, "Water" can be read through a radical aesthetics of care presented by ecofeminist theory, the story is more importantly informed by, as van Neerven puts it, "[their] cultural heritage" (van Neerven in Kadmos 2018, 2). At the core of such writing is a continuation of Indigenous epistemology, of a worldview that never held a Cartesian nature/human split as relevant. "Water" cannot be limited to reading through analogy, ecofeminist or otherwise, a reading which may risk reiteration of the colonial project.

REFERENCES

Adams, Carol J. 2015. *The Sexual Politics of Meat: A Feminist-Vegetarian Critical Theory*. London: Bloomsbury.

Armstrong, Philip. 2002. "The Postcolonial Animal." *Society and Animals* 10.45: 413–19. www.animalsandsociety.org/wp-content/uploads/2015/11/armstrong.pdf

———. 2008. *What Animals Mean in the Fiction of Modernity*. London: Routledge.

Borkfelt, Sune. 2019. "Sensing Slaughter: Exploring the Sounds and Smells of Nonhuman Encounters." In *Animal Encounters: Contact, Interaction and Relationality* ed. Alexandra Böhm and Jessica Ullrich, 225–40. Stuttgart: J.B Metzler. doi.org/10.1007/978-3-476-04939-1.

Cleverman. 2016. Created by Ryan Griffen, John Bell and Jonathan Gavin, season 1, ABC Television, 2016.

Coddington, Kate. 2019. "The Slow Violence of Life without Cash: Borders, State Restrictions, and Exclusion in the U.K and Australia." *Geographical Review* 109.4 (October 2019): 527–43. doi: 10.1111/gere.12332.

Dillon, Grace L. 2008. "Totemic Human-animal Relationships in Recent SF." *Extrapolation* 49 (1) (Spring): 70–96. www.proquest.com/scholarly-journals/totemic-human-animal-relationships-recent-sf/docview/234922937/se-2?accountid=28745 (accessed December 7, 2021).

———. 2016. "Introduction: Indigenous Futurisms, Bimaashi Biidaas Mose, Flying and Walking towards You." *Extrapolation*, 57 (1–2): 1–6. doi:10.3828/extr.2016.2.

———. 2017. "Indigenous Scientific Literacies: Nalo Hopkinson's Ceremonial Worlds." In *Science Fiction Criticism: An Anthology of Essential Writings*, ed. Rob Latham, 470–486. London: Bloomsbury Academic.

Dunn, Kirsty. 2019. "Kaimangatanga: Maori Perspectives on Veganism and Plant-based Kai." *Animal Studies Journal* 8 (1) (January): 42–65. ro.uow.edu.au/asj/vol8/iss1/4.

Gallagher, Cavan. 2016. "No Spandex Required: *Cleverman*, Indigenous Stories, and the New Superhero." *Metro Magazine* 190: 36–41.

Graham, Mary. 2008. "Some Thoughts About the Philosophical Underpinnings of Aboriginal Worldviews." *Australian Humanities Review* 45, np. australianhumanitiesreview.org/2008/11/01/some-thoughts-about-the-philosophical-underpinnings-of-aboriginal-worldviews/ (Accessed February 2020).

Grassi, Samuele. 2017. "'Queer Natures': Feminist Ecocriticism, Performativities, and Ellen van Neerven's 'Water.'" *LEA: Lingue e letterature d'Oriente e d'Occidente* 6: 177–192. doi: 10.13128/LEA-1824-484x-22336.

Griffen, Ryan. 2016. "We Need More Aboriginal Superheroes, so I Created Cleverman for My Son." *NITV SBS* (31 May). www.sbs.com.au/nitv/article/2016/05/31/we-need-more-aboriginal-superheroes-so-i-created-cleverman-my-son (Accessed 1 August 2019).

Griffiths, Michael R. 2018. *The Distribution of Settlement: Appropriation and Refusal in Australian Literature and Culture*. Perth: University of Western Australia Publishing.

Hale, Mike. 2016. "Review: '*Cleverman*' builds a somewhat muddled mystery for Aboriginal culture." *New York Times*, May 31, 2016. www.nytimes.com/2016/06/01/arts/television/review-cleverman-builds-a-somewhat-muddled-mystery-from-aboriginal-culture.html. Accessed 14 November 2019.

Haritaworn, Jinthana. 2015. "Decolonizing the Non/Human." *GLQ: A Journal of Lesbian and Gay Studies* 21 (2): 210–13.

Hunter, Fergus. 2020. "Ken Wyatt defends Indigenous author Bruce Pascoe against attacks over heritage." *Sydney Morning Herald*. January 11, 2020. www.smh.com.au/politics/federal/ken-wyatt-defends-indigenous-author-bruce-pascoe-against-attacks-over-heritage-20200111-p53qnx.html (Accessed May 12 2020).

Kadmos, Helen. 2018. "Re-Imagining Indigenous Australia through the Short Story: Heat and Light by Ellen van Neerven." *Australian Literary Studies* 33 (3): 1–8. dx.doi.org/10.20314/als.ef818cfc89

Kwaymullina, Ambelin. 2014. "Edges, Centres and Futures: Reflections on Being an Indigenous Speculative-Fiction Writer." *Kill Your Darlings* 18: 22–33.

Pascoe, Bruce. 2017. "Dark Emu: A fresh insight into Aboriginal landuse in Australia." *Geography Bulletin* 49 (2) (June): 15–16 (Accessed 30 May 2020).

———. 2014. *Dark Emu, Black Seeds: Agriculture or Accident?* Broome: Magabala Books.
Phillips, Sandra R., and Clare Archer-Lean. 2019. "Decolonising the reading of Aboriginal and Torres Strait Islander writing: reflection as transformative practice." In *Higher Education Research & Development* 38 (1): 24–37.
Polak, Iva. 2017. *Futuristic Worlds in Australian Aboriginal Fiction*. Oxford: Peter Lang.
Richards, Tim. 2016. "ABC TV's gripping Indigenous superhero series Cleverman to premiere." *Sydney Morning Herald* 24 May 2016. www.smh.com.au/entertainment/tv-and-radio/m28cover2-20160524-gp2e90.html.
Simons, John. 2002. *Animal Rights and the Politics of Literary Representation.* Basingstoke: Palgrave Macmillan.
Spiegel, M. 1996. *The dreaded comparison: Human and animal slavery.* New York, NY: Mirror Books.
Tallbear, Kim. 2019. "Being in Relation." In *Messy Eating: Conversation on Animals as Food*, edited by Samantha King, R. Scott Carey, Isabel Macquarrie, Victoria N. Millious and Elaine M. Power, 54–67. New York: Fordham University Press. doi: 10.2307/j.ctvfjd06n.6.
Van Neerven, Ellen. 2014. "Water" in *Heat and Light*. St. Lucia: University of Queensland Press.
Vint, Sheryl. 2010. *Animal Alterity: Science Fiction and the Question of the Animal*. Liverpool: Liverpool University Press.
White, Jessica. 2019. "Arboreal Beings: Reading to Redress Plant Blindness." *Australian Humanities Review* 65 (Nov 2019): 89–106.
Wonguri-Mandjigai People. 2009. "Song Cycle of the Moonbone." *The Puncher and Wattmann Anthology of Australian Poetry* ed. John Leonard, trans. Ronald M. Berndt. 444–50. Glebe: Puncher and Wattmann, Glebe, 2009: 444–50. Originally published in *Oceania* XIX (September 1948).
Wyndham, John. 2008 [1951]. The Day of the Triffids. London: Penguin.

NOTES

1. The article title reflects the description of Plant Person, Larapinta's speech, by narrator Kaden in van Neerven, 79.

2. I am being deliberately broad in nomenclature here, the figures all draw on First Nations' cultural beliefs, figures termed in colonial discourse "mythic." Yet they are also authorily imagined constructs. They are not human, nor therianthropic, material form is static. They speak as and resemble humans and simultaneously capture the qualities of diverse nonhuman animal or plant figures.

3. Sune Borkfelt is promoting a reading praxis whereby the phenomena of sound and smell are the analytical focus, heightening our proximity to animal suffering in slaughterhouses via literary representation, an approach that foregrounds the emotive and intuitive over the "rationalized."

4. Grace Dillon is arguing the trope or imaginative figuration of the "Native" has historically haunted science fiction, citing Frederic Jameson and his recall of Claude Levi-Strauss's "thinking Indians," whose totems provide metaphorical allegories necessary to bridge fantasy and science fiction (2017, 470).

5. The denoucement of the second series suggests engagement with other species that allows for alternative spaces of existence grounded in respectful kinship relations.

6. The year in which "Water" is set is 2022.

7. In Kaden's first-person narration there is no self-identification of a gender. It is overtly neutral. The only self-identification by the character is as queer. While Kaden is defined once as a daughter (by an Elder/uncle), I use the pronoun 'their' to acknowledge the text vexing of gender binaries, and avoid assumptions.

8. Arnhem Land Song cycles, originally translated by anthropologist Ronald M. Berndt, spring to mind; see Wonguri-Mandjigai People 2009.

PART IV

Mutation and Post-Apocalypse

Chapter 10

"We've Made Meat for Everyone!"

The Ideology of Distinction and Becoming Flesh in Cormac McCarthy's The Road *and Joseph D'Lacey's* Meat

Samantha Hind

Fires and floods rage across the world, destroying entire communities in the process. They leave behind ashy remnants and miry residues, as reminders of their power and destruction. One day, these remnants and residues might be all that is left of our civilization, as we know it—a crumbling wasteland littered with the cultural and ideological vestiges of a former world. A man and a boy might wander down the road, searching for food inside dusty ruins, paranoid about those who follow. A meat baron might survey his decaying town, full on flesh, deciding which townsfolk's status should be revoked next. These are the worlds that contemporary speculative fiction imagines; these are the worlds where disaster has struck, and people do what they have to do to survive—or so they say.

Such speculative fiction worlds, where whole cities have crumbled and starvation looms like an unwanted omen, are, at least for their creators, not such an inconceivable possibility, since the climate crisis puts the future of every species on Earth in danger. Cormac McCarthy's *The Road* (2006) and Joseph D'Lacey's *Meat* (2008) are speculative fiction novels that imagine the worlds that could emerge from our current inaction on climate change, with their desolate landscapes, widespread food scarcity, and absence of nonhuman animals. They postulate that lingering among these climate-changed environmental remnants are the hangovers of an anterior ideology: the ideology of distinction. This ideology insists on the biological and cultural separation of humans and nonhuman animals.

In laying bare these interwoven climate and ideological remnants, then, *The Road* and *Meat* share an interest in the production and consumption of flesh—both a large contributor to the current climate crisis and a process of applying an ideology of distinction in practice (Steinfield et al. 2006, xx-xxi). However, for many characters in the novels, it is not nonhuman animal flesh that keeps them fed, but instead it is human flesh that "becomes" edible. From small, family-run, basement operations to mass feedlot-factory farming establishments, human flesh production and consumption is a widespread practice in both *The Road* and *Meat*, constituting the staple food in many of their speculative diets. This choice of human flesh is perhaps surprising; as Nick Fiddes notes, "human flesh, nutritious as it may be, is not normally on our menus" (1991, 121). Cannibalism, specifically anthropophagy, exists as, arguably, the ultimate culinary taboo, supporting human flesh's inedible identity (Miller and Bowdoin Van Riper 2017, 4); however, both McCarthy's and D'Lacey's novels suggest that the lines between the distinct categories of inedible flesh and edible flesh are not stable, and we are only one power-hungry meat baron away from having human flesh on our plates.

McCarthy and D'Lacey negotiate the cannibalistic environment of the post-apocalypse, alongside the pre-apocalyptic remnants of an ideology of distinction. They question how these negotiations of human flesh consumption, in their speculative fiction worlds, contribute to broader critical questions about the role of an ideology of distinction in the current consumption of nonhuman animals. In both *The Road* and *Meat*, these critical questions are teased out and tested, through the characters' approach to flesh consumption and the parameters of who becomes edible. Lingering throughout these approaches is an ideology of distinction, which—whether it is manipulated or adapted—informs the divisions between the edible and the inedible, carrying itself from the pre-apocalypse to the post-apocalypse inside fleshy human vessels.

An ideology of distinction lingers in the minds and collective consciousness of speculative fiction characters, despite the shift from nonhuman animal flesh consumption to human flesh consumption. While a speculative post-apocalyptic world, where human flesh is eaten, seemingly provides a radical critique of current anthropocentric consumption, it is undermined by the residual presence of an ideology of distinction. Therefore, by focusing on the strangeness of the conditioning moments of flesh consumption, in *The Road* and *Meat*, we begin to see, fundamentally, how anthropocentric consumption is reinforced and maintained, both in speculative fiction and outside of it. In *The Road* and *Meat*, distinctions are made between edible and inedible flesh, and reinforced through what Matthew Calarco calls repeated enactments. During a discussion with Carol J. Adams about Derrida's concept of the carnophallogocentric subject, Matthew Calarco states that the subject "is never achieved once and for all. It must be repeatedly enacted, called into being in line with the conceptual-discursive-institutional ideal it invokes" (Adams and Calarco 2016, 43). As well as being crucial for the maintenance of the carnophallogocentric subject, this constant, repeated enactment is crucial for maintaining the ideology of distinction. The ideology exists, in part, through repeated enactments of nonhuman animal flesh consumption and the rejection of human flesh consumption. These enactments maintain not only the edibility of nonhuman animals, but also the inedibility of humans. However, while these repeated enactments suggest that the ideology they uphold is both prolific and stable, Calarco suggests, in reference to carnophallogocentrism, that, since these repeated enactments must take place, it means that, in fact, "it is unstable, structurally open to being challenged and contested" (2016, 44). Since an ideology of distinction follows these repeated enactments, it, too, is open to being challenged.

Close readings of flesh consumption in the novels, then, not only expose the workings of an ideology of distinction, but they also actively reveal counter-ideological possibilities, through their negotiations of both *becoming* and *consuming* human flesh. For the novels, before flesh can be consumed, it must first go through a process of becoming, of entering the identity of the edible. In *The Road*, this becoming is achieved through apparatus remnants and spatial conditions, in the form of nonhuman animal cooking equipment and housing. However, in *Meat*, this becoming takes a more gruesome turn, achieving its edible status through ritualized mutilations and graphic scriptures. Since the novels demonstrate a *becoming* that precedes a *consuming*, they reveal the constructed nature of an ideology of distinction and acknowledge that any being, regardless of species or status, is potentially edible. As such, the novels produce counter-ideological possibilities, in the form of what Matthew Calarco calls "indistinction." In this zone of indistinction, Calarco notes that "to see oneself as potentially edible [. . .] is to find oneself in a surprising, shocking alignment with animals; and to affirm and to live within the space of that alignment is ultimately to refuse the dominant culture's way of creating a sharp split between human and animal" (2015, 60). Through the revealing of human flesh's *becoming* and *consuming,* then, all flesh is shown to be indistinct. The challenges to the ideology of distinction that the novels provide, then, not only contest the prevalence of the ideology in their speculative fiction worlds, but they also contest the ideology, as it functions, outside of the speculative fiction world.

"RED AND SALTY MEAT INSIDE"

In the post-apocalyptic world of *The Road*, the man clings to the effigy of an ideology of distinction, maintaining an ontological distinction between humans and nonhuman animals, despite the apparent absence of the latter. Throughout the novel, the fear of cannibalism haunts the man and the boy—in terms of both *becoming* edible human flesh and *consuming* human flesh—yet, the man maintains that he and his son are not edible, and they will never resort to consuming other humans: "we wouldn't ever eat anybody, would we? [. . .] No. No matter what" (McCarthy 2006, 136). He maintains the pre-apocalyptic notion that "human flesh is the ultimate culinary taboo, and cannibalism the ultimate act of transgression" (Miller and Van Riper 2017, 80). In maintaining this notion, the man demonstrates, as Matthew Mullins notes, how "the refusal to satisfy hunger by eating humans signifies the adherence to a foundational set of beliefs that stipulates a good and bad, a right and wrong way to be human" (Mullins 2011, 80). However, McCarthy complicates the ontological distinctions that the man holds between human flesh and animal flesh, between "good" and "bad" consumption, by situating the man's consumption of, supposedly, nonhuman animal flesh, alongside cannibalized identifiers. In the post-apocalyptic world of *The Road*, then, the man's ideological beliefs are no longer stable, no matter how strongly he clings to them, and his re-enactments of the ideology begin to crumble.

In this new reality, the man and the boy spend their time on the search for food, rummaging around cupboards in derelict houses, hoping to find even the smallest morsel. Many of their searches yield very little, but sometimes they find leftovers from years gone by. These leftovers often include the remnants of canned goods, ranging from tinned fruit cocktail to tins of pork and beans. Since the man and the boy survive mainly on these products, Laura Wright suggests that they are "minimalistically vegan": "in the past world, they would have eaten animal meat; in the present, as no animals aside from humans seem to exist, survival is by and large minimalistically vegan" (2015, 73). However, the man and the boy live a far from vegan existence, maintaining a distinction between their inedible human flesh and the edible flesh of nonhuman animals, by repeatedly tucking into vestiges of flesh, wherever they can find them. While in a house, the man finds what he believes to be a piece of ham: "In an old batboard smokehouse they found a ham gambreled up in a high corner. It looked like something fetched from a tomb, so dried and drawn. He cut into it with his knife. Deep red and salty meat inside. Rich and good. They fried it that night over the fire, thick slices of it, and put the slices to simmer with a tin of beans" (McCarthy 2006, 16). Unlike many of the foods they find, which often come in labelled tins—and, if not labelled, at the very least, remain unopened—this piece of "ham" has no identifier. Visually, the flesh is indistinct, and it cannot be traced to a specific fleshy identity. The man does not pause to question the origin of this fleshy lump; he disavows its fleshy ambiguity and the possibility of it being human flesh, stating, categorically, that it is "ham," which he assumes to be the thigh of a dead pig. "Ham," however, is also used to refer to the back of the knee or thigh, more generally, regardless of species identity.[1] In reality, then, since only the leg remains, without other indicators, such as the rest of the body, the "red and salty meat inside" could be flesh from a number of species, including humans. Perhaps this conclusion appears speculative, since, after all, its fleshy indistinction could mean the flesh truly is the leg of a dead pig. Crucially, however, McCarthy continues to inscribe the "ham" with fleshy ambiguities, interweaving the discovery of the "ham" with telling puns, which reveal shared fleshy spaces, and repurposed cooking equipment, which combine fleshy renderings.

The man views the smokehouse as a sign that the flesh it contains comes from a nonhuman animal. Since the smokehouse would have traditionally been used to cure the flesh of nonhuman animals, the man's conclusion seems understandable, and he uses this conclusion to repeatedly enact an ideology of distinction. However, in this post-apocalyptic world, traditions do not mean certainty. During the same search for food, the man and the boy enter a barn, where there is "a boar-hide nailed to a barndoor. Ratty. Whisp of a tail" (McCarthy 2006, 16). The barn, traditionally used to house nonhuman animals, with its boar-hide-clad door acting as a signpost for nonhuman animal remains, suggests that what lies inside would once have belonged to nonhuman animals.

With this assumption, the man and the boy venture inside, expecting to find traces of nonhuman animals, which they might be able to use or consume; but, instead, "inside the barn three bodies hanging from the rafters, dried and dusty among the wan slats of light" (McCarthy 2006, 16). The barn's usual inhabitants have been replaced with the dried, dead bodies of humans, dangling inside their makeshift mausoleum. This makeshift mausoleum becomes the first of many indicators that there are connections between the human bodies in the barn and the flesh in the "tomb" of the smokehouse, casting doubt on the man's presumptions. These final resting place descriptors conflate one repurposed structure with another: the barn transforms from a holding place for nonhuman animals into a mausoleum for three human bodies, while, reflectively, the smokehouse transforms from a curing place for nonhuman animals into a tomb for a piece of unidentified flesh. Therefore, these repurposed structures, with their interwoven fleshy contents, cast doubt on the man's insistence on the hammy-nature of the smokehouse flesh—if the barn can house human flesh, so, too, can the smokehouse.

These human flesh indicators are not limited to the exterior structures of the barn and the smokehouse; their innards are equally revealing, with McCarthy employing puns and visual similarities to further complicate the fleshy identity of the "ham." The use of the pun "gambreled" is particularly telling because, while, in terms of the smokehouse, "gambrel" refers to the metal hanger, where carcasses are hung to be butchered, it also refers to the type of roof seen commonly on American barns.[2] The pun connects the bodies in the barn with the flesh in the smokehouse because they both, whether gambrel roof or gambrel device, hang from their gambrels, mirroring each other, with their placement of flesh. As such, whether explicitly human or ambiguously fleshy, they hang there, "dried and drawn" and "dried and dusty," as the man contemplates how to treat them: to shield them from his son's eyes or allow him to feast on the flesh.

The visual dryness of the flesh immediately links the barn bodies and the smokehouse flesh; but it is also a trope that McCarthy continues to return to, when regarding the bodies lying on roads and inside homes: "The mummied dead everywhere. The flesh cloven along the bones, the ligaments dried to tug and taunt as wires" (McCarthy 2006, 23). Since this dry, fleshy quality is something that McCarthy repeatedly uses to describe human flesh, whether in the barn or on the streets, its application to the smokehouse flesh, once again, raises questions of the "ham's" fleshy identity. Could it be that cutting into the barn bodies would also reveal "red and salty meat inside," ripe for consumption?

McCarthy continues to return to these repurposed structures and tools throughout the novel, using them as indicators of "all these things he saw and did not see" (McCarthy 2006, 115), imbuing each encounter with lingering doubts of fleshy identity. While scavenging around the grounds of the cannibal house, the man stumbles upon a makeshift stove, which he assumes is left over from the past, when they used it to cook nonhuman animals:

> In the yard was an old iron harrow propped up on piers of stacked brick and someone had wedged between the rails of it a forty gallon castiron cauldron of the kind once used for rendering hogs. Underneath were the ashes of a fire and blackened billets of wood. Off to one side a small wagon with rubber tires. All these things he saw and did not see. (McCarthy 2006, 115)

Despite his knowledge and paranoia about cannibals, the man assumes that the makeshift equipment has been used for nonhuman animals, like the smokehouse and its gambrel. Although, the cauldron may have once been used for cooking the flesh of nonhuman animals, since nonhuman animals no longer seem to populate the earth, it has now, clearly, been repurposed to cook the flesh of humans. Yet, the man is so controlled by an ideology of distinction, which views humans as inedible, that he misses the warning signs of the danger he is in and the flesh he has eaten. Even the ashy remnants do not seem to warn him, until it is already too late.

Brushing off the ashy remnants of the cauldron, the man leads the boy inside the cannibals' house and stumbles upon a hatch leading to a cellar. Thinking that it will contain "food," the man prises the hatch open. However, much to his dismay, there are no tins or prybars (McCarthy 2006, 114); instead,

> Huddled against the back wall were naked people, male and female, all trying to hide, shielding their faces with their hands. On the mattress lay a man with his legs gone to the hip and the stumps of them blackened and burnt. The smell was hideous.
>
> Jesus, he whispered.
>
> Then one by one they turned and blinked in the pitiful light. Help us, they whispered. Please help us. (McCarthy 2006, 116)

Although the man appears shocked to find the humans in the cellar, from the large cauldron to the recent fire, there were clear indications of their presence. McCarthy not only makes these connections between the equipment in the cannibal yard and the humans in the cellar, but he also reinforces the connections between the bodies in the barn and the "ham" in the smokehouse. There is a continuous, explicit connection between presently consuming human flesh and traditionally rendering nonhuman animal flesh. As such, McCarthy encourages the reader to return to the equipment in the yard, with its forty gallon cauldron and blackened fire, as the evidence for all the indicators that the man "did not see" (McCarthy 2006, 115). While the cauldron itself returns to the repurposing of nonhuman animal cooking equipment seen at the smokehouse, the association with "rendering hogs" makes this connection more tangible and explicit. Just like the boar-hide on the door, the image of rendering hogs connects these human flesh discoveries to the "ham" in the smokehouse. They are a set of piggy indicators that, together with the repurposed structures and equipment, cast doubt on the nonhuman animal nature of the "ham," since what is revealed, after the pig imagery, is always human flesh.

Furthermore, the humans in the cellar also encourage a return to the "ham" in the smokehouse, through their missing limbs. As the severed limbs from the still living body of a man show, these humans are kept alive so that their flesh can be removed, cooked, and eaten, in the quantities needed to feed the cannibals. Their cauterized flesh becomes a visible and odorous reminder of their edibility. However, it is not just that these severed limbs demonstrate the edibility of human flesh, but that those particular limbs severed, the legs, make striking connections to the "ham" in the smokehouse. By revealing the human legs as the source of eaten flesh, rather than omitting it entirely or selecting another body part, McCarthy encourages a connection to the leg of flesh in the smokehouse. Accordingly, when removed from the human body, the severed legs of the humans take on the same visible indistinction as the lump of leg flesh in the smokehouse. They, too, become another piece of flesh ready to be consumed by a hungry human. Therefore, while McCarthy denies the explicit knowledge of the "ham's" species, as viewed through the man's perspective, he reveals the origin of another lump of leg flesh, the human in the cellar, in order to determine the "ham's" speculative origin: human.

It has been suggested by Xavier Aldana Reyes that McCarthy's *The Road* offers "a wholesale condemnation of the practice of cannibalism" (Aldana Reyes 2014, 113); however, I have shown that such a suggestion offers a simplistic view of how McCarthy explores the consumption of human flesh in the novel. Instead of being a simple condemnation, McCarthy utilizes the taboo of cannibalism to explore the workings of an ideology of distinction and provide challenges to it. As such, by revisiting repurposed structures, tools, and visibly indistinct flesh, alongside the discovery of human flesh consumption, McCarthy not only complicates the fleshy identity of the "ham" that the man and the boy gladly consume, but he also complicates the man's maintenance of an ideology of distinction, whereby human flesh is inedible. He demonstrates both the ineffectiveness of such an ideology and the danger of it, since maintaining the inedibility of human flesh places the man and the boy in danger. However, the horror of consuming human flesh is never fully realized for the man and the boy, since the ham's identity is never confirmed, and they are never eaten. Yet, the cannibalized hints that McCarthy litters throughout this ashy wasteland actualize, if only in part, the horror for the reader. It is the readership's horror that is, all at once, actualised *and* transformed; what appears to be a nightmare of edible becoming and consuming is actually McCarthy's offer of transformation into a counter-ideological possibility: indistinction. The very fact that the man and boy inhabit a world where human flesh is eaten, and that they have most likely partaken in this fleshy meal, forces human flesh to become edible, much to the horror of the ideology of distinction. Readers are thrown into Calarco's "zone of indistinction," where acknowledging a shared edibility begins to deconstruct the distinctions that exist between humans and nonhuman animals (2015, 60). Indistinction, then, is offered as a counter-ideological possibility; the debased world of human flesh consumption, potentially, offers up a new way of life, where both humans and nonhuman animals exist "beyond the 'mere' meat to which the dominant culture tries to reduce them" (Calarco 2015, 59).

"WE'VE MADE MEAT FOR EVERYONE!"

Like *The Road*, *Meat* is haunted by the spectre of cannibalism; it threatens to pick off each inhabitant of Abyrne, one by one, until only the bones of the town remain. However, there is one group of Abyrne's residents that are selected for consumption, even before they let out their first scream in the world: The Chosen. Unlike the Townsfolk, the Chosen are farmed for their human flesh and kept in conditions similar to those of factory-farmed nonhuman animals. In order for Abyrne's leaders, Rory Magnus and The Welfare, to maintain the distinctions between the Chosen and the Townsfolk, which keep the Chosen eaten and the majority of the Townsfolk fed, they adapt an ideology of distinction, manufacturing distinctions by human-made mutilations. This residual but adapted ideology of distinction filters down, through newly created religious materials and capitalist advertisement, like the Gut Psalter and the Book of Giving. While the Book of Giving tells of how "the Father sent his own children down to Earth so that we, his townsfolk might eat" (D'Lacey 2008, 76), the Gut Psalter explains in fine details the mutilations that the Chosen must undergo, at birth, in order to *become* edible flesh. From the chemical removal of hair, to the slashing of vocal chords, the Chosen are stripped of any visual and audible similarities that might connect them with the Townsfolk; these mutilations are similar to those that nonhuman animals undergo in the factory farming process. Despite the obvious human species identity of the Chosen, then, *Meat* acts as an ideological allegory, placing mutilated humans in the conditions and positions typically reserved for farmed nonhuman animals. The Chosen, like the nonhuman animals they allegorize, exist in Abyrne as what Rebekah Sinclair calls "speciesed others" who are "always already edible, killable even before they are killed" (Sinclair 2016, 231).

In a rather disturbing interaction involving Hema and Harsha, the twin daughters of Richard Shanti, Magnus Meat Processing's best stunner turned Chosen rights activist, D'Lacey illustrates how an ideology of distinction works. The ideology is filtered down, through textual propaganda, into the minds of every townsfolk of Abyrne, and repeatedly enacted, through normalized actions. Hema and Harsha decide to hold a party for their toy guests, carefully selecting their meal for the evening. At first, their party appears to be like any other, with their mother, Maya, hoping to glimpse their imagined world "in which she could return to their simple innocence and in doing so briefly turn away from the realities of the town" (D'Lacey 2008, 95). However, in their town of horrors, the toys gathered around the table are not awaiting tea; instead, they await flesh:

> On each plate was a hollow portion of doll—an upper arm, a thigh, a calf, a foot, a hand. The torso had been cut into four slices like a small loaf. Hema and Harsha were 'sharing' them. It was the attention to detail that stunned Maya. The girls had prepared the doll before butchering her for their distinguished guests. They'd cut as much of her hair off as they could. Maya could see how they'd removed two thirds of each finger on her tiny hands and clipped her thumbs off altogether. On the platters where feet were served, she saw that the big toe had been severed. The shaven head lay to one side but in the top 'slice' of the torso, she saw the neck and the puncture wound in the centre of it where they'd silence the doll before slaughter. 'Hello, Mama,' said Harsha. 'Would you like to come to the party? We've made meat for everyone!' (D'Lacey 2008, 95)

In precise detail, Hema and Harsha carry out the mutilations to their toy doll, removing her hair and the required portions of finger. The childhood innocence—that Maya hopes to witness—vanishes under the ideological teachings of the Gut Psalter and the Book of Giving. Rather than existing outside of an ideology of distinction, where the production and consumption of the Chosen's flesh do not figure in their understanding of Abyrne, Hema and Harsha are at the centre of ideological conditioning; an ideology of distinction is infiltrating even the youngest of minds. In an interview, D'Lacey confirms this rationale, commenting: "I wanted to imply that the children were beginning to pick up and accept Abyrne's societal edicts as 'normal.' A scene in which they played out a meal for their toys seemed a good way of doing that" (Wilson 2013). Hema and Harsha's party, then, appears to be a form of repeated enactment—albeit an infantile one—whereby an ideology of distinction is reaffirmed and maintained.

The doll at the centre of their meal begins the party like any other of the toy guests, with a full head of hair and all her fingers intact; she is even accompanied by "the blind, balding bear, the toy soldiers, several dolls and even a rubber clown that smelled of chemicals—a toy they rarely played with" (D'Lacey 2008, 95). Gathered around the makeshift table, then, are a number of toys which Hema and Harsha could have "chosen"; there are even other dolls. There appears to be no rationale behind "picking out a plastic female doll with long blond hair" (D'Lacey 2008, 94–95), but she becomes their meal. This strange moment, then, where the parameters between the edible and the inedible fluctuate, signals a displacement of the ideology of distinction. Despite the repeated enactment of imagined consumption seemingly functioning as a maintenance of an ideology of distinction, then, Hema and Harsha's party has another function: the party provides a space for challenging the very ideology that they are enacting.

When their mother sees what they are doing, the girls proudly announce, "[w]e've made meat for everyone" (D'Lacey 2008, 95). The girls understand—

in part—that they must *make* meat; there is a *becoming,* before the consuming. In order for the doll to form a suitable meal for their distinguished guests, she must undergo a process of edible fleshy *becoming*. However, it is not just the mutilations and butchering of the doll's plastic flesh that constitutes this edible fleshy becoming; instead, after these physical enactments, there is an ideological becoming, whereby the doll stops being an inedible consumer and *becomes* an edible commodity. The doll makes the swift transition, from inedible toy—like the soldiers, clown, and other dolls—into delectable, plastic portions of edible foot, arm, and torso. By acknowledging this *becoming*, the girls' party exposes the workings of an ideology of distinction. It demonstrates that the ideology can only survive through repeated enactments; the distinctions of edibility are illusions created by an ideology of distinction.

Maya comments that this was "the second time she'd found the girls serving 'meat' to their toys and she wanted it to stop" (D'Lacey 2008, 109). Aside from being an exclusive game for the girls to play, then, there are suggestions that the girls have tried this before. The chemical smell that emerges from the clown, rather than simply being an identifier of its condition, alludes to a previous attempt at performing the mutilation ritual of chemical hair removal. The girls allow the toys with "failed" mutilations to re-enter the world of the inedible; they go through a process of *un-becoming*, no longer existing solely to be consumed.

This *un-becoming* is not confined to the realms of imagined play; instead, it takes centre stage, at the battle to free the Chosen. It is revealed that both Richard Shanti and prophet John Collins (the leader of the Chosen rights movement) bear the scars of failed mutilations:

> Collins bore a scar at his throat. Shanti was missing one thumb. Arnold Shanti had committed a crime of interference, a crime so grave it could never be acknowledged. He'd liberated twin male calves. He'd raised one as his own but both had grown up as townsfolk, neither knowing the other existed. "Brothers . . . " she whispered to John Collins. " . . . Chosen." (D'Lacey 2008, 340)

After a trail of indicators, throughout the novel, that there is something more to Shanti and Collins than Townsfolk, it is Parson Mary Simonson of The Welfare that finally connects the dots. Like the rubber clown, in Hema and Harsha's party, Shanti and Collins were granted an existence away from their birth as edible Chosen, by a member of the Townsfolk. Arnold Shanti, Richard Shanti's adopted father, facilitates Shanti and Collins' *un-becoming*, halting the mutilation rituals and moving them from the environment of the slaughterhouse to the environment of the town. Such an *un-becoming* shows the instability of the ideology of distinction and directly challenges it—despite taking many years to fully manifest. If Richard Shanti and John

Collins can exist within the town, even becoming, in Shanti's case, an admired member of MMPs workforce, the inherent difference between the Chosen and the Townsfolk, between the edible and the inedible, associated with an ideology of distinction, falls away. As such, any differences that exist between the Chosen and the Townsfolk are exposed as being illusory.

In the final moments of the novel, these illusory ideological distinctions are confirmed. The Chosen step into the light, revealing themselves, in their mutilated fleshy form, to Hema and Harsha: "There, for the first time, [Hema and Harsha] saw bulls and cows in the flesh, up close. There, too, they saw calves pressed close to their mothers. Some of the calves were the same size as the twins. Their eyes met. The twins saw the calves for what they truly were. Children" (D'Lacey 2008, 339). Unlike the horror of the "ham's" fleshy origin in *The Road*, which is never fully actualised, the horrors of the Chosen's fleshy identity are fully actualised for Hema and Harsha, who now understand the true identity of the flesh they have been playing with and consuming. Despite the Chosen's mutilated flesh, Hema and Harsha see that they are like the Chosen, and the Chosen are like them. They see that the distinctions they have been taught, through the ideological conditioning of the Welfare' scriptures, are human-made, serving as convenient justifications for the becoming and consumption of the Chosen. In the end, they are all the same flesh.

Aldana Reyes suggests that "*Meat*'s horrific premise is based on the possibility of humans being reduced to their flesh and on the subsequent loss of their rights as individuals" (2014, 116). While this is, in part, true, what Aldana Reyes does not acknowledge, here, is the role of nonhuman animals in the figuring of *Meat*'s horror. The horror of *Meat* is not simply a speculative imaging of human reduction; instead, the real horror of *Meat* is the exposition of an ideology of distinction, which perpetuates the very real, anthropocentric consumption of nonhuman animals. *Meat* shows us, in horrific detail, that the flesh of nonhuman animals is being butchered and consumed every day, on the basis of illusory ideological distinctions.

From unassuming children's parties to explicitly gruesome scenes of mutilation, D'Lacey posits that, behind the facades of repeated enactments, lies the real horror perpetuating the suffering and oppression of the Chosen and the nonhuman animals they represent: an ideology of distinction. D'Lacey conflates the disturbing, speculative practice of human flesh consumption with the very real, disturbing consumption of nonhuman animals, in order to negotiate the ideology of distinction that maintains the parameters of edibility. He forces us to question how human flesh *becomes* edible, in a speculative future, facilitating this application onto the edible *becoming* of nonhuman animals. These explorations of *becoming* and *consuming* flesh, then, demonstrate both the prominence and power of an ideology of distinction, as well as its weaknesses and instability. Indeed, the horror of consuming human flesh, in *Meat*, is fully realized, for every willfully ignorant Townsfolk of Abyrne. They see that they are like the Chosen, they see every mutilation as an application of distinction onto what was previously indistinct. By seeing the Chosen and acknowledging their connectedness to one another, they enter into this zone of indistinction, where, as Calarco notes, "to acknowledge oneself as inhabiting a shared zone of exposed embodiment with animals is to recognize that we are in deep and fundamental ways *like animals*" (2015, 58). Many of the Townsfolk are overwhelmed by the horrific realization of the indistinction of their flesh and the flesh of the Chosen: "a ripple of unease spread through the crowd. They began to retreat" (D'Lacey 2008, 341).

Nevertheless, there are those who embrace indistinction with cautious, but open, arms, acknowledging that inhabiting this zone of indistinction "means that we have ethical and ontological work to do" (Caffo 2013, 87). D'Lacey captures this movement into a zone of indistinction, in the final moments of the novel, allowing the Chosen to walk free, alongside one another and Hema and Harsha, led by Moses-esque Richard Shanti: "They only knew that they were free now and that with Shanti's knowledge and the knowledge of the followers, they would survive until they reached the land where pain was no longer a memory, a land where what they had given would never be asked for again. They knew it existed" (D'Lacey 2008, 343). Not only has the Chosen's flesh been freed from the confines of MMP's slaughterhouse walls, but they have been freed from an ideology of distinction, too. In this new land that they long for, they will be free from the bonds of the ideology of distinction, no longer forced to relinquish their lives for the greed of others. Since we are not granted the same hopeful ending in *The Road*, we can only hope that the boy, a product of the post-apocalypse, not only survives, but leads the rest of humanity to a new land, where an ideology of distinction is but a distant memory.

"NO ONE EXISTS OUTSIDE THAT SIMPLE TRUTH"

I will conclude this chapter with a quote from *Meat*'s John Collins: "'In the flesh, as we sit here, as *people*,' he would sometimes say, 'we've all come from the same place, from the same beginning. That beginning is where we're all going back to sooner or later. That makes us all brothers and sisters. *All* of us. No one exists outside that simple truth. Can you see that much?'" (D'Lacey 2008, 28).

Negotiations of human flesh's edible *becoming* and *consuming*, in *The Road* and *Meat*, offer us more than just a grisly spectacle of the extremes of flesh consumption; instead, they actively encourage explorations of counter-ideological possibilities, showcasing the possibilities of an alternative, speculative future. While some may argue that human flesh consumption simply reduces humans to calorific constituents and leaves them to rot in a space of abject horror, human flesh consumption, through its acknowledgement of human edibility, offers the possibility for humans to ascend from this debased place of edibility, alongside other fleshy beings. As Calarco notes, "inasmuch as we share embodiment with animals, we know that their bodies and our bodies can become something more, something beyond the 'mere' meat to which the dominant culture tries to reduce them" (2015, 59).

The counter-ideological possibilities of indistinction, explored by these awkward and strange moments of flesh consumption and becoming, demonstrate the instability of an ideology of distinction, both within the novels and outside of them. Although it appears that all that survives at the end of the world are humans and an ideology of distinction, both clinging to the fleshy vestiges of a bygone era, McCarthy and D'Lacey do not simply comply. Instead, they work within an ideology of distinction to weaken the repeated enactments that maintain it, exposing the workings of the ideology and providing counter-ideological possibilities like indistinction.

Therefore, while the climate crisis offers us an insight into what it means to eat flesh in a world desperate for a sustainable alternative, and Calarco's indistinction approach offers us an insight into what it means to be flesh, crucially, the speculative fiction worlds of *The Road* and *Meat* offer us an insight into what it means to both eat *and* be flesh in a world where everything is on the menu.

REFERENCES

Adams, Carol J., and Matthew Calarco. 2016. "Derrida and *The Sexual Politics of Meat.*" In *Meat Culture*, edited by Annie Potts, 31–53. Boston, MA: Brill.

Aldana Reyes, Xavier. 2014. *Body Gothic: Corporeal Transgression in Contemporary Literature and Horror*. Cardiff: University of Wales Press.

Caffo, Leonardo. 2013. "We Are Made of Meat: An Interview with Matthew Calarco." *Relations* 1 (2): 85–90. doi.org/10.7358/rela-2013-002-caff.

Calarco, Matthew. 2015. *Thinking Through Animals: Identity, Difference, Indistinction*. Stanford, CA: Stanford University Press.

D'Lacey, Joseph. 2008. *Meat*. London: Bloody Books.

Fiddes, Nick. 1991. *Meat: A Natural Symbol*. London: Routledge.

McCarthy, Cormac. 2006. *The Road*. New York, NY: Picador.

Miller, Cynthia J., and A. Bowdoin Van Riper. 2017. "Introduction." In *What's Eating You?*, ed. Cynthia J. Miller and A. Bowdoin Van Riper, 1–12. New York, NY: Bloomsbury Academic & Professional.

Mullins, Matthew. 2011. "Hunger and the Apocalypse of Modernity in Cormac McCarthy's *The Road.*" *Symploké* 19 (1–2): 75–93. dx.doi.org/10.5250/symploke.19.1-2.0075.

Sinclair, Rebekah. 2016. "The Sexual Politics of Meatless Meat: (in)Edible Others and the Myth of Flesh without Sacrifice." In *The Future of Meat without Animals*, ed. Brianne Donaldson and Christopher Carter, 229–248. London: Rowman & Littlefield International, Ltd.

Steinfeld, Henning, Pierre Gerber, Tom Wassenaar, Vincent Castel, Mauricio Rosales, and Cees de Haan. 2006. *Livestock's Long Shadow: Environmental Issues and Options.* Rome: Food and Agriculture Organization of the United Nations. www.europarl.europa.eu/climatechange/doc/FAO%20report%20executive%20summary.pdf.

Wilson, Michael. 2013. "Interview: Joseph D'Lacey on the rerelease of MEAT, Part II." *This is Horror*, 19 December 2013. www.thisishorror.co.uk/interview-joseph-dlacey-rerelease-meat-part-ii/.

Wright, Laura. 2015. *The Vegan Studies Project: Food, Animals, and Gender in the Age of Terror.* Athens, GA: University of Georgia Press.

NOTES

1. *Oxford English Dictionary*, online edition, "ham, n.1 and adj." www.oed.com/view/Entry/83690.

2. *Oxford English Dictionary*, online edition, "gambrel, n. 1a, n. 3a." www.oed.com/view/Entry/76464.

Chapter 11

"There Would Be Monsters, Some Hopeful"

Viral Agencies and Mutational Posthuman Politics in Post-Millennial Science Fiction

Clare Wall

Climate change fiction offers multiple approaches to portraying "Nature" as an active force possessing an unpredictable agency. By imagining the transformative effects of global warming and the unpredictability it injects into future ecologies, climate fiction also draws attention to its complex effects through future plagues, species collapse, and invasive or "unnatural" technoscientific creatures. Peter Watts's *Rifters* trilogy (1999, 2001, 2004), Paolo Bacigalupi's *The Windup Girl* (2009), and Margaret Atwood's *MaddAddam* trilogy (2003, 2009, 2013) are all plague narratives and examples of ecofiction containing climate-changed futures and genetically modified beings. Their texts also undermine anthropocentric attempts at mastery over nature through environmental instabilities caused by infections and ecological disasters. Exploring the agencies and mutational potentialities of nonhuman life in these narratives and their ability to generate transformative posthuman connections, I argue that their focus on the agentic potentials of nonhuman life to shape and transform bodies, environments, and subjects generates a space where humans might be resituated as entangled and ever-evolving with the biosphere. Additionally, these texts facilitate a shift towards an embedded ecological consciousness through interspecies partnerships which contest the lines we draw in terms of "nature" and the "unnatural" and who, or what, belongs in any given ecosystem. In doing so, these narratives invite the reader to undergo a mutational reorientation away from an anthropocentric understanding of nature.

Examining Watts's, Bacigalupi's, and Atwood's post-millennial plague narratives through a posthumanist lens, it becomes clear how their nuanced accounts of interspecies partnerships, nonhuman entanglements, and transformative "mutational politics" decenter the human subject and position the human as part of an environmentally situated assemblage. Thinking the human as an assemblage positions it to better relate to the environment through new forms of partnership, becoming-with, and knowledge attained through such practices. Andrew Pickering (2005) argues that posthumanism brings into focus "the idea of a *mutual* becoming or coproduction or coevolution of people and things" (31). The human is therefore already a mutational being, one that is always adapting and changing in the shifting series of relations we belong to in the world. Focusing on events in *Maelstrom* and *βehemoth*,[1] I examine how Watts's narrative draws attention to the powers of pathogens and their destabilization of traditional boundaries between bodies, environments, and real and virtual spaces to underscore the transformative potential partnerships one might form with microbes and pathogens. I then compare this with how the violent politics against genetically modified life is depicted in Bacigalupi's *The Windup Girl*. Additionally, I examine how Bacigalupi's novel presents the need to critically rethink nature-culture binaries including born versus made and natural versus unnatural to navigate the world under climate change through its portrayal of transgenic species. This paradigm shift and the agential power of the environment to adapt is shared in Atwood's *Oryx and Crake* and *MaddAddam* through the becomings of the posthuman Crakers, which undermines the genetic foreclosure attempted by their creator, Crake. Both Atwood's and Bacigalupi's endings offer ambiguous hope in the form of posthuman and hybrid life thriving which further challenges concepts of nature as static. By resisting technoscientific controls over environments in favour of interspecies partnerships and dynamic ecologies, these narratives invite readers to contemplate an embedded ecological consciousness, in turn offering an inoculation against an anthropocentric reading of nature.

THE *RIFTERS* TRILOGY: THE POWER OF PATHOGENS

Bacteria and viruses tend to conjure negative associations despite their many beneficial partnerships and roles in the development of complex life.[2] Watts's *Rifters t*rilogy follows Lenie Clarke's experiences as a rifter initially employed by the Grid Authority to maintain its geothermal power generators in the Pacific Rift. Rifters like Lenie are cyborgs whose bodies have been augmented genetically and technologically to enable survival in the rift.

While they are modified to survive there, the rift is also an agent in shaping the rifters (Wall 2015, 73). Lenie unwittingly becomes an ideal host for the extremophile bacteria βehemoth that has evolved in the rift as a more efficient "competitor" to complex life (Watts 1999, 258). Despite her employer setting off a nuclear detonation to contain the infection and all possible vectors, Lenie survives and seeks vengeance by spreading it across North America. After hiding in the Atlantic for five years while billions died, Lenie re-emerges, this time to seek redemption by trying to stop a newly modified, deadlier form of the pathogen that threatens what remains of the biosphere.

Watts draws on Lynn Margulis's theory of endosymbiosis—the process whereby eukaryotic cells evolved to their present form through symbiotic partnerships formed with other cells they consumed, allowing them to develop useful organs such as mitochondria and chloroplasts (Sagan 1967, 228).[3] Like the partnership between eukaryotic cells and mitochondria, βehemoth offers additional stamina and energy to hosts like Lenie, but because it has not undergone millions of years of symbiotic evolution, its benefits are temporary and far outweighed by the eventual death toll it extracts (Watts 2001, 286). Utilizing this theory of symbiotic and evolutionary adaptation, Watts's depictions of contagion emphasize the mutual becomings and exchanges across life forms, presenting an ambiguous space for potential change rather than a purely negative image of infection. Heather Paxton suggests our lack of attention to microorganisms limits and warps our understanding of human society (2008, 18–19). Watts's narrative foregrounds infections and adaptive becomings, drawing attention to the roles of nonhuman agency and embedded subjectivity, especially through the ambiguous space of symbiotic partnerships.

Alphonso Lingis suggests that many symbiotic movements are not goal-oriented in the sense of a conscious mind or agent but lead to intense becomings with others (2003, 167–8). The recognition of nonhuman agencies and the complex interrelationships between species are similarly articulated in Karen Barad's materialist politics of agential realism which offers a means of considering material relations and forms of agency through the "intra-actions" of bodily production.[4] Here, agency is defined as the "reconfigurings of the world" (2008, 135). Conceptualizing agency in this way resists privileging an anthropocentric unified subjecthood. It also facilitates a posthuman ecopolitics because it acknowledges that bodies "are not simply situated in, or located in, particular environments. Rather 'environments' and 'bodies' are intra-actively co-constituted" (2006, 170). Watts repeatedly underscores the significance of nonhuman agencies through frequent motifs of unintended symbiotic exchanges and coevolutions occurring between virtual and physical forms of life and environments.

Maelstrom first introduces the concept of symbiogenesis through observations on the partnerships between sea creatures in an aquarium made by Sou

Hon Perrault, a disaster responder assigned to virtually observe the refugee strip who becomes invested in helping Lenie. While watching the aquarium's denizens, Sou Hon is awed by the fact "that the whole crazy alliance—algae, anemone, fish—hadn't even been engineered. It had evolved naturally, a gradual symbiosis spanning millions of years. Not one gene had been tweaked in its construction" (2001, 25). The evolved partnerships between the sea creatures emphasize their environmentally embedded interconnections. Moreover, the anthropocentric tendencies to consider humans the master shapers of the world and lifeforms as singular rather than interdependent entities are reflected in Sou Hon's wonder at it not being modified by humans. Watts effectively builds on this motif of unexpected, co-constituted partnerships by repeating it through the physical and virtual entanglements formed between Lenie, βehemoth, and the evolving virtual meme/program Anemone that seeks to ensure βehemoth's survival.

In addition to drawing attention to the power of microbial agencies to shape events and even the direction of life itself, the *Rifters* trilogy effectively critiques anthropocentrism by foregrounding the flow between the agential becomings in the material and virtual worlds. The trilogy features chapters from the perspectives of several human and virtual characters, such as Lenie Clarke (human), the viral program (Anemone), and the Madonnas (virtual malware). By intersplicing chapters from Anemone's perspective as it undergoes its own Darwinian selection, *Maelstrom* offers a unique vision of the virtual environment Anemone inhabits and its interactions with other virtual life. Lenie's vengeance-filled travels across North America spreading βehemoth unwittingly contribute to the symbiotic development of the Maelstrom's/internet's wildlife into "some kind of–Lenie Clarke interdiction network" (Watts 2001, 345), unintentionally driving Anemone's emergence from simpler viral programs. In turn, Anemone creates a real-time following for Lenie by seeding viral myths of her as the "Meltdown Madonna" and "Mermaid of the Apocalypse" (241), further fueling it's evolution. Much like Lingis's claim regarding the lack of conscious agency in many cross-species partnerships, the *Rifters'* narrative emphasizes the all too often unnoticed nonhuman agencies that can have significant effects.

Through the chapters from the evolving viral program's perspective, it becomes apparent that it has no concept of Lenie as a human being. Interacting with her benefits its survival and reproduction which, in turn, helps its virtual passage and infection of Maelstrom/the internet. In a scene depicting one of Anemone's prior evolutions as 400 Megabytes, Watts emphasizes the disconnect between the factors driving 400's "choices" and the reality occurring in Lenie's world, stating "[y]ou want to get around fast in Maelstrom, the name you drop is *Lenie Clarke*. 400 doesn't know why this should be . . . . What it *does* know is, that particular string of characters gets you in *anywhere*" (2001, 183). Writing Lenie's name into its code ensures 400's proliferation in much the same way that βehemoth thrives through Lenie acting as both a host and a vector. 400's actions parallel the world of the infection which itself is striving to survive. Discussing her posthuman theory of understanding agency and matter, Barad argues "[t]he world is a dynamic process of intra-activity and materialization in the enactment of determinate causal structures with determinate boundaries, properties, meanings, and patterns of marks on bodies" (2007, 140). As 400 evolves into Anemone, it actively promotes the Meltdown Madonna memes that inspire a doomsday cult following for Lenie, thus emphasizing the ongoing mutually beneficial exchanges occurring between βehemoth, Lenie, and Anemone. Additionally, Ben Eldridge observes that Watts's vivid use of physical language personifies and anthropomorphizes 400's perspective (2019, 225). Ascribing greater agency to 400 makes it a character rather than an object viewed by a human interpreter.[5] By emphasizing its dynamic agencies, Watts models the significance of nonhuman agential becomings.

Watts thus illustrates the complex entanglements of virtual and material production by human and nonhuman agents by demonstrating how βehemoth's effects leak across both the biosphere and Maelstrom. As Pramod Nayar argues in his discussion of posthumanism, "[l]ife" is "a process of *becoming* through new connections and mergers between species, bodies, functions, and technologies" (2014, 30). Humans, according to Nayar, are part of that becoming with beings outside themselves (31). Stacey Alaimo similarly asserts in her trans-corporeal posthuman ethics that "human bodies and nonhuman natures transform, unfold, and thereby resist categorization, complete knowledge, and mastery" (2008, 253). Lenie's translation into a digital assemblage extends her beyond herself, infecting the internet by shifting her from a physical vector into an equally infectious circulating meme as her actions unintentionally influence Anemone's emergence as "a colonial superorganism" (Watts 2001, 346). By depicting the entangled flow of human and nonhuman agencies, Watts underscores their power to enact dynamic global transformations.

While such symbiotic partnerships may ensure Lenie, Anemone, and βehemoth's survival, they also lead to a thanatopolitical destruction of both human and nonhuman life. It is only in the latter half of *βehemoth* that some of the more redemptive potentialities of such partnerships are revealed. Returning to the surface five years after her plague pilgrimage across North America, Lenie encounters the Lenies/Madonnas—modified and degraded forms of Anemone that savagely attack virtual ecologies and any systems they infect. Her connection with the destructive Madonnas that manifest with her rifter appearance and name becomes a further demonstration of the ongoing co-constitutive exchanges between virtual and physical agents as well as a destabilization of the liberal human subject. After quarantining a Madonna that infected the mobile medical van Lenie and her allies were operating out of, Lenie identifies with it as an extended part of her former fury-driven self; she acknowledges that "back at the beginning, she'd been the template. This thing had taken its lead from *her*" (2004b, 143). However, instead of erasing the Madonna, Lenie seeks a means to rehabilitate it; she enlists aid to help "tweak" it to "Make Lenie *like* Lenie" (192). Examining recent research in interactions between the immune system, body, and bacteria such as gut flora and fauna, Nayar argues that the self is not coherent but symbiogenetic (2014, 45–6). In other words, the "self" is in part determined by the interactions between your cells, genes, and the bacteria your body hosts, and therefore, is ever-evolving and changing. Lenie's confrontation with her past and her acceptance of her virtual doppelganger offer examples of how kinship relations can better situate the self to connect across species and bodies and to take greater responsibility.

Through Lenie's virtual and bacterial entanglements, Watts's narrative challenges the notion of the autonomous self, suggesting that being is itself mutational and infectious. Lenie's becomings of self with other lifeforms and entities are heavily shaped by contagion. The Madonnas are altered by means of a counter-infection that restores their cooperative capacity. It does so by causing them to again recognize all descendants of Anemone with "Lenie Clarke" in their coding as kin, which they then counter-infect with that cooperative code (Watts 2004b, 197). Acting together as a united assemblage, the Madonnas possess vast transformative power to destroy virtual containment measures, including those that threaten Lenie and her rifter ally, Ken Lubin. The Madonnas' destructive virtual presence also mirrors Lenie's past actions which devastated countless lives and ecologies. The only form of restoration for both the Madonnas and βehemoth is by performing a retrofit of infectious new kin relations. The Madonnas' rehabilitative mutation reopens it to forms of virtual community; the extension of kin and self through infectious and virtual becomings destabilize the nature/culture and human/animal/machine boundaries used to define and empower the human subject and facilitate an inter-meshed posthuman one.

The potential promise offered through mutational becomings also plays out in the physical world through Seppuku, an entirely new manufactured pathogen and untested cure being forced into North America by foreign missiles. Taka Ouellette, the doctor Lenie befriends after commandeering her mobile clinic, eventually realizes Seppuku is designed to immunize the biosphere against βehemoth and β-Max, conceiving of it as "[t]he end of Life As We Knew It. The beginning of Life As We Don't" (Watts 2004b, 244). Seppuku offers ambiguous hope by introducing viral symbionts which will keep βehemoth out by redesigning its hosts internally (242). Life will continue, but in new and unimaginable forms, offering an open possibility—one that rejects the humanist fixation on thriving at all costs. Even if humanity does not survive, some species will live on to evolve new partnerships. This position may be especially jarring to readers because it resists granting any privilege to human survival, making Watts's narrative highly effective in its potential to reorient the reader towards a multispecies perspective—one where humanity is not at the epicentre.

In making the cure to βehemoth's destruction of the biosphere also be an infection, survival is opened to unpredictable new collaborations between the viral codes introduced by Seppuku and its new hosts. Like the ancient merger of proto-eukaryotic cells with mitochondria, Seppuku offers a means of "life within life" (240). By forming new symbiotic partnerships with others, enough aspects of the biosphere may survive to regenerate anew. According to anthropologist Stefan Helmreich's observations on the foundational microbial becomings of ocean life, "viruses have not only or merely parasitized organisms in which they have taken up tenancy but also laterally contributed—think tangled tree of life—to the genomes of those creatures, as viral material has been transduced into host DNA" (2009, 192). Similarly, Taka finds the possibilities and consequences produced by Seppuku's counter-infection overwhelming:

> What simulation could predict the behavior of a multimillion-species system when every living variable was perturbed at once? How many carefully-selected experimental treatments would it take to model a billion simultaneous mutations? Seppuku—whatever Seppuku was poised to become—threw the very concept of a *controlled experiment* out the window.
>
> [. . . .]
>
> And maybe it wouldn't fail. Maybe everything would change for the better. There would be monsters, some hopeful. (Watts 2004b, 243)

Despite the uncertain and apocalyptic setting in the *Rifters* trilogy, symbiotic kinship offers "hopeful monsters" and the potential to shift human thinking towards ecological situatedness. Alaimo contends that understanding nonhuman agencies "catalyzes an environmental ethics of partnership" (2008, 245). By foregrounding the power of kinship exchanges, Watts's narrative shows one way of catalyzing such an ethics. In order to achieve an ecological consciousness necessary for survival, *Rifters* suggests the concept of "humanity" must become infected and redesigned with cross-species kinship.

By *βehemoth's* conclusion, the environment is in a dire and unstable state, tempering utopic hope and denying the promise of guaranteed salvation through bioengineering. However, from a posthumanist perspective, the short epilogue that reads "FAILURE TO CONVERGE. CONFIDENCE LIMITS EXCEEDED. FURTHER PREDICTIONS UNRELIABLE" offers some optimism through its denial of closure (Watts 2004b, 287). The all-capitalized prediction implies an algorithmic model which has, as Taka imagined, failed to determine the outcome. Neither survival nor annihilation is assured. New becomings and kin alliances forged through cross-species contamination and infectious partnerships prevent a foreclosed future by opening an ambiguous space of possibility. Even if humanity does not make it, the "hopeful" likelihood remains that life will continue evolving and, in the grand scale of evolution, something—or a number of things—will live on.

THE WINDUP GIRL: **NICHES OF THE FUTURE**

While Watts's narrative hinges on the ambiguous symbiotic potentials of evolutionary partnerships and infectious becomings, Paolo Bacigalupi's *The Windup Girl* explores the implications of biotechnological adaptation and adaptive niches. *The Windup Girl* is set in a future post-scarcity Thailand after global warming and corporate bioengineered life forms and diseases have caused extensive multi-species collapse. The novel follows multiple character perspectives during the events that lead to a Western seed corporation's attempted coup to gain control of the Thai's treasured seedbank and its valuable unpatented genetic material. Agricultural corporations had previously unleashed various plagues against each other's genetically modified products; their sterile seeds and the uncontrolled mutations of those infections, coupled with invasive species and climate change, resulted in widespread extinctions and a heavy loss of human life. Like the *Rifters* trilogy, *The Windup Girl* also emphasizes the agential powers of infections through their impact on reshaping life for humans and nonhuman species; however, Bacigalupi foregrounds the need to critically re-examine traditional definitions of natural versus unnatural and born versus made. The novel especially emphasizes the importance of critically examining these binaries and the implicit biases they harbor when approaching ecological management to better understand how they are shaped by anthropocentric models of control that legitimize thanatopolitical biogenetic violence rather than potential symbiotic partnerships.

Invasive species and biogenetic plagues have resulted in the Thai perceiving foreign technologies as contaminating nature/"niche." While the Thai employ Gibbons, a Western gene-hacker, to help them resurrect lost species from their seedbank, their foods do not contain the proprietary controls the

Western companies use to render their seeds infertile. Daniel Dinello suggests technology in science fiction often behaves like a virus in that it "metamorphoses itself, as a result of unintended and uncontrollable consequences, progressively transforming the human world in the wake of its own changing structure" which "undermines the techno-utopian dream of mastery" (2005, 247). In *The Windup Girl*, the plagues undermine such fantasies of techno-mastery by originating from the seed corporations' own acts of biogenetic sabotage which have—once released into the world—mutated out of control. The agential powers of these mutating infections thus subvert the corporate and utopian technophilic positions embraced by characters like Gibbons and the AgriGen seed company spy, Anderson Lake.

After attempting to destabilize the Thai government to gain access to its seedbank, Anderson is ironically killed by the "tropical" disease that has formed in his factory's contaminated algae vats (Bacigalupi 2009, 346). This illness is a new strain of blister rust, one of the Western-manufactured diseases that formerly only affected crops but managed to jump "the animal kingdom barrier" to infect humans (217) because of the environmental conditions in Anderson's factory. The infection's new adaptation further highlights the permeability of plant, animal, and human genetic cell-lines, something the seed companies overlooked, and which is often forgotten in the conceptual separation of humans as "separate" from other species. Stefanie Fishel argues that the traditional image of the self-contained human body is challenged by new understandings of how "organs and genomic information flow across borders and bacterial and viral communities, both symbiotic and pathogenic, clearly affect our bodies, and through our bodies, politics. It is becoming more and more difficult to uphold the fiction of autonomous selfhood, or the figure of the human body as a Newtonian entity with boundaries" (2017, 7). The uncontrolled spread of the engineered plagues has also driven new technological becomings, resulting in continual exchanges between the infections, their hosts, and the constantly re-engineered crops that must be produced to stay ahead of the ever-adapting mutational exchanges between the diseases, their hosts, and the environment.

The power of Bacigalupi's imagined infections to subvert Western corporate attempts to control the environment helps highlight nonhuman and environmental agencies. Erika Cudworth and Stephen Hobden define *affective agency* as the potential to cause significant changes to "natural systems and the beings and things caught up in them" (2018, 47). The uncontrolled mutations of the bioplagues offer one potent example of how nonhuman agencies can transform the world. Like the virtual programs and mutational and adaptive powers in the *Rifters* trilogy, diseases in *The Windup Girl* underscore the critical importance of recognizing the abilities of nonhuman agencies to affect others. The impact of the diseases in these narratives at the human, animal, and ecological levels enmesh humanity in a matrix of connections with other species and resist ideas of mastery through genetic technologies. By depicting the complexities of ecological systems and their interactive agencies, Bacigalupi effectively conveys how destabilizing one aspect affects the entire system, including human beings.

The Windup Girl's focus extends beyond merely invasive microbes to also include invasive animals. In her discussion of the historical relationship between pigeons and humans, Donna Haraway recognizes pigeons as one of many animals with a European colonial history that altered ecologies (2016, 15). Haraway highlights the stark binaries involving our relationship with pigeons as having been "treasured kin and despised pests, subjects of rescue and of invective, bearers of rights and components of the animal-machine, food and neighbor, targets of extermination and of biotechnological breeding and multiplication, companions in work and play and carriers of disease" (2016, 15). One of the main narrative perspectives is from Emiko, a Japanese New Person/windup—manufactured people genetically customized for different forms of labor and considered private property—who has been abandoned by her owner and is forced to work as a prostitute due to being an illegal nonperson in Thailand.[6] Both New People and the chameleon-coated Cheshire cats are perceived as forms of biogenetic imperialism by the Thai; foreign gene-hacked beings are considered invasive species symbolic of globalization and biogenetic warfare. The cheshires have strong associations with being a "plague" due to their destructive transformation of the local ecosystem by out-competing other cats and decimating local bird species (Bacigalupi 2009, 114). As a cat, the cheshire is an animal that has occupied multiple contrasting representations similar to those of Haraway's pigeon. Cats have been positioned as both beloved family members/companions, destructive nuisances when wild, carriers of diseases such as toxoplasmosis, and invasive threats to already established wild ecologies. Much like historic perceptions of "foreign diseases," as invasive, genetically modified predators, the cheshires are considered a killable invader brought by foreign trade.

Arguably, one of the most sobering things Bacigalupi depicts is how, in a time of multispecies loss, new species are not welcomed even as empty niches are mourned. Jaidee, the Environment Ministry Captain, acutely feels the loss of species like the sacred Bo tree (2009, 168), yet when he witnesses a pair of cheshires preening themselves in plain sight, he intends to kill them because he perceives them as a symbol of "what Trade has given us" (173). Like most Thai, Jaidee believes they are "unnatural" and therefore soulless and killable. On the surface, his desire to kill the cheshires appears cruel, but his associating them with the suffering that globalized trade and biogenetic warfare have brought upon his people makes it more complicated. Building on Alfred W. Crosby's argument that weeds brought to North America were essential in facilitating Europe's colonization of it (2004, 170), ecocritics Jodi Frawley and Iain McCalman observe that historically, colonization included the intentional relocation of useful/profitable plants and animals to other lands (2014, 7). They also assert that "invasion ecologies" involve species where their reproduction is out of sync with the host community, arguing that it is not that the species is inherently invasive but how they "interact with their biocultural environment" that makes them become perceived as invasive (2014, 4–5). As a transplanted companion species brought by foreigners, the cheshires are an example of an invasion ecology—albeit an accidental one. Their Western gene-hacked origin means they are perceived as inseparable from the genetically created diseases that have ravaged the Thai. Much like the legitimization of lethal pest control in Australia for invasive species, despite "no pre-existing 'native' ecosystem to which Australia would return—even with rewilding" (Hillier 2017, 715), the Thai also engage in violent forms of cheshire extermination even though their environment has already been irrevocably transformed by successive waves of invasive species, diseases, and climate change. Conversely, Jaidee's comrade, Somchai, asks him not to shoot the cheshires because "[t]hey bleed like any other animal," further arguing that "[t]hey breed. They eat. They live. They breathe. . . . If you pet them, they will purr" (Bacigalupi 2009, 173). Somchai's experiences on cheshire detail where he killed thousands of them have caused him to recognize that their helplessness and ability to suffer transcends the categories of natural versus unnatural. Against Jaidee's perception of the cheshires as an unnatural plague, Somchai's assertion that they are no different than a "natural" cat exposes the superficiality of such binary distinctions and invites reconsideration of terms like "natural" and "invasive"—especially in the era of global warming.

Emma Maris's critique of the concept of wilderness proposes embracing a "rambunctious garden" as a new paradigm to confront species preservation efforts under climate change. In this paradigm, rather than trying to preserve a "stable, pristine, wilderness" that has no "natural baseline" due to waves of colonization, one must embrace conservation efforts that recognize nature as diverse and existing everywhere, including in areas with human habitation (2011, 2–3). I suggest that Bacigalupi's interrogation of what is natural or unnatural offers a similar line of critique. Observing the symbolic significance of the flood, Andrew Hageman argues that a reconsideration of and the potential for a "new ecological paradigm" is supported by the "heterogenous group" remaining in the evacuated Bangkok after the flood (2012, 300). He further contends that when Emiko, Gibbons, and his transsexual lover, Kip, remain in the city, they "disrupt any conventional sense of 'human' purity" (2012, 300). While Hageman does not include the cheshires, they are also present in the city after the flood (Bacigalupi 2009, 355). Their presence further supports this potential for a new line of ecological thinking in its depiction of species niches as dynamic and adaptive places of multispecies becomings rather than static spaces—something that is vital for approaching environmental uncertainties of the Anthropocene and to preserve biodiversity in as many forms as possible. Facilitating acceptance that a reclamation of lost niches with species that may be "unnatural" or even genetically modified might be a part of that preservation process and requires recognizing nature as neither static nor something that can be contained in designated areas.

POST-PLAGUE ECOLOGIES: ATWOOD'S *MADDADDAM*

Atwood's *MaddAddam* trilogy also depicts a world that has been badly damaged by the overuse of resources, climate change, and corporate-engineered infections. The world before Crake's plague is well on its way to catastrophe through overconsumption and pollution. While Watts and Bacigalupi treat the outcomes of their plagues as stemming from an unfounded faith in technology to contain the adaptive agential power of nature, Atwood differs in presenting her narrative's apocalyptic plague as an intentional act committed by the corporate scientist Crake to save the planet from humanity. Crake firmly believes that humanity is inherently flawed and chooses to wipe it out to both preserve the planet and make way for his genetically "perfected" replacement species, the Crakers. In *Oryx and Crake*, the narrative travels between the post-plague present from the perspective of Crake's friend and "last man" figure, Jimmy (nicknamed Snowman), and his memories of the events that led up to his situation as he tries to survive and watch over the Crakers. *Year of the Flood* and *MaddAddam* shift to other survivor accounts of the "sick" world of the past and their challenges to form a community in the aftermath of Crake's plague—often offering a counter-narrative to Jimmy's accounts. Like Bacigalupi and Watts, Atwood challenges readers with the possibility that we may have to embrace radical changes to drastically curb our destructive tendencies; however, her trilogy is the only one that imagines an embedded way of living with other species through its depiction of the formation of a posthuman community.

One of the ways in which Atwood underscores the power of nonhuman agencies and mutationality is through the scientist Crake. Crake is very similar to Bacigalupi's character Gibbons in that neither of them draw specific distinctions between natural and nonnatural and both believe the genetically modified posthuman "models" of Crakers and New People are superior to humanity. Gibbons suggests it is easier to build a disease-resistant person adapted to the environment than protect existing humans (Bacigalupi 2009, 243), and Crake believes the natural next step to make humans ecologically sustainable is to radically change the species by genetically editing out its "destructive features" and designing these modified people to be "perfectly adjusted to their habitat" (Atwood 2004, 366–7). Crake's act of genocide is reprehensible, but his questioning of the assumptions of anthropocentric superiority that humans should hold value above other species and ecologies challenges the givenness of these hegemonic norms, especially in proposing that we may have to recode ourselves if we are to truly achieve a sustainable ecological existence not limited by anthropocentrism or capitalist greed. Hannes Bergthaller's reading of Atwood's narrative contends that it challenges readers to embrace a posthuman politics by asking: "why (and under what conditions) the survival of the human species should be regarded as an ethical good to begin with" (2010, 742). Atwood's and Watts's narratives both suggest a critical look at anthropocentrism is necessary, especially during a time when so many proposed environmental actions are rejected because of a general unwillingness to change Western consumption habits that come at a great cost to other species.

Claire Colebrook's discussion of Anthropocene futures contends that human extinction is frequently portrayed as the end of the world, leaving "no conception of extinction as an inhuman event, either as a sense of the loss of life beyond what it means for humans and their recent attachment to biodiversity, or a sense of a certain mode of humanity reaching its end and giving way to other forms" (2019, 267). Atwood's portrayal of a world where its apocalypse leads to a restorative end to the ecological blight of capitalist consumption underscores Colebrook's point. The world does not end just because human society goes extinct. Jimmy and other survivors must live alongside wild creatures (including the hybrid wolvogs, bobkittens, and pigoons)[7] as biodiversity reclaims the remnants of human society. In this sense, both Watts's and Atwood's narratives resist anthropocentric apocalypticism by recognizing that what survives may not be human beings—at least not as we know them—and that a restoration of biodiversity, even if it is radically different than it was before, is still worth celebrating. Crake acts as a kind of *pharmakon* in that he kills through his plague, yet also cures the dysfunctional biocapitalist relationship to the planet (Canavan 2012, 154). However, much like the uncertainty and violence associated with achieving survival in *Rifters*, Crake's utopic vision is tainted by his belief that he can control nature through bioengineering and by harnessing his marketed BlyssPluss pleasure drug to spread a hemorrhagic infection to the world's population (Atwood 2004, 389).

While Crake designed the Crakers to be incapable of symbolic thinking or imagination, the stories Jimmy tells the Crakers to help them understand the world end up inspiring a pseudo-religion around Crake and his deceased lover, Oryx. On a visit, Jimmy observes the Craker women deciding to hold a communion ritual with Oryx. He is astonished that "they're conversing with the invisible, they've developed reverence" (192). Alaimo argues that belief in genetic mastery results in an erasure of the "multiple material agencies and the unpredictable transformations that these living forces will effect" and places the environment in a passive role (2010, 150). The Crakers are also supposed to be incapable of acquiring literacy, yet Toby, a former member of the God's Gardener eco-cult who becomes a primary narrative perspective in the latter two novels, effectively teaches the young Craker Blackbeard to read and write. Jimmy's and Toby's storytelling and teaching of writing acts as a counter-code to Crake's genetic foreclosure. Like a virus, their language figuratively infects the Crakers, performing its own transformations and injecting an element of unpredictability into their future. This is especially true for Blackbeard who closes *MaddAddam* after having inherited the role of storyteller from Toby (Atwood 2013, 385). While still a humanoid voice, Blackbeard's written perspective acts as a significant destabilizing force to Crake's project to genetically erase anything he deemed irrational in humanity. His reporting that some Crakers and humans have had children together (379) also leaves readers to consider what traits these future hybrid children may possess. Discussing the implications of the Crakers' emerging religion, Theodore F. Sheckels argues that it leaves it uncertain what else Crake failed to engineer away; jealousy, distrust, or possessiveness could also return (2012, 151). The Crakers' emergent abilities and those promised by their hybrid young subverts human mastery through technoscience and underscores the complex and unpredictable changes that can occur through becomings in the material world.

After the fall of consumer society, the ecological system also shows signs of regeneration. Discussing the moment in *MaddAddam* when the pigoons are swimming in an old pool now teeming with algae, weeds, and frogs (Atwood 2013, 284), Courtney Traub contends that "[l]ife thrives" after Crake's plague, "suggesting that 'nature' (even the genetically modified kind) can find its stubborn way in spite of human destructiveness" (2018, 97). Similarly, Lucy Rowland observes that in the hybrid state of the post-plague landscape "both genetically modified and 'natural' animals and plants remain as well as genetically modified humans [Crakers] and 'natural' humans" (2015, 52). Instead of perpetuating a division between nature and technologically created life, this hybrid ecosystem presents a thriving and positive vision of regeneration as gene-spliced creatures find niches outside the lab, contributing to a figurative and literal posthuman ecology that encourages a reassessment of such divisions through its emphasis on nonhuman adaptability and fluidity.

Discussing the meaning of responsibility in a materialist politics, Barad explains that all phenomena are a part of the dynamic becomings of the world, and that while humans do not control them, "through our advances, we participate in bringing forth the world . . . including ourselves" (2007, 353). A materialist ecopolitics thus reinserts humans into an inter-connected world system that requires our responsibility to others due to our participation in the processes of becomings that shape it. Much like the end of *The Windup Girl,* Atwood's narrative concludes with an image of a reinscribed nature where humans, nonhumans, and transgenic beings exist through negotiating a multi-species ethics of responsibility and partnership. With Blackbeard's mediation, the human survivors have formed an alliance with the sentient pigoons where both parties agree not to harm or eat each other and to even work together in a mutual rescue effort (Atwood 2013, 270). They also hold a joint funeral where the pigoons even carry Jimmy's body "as a sign of friendship and interspecies co-operation" (373). This posthuman garden is not a return to an idealized untouched Nature; instead, it shows a thriving community of "natural" and genetically modified wildlife. Atwood's narrative ends with an image of an uncertain fate for humanity but also comes with the potential renewal of the ecosystem through new becomings that do not distinguish between born and made and a politics of responsibility towards a diverse community of agents, most of whom are not human. In doing so, Atwood's trilogy offers a version of a hopeful future that embraces an ecologically situated ontology.

Ecocritics Andrew Belyea and Nannette Norris suggest humanity has quickly become "the planet's most treacherous virus" (2013, 8). *The Rifters t*rilogy, *The Windup Girl,* and the *MaddAddam t*rilogy all share a fixation with infection and connect humanity with pathogens in our willingness to colonize and modify the biosphere through biotechnology, without considering the lasting potential consequences of doing so. Discussing the posthuman in terms of a radical mutation in the human, Antonia Peroikou suggests it becomes "the site of a mutational, a viral, or better yet, a parasitic way of thinking that calls for the necessity of a different logic" (2017, 38). By challenging anthropocentric biases in their narratives, Watts, Atwood, and Bacigalupi underscore the importance of imagining potential new symbiotic partnerships and hybrid ecologies that negotiate environmental effects under climate change with attention to our entanglements with nonhuman agencies. Through their narratives' adaptive and infectious posthumanist politics, they invite the reader to themselves undergo a mutational change, one that requires embracing an ecologically situated consciousness and embedded posthuman ethics.

REFERENCES

Alaimo, Stacy. 2008. "Trans-Corporeal Feminisms and the Ethical Space of Nature." In *Material Feminisms*, ed. Stacy Alaimo and Susan Hekman, 237–64. Bloomington, IN: Indiana University Press.

Alaimo, Stacy. 2010. *Bodily Natures: Science, Environment, and the Material Self*. Bloomington, IN: Indiana University Press.

Atwood, Margaret. (2003) 2004. *Oryx and Crake*. Toronto: Seal.

———. 2009. *The Year of the Flood*. Toronto: McClelland & Stewart.

———. 2013. *MaddAddam*. Toronto: McClelland & Stewart.

Bacigalupi, Paolo. 2009. *The Windup Girl*. San Francisco, CA: Night Shade Books.

Barad, Karen. 2007. *Meeting the Universe Halfway: Quantum Physics and the Entanglement of Matter and meaning*. Duke University Press.

———. 2008. "Posthumanist Performativity: Towards an Understanding of How Matter Comes to Matter." *Material Feminisms*, ed. Stacy Alaimo and Susan Hekman, 120–154, Bloomington, IN: Indiana University Press, 2008.

Belyea, Andrew and Nanette Norris. 2013. "Introduction: Ecocritical Spring and Evolutionary Discourse." *Words for a Small Planet: Ecocritical Views*, ed. Nanette Norris, 1–16, Lanham, MD: Lexington Books.

Bergthaller, Hannes. 2010. "Housebreaking the Human Animal: Humanism and the Problem of Sustainability in Margaret Atwood's *Oryx and Crake* and *The Year of the Flood*." *English Studies* 91 (7): 728–43.

Canavan, Gerry. 2012. "Hope But Not For Us: Ecological Science Fiction and the End of the World in Margaret Atwood's *Oryx and Crake* and *The Year of the Flood*." *LIT: Literature Interpretation Theory* 23 (2): 138–159.

Colebrook, Claire. 2019. "The Future in the Anthropocene." *Climate and Literature*, ed. Adeline Johns-Putra, 263–80. Cambridge UP, 2019.

Crosby, Alfred W. 2004. *Ecological Imperialism: The Biological Expansion of Europe, 900–1900*, 2nd ed. Cambridge: Cambridge University Press.

Cudworth, Erika, and Stephen Hobden. 2018. *The Emancipatory Project of Posthumanism*. New York, NY: Routledge.

Dinello, Daniel. 2005. *Technophobia!: Science Fiction Visions of Posthuman Technology*. Austin, TX: University of Texas Press.

Eldridge, Ben. 2019. "A *Maelstrom* of Replication: Peter Watts's Glitching Textual Source Codes." *Canadian Science Fiction, Fantasy, and Horror: Bridging the Solitudes*, ed. Amy J. Ransom and Dominic Grace, 221–238. Cham: Palgrave Macmillan.

Fishel, Stephanie. 2017. *The Microbial State: Global Thriving and the Body Politic*. Minneapolis, MN: University of Minnesota Press.

Frawley, Jodi, and Iain McCalman. 2014. "Invasion Ecologies: The Nature/Culture Challenge." *Rethinking Invasion Ecologies from the Environmental Humanities*, ed. Jodi Frawley and Iain McCalman, 1–12. New York, NY: Routledge.

Hageman, Andrew. 2012. "The Challenge of Imagining Ecological Futures: Paolo Bacigalupi's *The Windup Girl*." Science Fiction Studies 39 (2): 283–303.

Haraway, Donna. 2016. *Staying with the Trouble: Making Kin in the Chthulucene.* Durham, NC: Duke University Press.
Helmreich, Stefan. 2009. *Alien Oceans: Anthropological Voyages in Microbial Seas.* Berkeley and Los Angeles, CA: University of California Press.
Hillier, Jean. 2017. "No Place to Go? Management of Non-human Animal Overflows in Australia." *European Management Journal* 35: 712–21. dx.doi.org/10.0116/j.emj.3027.03.004.
Lingis, Alphonso. 2003. "Animal Body, Inhuman Face." *Zoontologies: The Question of the Animal*, ed. Cary Wolfe, 165–82. Minneapolis, MN: University of Minnesota Press.
Marris, Emma. 2011. *Rambunctious Garden: Saving Nature in a Post-Wild World.* New York, NY: Bloomsbury.
Nayar, Pramod K. 2014. *Posthumanism.* Malden: Polity.
Paxton, Heather. 2008. "Post-Pasteurian Cultures: The Microbiopolitics of Raw-Milk Cheese in the United States." *Cultural Anthropology* 23 (1): 15–46. www.jstor.org/stable/20484494.
Peroikou, Antonia. 2017. "Of Crakers and Men: Imagining the Future and Rethinking the Past in Margaret Atwood's *MaddAddam* Trilogy." *Posthuman Gothic*, ed. Anya Heise-von der Lippe, 36–53. Cardiff: University of Wales Press.
Pickering, Andrew. 2005. "Asian Eels and Global Warming: A Posthumanist Perspective on Society and the Environment." *Ethics and the Environment* 10 (2): 29–43. www.jstor.org/stable/40339103.
Rowland, Lucy. 2015. "Speculative Solutions the Development of Environmental and Ecofeminist Discourse in Margaret Atwood's *MaddAddam*." *SLC/ELC Studies in Canadian Literature/ Études en Littérature Canadienne* 40 (2): 46–68.
Sagan, Lynn. 1967. "On the Origin of Mitosing Cells." *Journal of Theoretical Biology* 14 (3): 225–74. doi.org/10.1016/0022-5193(67)90079-3.
Shecels, Theodore F. 2012. *The Political in Margaret Atwood's Fiction: The Writing on the Wall of the Tent.* Farnham: Ashgate Publishing Ltd.
Traub, Courtney. 2018. "From the Grotesque to Nuclear-Age Precedents: The Modes and Meanings of Cli-Fi Humor." *Studies in the Novel* 50 (1): 86–107.
Wall, Clare. 2015. "Here Be Monsters: Posthuman Adaptation and Subjectivity in Peter Watts' *Starfish*." *The Canadian Fantastic in Focus: New Perspectives*, ed. Allan Weiss, 67–80. Jefferson: MacFarland and Company Inc.
Watts, Peter. 1999. *Starfish.* New York, NY: Tor.
———. 2001. *Maelstrom.* New York, NY: Tor.
———. 2004a. *Behemoth: β-Max.* New York, NY: Tor.
———. 2004b. *Behemoth: Seppuku.* New York, NY: Tor.

NOTES

1. Watts intended *Behemoth* to be one novel, but it was published in two volumes, *β-Max* (2004a) and *Seppuku* (2004b). This article treats them as one narrative but cites them separately.

2. While the ongoing COVID-19 pandemic has likely increased negative associations of viruses, it has also possibly raised awareness of nonhuman agencies in it being a zoonotic infection that has globally reshaped many aspects of our lives.

3. Margulis published "On the Origin of Mitosing Cells" under the name Lynn Sagan.

4. Barad uses the term "intra-actions" rather than interactions to refer to the material entanglements, arguing that the latter assumes a separation of subject and object before the exchange, whereas intra-action emphasizes that they are already entangled as matter (2008, 133).

5. See Eldridge 2019 for a detailed structural analysis of Watts's personification of 400.

6. New People/"windups"—called so due to their stutter-stop movements—are considered a soulless unnatural threat by the Thai (Bacigalupi 2009, 35).

7. The pigoons are genetically modified pigs with human neocortex tissue designed to grow human-compatible organs. The wolvogs (wolf-dogs) and bobkittens (bobcat-kittens) are lab-created hybrids of domestic pets and wild animals which have escaped the labs they were created in and now roam the landscape as new apex predators.

Chapter 12

"A Reign of Community and Harmony"

Envisioning a Multispecies Society in a Post-Nuclear World

Elizabeth Tavella

Imagine: the planet is destroyed by atomic devastation and transformed into a desert of radioactive ashes. Shifts in climate conditions threaten survival. Wild birds are extinct; rain falls incessantly. This is the atmosphere that saturates the opening scene of *Il Pianeta Irritabile* (Irritable Planet), a novel published in 1978 by Italian writer Paolo Volponi during the unsettling political context of the Cold War and a period of constant nuclear threat.[1] However, rather than relying on the sense of hopelessness incited by apocalyptic imagery, the narrative of ecological devastation is intended to create an opportunity for renewal and systemic change. After describing a landscape radically altered by the destructive consequences of human activity, the author introduces the main protagonists: a monkey, an elephant, a domesticated goose, and a dwarf.[2] Following a dramatic circus escape, the four survivors embark on a transformative journey across a devastated world in search of a land where they can start a post-human civilization. As they build a new society, the planet is also revitalized and begins to recover from humans' violent will for domination.

Lying at the intersection of critical animal studies, disability studies, and ecocriticism, this chapter examines Volponi's provocative political and philosophical stances aimed at highlighting the inherent limits of the nature/culture dichotomy as well as the urgent need to build a society based on new ethical foundations. By analyzing the author's ideal of community and his profound critique of the capitalist system, I argue that *Il Pianeta Irritabile*, imbued with utopian elements, stimulates new theorizations of multispecies coexistence that can inspire an alternative approach to responding to the present global climate emergency. In particular, I first explore the nexus between capitalist logic and the institutions that exploit nonhuman animals and other disempowered beings, a logic that in the context of this novel is emblematically represented by the circus. Moreover, a close reading of the characters' process of liberation from human oppression highlights the impact their identities hold for the speciesist, ableist, and sexist assumptions that humans have placed onto them, and the need to disrupt these assumptions in order to establish truly new rules for communal living based on care and the abolishment of hierarchal social structures.

In order to accomplish this, I will focus on the liminal properties between "human" and "animal" that distinguish each of the four main characters, who I intend to rescue from the cage of allegory, as they redefine their ontological status in the course of their turbulent adventures. In fact, while the novel is often read exclusively as allegorical and through an anthropocentric lens, similarly to the destiny that has befallen George Orwell's *Animal Farm*, I will instead examine the author's ability to explore the *real* nature and place in the world of nonhuman animals, who should not be understood, within this theoretical framework, as mere projections of the renewal of "humans."[3] In addition, I explore the author's celebration of animality and corporeality on a narrative and linguistic level, including the role of his lexicon of bodily functions in the great scheme of redefining social and cultural norms, conventions, and behaviors. Ultimately, this chapter is concerned with broad questions of multispecies justice and the role of literature: how can agency, bodily autonomy, and liberation be redefined beyond the human-animal binary? What does a just multispecies society look like? How can literature inspire radical social and ecological change?

IN SEARCH OF FREEDOM: RECLAIMING ANIMALITY AND BREAKING BINARIES

As Sherryl Vint has shown, apocalyptic science fiction novels share recurrent patterns in the representation of nonhuman animals: "a recurrence of war with fellow creatures, human and non-human; the threat of human annihilation and a vision—sometimes fearful, sometimes optimistic—about another species replacing us as the dominant form of life" (2010, 208). Paolo Volponi's narrative of extinction is a clear manifestation of this definition. In fact, by imagining a world in which social and ecological roles are gradually being reestablished within the novel, it forces readers to reevaluate the place that humans and other animals hold on the planet. In the context of a degraded environment then, four individuals join forces and set out on the path towards a place where they can have a fresh start. In order to find a new ecological balance, they must first go through dystopia before building their own utopia that will lead to a radical disruption of the categories of "human" and "animal."

When the characters are first introduced, they are described as motionless figures situated in the center of a cave: a monkey sits on an elephant's back while holding a chain used to restrain a dwarf by his neck as he lies on his side, and a white goose stands under the elephant with her wings spread open. Already from their arrangement, the power dynamics of the group are made clear. While they manage to escape the material cages of the circus, the process of liberation from human oppression is far from complete; in fact, they still need time to break out of the cultural and social cages that had prevented their freedom in the first place. As a consequence, once they set off on their journey, they reinstate a similar structural hierarchy to the one found in the circus: "the baboon commands, the others are servants."[4] Being the only individual of his species in the whole circus, the monkey, who was given the name Epistola, takes humans as an example to learn from and ends up reproducing their most violent and authoritative behaviors based on his interactions and experiences.[5] Yet, even with all the behavioral similarities, he still remains distinctly segregated to the category of "animal" due to his lack of human speech, which is framed as a form of cognitive impairment, and for his repeated acts of masturbation that are meant to symbolically represent a descent into bestiality. Initially then, animality is constructed as inferior and other, and reinforced by the harmful mindset that takes the abled human body as the default cross-species measure to conform to. However, as the monkey's past of abuse slowly unravels, his "fury against the cage" is also made explicit through the tale of his attack on a trainer, a reaction caused by a life in captivity during which he "did not know anything about free forests or simian families" that demonstrates his longing for bodily freedom.[6] This scene of animal resistance shows that the monkey has a clear sense of agency that has been repressed by living in a system meant to keep under control his essence and vitality.

In contrast, the elephant, who has lived a life "without freedom and independence" and is known by the name of Roboamo, is the only member in the group who has learned to articulate words of a human language, a skill that is herein connected to rationality and philosophical reasoning.[7] While living in the circus, he was taught to learn Dante's *Divine Comedy* by heart, and he was able to read and interpret texts, all skills that he kept secret to avoid being further exploited. As in the case of the monkey, the elephant's hybrid characteristics function as a destabilizer of the human-animal binary: his speaking abilities draw him nearest to the "human" category, yet his species and apparent submissive behavior keep him conveniently associated with the "animal" category. The absence of an overt reaction to his oppression should, however, not be regarded as consent for abusive treatment, but rather as a consequence of systemic human dominance taking advantage of his resignation. For example, a subtle form of resistance can be detected when he is practicing Dante's verses with the director of the circus who had domesticated him. Even when aware of making a mistake, he still adds the vocative expression *oh!* and a final *e* to the truncated word *color* for his own pleasure when reciting the first line of the *Purgatory* "Dolce color d'oriental zaffiro" (100) therefore purposefully disrupting the canonical rhythm and meter of the poem. To counter the process of assimilation into human culture, the elephant thus initiates a process of decolonization from imperialist domination that is rooted in language, first by using the same words he had learnt in the circus to make sense of the world, then by appropriating the language of the oppressor to think independently and guide the group in making decisions and facing obstacles along the way. Towards the end of the novel, as a sign of his complete rejection of assimilation, he dismisses the idea that nonhuman animals voluntarily resign themselves to human domination by asserting: "No animal repeats! Keep that in mind, even if everyone has always said otherwise."[8]

The goose, called Plan Calcule due to her calculus skills, is perhaps the most misunderstood member of the group and is often coded as inferior compared to the others due mostly to group dynamics. The lack of affirmation of her individual existence extends also within literary criticism, where she is often misgendered, thus reinforcing the pervasiveness of a male default and a patriarchal linguistic norm.[9] A trait that distinguishes her characterization is that she is depicted as constantly defecating, a bodily function that is at first tied to grotesque and shameful animality, but that later in the novel turns into a symbol of regeneration and acceptance of abject corporeality. Similarly to the elephant, she learned to count and perform numerical operations in the circus for the sake of human entertainment. Her bird-ness is therefore suppressed not only by the exploitative system that the circus actively supports, but also by the centuries-long process of domestication that, besides stripping her of her freedom, is responsible for her conceptual disconnection from the natural world.[10] Because of this mode of thinking, the evocative narrative of bird extinction that permeates the novel completely erases her presence as a bird. Nonetheless, she still plays a pivotal role in the narrative by becoming the reconnoiterer responsible for exploring new territories before the group can safely advance on their journey. Additionally, in several instances her individual traits and agency prevail over the other members of the group, such as when the dwarf orders her to go explore in a certain direction, with assertiveness and confidence, "she took off in the opposite direction of the one indicated to demonstrate her autonomy and erudition."[11] She also visibly reacts to preserve her bodily integrity when the dwarf approaches to hug her and "she pushed that colonial aggressor away with her wings because she felt not recognized, but rather threatened with death . . . with the ancestral, vulgar pulling of the neck."[12] The goose's body is conceptualized here as a site of settler coloniality that is being violated against her will, which leads to the rejection of an invasive and unwanted physical contact. In this passage, besides identifying the goose as a colonial subject, the author is thus also alluding to the practice of killing birds by manual neck dislocation, which is still considered "humane" and systematically normalized across cultures. By bridging colonial thinking with the embodied experience of a nonhuman animal, this literary scene clearly elucidates the deep intersections between colonialism and speciesism. In fact, as Dinesh Wadiwel attests, "the colonial project—encompassing diverse rationalities of elimination, exploitation, and assimilation—cannot be easily disentangled from our prevailing relationships with animals" (2020, xvii). The goose's act of resistance, then, represents the refusal of oppressive systems and consequent affirmation of her liberated identity.[13]

The fourth element of the group, the dwarf, has generally been regarded as the main character of the story through readings that tend to promote anthropocentric criticism.[14] Due to his biological affiliation to the human species, he holds a privileged position in terms of visibility and attention. However, because of how his condition is perceived, combined with his disfigured face due to an acid attack, he is constructed as victim to animalistic instincts, and therefore comes to embody an uncanny ambivalence between "human" and "animal." Using disability as a dehumanizing metaphor not only reinforces negative stereotypes of disability that conceal the struggles of people with disabilities, but it also reiterates the representation of the "animal" in derogatory terms, concurrently perpetuating speciesist thinking. At the same time, however, the use of a stigmatizing portrayal of disability highlights the commodification of "freakery" intrinsic to the logic of the circus. As Sammy Jo Johnson notes, the circus and the freak show are not distinct phenomena, nor distinct systems of oppression. Instead, they are intrinsically connected due to "shared narratives of non-agency" (2020, 57).[15] While the identities of the four characters are indeed framed around ableist/speciesist discourses, their agencies and refusal to comply with oppression are also developed to highlight the silencing of non-normative identities within capitalist society.

The dwarf's process of liberation, then, includes coming to terms with the boundaries of humanity that are defined by normative bodily and cognitive standards while also dealing with his sense of guilt for belonging to the human species. Becoming "animal" is a liberating act—not a process of animalization—that eventually removes the last vestiges of anthropocentrism.

As he reclaims his own identity, which includes questioning his past, his attachment to material possessions, as well as the various names he was given, from *Zuppa* (Soup) to *Mamerte* and the highly charged *Man*, at times he must grapple with the difficulties of renouncing his privileges and attempts to detach himself at an ontological level from the other members of the group.[16] For instance, in his reenactment of the typical urge of human beings to classify the world into separate compartments based on the nature/culture dichotomy, "he wanted to distinguish himself from the goose and catalog her as a bird."[17] As he struggles to reconcile with his own animality, at first he still resorts to ideas of superiority and inferiority, especially when he proudly affirms that he is *more animal* than the other members of the group. Ultimately, though, in his attempt to redefine his own ontological status, the dwarf's epistemological approach based on hierarchical thinking is destined to fail; the only way for him to go beyond hierarchical constructs is to break out of binary thinking. In fact, towards the end of their adventures, he comes to the conclusion that he is not that much different from the others: he is just as disempowered as them.

Volponi's attempt to challenge the human-animal divide gives birth to a fictional group of beings whose bodies represent nonhegemonic corporealities premised on capitalist exploitation. While the characters can be considered as anthropomorphic types operating within an allegorical framework, viewing them exclusively as "mannequins of an allegorical intent" (Zinato 2001, 62) erases the nuances of their subjectivities; it also risks extending their objectification beyond the literary page to include those individuals across species whose lived experiences stand outside the boundaries of normalcy. The prominent role given to the senses, which is emphasized from the opening scene of the novel through highlighted perceptions and sharpened sight, represents a clear sign of the emergence of animality, which is celebrated by embracing a corporeal lexicon that abounds with synesthetic metaphors. The search for liberation from social constraints is expressed also through the author's transgression of the hierarchy of linguistic registers and lexical conventions. While the scenes of sexual intercourse between the dwarf and the goose are at times disturbingly violent, especially as long as the dwarf is carrier of the remnants of human dominance and patriarchal values, the violence of the actions and interactions weakens, until it disappears. Thus, a language of excess made of derogatory expressions, along with vivid descriptions of interspecies sexuality, is used as a means to generate discomfort and push the boundaries of socially accepted normalcy and conformity.

The artificial separation between nature and culture is further challenged through language on a narrative level. In fact, instead of conceiving *logos* as an exclusive "human" ability connected to rationality, the diverse group of characters engages in various forms of verbal and nonverbal communication that forces us to reconceptualize language beyond anthropocentric narratives of nonhuman voicelessness. On the one hand, the monkey and the goose clearly communicate their desires, needs, and emotions, without having to express them by articulating human speech; on the other, the anthropomorphic qualities of the speaking elephant unsettles the linguistic divide even further.[18] By playing with multiple variations of voice and speech in a fictional realm, Volponi's novel raises important questions regarding power and discourse within interspecies relations and facilitates the maturation of a non-anthropocentric view of language by making space for normatively silenced voices.

As readers learn about the past abuses and systemic discrimination experienced by the four main characters, their journey turns into a liberation process from dominant and oppressive systems. The novel in fact stages the harmful consequences of reducing the natural world to an artificial and distorted simulation of human culture and, by pushing the boundaries of imagination, it makes the struggle against human hegemonic discourses more readily accessible.

THE FORMATION OF A NEW ECOLOGY: A COMMUNITY OF INTERSPECIES CARE

Volponi's novel participates in the long tradition of eco-apocalypse novels, which has recently acquired popularity especially with the emergence of the "cli-fi" literary genre.[19] While the concern for our planet's survival is not new, the author offers an uplifting vision of renewal and hope that has tangible repercussions in terms of shifting our thinking. In fact, the vibrant revival of natural life expressed through a disorienting and nonlinear narrative echoing the ever-changing natural landscape, is a direct response to catastrophic anthropogenic actions symbolized by the atomic bomb.[20]

Initially, the four main characters wander through hostile landscapes of fire and ice, and through a magmatic and deserted territory, whose ecology and even astronomy have been radically subverted.[21] Besides describing the planet's fierce transformations, Volponi also draws attention to the wounds of the land by infusing his narration with references to ecological disasters contemporary to his time of composition, particularly oil spills and their devastating effects on nonhuman animals. For instance, while the dwarf and the goose are on one of their reconnaissance ventures, a chasm suddenly opens up in the ground and petroleum starts flowing out of the earth. The goose "observed in dismay the whiteness of her plumage and feathers that were once again endangered by petroleum."[22] From the goose's emotional reaction, the imminent danger of oil pollution is a daunting reminder of similar past traumatic events, and her jeopardized body becomes a symbol of the assertion of power of the western capitalist system over the land. The consequences of this system are brought to the extreme by imagining skies with no birds, emptied entirely of bird songs. When the dwarf becomes aware of this reality, he suddenly realizes that in his life, he "had seen very few birds, and only in the cages of zoos and in the offices of the powerful; they were almost all parrots, ravens, and Indian blackbirds who mumbled or even spoke rather than emit a single note of a song."[23] The brutal attempt to control nature is exemplified by the reference to imperialist institutions, such as the zoo, whose oppressive ideology is replicated in miniature with every birdcage or aquarium placed in a human-made environment. Further, the choice of bird species is also not fortuitous since they are typically known for their ability to mimic human speech, which once again underlines the author's intention of destabilizing the illusory human-animal opposition based on language. This process of forced assimilation, emphasized through language, leads to a state of alienation and artificiality that is perfectly summed up by Volponi in an interview in which he discusses the automation of nature as a consequence of capitalist logic: "Everything is reduced to an instrument, a means, a resource [. . .]. Nature appears as the keyboard of a simulation, its elements, its seasons are reduced essentially to buttons, switches, inputs of this simulation plan" (Volponi and Leonetti 1995, 101).[24]

Besides the group of circus survivors, in this post-atomic world, "the enemy of humans and dwarfs, of animals and plants" continues to live on, personified in a merciless governor they emblematically name *Moneta* (Coin) after having discussed other options such as Rovina (*Ruin*), Catena (*Chain*), and Macello (*Slaughterhouse*).[25] He is protected by his submarine and a task force of scuba-divers who, when they first see the elephant, think he must be used to pull carriages and that they should take him, if only to repurpose him as meat.[26] Such a mindset perpetuates ideas of animal exploitation and ownership as well as the practice of killing other animals for human consumption, intrinsic to profit-based economy. When the two parties meet, Moneta calls the dwarf "a fake man" whom he wants to save "by making him a hu*man*, worthy of hu*man* civilization."[27] While the group of four is still hiding, in order to trick them into coming forward, Moneta proposes to those who are still alive that they accompany him on a rocket that will bring them to "a new and better world."[28] The colonizing drive toward the exploitation of living beings and natural resources extends now to outer space, prefiguring the idea of a multiplanetary capitalism. Following a series of Moneta's proposals mixed with insults, the dwarf delivers an invective against him and, more broadly, against the capitalist system he represents:

You are and always will be shit. But not the good shit, honest manure of the body: satisfaction and waste of an easy life, day by day, even defecating and fertilizing, taking and eating. You are surely not the shit of a natural cycle, but a pile [of shit], the hoarded turd of forced circulation. Just like the unnatural, you confuse gold with shit, and not the gold metal used for teeth, or the shit used to fertilize, but the golden coin with the shit coin! [. . .] Artificiality as in a factitious source of power, but not as in research and science. Because scientific artificiality is destined to return to a natural state: close even to good shit! Whereas your artificiality is just artificial and, to remain as such, it has to continue to intensify its artifices and detach itself from the natural.[29]

As Andrea Inglese notes, it is through this invective that the dwarf finally achieves his liberation from a system that forced him to separate himself from his animalistic nature (2008, 356). The triumph of corporeality and bodily functions, expressed through linguistic liberty and the verbal breaking of taboos, thus serves the purpose of marking the distance between reclaimed animality and the artificial manipulation of ecosystems for profit and greed. As a consequence of the dwarf's words, Moneta violently reacts by shooting in every direction, which triggers the monkey to attack out of anger and scorn. Once their eyes meet, a fight to the death begins and ends soon thereafter with their mutual destruction.

What at this point may seem as the overall victory of the circus survivors, actually turns out to be the result of the hidden intervention of the imitator of birds, a mysterious—almost mythological—person who has been acting in the background in the course of their adventures. In fact, readers discover only towards the end of the novel that he had been silently following the group along their journey helping them overcome a series of obstacles, including this final battle by sabotaging the submarine, which allows the group to defeat the last Man embodying their oppressor. Originally hired by the circus for his ability to replicate the songs of extinct birds, therefore bringing spectators closer to a lost nature, he functions as a reminder of the alienation of human beings from a natural state. While he never articulates human words, he still holds the privilege of being considered a member of the "human" species and, in stark contrast with the elephant who is involuntarily assimilated into human culture through language, he incorporates the natural world within himself thanks to the mimetic skills of his voice. Despite the different levels of agency, his quiet presence is also meant to further destabilize the clear-cut distinction between species not only by presenting yet another example of language beyond anthropocentric views, but also by becoming a corporeal manifestation of hybridity through his gradual metamorphosis into a bird.[30] While the narrative occasionally acquires key features of saviorist discourses, somewhat diminishing the potential of the main characters to liberate themselves without the interference of an external human force, all forms of centralized power have gone extinct and the three survivors are finally in the position to inaugurate a multispecies society based on egalitarian values, interspecies care, and ecological respect.

As they become increasingly more aware of the importance of serving the totality of existence, they also must learn "to stay with the trouble of living and dying together on a damaged earth," to quote Donna Haraway's words, which requires "making oddkin; that is, we require each other in unexpected collaborations and combinations, in hot compost piles" (2016, 4).[31] This is precisely the guiding principle of the survivors' restructuring of the social order. With the death of the monkey, the hierarchy that was originally established dies with him and they resume their journey in the direction that instinctively felt right, "without needing any warning or order."[32]

While they walk through a landscape made of hills, ponds, and deserts of rocks, they start to alternate synchronous and individual gestures,

> The gestures were carried out, individually or combined, to test the character of the new group and of the new relationships, in order to determine the ideal conditions within the new social conformation, especially since no one thought they could guide or govern as the absolute chief. In these gestures each one of them wanted to try and exist for what they were, and further wanted to declare and express their sense of equality towards the others.[33]

As they gradually abandon a capitalist value framework rooted in alienating individualism, they learn to face the precarity of the shifting ecology surrounding them by creating moments of harmony and dissonance together, by moving polyphonically, collaboratively, which can only be accomplished through cross-species coordination, as suggested by Anna Tsing (2015, 22–24, 155–56). However, as part of the progressive rejection of anthropocentrism, the dwarf must let go of the last object belonging to his past that he had been secretly carrying with him since the very start: a sheet of rice paper containing a poem in ideograms that a nun had gifted him while they had an affair. On one hand, the physical object is a symbol of human eagerness to accumulate capital now transformed into a common good; on the other its mysterious content represents a final remnant of human culture, embodied by an item bearing a linguistic message. At the end of the novel, in a moment of solemn communion, the dwarf divides the sheet of paper into three parts, one for each member of the group, and he starts eating it.[34] Human culture is therefore reinserted within a natural cycle; a corporeal act stipulates the end of human cultural history and of speciesist discourses of linguistic exceptionalism. The Word then literally becomes flesh, losing its meaning and aura of sacredness. By sketching out the beginnings of a new non-hierarchical order,

Volponi lays the foundations of a multispecies society whose future resides in the readers' imaginative vision of justice.

While the journey of liberation of the circus survivors unfolds, the planet also undergoes a process of renovation and transformation. In fact, the earth acts throughout the novel as an additional resilient character that, thanks to its self-healing properties, resurges from the ashes. Blooming vegetation gradually takes over the harsh landscapes, once the heavy rain stops falling. As a consequence of the split between nature and culture, combined with the insurgence of patriarchal values advanced by a capitalist framework, the planet's response to harmful anthropogenic actions is associated with generative properties and imagery of irritability and mutability, socially labeled values that are normatively associated with femininity. As ecofeminist scholars have profusely demonstrated, there is a long tradition of depicting Earth as "a nurturing mother who will clean up men's toxic wastes, as a bad and unruly broad who brings hurricanes and other 'bad' weather" (Gaard 2014, 233). Volponi's representation of the planet reproduces this damaging stereotype then and, by gendering nature according to stereotypical generalizations, it reinforces a false dichotomous construction of gender. Nevertheless, the metamorphic logic that governs the ecosystem's recovery from human domination is a sign of radical ecological thinking, especially within the Italian context of the 1970s.[35] Even the dwarf's jacket participates in this process of renewal: its human-made textile turns into a vegetal fabric, as an additional proof of the vitality of nature taking over the lurking remains of human culture. For Volponi, "nature, animals, and humans are intimately connected. They are not distinct phases of world creation, but rather entities made up of the same explosion and substance, in their interaction with one another" (1999, 157).[36] While the ecosystem is still conceived as made of three separate and absolute categories, the recognition of the interconnectedness of all elements demonstrates an epistemic shift based on a symbiotic bond between all forms of life, which this novel powerfully dramatizes.

CONCLUSIONS

With *Il Pianeta Irritabile*, Volponi manages to disrupt the conventional binaries of nature/culture and human/animal, particularly through linguistic experimentation and metamorphic processes extending to the corporeal dimension and the natural environment, which leads to the obsolescence of hierarchies and the establishment of a new social and ecological order. By taking full advantage of the potential of world building within a fictional realm, he also explores themes relevant to political ecology that deeply resonate with the ongoing climate crisis. The novel also mobilizes the collective imagination to speculate on a social structure beyond capitalism, finding possibilities of transformation within ecological disturbances. In order to fully understand the author's choice of using the circus as a paradigmatic site of capitalist ideology it is fundamental to recover its literal meaning and social function as a place that exploits nonhuman animals and othered non-normative bodies for human entertainment. Capitalist logic, however, is not exclusive to the circus but is indeed intrinsic to all the industries that rely on animal exploitation, such as food production, fashion, biomedical research, and pet-trade, just to name a few. Certainly, using nonhuman animals in a literary text to allegorically represent human exploitation and alienation under capitalism might normalize the erasure of their lived experiences by rendering them mere signifiers; yet this popular narrative device can also inadvertently denounce the *real* injustice that actual living beings of other species are subjected to. Volponi's novel is indeed an excellent example of this cultural practice and—perhaps unintentionally—also testifies to the need to build solidarity across species in order to eradicate interlocking oppressive systems.

In the pages of this book then lies a powerful warning that invites us to rethink the way resources are distributed, to radically change our consumption habits, and to prioritize justice over profit, a concern Volponi addressed frequently in his works and advocated for in interviews up until his death.[37] However, instead of resigning ourselves to the inevitability of collapse, Volponi views destruction as an opportunity for social and moral renewal and presents a transformative vision of a world that eventually matures past anthropocentric domination. Therefore, by recuperating Volponi's firm belief in the role of literature to keep consciences alive and to advance new forms of communication and representation that challenge dominant power structures, literary criticism consequently becomes a powerful means to critically examine reality and contribute to promoting change.[38]

REFERENCES

Belcourt, Billy-Ray. 2014. "Animal Bodies, Colonial Subjects: (Re)Locating Animality in Decolonial Thought." *Societies* 5 (1): 1–11. doi.org/10.3390/soc5010001.

Colling, Sarat. 2021. *Animal Resistance in the Global Capitalist Era*. East Lansing, MI: Michigan State University Press.

Fioretti, Daniele. 2014. "Foreshadowing the Posthuman: Hybridization, Apocalypse, and Renewal in Paolo Volponi." In *Thinking Italian Animals: Human and Posthuman in Modern Italian Literature and Film*, ed. Deborah Amberson and Elena Past, 145–58. New York, NY: Palgrave Macmillan.

Fioretti, Daniele. 2017. *Utopia and Dystopia in Postwar Italian Literature: Pasolini, Calvino, Sanguineti, Volponi*. Basingstoke: Palgrave Macmillan.
Gaard, Greta. 2014. "Toward New EcoMasculinities, EcoGenders, and EcoSexualities." In *Ecofeminism: Feminist Intersections with Other Animals and the Earth*, ed. Carol J. Adams and Lori Gruen, 225–239. New York, NY: Bloomsbury Publishing.
Haraway, Donna Jeanne. 2016. *Staying with the Trouble: Making Kin in the Chthulucene*. Durham, NC: Duke University Press.
Inglese, Andrea. 2008. "L'Amano e l'Animale in *Il Pianeta Irritabile* Di Paolo Volponi." *Cahiers d'études Italiennes* 7 (May): 347–57. doi.org/10.4000/cei.943.
Jenkins, Stephanie, Kelly Struthers Montford, and Chloë Taylor. 2020. *Disability and Animality Crip Perspectives in Critical Animal Studies*. Abingdon: Routledge.
Johnson, Sammy Jo. "Zoos, Circuses, and Freak Shows: A Cross-Movement Analysis." In *Disability and Animality: Crip Perspectives in Critical Animal Studies*, edited by Stephanie Jenkins, Kelly Struthers Montford and Chloë Taylor, 57–74. Abingdon: Routledge.
Marcoaldi, Franco. 1993. "Volponi Lascia e Raddoppia." *La Repubblica*, January 19, 1993.
Meijer, Eva. 2019. *When Animals Speak: Toward an Interspecies Democracy*. New York, NY: New York University Press.
Mobili, Giorgio. 2008. *Irritable Bodies and Postmodern Subjects in Pynchon, Puig, Volponi*. New York: Peter Lang.
Monserrati, Michele. 2016. "The Atomic Fear: Translating (Post)Marxist Fantasies About the End of Times." *Italian Studies* 71 (4): 515–34. doi.org/10.1080/00751634.2016.1222763.
Moore, Bryan L. 2017. *Ecological Literature and the Critique of Anthropocentrism*. New York: Springer Berlin Heidelberg.
Nocella, Anthony J., Amber E. George, and John Lupinacci, eds. 2019. *Animals, Disability, and the End of Capitalism: Voices from the Eco-Ability Movement*. New York: Peter Lang.
Papini, Maria Carla. 1997. *Paolo Volponi: Il Potere, La Storia, Il Linguaggio*. La Nuova Meridiana 27. Firenze: Le lettere.
Pifferi, Stefano. 2020. "L'Uomo è l'Animale Irritato. Una Rilettura Distopico-Odeporica de *Il Pianeta Irritabile* di Paolo Volponi," *California Italian Studies* 10.1: 1–14. escholarship.org/uc/item/4ns1d81v.
2021. "Contro l'Umanità: 'Eco-criticism,' Anti-Antropocentrismo, Odeporica nel «Pianeta Irritabile» di Volponi." *Griseldaonline* 20.1: 205–218. doi.org/10.6092/issn.1721-4777/11457
Raffaeli, Massimo. 1997. *Paolo Volponi: il Coraggio dell'Utopia*. Ancona: Transeuropa.
Ritrovato, Salvatore, Tiziano Toracca, and Emiliano Alessandroni, eds. 2015. *Volponi Estremo*. Studi 31. Pesaro (Italy): Metauro.
Shukin, Nicole. 2009. *Animal Capital: Rendering Life in Biopolitical Times*. Posthumanities 6. Minneapolis: University of Minnesota Press.
Taylor, Sunaura. 2017. *Beasts of Burden: Animal and Disability Liberation*. New York: New Press.

Toracca, Tiziano. 2020. "Il Pianeta Irritabile Di Paolo Volponi: Un Pianeta Senza La Merda Moneta." *Studi Novecenteschi* 99 (1): 127–145. doi.org/10.19272/202003001006.

Toracca, Tiziano. 2013. "La Favolistica nella Narrativa di Paolo Volponi: una Filigrana Ideologica." *Rivista di Letteratura Italiana* 42 (1): 145–164.

Tsing, Anna Lowenhaupt. 2015. *The Mushroom at the End of the World: On the Possibility of Life in Capitalist Ruins.* Princeton: Princeton University Press.

Vint, Sherryl. 2010. *Animal Alterity: Science Fiction and the Question of the Animal.* Liverpool: Liverpool Univ. Press.

Volponi, Paolo. 1978. *Il Pianeta Irritabile.* Torino: Einaudi.

1989. *Il Diavolo dell'Avvocato.* Interview by Franco Marcoaldi. In *L'Espresso*, April 16, 1989.

1999. *Del Naturale e Dell'Artificiale*, edited by Emanuele Zinato. Ancona: Il Lavoro Editoriale.

and Francesco Leonetti. 1995. *Il Leone e la Volpe: Dialogo nell'Inverno 1994.* Torino: Einaudi.

Wadiwel, Dinesh Joseph. 2020. "Foreword." In *Colonialism and Animality: Anti-Colonial Perspectives in Critical Animal Studies*, edited by Kelly Struthers Montford and Chloë Taylor. Abingdon: Routledge.

Zinato, Emanuele. 2001. "Volponi." Palermo: Palumbo.

Zinato, Emanuele. 2002. "Introduzione." In *Romanzi e prose* 1, edited by Emanuele Zinato, XXI-XXII. Torino: Einaudi.

NOTES

1. All translations of citations from the novel are mine.

2. I will predominantly use the term "dwarf" for the sake of consistency, instead of the terms "person with dwarfism," "little person" or "person of short stature."

3. For examples of allegorical readings see: Toracca 2013; Pifferi 2020.

4. "Il babbuino comanda gli altri eseguono" (Volponi 1978, 21).

5. Volponi describes this character as a hamadryas baboon but uses the terms baboon and monkey interchangeably throughout the novel.

6. "Furore contro la gabbia"; "Non sapeva niente di libere foreste, né di famiglie scimmiesche" (Volponi 1978, 9).

7. "L'elefante [. . .] non sapeva cosa fossero libertà e indipendenza" (Volponi 1978, 11).

8. "Nessun animale ripete! Tienilo presente, anche se si è sempre detto il contrario" (Volponi 1978, 160).

9. As an example, they are often defined as "the horsemen of the apocalypse," turning them into a homogeneous group of male figures. See for instance Raffaeli 1997, 100; Pifferi 2021, 209.

10. Volponi discusses more directly the pervasiveness of animal exploitation—in conjunction with the exploitation of natural resources—in the famous article "Natura ed Animale" where he declares, "Nature and animals are actually very distant from

our world, separated and partially forgotten, under investigation, used, conditioned, exploited, domesticated, surely removed from their reality, from their original condition. [. . .] The animal is intended as domesticated, slave, but mainly as food, fur, etc." "La natura e l'animale sono in realtà molto lontani dal nostro mondo, spezzati e in parte dimenticati, indagati, usati, condizionati, strumentalizzati, allevati, certamente tirati fuori dalla loro realtà, dalla loro condizione originaria. [. . .] L'animale è inteso come un domestico, un servo, ma più che altro come cibo, pelliccia, ecc" (Volponi 1999, 155–156).

11. "Si alzò in volo nella direzione opposta a quella indicatale per dimostrare la propria autonomia e sapienza" (Volponi 1978, 127).

12. "Spingeva via quel colono aggressore con le ali sentendosi non riconosciuta, ma piuttosto minacciata di morte . . . addirittura della ancestrale, volgare tirata di collo" (Volponi 1978, 118)

13. For the most recent and complete theorization of animal resistance see Colling 2021.

14. Among the various anthropocentric readings of the novel centered on the dwarf see for instance Papini 1997, 88–89.

15. On the intersection between disability and animal studies see Jenkins, Struthers and Taylor 2020; Nocella, George, Lupinacci 2019; Taylor 2017.

16. His names evoke several meanings: Mamerte can be interpreted as a reference to the Italic deity of war, from which the Romans derived *Mars*, or as an echo of *ma merde*, literally "my shit" or more figuratively "my stuff" in French, thus insisting on the lexical field associated with bodily waste and on capitalist accumulation processes; the name Man was given to him by the nun he had an affair with, who chooses the English version of the word (Volponi 1978, 104).

17. "Volle distinguere l'oca da lui, e catalogarla come uccello" (Volponi 1978, 49).

18. For a recent theorization of political animal voices see Meijer 2019.

19. The *topos* of ecocatastrophe has a long history traceable back to Ancient Greek and retraced by Moore 2017. Within the Italian context, this book belongs to a cluster of post-apocalyptic novels published around the same time, which includes Guido Morselli's *Dissipatio H.G.* and Carlo Cassola's so-called "nuclear trilogy." For more examples see Fioretti 2017.

20. For a discussion of the influence of a nuclear threat on Volponi's writings and imaginary see Monserrati 2016: 515–534; Papini 1997, 67–104.

21. A sign that astronomical objects are also going through a phase of transformation is the presence of three moons now visible in the sky.

22. "Considerava sbigottita che il biancore del suo piumaggio e delle sue penne veniva un'altra volta minacciato dal petrolio" (Volponi 1978, 122).

23. "Ne aveva visti pochissimi in vita sua di uccelli, e solo nelle gabbie degli zoo e degli uffici dei potenti. Ed erano quasi tutti pappagalli, corvi, merli indiani che borbottavano o che addirittura parlavano piuttosto di emettere una sola nota di canto" (Volponi 1978, 36).

24. "Tutto è ridotto a strumento, mezzo, risorsa, energia [. . .]. La natura appare ormai come la tavola, la tastiera di una simulazione, i suoi elementi, le sue stagioni

ridotti essenzialmente ad essere i tasti, i commutatori, gli input di questo piano di simulazione."

25. "È il nemico degli uomini e dei nani oltre che degli animali e delle piante" (Volponi 1978, 92).

26. "He must belong to the enemies, and he must pull wagons. [. . .] He can be useful, if nothing else as fresh meat." "Deve appartenere al nemico e deve trainarne i carri. [. . .] Potrà esserci utile, se non altro come carne fresca" (Volponi 1978, 163).

27. "Falso uomo"; "Ti salvo rendendoti uomo, degno della civiltà degli uomini" (Volponi 1978, 165). The cursive is mine to highlight how, in Italian, the word "uomini" (men) is used to encompass the entire human species, thereby reinforcing the dominant male standard within human societies.

28. "Chi è vivo può salire con me sul razzo che ci porterà su un mondo nuovo e migliore" (Volponi 1978, 156).

29. "Merda eri e sei e merda sarai! Ma non la buona merda, onesto sterco di un corpo: soddisfazione e rifiuto di una esistenza appagata, giorno per giorno, anche defecando e mangiando. Tu non sei certo la merda di un ciclo naturale; ma il mucchio, lo stronzo tesaurizzato di una circolazione forzata. Come nell'innaturale tu confondi l'oro con la merda, e non l'oro metallo utile per i denti e non la merda utile come concime; ma l'oro moneta con la merda moneta! [. . .] L'artificiale come artificiosa ragione del potere e non come ricerca e scienza. Perché l'artificiale scientifico ritorna naturale; vicino anche alla buona merda! Mentre il tuo artificiale resta sempre e solo artificiale, e per reggere come tale deve continuare ad aumentare i propri artifici e a staccarsi come potere del naturale" (Volponi 1978, 170). For a more detailed discussion of Moneta's role in the narrative through a Marxist lens see Toracca 2020: 127–145.

30. On the role hybridization plays in the novel see Fioretti 2014, 145–158; 2017, 155–194.

31. "Occorreva invece affermare e servire la totalità, integra e presente, dell'esistenza: di tutto e di ciascuno" (Volponi 1978, 174).

32. "Senza bisogno di avvertimenti o di comandi" (Volponi 1978, 185).

33. "I gesti venivano compiuti, singolarmente o insieme, per saggiare la dimensione del nuovo gruppo e quella dei nuovi rapporti. Perché ciascuno potesse trovare la propria posizione e la misura adatta dentro la nuova figura sociale. Tanto più che nessuno pensava di poter guidare e governare come capo assoluto. In quei gesti ciascuno voleva provare di esistere per quel che era, e intendeva inoltre dichiarare ed esprimere il proprio senso di parità con gli altri" (Volponi 1978, 184).

34. Carla Maria Papini has interpreted this scene as a parody of the Eucharist (Papini 1997, 90). On the same subject see also Zinato 2002, XXI-XXII.

35. On the concept of metamorphic logic see Mobili 2008, 148.

36. "La natura l'animale e l'uomo sono quindi intimamente connessi e stretti. Non sono fasi diverse e distinte della creazione del mondo; ma entità comprese nella stessa esplosione e materia, interagenti tra loro."

37. "Maybe the moment will come when we realize that we cannot continue like this, and that we must find a way to distribute resources differently, to think of consumption differently, and facilitate greater justice." "Forse arriverà il momento in cui

capiremo che non possiamo andare avanti così; e che bisognerà pensare a una diversa distribuzione planetaria delle ricchezze, a un'idea diversa di consumo, a una maggiore giustizia" (Marcoaldi 1993).

38. "Literature has always had—and should have—a clear role: to keep consciences alive, help people not lose their minds and languages. It has the duty to be what it has always been: conflict, a challenge to dominant power, an attempt to find new forms of communication and new languages." "La letteratura ha sempre avuto e dovrebbe avere un compito preciso: quello di tenere vive le coscienze, di aiutare la gente a non perdere la propria testa e la propria lingua. Ha il dovere di tornare a essere quella che è sempre stata: conflitto, sfida contro il potere dominante, tentativo di trovare nuove forme di comunicazione e nuovi linguaggi" (Volponi 1989, 161).

Index

Aboriginal: culture, 184, 187–189; identity, 184; knowledges, 184–185, 191; literature, 183, 188, 190; narratives, 187–188; people(s), 19, 184, 187, 194; perspectives/worldview, 186. *See also* First Nations, Indigenous
activism, 155; activist, 86, 148–149, 176, 213
Adams, Carol J., 195, 206–7
adaptation, 71–72, 84, 104, 107, 197, 222–223, 228, 229
adventure stories, 71
aesthetics, 119, 127n6, 199
agency, 16–19, 71, 77, 127n1, 150, 153–154, 156, 158–160, 174, 183, 221–226, 229, 232, 240–242, 247; affective, 159, 229; nonhuman, 7, 10, 13, 15–19, 34, 53, 62, 93, 98–99, 193, 147–149, 159, 160–161, 166, 191, 223–224; viral, 225; virtual, 224–225
agriculture, 4, 40–41, 73–4, 184–5
Alaimo, Stacy, 225, 227, 234
Aldana Reyes, Xavier, 212, 216
algae, 114, 224, 229, 234
aliens, 18, 21, 155, 165–179, 187; alien, 143, 189, 191; alien topography, 46

alienation, 63, 70, 246–7, 250; alienating, 248
allegory, 2, 9, 24, 33–34, 43–48, 188, 213, 240; allegory, national, 9, 33–34, 43–45. *See also* counterallegory, pseudo–allegory
alterity. *See* otherness
altruism, 72, 74, 76, 81
American revolution, 43–44
anemone(s), 224
animality, 240–244
animal studies, 7, 12, 16, 25, 63, 73, 91, 93, 107, 149, 166, 194, 239, 253n5
animals, 1, 4–8, 11–13, 16–19, 21, 24–26, 39, 53–56, 63–64, 73–74, 76, 81–82, 91–96, 99–100, 102–107, 115, 117–119, 130–131, 137–140, 149, 156, 159, 161, 165, 168–169, 171, 173–175, 179, 182n1, 186, 188, 191, 195–197, 205–218, 231, 234, 238, 240–246, 249–250, 252n10; domesticated, 11, 63, 92; invasive, 230; wild, 56, 75–77, 100, 233, 238n7. *See also* individual species
anteater, 115
Anthropocene, 2–6, 8, 10, 19, 21, 26, 33–34, 48–49, 57, 61, 64, 70–73, 86, 109, 127n1, 149–50, 154, 184, 232–3

anthropocentrism, 2, 5, 8, 10–12, 17, 19, 22–24, 26, 35, 40, 49, 61, 73, 86, 93, 109, 115, 140, 147–161, 163n1, 166–167, 169–170, 174, 177–178, 184–185, 192, 206, 216, 221–224, 228, 233, 235, 240, 243–244–5, 247–248, 250, 253n14; anti-anthropocentrism, 25, 72, 130; non-anthropocentrism, 25, 245; post-anthropocentrism, 150, 194, 248–250
anthropomorphism, 15, 81, 84, 98, 113, 123, 137, 156–157, 179, 184, 192, 225, 244–245,
anthroponormativity, 18, 169–170, 175, 179
apocalypse, 73, 80, 85–86, 233, 245, 252n9
Aquinas, St. Thomas, 115
Aristotle, 197
artificial intelligence (AI), 20, 25, 170, 172, 177–178
ass, small grey, 46
assemblage(s), 4, 6, 16, 25, 160–161, 222, 225–226
Atwood, Margaret, 24–25, 69, 221–22, 232–35; *MaddAddam,* 222, 234; *Oryx and Crake,* 222, 233; *Year of the Flood,* 232; *MaddAddam* trilogy, 69, 221, 232–235

baboon, 241, 252n5
Baccolini, Raffaella, 23
Bacigalupi, Paolo, 24–25, 221–222, 228–235, 238n6; *Windup Girl, The,* 222, 228–235, 238n6
bacteria, 223, 226, 229
Bagnold, Enid, 75; National Velvet, 75
Barad, Karen, 16, 57, 223, 225, 235–36, 238n4
Barnes, Richard, 106
Barrington, Samuel, 42
Baumgarten, Alexander Gottlieb, 119
bear, 94, 117, 214
beauty, 110, 117–120, 123–124, 127n6, 135, 141–143

becoming, 11, 24, 25, 40, 79, 99, 113, 120, 122, 124, 153, 155, 161, 206–218, 222–235, 242–243, 247
bee(s), 117
Beier, Jesse, 71–12
being-with, 10–11, 17, 70–76, 79–86
Bekoff, Marc, 15–16, 130
Bell, Julian, 57
Belyea, Andrew, 235
Benford, Gregory, 169
Benjamin, Walter, 44–5
Bennett, Jane, 16, 159–160
Bentley, Joseph, 127n7
Berger, John, 19, 35
Bergthaller, Hannes, 127n1
Bickley, R. Bruce, 52n13
bioengineering, 228, 233
birds, 26, 36, 55, 57, 69, 112, 118, 129, 132, 134, 137, 230, 239, 242–244, 246–247. See also individual species
Birke, Linda, 11, 79–81
Bishop, Elizabeth, 117, 127n5
bison, 92
blackbirds, 119
black skimmer bird, 131
Blakeslee, Nate, 13, 91–96, 102–107; American Wolf, 91, 94, 102–103
blood, 54, 112, 119–120, 122
Borkfelt, Sune, 16, 185, 201n3
born vs. made, 222, 228, 235
Boscacci, Louise, 11
Bo tree, 153, 230
boundaries, 1–2, 4, 6–7, 11, 15–18, 24, 46, 60, 79, 96, 102, 109, 121–122, 124, 130, 136, 143, 147, 151, 159, 165–166, 168, 184, 192, 225, 229, 243–245; human/animal, 1, 7, 11, 20, 189, 226; human/nonhuman, 1–2, 16, 20, 24, 110, 147, 159, 184, 189, 226; real/virtual, 1, 20, 222; territorial, 3, 8, 13, 104–106, 130
Braidotti, Rosi, 17, 147–152, 159–161, 163n1, 163n2
Brandt, Keri, 79
Bratton, Susan Power, 130, 132

Brooker, Jewel Spears, 127n7
Brooks, S. C., 134
Bryant, Bonnie, 79, 88n2; *Saddle Club* book series, 79, 88n2
Bryson, J. Scott, 110, 116
Buber, Martin, 113
Buddha/Buddhism, 121, 123, 127n7, 153
Budiansky, Stephen, 52n8
Buell, Lawrence, 55, 154
butterflies, 118

Calarco, Matthew, 23–25, 206–207, 212, 217–218
Callicott, J. Baird, 119, 151
camel, 122
cannibalism, 206–213
capitalism, 4, 246, 250
Capitalocene, 3–8, 26
Card, Orson Scott, 18, 165, 169, 171; *Ender's Game*, 172; *Speaker for the Dead*, 165, 169, 172–178; *Xenocide*, 171, 179; Ender Tetralogy, 165–167, 169–171, 176, 179
carnophallogocentrism, 206–207
Carson, Rachel, 13–15, 26, 69–71, 92–93, 97, 129–143; *Edge of the Sea, The*, 129–131, 133–143; *Sea Around Us, The*, 129–131, 133–143; *Silent Spring*, 26, 69, 97, 129–130, 132, 140; *Under the Sea-Wind*, 129–131, 134, 137–138
Carter, Bob, 16–18
Cartesianism, 15, 115, 174; Cartesian split, 174, 199
Catlin, George, 92
cattle, 140, 178
Chakrabarty, Dipesh, 3, 109
characters; nonhuman, 15, 20, 26, 37, 46, 70, 131, 134, 137, 139, 143, 224, 240–245, 247; human, 37, 46, 51n2, 70–71, 74–75, 79, 147–152, 155–156, 158, 161, 168, 170, 179, 206, 224, 229, 240–241
King Charles II, 42

Charles, Nickie, 16–18
chestnut tree(s), 155
chickens, 101
children's literature, 74
Christ, 46, 112, 118; Christian allegory, 45; Christian incarnation of the Word, 113; Christian beliefs, 115
Christensen, Laird, 113, 127n3
Chura, Patrick, 36
civilization, 9, 34, 37, 39–41, 44, 52n9, 53, 56, 67n2, 72, 101, 205, 239, 246
Clark, Timothy, 10, 54, 61–64, 109, 150, 155
Cleverman, 19, 183–191, 198
climate change fiction, 9, 21, 53–54, 57, 60, 62–64, 221, 245
climate crisis, 3, 9, 20–21, 23–25, 33, 53, 205–206, 218, 249
cli–fi. *See* climate change fiction
Colebrook, Claire, 233
colonialism, 3, 8, 187, 189, 195, 199, 243
colonization, 18, 37–39, 41, 43, 179, 185, 192, 195–6, 231, 242
Columbus, Christopher, 42
comb jelly, 138
conservation, 9, 22, 72, 95, 192, 104–106, 231
coyote, 13, 91, 93–94, 96–102, 106
counterallegory, 45. *See also* allegory, pseudo–allegory
counter–apocalypse, 72, 80
cows, 216. *See also* cattle
Cowan, Bainard, 45
Crosby, Alfred W., 92, 230
Crutzen, Paul J., 2, 5
Cudworth, Erika, 229
cyborgs, 222

dairy, 195
Dante, 26, 44, 46, 241; *Inferno*, 44, 46, 52n12
Dark Emu controversy, 184–185
Darwin, Charles, 51n1, 52n11, 97, 154, 195, 224

death, 6, 12, 35, 39, 42, 47–48, 61, 70, 94, 102, 105–106, 110, 114–116, 118–124, 138, 159, 171–172, 187, 193, 223, 243, 247–248, 250
decolonization, 12, 195, 242
deer, 121
Delany, Samuel, 21
De Lauretis, Teresa, 20
Deleuze, Gilles, 122, 159–160
DeLoughrey, Elizabeth M., 2–3, 33, 45, 48
Derrida, Jacques, 6, 174–175, 206
Descartes, René, 15, 171. *See also* Cartesianism
dietary culture, 194
Dillon, Grace, 185–186, 188–190, 196, 201n4
Dillon, Sarah, 22–23
Dinello, Daniel, 229
disability studies, 25, 239
D'Lacey, Joseph, 23, 205–206, 213–218; *Meat*, 205–207, 213, 216–218
DNA, 18, 175, 227
Dobie, J. Frank, 96–97; *Voice of the Coyote*, 96
dodo, 107
dog(s), 39, 83, 99–100, 140, 238
domestication, 72–73, 77, 242
dugong, 193–194
Dunn, Kirsty, 196
Dutton, Peter, 184, 187
dystopia, 8, 20, 23–24, 33, 59, 186–187, 241

Eagleton, Terry, 34–35, 48
Easterbrook, Neil, 170
eating, 117–118, 195, 208, 247–248
Ebbatson, Roger, 56, 63, 67n1
ecocriticism, 10, 25, 54, 61–64, 156, 239
ecofeminism, 23, 26, 190, 199, 249
ecological crisis, 48, 54, 221
ecological destruction, 12, 148–149, 151, 156, 239, 245
ecological imperialism, 38–41

ecological relationships, 7, 94, 142, 228
ecologies; material, 230; virtual, 225–226
ecology, 2, 17, 25–26, 40, 54, 67n1, 69, 70, 72, 86, 91, 105–107, 129–131, 137, 148, 150, 160, 197, 221–222, 230–235, 240–241, 245, 249–250
ecopoetry, 14, 110–113, 124
edibility, 24, 207, 211–212, 215–216, 218
eel, 131, 137–138
egg(s), 138, 194–195
Elder, John, 116
Eldridge, Ben, 225, 238
elephant, 26, 73, 239, 241–242, 245–247
Elmore, Jonathan, 21
Embeddedness, 152, 154
Emerson, Ralph Waldo, 111
empathy, 18, 74–75, 79–80, 92, 113, 117, 165–171, 173, 176–177, 179, 182n1, 189
empire, 2, 8, 33, 92, 172, 179, 199
empirical ecocriticism, 10, 54, 61
entanglement, 6–7, 10–11, 14, 21, 22, 24–25, 54, 149, 191, 197, 222, 224–226, 235, 238n4
Eremocene, 8, 69–70, 73
Estes, Allison, 78; *Friends to the Finish*, 78
ethics, 18, 67n1, 73, 119, 127n6, 130, 167, 170–171, 176, 195–196, 225, 227, 235
Ettinger, Bracha, 11
exceptionalism, 10–11, 37–40, 54, 58, 72–73, 80, 86, 127n1, 149, 151, 154, 157, 159–160, 163n1, 248
extinction, 1–2, 34, 44–45, 47, 58, 64, 69–70, 72, 92, 99, 140, 173, 176, 228, 233, 240, 242

Farley, Walter, 76; *Black Stallion* book series, 76
Fast, Robin Riley, 127n5
Fiddes, Nick, 206

First Nations; culture, 188–189; knowledges, 193, 199, 201n2; literature, 186, 188, 194; narratives, 186, 188, 194; people(s), 186, 188–189, 192; perspectives/worldview, 186, 198. *See also* Aboriginal, Indigenous

fish, 117, 118, 127n5, 129, 134, 138, 193, 196–197, 224. *See also* individual species

Fishel, Stefanie, 229

flesh, 33–34, 54, 60, 118, 120, 122, 205, 218, 248

Flores, Dan, 13, 91–93, 95–102, 104, 106; *Coyote America*, 91, 94, 96–102

flower(s), 111, 113–116, 122, 197. *See also* individual species

Fludernik, Monika, 136

Forster, E. M., 9–11, 54, 57–64, 67n2–4, 67n6; "Machine Stops, The," 9, 54, 57–64, 67n3–4

fox(es), 122

Frawley, Jodi, 231

Freud, Sigmund, 116

frog(s), 154. 234

Fromm, Harold, 109

Frost, Mark, 63–65

Frost, Robert, 111

Futurism, 10

Gadamer, Hans–Georg, 127n6

Galapagos, 8, 22, 33–34, 37–39, 41, 44–47, 51n1

Galapagos tortoise, 34, 38

Gallagher, Cavan, 186–187

Garnett, David, 56–58, 61

gender, 75, 80, 106, 168, 193, 194, 197, 242, 249; ambiguity, 193; binaries, 197; cross–gender, 80; identity, 168; misgendered, 242; morality, gendered, 88; norms, 75

genetic; biogenetic, 228–230; foreclosure, 222, 234; gap, 176; material, 6; modification, 177, 221–222, 228, 230–231, 234–235, 238n7; neighbors, 161; purity, 101; symbiogenetic, 226

Ghosh, Amitav, 21, 23

Gidmark, Jill B., 51n1

Giles, Paul, 34, 46

Gillespie, Kathryn, 15

Goats, 140

Gomel, Elana, 166, 171–172

goose, geese, 26, 117, 239, 241–246

Graham, Mary, 186

grass, 60, 74, 103, 11, 115–116, 121–123, 197

Grassi, Samuele, 190, 192, 197, 199

Griffen, Ryan, 183, 187–188, 198

Griffiths, Michael, 184–185

Gruen, Lori, 93

Grusin, Richard, 152, 157–158

Guattari, Félix, 122, 159–160

gulls, 138

Hageman, Andrew, 231

Hagood, Amanda, 130, 133–134

Hale, Mike, 188

Halley, Jean O'Malley, 75, 77, 79–80

Hanson, Natalie Corinne, 74

Haraway, Donna, 2, 4–6, 16, 25, 122, 124, 230, 248

Haritaworn, Jinthana, 183

Harper, Amie Breeze, 196

Hartley, L. P., 58

Hatley, James, 12–13, 15

Hattenhauer, Darryl, 37

Hayles, N. Katherine, 51–52n5

Haynes, Patrice, 159–160

hearing, 16, 36, 139, 148, 160

Hearne, Vicki, 81–82

hedgehog, 122

Heidegger, Martin, 70, 73

Heise, Ursula K., 21–22, 26, 110

Helmreich, Stefan, 227

heron, 122

Herz, Judith Scherer, 58–59

Hewitt, W. G., 138

Heyerdahl, Thor, 133

Hillegas, Mark, 59

Hlavajova, Maria, 163n1
Hobden, Stephen, 229
hogs. *See* pig(s)
Hogan, Patrick Colm, 168
Hood, Samuel, 42
Horn, Eva, 127n1
Hornberg, Alf, 3
horse(s), 8, 10–11, 70–86, 88n2; stallion, 75–78
horsemanship, 11, 79–81
human–horse relations, 8, 70–71, 73–76, 78, 80–81
humanism, 9–10, 17, 54, 58–60, 148–150, 152, 159, 163n1, 163n2; anti–humanism, 58, 150. *See also* posthumanism; transhumanism
human–animal binary, 20, 240–241, 244, 246
human–animal relationships, 10, 63, 96
hunting, 37–38, 73, 75, 105–106, 118–119
hybridity, 192, 247

ideological conditioning, 214, 216
ideology of distinction, 24, 205–209, 212–218
immersion, 124, 131, 198
imperialism, 3, 38, 40–42, 44, 52n7, 52n10
indigenous; culture, 22, 184, 186, 191, 196; genocide, 45; identity, 185–186; kinships, 190; knowledges, 190; languages, 176; logic, 22; narratives, 185, 188–191, 196; people(s), 22, 92, 96, 183, 196, 188, 190; perspectives/worldview, 2, 19, 184, 186–188, 191, 196–197, 199; traditions, 19, 183. *See also* Aboriginal, First Nations
indiscernibility, 1
indistinction, 21, 207, 209, 212, 217–218
infection, 223–227, 233, 235, 238n2
Inglese, Andrea, 247
insect(s), 116. *See also* individual species

intersectionality, 168, 190
interspecies care, 248
interspecies connection, 183
invasion ecology (ies), 231
Iovino, Serenella, 156
Ishikawa, Norburu, 5
Italian literature, 25, 239, 249, 253n19

James, Will, 76; *Smoky the Cowhorse*, 76
Jameson, Frederic, 201n4
Jefferies, Richard, 10, 53–57, 61–65, 67n1; *After London, or Wild England*, 10, 53–57, 61–64, 67n1, 68n6
jellyfish, 136
Johnson, Sammy Jo, 243
Johns–Putra, Adeline, 9, 53–54, 62–63
Jonsson, Emelie, 58, 63
Joon Ho, Bong, 20
Joyce, Stephen, 22–23
Jung, Carl, 112

Kadmos, Helen, 189–190
Kant, Immanuel, 119, 148, 151
Kearns, Cleo McNelly, 127n7
Keith, W. J., 56–57
Kennedy, John F., 132
kinship, 100, 190, 192, 194–195, 201n5, 226, 227
Klingopulos, G. D., 58
Kwaymullina, Amberlin, 186, 191, 196
Lamb, Rick, 81

Landon, Brook, 59–60
language, 17, 36, 51n4, 73, 81, 91, 95–96, 100–101, 103, 111–114, 124, 139, 159, 161, 165–166, 169, 172, 175, 178, 186, 191, 198, 225, 234, 241, 244–247, 255n38; limitations of, 36, 95, 110, 197; organic, 14, 110
Lazo, Rodrigo, 52n7
Lear, Linda, 130–131
Leavis, Q. D., 61
Leopold, Aldo, 13, 92–93, 97

Levi–Strauss, Claude, 201n4
liberation, 60, 156, 240–241, 243–245, 247, 249
Lidskog, Rolf, 71, 86
lilies, 113, 118, 124
limpet(s), 138
Lingis, Alphonso, 223–224
lion(s), 94, 120
Lodge, David, 62
London, Jack, 91
love, 35, 70–71, 84–85, 92, 107, 114–115, 117–118, 120, 124, 130, 135, 177, 190–191, 197
Lyotard, Jean–François , 166

mackerel, 131, 134, 137
Macy, Joanna, 151
magpie(s), 197
Malm, Andreas, 3
Malmgren, Carl D., 165, 169, 174
manifest destiny, 34, 38
mapping, 9, 20, 34, 36, 41, 43, 48, 98, 133
Marchand, Jeffrey Scott, 159
Maris, Emma, 231
material ecocriticism, 156
Mayer, Jed, 63
Mazel, David, 63
McCalman, Iain, 231
McCarthy, Cormac, 23–24, 26, 205–212, 218; *Road, The*, 23, 26, 205–208, 212–213, 216–218
McFarland, Sarah, 18
McKibben, Bill, 86
meat. *See* flesh
Medalie, David, 58, 60, 67n2
Melville, Herman, 2, 8–9, 12, 33–49, 51n1, 52n7, 52n13; "Encantadas, or Enchanted Isles, The," 8, 12, 33–49, 51n1, 51n2, 52n7, 52n13; *Moby-Dick*, 45, 51n1; *Pierre*, 34, 46, 51n1
Merleau–Ponty, Maurice, 116
metamorphosis, 122, 247

metaphor, 8, 16, 26, 33, 46, 113, 116, 118, 122–123, 156, 177, 194, 201, 243–244. *See also* symbol
microbes, 5, 222, 224, 227, 230
Miller, J. Hillis, 41, 43, 51n3
Miller, Perry, 35, 52n6
Miller, Robert, 81
monkey, 239, 241, 245, 247–248, 252n5. *See also* baboon
Moore, Jason, 3–4
Moore, Marianne, 127n5
Morris, Brian, 63
Morrison, Ronald D., 63
Morton, Timothy, 67n1
Moss, Thylias, 132
moth(s), 116
mountain lion(s), 94
Moylan, Tom, 23
Mullins, Matthew, 208
multispecies, 230, 232, 240; community, 21, 240, 248–249; justice, 235, 240; perspective, 227
mushroom(s), 124
mutation, 21, 24–25, 221–222, 226–229, 232, 235

naming of animals, 82; of places, 9, 34, 41, 43, 48, 107,

narratives, human–horse, 10–11, 86
narrative form, 54
narrative style, 139
national allegory, 9, 33–34, 43, 46, 48
nationalism, 8–9, 34, 43–44, 192,
nation formation, 9, 33–34, 37, 45–48
Nattermann, Udo, 63
nature's nation, 35, 42–43, 46, 52n6
Nayar, Pramod, 6–7, 225–226
Nealon, Jeffrey T., 149
Nietzsche, Friedrich, 116, 166
Nixon, Rob, 21, 154–155
nonhuman, 1, 5–7, 11, 14–17, 19, 21–26, 34–35, 41, 47, 49, 53–58, 70–73, 79–80, 85–86, 94, 147–149, 153–156, 159–161, 166, 168–178,

182n1, 183–189, 191–192, 194, 199, 222, 228, 234, 244; agency/agencies, 10, 15–18, 25–26, 39, 54, 62, 159–161, 223–227, 229, 232, 235, 238n2; animals, 1, 4–8, 11, 14–16, 18–19, 24, 53–54, 64, 73, 94, 156, 165, 168, 171, 174, 176, 178–179, 182n1, 185, 196, 201n2, 205–221, 240, 243, 245, 250; boundaries of, 2–3, 11, 152, 156
Norris, Nannette, 235
Nowak, Martin, 72
nuclear, 26, 223, 239, 245, 253n19, 252n20
Nystrom, Jan, 130

oak, 197
ocean, 2, 14–15, 35, 48, 69, 92, 112, 129–143, 154, 198, 227
oceanalia, 14, 131
Okorafor, Nnedi, 22
Oliver, Kelly, 13
Oliver, Mary, 14, 109–125, 127n2, 127n5; *American Primitive*, 110, 116–117, 127n5; *Blue Horses*, 110; "Owls," 119–120, 123
onomatopoeia, 34–36, 111
Oppermann, Serpil, 156
orchid(s), 198
Ortiz Robles, Mario, 93
Orwell, George, 240
O'Sullivan, Marnie, 15
Oswald, John, 15
otherness, 20–21, 54, 81, 82, 109–110, 113, 125, 156–157, 166–167, 185, 193, 197
Ovid, 157
owl(s), 119–121, 123–124

Page, Norman, 67n3
Papini, Carla Maria, 254n34
Parrinder, Patrick, 170
Pascoe, Bruce, 184–185, 187, 198
pathetic fallacy, 113
pathogens, 222–223, 226, 235
Paxton, Heather, 223

peculiar associations, 9, 34, 36–38, 49
Peggs, Kay, 168, 174
Peroikou, Antonia, 235
personification, 113, 138–139, 238n5
Peters, John Durham, 13, 132–133
Pick, Anat, 1
Pickering, Andrew, 222
picturesque, the, 34–35
pig(s), 140, 209–211, 238n7
pigeon(s), 107, 230
pine tree, 153, 160
plague, 24, 175, 221–222, 225, 230–234
Plantationocene, 5, 8
Plato, 119
Plotinus, 119
Plumwood, Val, 23
point of view, 62, 134–135, 141, 143; 1st Person, 131, 134–135, 139; 2nd Person, 131, 134–136, 139; 3rd Person, 55, 131, 134–135, 137, 139–140
Polak, Iva, 190–191, 193
pony books, 70, 74–75
Pony Boy, GaWaNi, 81
post–Anthropocene futures, 71–72, 233
post–apocalypse, 22–25, 56–7, 206, 208–209, 217
post–apocalyptic fiction, 20, 24, 26, 61, 253n19
posthuman, the, 6, 63, 147, 152, 157–158, 160, 163n1, 163n2, 188, 222
posthumanism, 127n1, 147, 152, 154, 163n1, 163n2, 196, 222, 225; ecological posthumanism, 127n1, 234
Powers, Richard, 17–18, 147–162; *Overstory, The*, 147–153, 157–161
predators, 92, 98, 100, 102, 104–106, 119–120, 230, 238n7
Preece, Rod, 113
Prometheus, 72
progress, 8, 57, 60, 91, 147–152, 157–158, 162
pronouns, uses of, 134–135, 137, 143

pseudo–allegory, 33, 43–48. *See also* allegory, counterallegory
Pullein–Thompson, Christine, 75–76; *Phantom Horse* book series, 75–76, 82
Putnam's Magazine, 51n1

rat, 140
reader positioning, 14–15, 26, 35–36, 47–49, 55, 58, 61–62, 64, 71, 73, 77, 80, 96–104, 107, 110–120, 124, 129–143, 165–166, 185, 194, 212, 222, 232–235, 241–245
reception studies, 10, 80, 130, 184, 188–189, 199
representation, 20, 34, 41, 45, 49, 189, 201n3, 249, 250; of animals, 13, 240, 243; of flesh, 23; of humans, 10, 19, 70, 184; of nonhumans, 18–19, 183, 184; of sea, 15, 129, 131, 143
redwood(s), 148, 158
reptiles, 36
Ritchie, D. G., 119
Robinson, Margaret, 196
Rogin, Michael Paul, 45
romance, 70, 78–79, 83, 86, 88; interspecies, 70, 77
Roosevelt, Theodore, 91
rose(s), 123
Rose, Deborah Bird, 12–13, 15, 190
Rose, Mark, 167
Rowland, Lucy, 234

Saint Francis, 112, 127n4
Salt, Henry Stephens, 55
sand, 142
sanderling(s), 138
science fiction, 2, 6, 18, 20–22, 25, 59–61, 69–73, 155, 165–169, 188, 190–191, 196, 201n4, 221, 229, 240
scientific knowledge, 133, 142
Schneider–Mayerson, Matthew, 10, 54–55, 62, 64
Schopenhauer, Arthur, 116
Schullery, Paul, 95

Scigaj, Leonard, 110, 112
Scott, Heidi C. M., 63
sea. *See* ocean
sea baskets, 141
Seabury, Marcia, 59
sea hare, 141
seals, 139
seaweed, 138, 141
senses. *See* smell, hearing, sight
Sewell, Anna, 73–74; *Black Beauty*, 73–74
Sharpe, Jenny, 45
Sheckels, Theodore F., 234
Shoptaw, John, 14
sight, 13, 20, 35, 68n4, 106, 113, 116–117, 129, 139, 163n1, 191, 217, 230, 244
Sinclair, Rebekah, 213
Sitwell, Edith, 68n4
skink(s), 197
slavery, 5, 8, 37–41, 43, 45, 177, 187; slave(s), 40, 48, 253n10; slave agriculture, 4; slave trade, 5; slave labor, 5; enslaved, 176–177
Slotkin, Richard, 40
Smart, Alan, 26
Smart, Josephine, 26
Smell, 139, 201n3, 211, 214–215
Smiley, Jane, 11, 81, 83, 85–86; *Horses of Oak Valley Ranch* book series, 11, 80–81, 83, 85–86
snail(s), 135
snake(s), 117, 119
social Darwinism, 195
Soper, Kate, 51n4
soul(s), 59, 113, 115, 121, 123, 230, 238n6
sound, 36, 111, 139, 159, 201n3
species, 1–4, 6–7, 18–19, 22–24, 60, 63, 70–73, 81, 86, 92–107, 109, 113, 118, 140, 147, 151, 156–157, 163n1, 165, 167–178, 182n2, 183, 187–193, 197, 201n5, 205, 207, 209, 212–213, 221, 223–233, 240–248, 250, 254n27; cross–species relationships,

73, 224, 227, 248; extinction, 34, 45, 69; invasive, 228, 230–231; transgenic, 222
speciesism, 19, 183, 187, 189, 195, 199, 243
speculative fiction, 20, 22, 24, 26, 168–169, 186, 189–191, 205–207, 218
Spenser, Edmund, 46
spider, 119
squirrel, 139
stallion. *See* horse(s)
Steuer, Jonathan, 132
stillness, 17, 147–148, 152–162
Stoermer, Eugene R., 2, 5
Stone, Christopher D., 151
Streeby, Shelley, 20, 22, 26
subjectivity, 7, 13, 16, 82, 98, 101, 103, 148, 150, 152, 159–161, 194, 197, 223; posthuman subjectivity, 148, 150, 160–161, 163n1
sublime, 119, 120, 124
survival, 17, 25, 70–72, 76, 86, 99, 101, 104, 138, 158, 172–173, 188, 208, 222, 224–225, 227–228, 233, 239, 245
Suvin, Darko, 20, 166
sycamores, 156
symbiosis, 8, 224–228, 235; endosymbiosis, 223
symbiotic partnerships, 11, 25, 223–228, 235
symbol, 34, 40, 43–44, 47, 52n13, 120–121, 194, 199, 230, 242, 246, 248. *See also* metaphor

Tallbear, Kim, 196
technology, 3, 8, 20–21, 25–26, 51n4, 53–54, 57, 59, 60, 63–64, 69, 93–5, 99, 107, 109, 140, 158, 163n1, 165, 177, 190, 222, 225, 228–230, 232, 234; biotechnology, 69, 228, 230, 235; techno–determinist, 3; techno–optimism, 4, 10, 158, 229
texturization, 131, 141–2
timescales, 18, 148, 154–155, 158

thrush(es), 119
Thomas, Edward, 55–56
tofu, 195, 197
tortoise, 34, 37–39, 46–47, 51n2, 52n13
transhumanism, 152, 163n1
Traub, Courtney, 234
travel literature, 33
travelogue, 8, 33–34. 37
tree(s), 17, 117, 139, 147, 149, 151, 153–160, 191, 198, 230. *See also* individual species
Trexler, Adam, 64
Tsing, Anna, 5, 248
Tucker, Nicholas, 77, 79

U.S.S. Essex, 37–38, 43, 51n2

van Neerven, Ellen, 19, 22, 183–184, 186, 189–199, 201n1; "Water," 19, 183–184, 187–189, 201n1, 202n6
veganism, 196
vegetarian foods, 184
Vint, Sherryl, 20–22, 166, 185–186, 189, 240
virus, 6–7, 18, 21, 25, 73, 175–177, 184, 222, 227, 229, 234–235, 238n2; COVID–19, 184
vital materialism, 159
Volponi, Paolo, 25–26, 239–240, 249, 252n10, 253n16, 252n20; Pianeta Irritabile, Il, 25–26, 239–240, 249
vulnerability, 12, 17, 61, 65, 72, 173; invulnerability, 71

Wadiwel, Dinesh, 243
Walker, Margaret Urban, 76–77
Waterton, Claire, 71, 86
Watt, Ian, 21
wattle tree, 198
Watts, Peter, 24–25, 221–228, 232–235, 237n1, 238n5; *βehemoth*, 222, 225, 228, 237n1; *βehemoth: β–Max*, 237n1; *βehemoth: Seppuku*, 237n1; *Maelstrom*, 222–224
War of 1812, 37–38, 43

weeds, 116, 123, 230, 234
Weil, Kari, 156
Welshman, Rebecca, 63
Wertheimer, Eric, 37
Westerns, 76
whale(s), 45, 122, 139,
whelks, 118
White, Jessica, 190
Whitman, Walt, 115
Williams, Raymond, 39, 51n4,
Williamson, Henry, 56, 137
Wilson, Edward O., 8, 69–71
witnesses, 11–15, 37, 74, 84, 95, 97, 131, 133, 194, 214; bearing witness, 12–13, 74, 95; called to witness, 12, 194; eyewitness(ing), 37, 113
witnessing, 7, 11–15, 17, 132–133, 136
Wright, Laura, 208

Wolfe, Cary, 6, 16, 152, 163n1, 163n2, 182n2
wolves/wolf, 13, 91, 93–95, 102–106; wolf–dog, 238; wolf, prairie. *See* coyote; wolf watchers, 103–105; wolves, Yellowstone, 102
wonder, 116, 129–133, 135, 139, 141–143, 193, 224
Wood Wide Web, 147
worms, 119
Wyndham, John, 190

Yellowstone; National Park, 95, 102–107; Wolf Project, 95, 105
young adult literature, 70, 73, 78–9

Zipes, Jack, 88n1
Zoomorphism, 184
Zylinska, Joanna, 10, 71–73, 80, 85–86

About the Editors

Dr. Sune Borkfelt has lectured at Aarhus University, Denmark, since 2007. He is author of *Reading Slaughter: Abattoir Fictions, Space, and Empathy in Late Modernity* (Palgrave, 2022). His research on topics such as nonhuman otherness, the naming of nonhuman animals, postcolonial animals, and the ethics of animal product marketing, has appeared in *English Studies*, *Animals*, and *Journal of Agricultural and Environmental Ethics* as well as in a number of edited collections. He is also editor of a 2016 special issue of the journal *Otherness: Essays and Studies* focused on animal alterity.

Matthias Stephan (Aarhus University, Denmark) researches postmodernism, and its implications in Gothic, sf, and crime fiction, and intersections of these fields as they represent and consider global climate change. His work has appeared in *Science Fiction Studies*, *Scandinavian Studies*, *Coolabah* and in a number of edited collections. His monograph *Defining Literary Postmodernism for the Twenty-First Century* is available at Palgrave. He is general editor for *Otherness: Essays and Studies*, and coordinator of the *Centre for Studies in Otherness*.

About the Contributors

Clare Archer-Lean is discipline leader of English Literature at the University of the Sunshine Coast, Queensland Australia. Clare's research is on the ways in which literary and cultural representations of animals inform human perceptions of their own identities and their place in the natural environment. Her work includes textual analysis and applied trans-disciplinary methods to interrogate the implications of human stories on animal lives. Clare has recent publications in this space *The Routledge Companion to Australian Literature, ISLE, Geofrum, Pacific Biology, Journal of Australian Studies, Australian Literary Studies* and *JASAL*.

Anastasia Cardone received her BA and MA with honors in European and Extra-European Languages and Literature at the Università Statale di Milano (Italy) with two dissertations on American literature and ecocriticism. In particular, her MA thesis (2015) won the prize for best dissertation in American literature from the AISNA association. It analyzed Annie Dillard's *Pilgrim at Tinker Creek* and Mary Oliver's ecopoetry from a biosemiotic perspective. She is currently finishing her PhD at the University of Leeds in the School of English, with a thesis on bird vocalising and avian soundscapes as symbols of (an) American identity in US non fiction. She is working on politicians' correspondence, ornithological writing, and Transcendentalist works, ranging from Thomas Jefferson to Henry David Thoreau. Among others, she published two essays on Annie Dillard: 'Where the Twin Oceans of Beauty and Horror Meet' (2016) in *Ecozon@* and 'Bringing Culture Back to Nature' (2020) in the volume *Avenging Nature*.

Kristen R. Egan is an Associate Professor of English at Mary Baldwin University, where she teaches courses on American Literature, literature and science, and writing. She has an interdisciplinary background with a B.S. in Biology and a Ph.D. in English. Her work on Charlotte Perkins Gilman, Ellen Richards, and environmental conservation is available in Women's Studies

Quarterly, and she has an article on Willa Cather, bathing, and racial degeneracy forthcoming in *Studies in American Fiction*.

Owen Harry is a PhD candidate in English Literature at the National University of Singapore. His research focuses on the relationship between religion and the environment in contemporary American literature. He has published an article on Buddhist impermanence and environmental ethics in the work of Gary Snyder.

Samantha Hind is a WRoCAH-funded PhD researcher at the University of Sheffield. Her thesis, *Speculative Flesh Ecologies: Researching Flesh Consumption in 21st Century Speculative Fiction*, explores the construction of flesh as a facilitator for human and non-human indistinction in twenty-first century speculative fiction, questioning what it means to both be and eat flesh in the fragile flesh ecologies of speculative futures. She is also a member of Sheffield Animal Studies Research Centre (ShARC).

Dr. Lauren O'Mahony is a senior lecturer in Global Media and Communication at Murdoch University in Western Australia. Much of her research focusses on Australian women's literature as well as the analysis of popular television, creativity, media audiences, and creative non-fiction. Her research has been published in *The Journal of Postcolonial Writing*, *The Australasian Journal of Popular Culture*, *The Journal of Popular Romance Studies*, *Communication Research and Practice*, and *Text Journal* as well as the edited books *Theorizing Ethnicity in the Chick-Lit Genre* (2019) and *The Routledge Research Companion to Popular Romance Fiction* (2021).

Lauren E. Perry earned her Ph.D. in English from the University of New Mexico in May, 2021, and has contributed to several literary animal publications, including *Posthumanist Perspectives on Literary and Cultural Animals* (Springer Nature 2021) and *Contagions and Nonhuman Animals* (Forthcoming). Dr. Perry currently serves as Faculty at Central New Mexico Community College.

Adrian Tait, Ph.D., is an independent scholar and ecocritic with a particular interest in Victorian and early modern literary responses to environmental crisis. He has published related papers in a number of scholarly journals, including *Green Letters: Studies in Ecocriticism*, the *European Journal of English Studies*, and *Cahiers victoriens et édouardiens*, and contributed to essay collections such as *Nineteenth-Century Transatlantic Literary Ecologies* (2017), *Victorian Ecocriticism: The Politics of Place and Early Environmental Justice* (2017), *Perspectives on Ecocriticism* (2019), *Literature and Meat*

Since 1900 (2019), and *Gendered Ecologies: New Materialist Interpretations of Women Writers in the Long Nineteenth Century* (2020).

Elizabeth Tavella is a Postdoctoral Teaching Fellow at the University of Chicago, affiliated with the Center for the Study of Gender and Sexuality, and is currently finalizing a monograph on spaces of animal confinement, from slaughterhouses to zoos and laboratories, in contemporary literature and media. As a transdisciplinary researcher, Elizabeth's work builds on critical animal studies, decolonial methods, critical theory, and queer ecology to investigate interlinked systems of oppression and power hierarchies from an artistic and cultural perspective.

Mary Trachsel has been a member of the Rhetoric faculty at the University of Iowa in the U.S. since 1989. In the field of animal studies, her academic interests in literature, language, and communication join her personal interests in interspecies relationships and ecology. Her studies of human-nonhuman animal communication and coexistence have explored literary representations of human-nonhuman relationships, historical records of interspecies agricultural relationships, and discursive constructions of humans and other lifeforms. Her work has appeared in *Society and Animals, Social Sciences, Transpositiones,* and in several essay collections.

Dr. Vera Veldhuizen is Assistant Professor in European Languages and Cultures at the University of Groningen, the Netherlands. She previously finished her PhD on empathy, ethics and justice construction in children's war literature at the University of Cambridge, supervised by Maria Nikolajeva. Her current research project is on cognitive approaches to conflicting truth narratives in children's literature. Her most recent publications include "Empathy Across Time in Speculative Children's Shoah Fiction" in *English Association: Issues in English* and "Narrative Ethics in Robert Westall's *The Machine Gunners*" in *Children's Literature in Education*. She is the recipient of a research fellowship position at the International Youth Library in Munich, and an invited jury member for the iBBY Netherlands MA thesis prize.

Clare Wall is a Toronto-based educator and independent scholar. She holds a PhD from York University in English Literature. Her research interests include contemporary posthuman climate fiction, nonhuman agencies, and ecologies of the future. Her academic writing and poetry appear in the *Canadian Fantastic in Focus* anthology and *Philament: A Journal of Arts and Culture.*

www.ingramcontent.com/pod-product-compliance
Lightning Source LLC
Chambersburg PA
CBHW020112010526
44115CB00008B/799